Lead the Way

Following the words and examples of
Jesus in leading the charge toward
positive cultural change

Elaine Elkins

WESTBOW
PRESS®
A DIVISION OF THOMAS NELSON
& ZONDERVAN

WestBow Press books may be ordered through booksellers or by contacting:

WestBow Press
A Division of Thomas Nelson & Zondervan
1663 Liberty Drive
Bloomington, IN 47403
www.westbowpress.com
1 (866) 928-1240

ISBN: 978-1-9736-1630-6 (sc)
ISBN: 978-1-9736-1629-0 (e)

Library of Congress Control Number: 2018901372

Print information available on the last page.

WestBow Press rev. date: 06/24/2019

Foreword

If we are honest, the idea of being an agent of cultural change for Jesus is overwhelming. We want to be kingdom bringers, but we're consumers. We want to be helpful to other people, but we're busy. We want God to be the Lord and Leader of our lives, but we like to be in control. It's tough to be human. We painfully know that in this world, we will have struggles. But that's why the good news of Jesus is so wonderful. His grace is sufficient for us. We are more than conquerors because He has already overcome this world!

Do you believe that God has created you to do amazing things? Do you believe that God can transform you into the person He created you to become? Are you willing to trust in God's promises? If so, get ready for true spiritual adventure. You can be an agent of cultural change for Jesus, and you can bring God's kingdom to earth, because He created you for this adventure.

This book, *Lead the Way*, is more than a devotional. It is an invitation for you to join God in the redemptive work He wants to accomplish in your heart and through your life. By His power, you can contribute to the restorative action that this world desperately needs. In each daily entry, you will read the words of Jesus and the setting in which they were said. You will be guided to "step in" and allow God to refine your heart, and then "step out" in faith with the personal invitations God has already prepared for you. Don't be daunted; it's God's work. He promises to carry it to completion. You will need to ask yourself, "Is God capable of taking my life, shaping it, and using it for His purposes?" If your answer is yes, get ready—true spiritual adventure awaits.

The author, Elaine Elkins, is a wonderful example of God accomplishing His work through her life. Elaine received the vision for this book—the title, concept, and structure—in a single holy moment. It was God's call for her to step forward in faith with the largest endeavor of her life so far. She had the right attitude because she embraced her inadequacy. God gifted her with faith to undertake this book project and reminded her that He would hold her together and accomplish more than she could ever ask or imagine. As Elaine's husband, I am overflowing with respect and admiration. She trusted God, and with His guidance has crafted 366 amazing entries. She knew that she wasn't qualified by any human standards, but she believed that God would enable His servant. He protected her from the enormous size of this undertaking and gave her strength when she was weak. He empowered her to step into what He had prepared in advance for her to do. It was always God's work, always God's power, and He gets all the glory.

So, I ask you again, do you believe God has created you to do amazing things? Do you believe that God can transform you into the person He created you to become? If you are ready to allow God's Holy Spirit to work in your heart and through your life, then I am honored to pray for you. Please pray with me.

> Lord, our Heavenly Father, we praise you for who you are. You know every detail of who we are. By your love, you call us to yourself and give us the faith to trust you as the Lord and the Leader of our lives. We surrender everything to you and humbly accept your supernatural power into our lives. Grant us an extra portion of your Holy Spirit to open our eyes, our ears, and our hearts. It is your business that we want to

participate in. In the name of Jesus, protect us from anything that could try to steal away the good work you want to accomplish in us and through us. We fix our eyes on you, we place our hope in you. We ask you Lord, to have your way in us.

May God bless you and protect you as you step into the spiritual adventure you were created for.

Jeffrey Elkins
Loving husband of Elaine Elkins

Introduction

Most people believe that the Holy Bible contains many spiritual and moral lessons that have stood the test of time. Christians and non-Christians alike have been entertained by and even gleaned wisdom from the stories therein. Many would even venture to say that Jesus was one of the wisest teachers this world has ever known. Some would go so far as to call the Bible "the owner's manual for life." But, like any set of written instructions, one must open them up and read them. So, where to begin? I suggest choosing a Bible that suits your learning style. Some prefer the more traditional and literal translations, like the King James Version. Others relate to the Message Bible because it is written in a more contemporary style and is more conceptual than literal. Every Holy Bible is the written word of God, so choose the one that is easy for you to read and understand. In *Lead the Way (LTW)* I have chosen to reference the New International Version (1995 and 2011 editions) because it is one of the more common Bible version used today, and because the language makes sense to me. Whichever Bible you choose, know that a treasure trove of knowledge lies between its covers. So, open it up and dive in. Let LTW guide you along this journey of discovery and faith as we sit at the Master's feet together.

Because this book is meant to be both a devotional and a discipleship tool, you should approach it as such. You should expect to be informed and challenged by the information provided, but also inspired to put what you learn to use in your life and ministry. As with any method designed to help a person draw nearer to God, LTW will be best utilized by persons fully surrendered to His will. The best way to ensure you are in a proper head and heart space is to pray. Always begin each session of this devotional in a time of acknowledgment of, praise of, and supplication to God. In that way, you dim the influences of the encroaching world and focus your attention on what God wants to tell you in your time together. This is key! Aligning with the Holy Spirit is essential to achieving your potential in anything in life—this devotional included.

Upon preparing your heart and mind for what Jesus wants to teach you through His words and examples, it will be beneficial to pause after reading the attribute at the top of the page. The attribute is the one-word title of each day's entry. It is meant to be a prompt or reminder of the type of character Jesus wants His disciples to develop. The attribute will help to bring into focus the theme of His lesson. Take some time to consider what the word means in a general context, and in how it applies to your life. You may wish to look up its definition and think about how Jesus might have used similar terminology in His teachings. Then, as you read the verses that follow, apply the attribute to the lesson He is teaching you today.

Next, read through the day's verse(s) one or two times. You may want to read Jesus' words in a few different translations to glean the most meaning from them. Also, it is always wise to read any section of scripture in its greater context. Thus, wherever it seemed relevant, I have included (in parenthesis) additional verses that should help you to paint the day's scripture into a more complete picture.

Following the day's verse(s), you will find an overview of the political, cultural, and religious climate in which Jesus first spoke those words. I hope this overview will help you understand why He chose the words He spoke, the tone in which He spoke them, and their intended purpose for His first-century audience. It is meant to be a synopsis, *not* an exhaustive analysis of doctrine or history. If you are less familiar with ancient society or the setting in which Jesus lived and taught, this overview should paint a picture of the scene each passage depicts.

After the historical scene is set, I offer relevant, modern-day examples of how Jesus' words apply to us today. Again, this is not an exclusive or exhaustive list, but a starting point from which to begin applying His teachings in your life. Every teaching of our Lord and Savior contains a relevant lesson for each of us, if we take the time to listen and learn.

Once you have had a chance to consider Jesus' words from historical and present-day perspectives, LTW suggests you reflect more closely on what His teaching means to you personally. Under the heading "Stepping In," I have suggested ways to take to heart Jesus' words and to get to know God more intimately. Thought-provoking questions, pray prompts, and further scripture references are provided to encourage spiritual growth and discovery. The deeper you venture into God's truth, the more He will reveal His plan and His purpose for you. Be brave and dive in!

Filled with information and spiritual insight, you are now encouraged to apply what you have learned to your life and ministry. Under the heading "Stepping Out," I offer suggestions for how you may begin to put the day's teaching into tangible action. These are only suggestions. If God is prompting you to respond in a different way, that is fine. The point of this section is to inspire you to go and be the hands and feet of Christ; to move learning from your head to your heart, and then from your heart to your body. Remember, each leap of faith started with a single step.

At the back of this book, you will find the "Action Plan Tracker" chart. Make copies of this or cut it out and laminate it so that you can keep track of your thoughts (brain), your feelings (heart), and your actions (hand) in response to Jesus' teachings over the course of a week. If you choose to laminate and reuse it weekly, take a photograph (or make a copy) of this chart so that you can track your progress. Keep it where you can see it each day. Use it to motivate your actions. Keep it simple and fun.

The purpose of this book is to help Christ followers turn their devotion into a lifestyle of faith. And, though God is pleased when hearts and minds are attuned to Him, He receives the ultimate glory when our actions show others that we belong to Jesus. Jesus gave His life to initiate a *movement*, not a philosophy or religion. We pay Him the greatest honor when we heed His words and learn from His example. LTW is a call to listen, learn, and lead. Jesus didn't train His disciples to remain mere students; He prepared them to be apostles. This work continues today. We are Christ's legacy—should we choose to accept our callings!

Still encouraging for us today is the advice the apostle Paul gave to newly converted Jewish Christians long ago, to support one another through fellowship and the spurring on of good deeds (Heb 10:19–25). God never intended for His children to walk this journey of life and faith alone. Jesus reiterated the same encouragement to His own disciples shortly before He went to the cross to face the agony of utter aloneness: "Love one another … as I have loved you" (Jn 13:34). If that were not reason enough to obey this new command, Jesus tells them, and us, another reason to love: "By this all men will know that you are my disciples, if you love one another" (Jn 13:35).

Leading the way toward positive cultural change can be done in no other way. We need Jesus, the Father, the Holy Spirit, the Word of God, *and* each other to achieve this big, audacious, but entirely worthy goal. Are you in? If so, please join us as we follow Jesus and lead the way for others while marching toward eternity, where we will hear those wonderful words, "Well done, good and faithful servant!" (Mt 25:23).

Resolved

"Now my heart is troubled, and what shall I say? 'Father, save me from this hour?' No, it was for this very reason I came to this hour. Father, glorify your name!"

—John 12:27–28 (Jn 12:20–36)

On the first day of the week, just five days before Jesus would be arrested, falsely tried, convicted, and led to His death, He entered Jerusalem for the last time. Crowds of hopeful spectators lined the streets, welcoming their new king with waving palm branches and shouts of praise. As Jesus wound His way through the expectant crowd, the Twelve looked on with wonder and amazement. From along the fringes, the Jewish leaders watched with increasing disdain as the people cheered on the one "who comes in the name of the Lord." Even some newly converted Greek Jews came to catch a glimpse of the purported Messiah.

This came as no surprise to Jesus. It was all a part of the Father's plan. However, seeing the confusion that still plagued His disciples, Jesus clarified what was happening: "The hour has come for the Son of Man to be glorified" (Jn 12:23). Jesus hoped His men would understand that all He had been preparing them for was about to transpire. He reminded them that, for the kingdom to expand, He had to die. He reiterated that His death was not the end, but only the beginning of their life of faith. In a moment of raw honesty, He invoked the Father to describe the reason why He came. To the surprise and benefit of those present, the audible voice of God answered, "I have glorified it, and will glorify it again." (Jn 12:28).

While Jesus was on earth, He was both fully human and fully God. This is one of the marvelous mysteries of our triune God. Now that He is again in heaven (for the time being), His Spirit lives on in us, His believers. From the creation of the world, God made all things to glorify Himself. When He created humans in His image, it was the pinnacle of His masterwork. Not only does our very existence prove intelligent design, but our lives stand tribute to our glorious Creator. We were made to worship, love, serve, be in relationship with, and glorify God with our thoughts, words, and actions.

As Jesus' kin, we have a wide range of emotions that drive our attitudes, desires, and behaviors. Unlike Jesus, when we are faced with troubling decisions, we generally opt for the easiest alternative. Jesus gives us a beautiful example of resolving to remain faithful, even to the bitterest end. The lesson for us is to do the same. We must resolve to do God's will—not for our own gain, but for the glory of God. To do this, all of God's children, including Jesus, must listen to and obey the Father's commands.

Stepping In: Read Matthew 3:17, 6:9-10, 26:42 Luke 9:51; John 3:16–17; and Romans 12:2–3. How do these verses encourage you to remain resolute in your faith, as Jesus did? What is troubling your heart and keeping you from glorifying God? Talk to Him about it.

Stepping Out: This week, begin to root out any area of your life that does not bring glory to God. Prayerfully confess it to God, ask Him to remove it, and repent of it. For best results, get the assistance of an accountability partner to help you.

Honest

"Yes, it is as you say," Jesus replied. "But I say to all of you: In the future you will see the Son of Man sitting at the right hand of the Mighty One and coming on the clouds of heaven."

—Matthew 26:64 (Mt 26:47–68)

Many things transpired on the night Jesus was arrested. It started in an upper room in a stranger's house in Jerusalem, where Jesus and His disciples ate their Passover meal. During the course of the evening, Jesus professed His intention to sacrifice His life for the atonement of sin, initiated the institution of Communion, proclaimed one of His own a traitor, and performed the unthinkably subservient act of washing His disciples' (even His betrayer's) feet.

In a confused state and filled with grief, all but Judas Iscariot accompanied Jesus into the garden of Gethsemane outside the city wall. There, while even His closest companions slept, Jesus prayed His most anguished prayer. Yet He remained obedient to God's will. Judas handed his Master over to the hired mob and then slipped away with the other apostles as they fled in fear.

Alone, Jesus faced a series of unjust trials that led to His death sentence. When asked by the members of the Sanhedrin if He was the Christ, Jesus gave them an honest response: "Yes, it is as you say." By so doing, Jesus informed His captors that He was indeed the Son of Man—and that they had not seen the last of Him.

In only one other instance does Jesus admit that He is the Christ. Though He implied it frequently by telling people that He and the Father are one, and that He has the power and authority to forgive sins, He was careful not to divulge this incriminating truth too soon. However, when the time came for Him to go to the cross, these were the words it would take to prove His guilt in the eyes of His accusers. Adding to His blasphemous claim, Jesus was completely honest about His heavenly destination and redemptive plans. Though Christians today take the knowledge that Jesus is God as well-established fact, it was indeed privileged information in His day.

Throughout His human life, we see Jesus divulging surprising truths to the least likely of sorts, the story of the Samaritan woman being one (Jn 4:1-42). This speaks clearly to the beautiful inclusivity of our Lord's grace and wisdom. The lesson for us today is to follow Jesus' example of offering this revelation of saving grace to all, spoken in love and humility. Our Lord has shown that honesty is always the best policy.

Stepping In: Read Psalm 110:1, Daniel 7:13–14, John 4:25-26; and Revelation 1:7. Do you believe that Jesus is who He says He is? If so, thank Him by praying today's verse back to Him. Let Him know you look forward to when you get to meet Him face-to-face. If you do not yet believe, ask Him to reveal Himself to you personally.

Stepping Out: This week, do not keep this revelation to yourself. Be honest about your faith. Share the hope you have in Jesus by sharing His love with even the most unlikely of recipients—if only to tell them that Jesus loves them.

Counseled

"But I tell you the truth: It is for your good that I am going away. Unless I go away, the Counselor will not come to you; but if I go, I will send him to you."

—John 16:7 (Jn 16:1–16)

On the last night of His earthly ministry, Jesus utilized every teachable moment He had with His disciples. As they enjoyed their last Passover meal, He taught them about the necessity of His death. He said that they should remember His broken body and spilled blood each time they took Communion together. By washing their feet, Jesus taught His men about humble servanthood and brotherly love, which would be markers for their identities in Christ.

After Jesus had predicted His betrayal and denial, He sat down to teach one final time. Speaking plainly about what was to come, Jesus sought to warn, encourage, and comfort the apostles. He needed them to know without any doubt that the connection He had with His Father was the connection the apostles must have with Him, through the link of faith, prayer, and love. He promised them that although He would soon not be with them physically, they would not be alone. The Spirit of truth would be with them to guide and to help. They would be counseled. Help was on the way.

Anyone who has suffered the loss of a loved one can relate to the fear and grief the disciples must have felt on the night Jesus was arrested and taken away. He was their teacher, their leader, their friend, their Lord, and their only source of truth and hope. Because they could not imagine life without Him, Jesus spoke the words we find in the book of John (chapters 14–17).

When we read those words today, we as disciples hear Jesus' honest plea to trust Him. We are reminded that we are chosen by Him to continue the work of the apostles in bringing the good news to the world. He warns us that because of His name, we will experience resistance and persecution. But we are not to fear, because our pain and efforts serve important purposes: bringing glory to God and bringing salvation to those who accept our testimony.

Together, God's words, Jesus' examples, and our demonstrated faith leave the observer with ample reasons to believe. But Jesus knows that it will not be easy for us to persevere. He gives us more than we need to overcome and carry on: Himself in Spirit, living in us. Through the power of the Holy Spirit, all believers are counseled in the wisdom and will of our Father in heaven. Thus, we can stay confidently on our mission's course.

Stepping In: Read Deuteronomy 31:8, Joshua 1:9, Psalm 139, Isaiah 9:6, 63:11–14, Romans 8:22–27, and Galatians 5:25. How have you been counseled by the Holy Spirit? In what ways has He influenced your attitude or behavior? Pray for Him to draw you closer still so you can hear and respond to His voice.

Stepping Out: This week, as you have been counseled by the Spirit of truth, gently counsel others.

Evangelical

"And this gospel of the kingdom will be preached in the whole world
as a testimony to all nations, and then the end will come."
—Matthew 24:14 (Mt 24:1–14)

In Jerusalem's temple during His third year of ministry, Jesus spoke some harsh words of rebuke and accusation to the Pharisees and the teachers of the Law. Afterward, Jesus and His disciples retreated to the Mount of Olives. Jesus' men had many questions for Him, and He had much still to teach them in the limited time He had left before going to the cross.

The disciples were puzzled over His comments about the destruction of the temple, and asked Him to explain. They were also anxious to know when He would return after going to the Father. Trying to imagine how everything was going to unfold, they asked Him for a sign that would signify these imminent events. Clearly, the disciples needed guidance and comfort from their Master.

Thus, Jesus explained everything to them in detail, starting with an admonition to stay strong in their faith and not to be deceived by false Christs and prophets. He held nothing back. The future would be bleak, but their eternity was secure. Above all, they were to remain faithful to their evangelic callings until the very end. Jesus gave the disciples a glimpse of how their kingdom work would have far-reaching effects, beyond what they could possibly imagine.

This evangelic movement continues today, with no sign of slowing down in sight. In fact, there are still many dark places in the world yet to be exposed to the light of the gospel. That means that the work of Christian evangelism is far from over. Simply put, we still have plenty of work to do. However, as Jesus said, "The harvest is plentiful, but the workers are few" (Mt 9:37). Indeed, a minority of people still do the majority of the missional workload.

That said, there are two important things to remember. First, we should never underestimate the power of our Christian influence. Our faith-filled example, and the big and small things we lovingly do for others, can send a wide ripple effect of positive cultural change. Even if we cannot travel to remote areas and bring the gospel to those who have never heard it, we can help right where we are. We can help local missionary efforts; we can contribute financially to global missions; we can pray.

Second, never underestimate the power of God. If He calls us to share the gospel, no matter where that might be in the world, He will also equip us to make it happen. In fact, the more impossible the task is from a human perspective, the more glory God gets when it comes to fruition. If Jesus will not be satisfied until all have heard the gospel, then we should not be either.

Stepping In: Read Romans 8:28-30, 10:12-18 and Revelation 3:7-10, 16:12-15. How do these verses help you understand your role in bringing the gospel to the whole world? How do you feel, knowing that your influence will help usher the day of Jesus' return? Pray for a clear calling from God so that you can know your part in His plan.

Stepping Out: This week, pray about and consider what evangelic work God might be calling you to. In the meantime, contribute to missionary efforts through financial support, prayer, or both.

Patient

> "Do not leave Jerusalem, but wait for the gift my Father promised,
> which you have heard me speak about. For John baptized with water,
> but in a few days you will be baptized with the Holy Spirit."
> —Acts 1:4–5 (Acts 1:1–11; 2:1–12)

After Paul's encounter with the resurrected Jesus on the road to Damascus, this former persecutor of Christians became one of the faith's most avid proponents. As one of Jesus' unlikely (yet chosen) apostles, Paul boldly proclaimed the gospel to an ever-broadening sphere of influence during his lifetime. A person who was very much impacted by Paul's zealous faith was Luke, the writer of the book of Acts as well as a gospel account. A physician by trade, Luke used his intelligence and literary skills to write a detailed account of Christianity's first missionaries, creating an historical record of how the new faith was spread. Through the help of his friend and publisher, Theophilus, Luke intended for his account to provide solid proof of Jesus' power, and to encourage resilient faith among fledgling believers far and wide.

Luke was quoting a disciple's recollection of Jesus' words in the above verses. Knowing that His men would be inspired by His reappearance, and anxious to share the wonderful news of His victory over death (for Himself and all of humanity), Jesus commanded patience and obedience. Then the disciples became the first people in history to receive the indwelling Holy Spirit of truth.

In our stimulus-crazed world, the idea of waiting for anything leaves many of us feeling anxious. Patience, especially for people in this digital age, is not one of our virtues. Like children before Christmas, having to wait for what has been promised (if we are good), we restlessly fidget and pace, shaking the packages under the tree to decipher their contents, and incessantly ask our parents, "Is it time yet?"

As much as any expectant child, the despondent disciples longed for the gift of Jesus' promised presence and the security and comfort it would bring. When that moment was realized, these men were ready to spring into action, eager to heed their calling to spread the good news that Jesus had conquered death and was alive. Patience was not on their radar!

Yet Jesus told them to wait. They were asked to believe that God knows best, and to trust that His timing is always perfect. So wait they did, setting for us an example of obedience and patience for which they were richly rewarded. Jesus often asks us to wait—not for the Holy Spirit to come, but for the Spirit to move. We would be wise to learn from innumerable Bible examples that taking action before God gives the clear go-ahead never bodes well. However, with the help of the Holy Spirit, we can endure waiting for our next assignment in God's timing and in His way.

Stepping In: Read Acts 1 and 2, then look up names and titles of the Holy Spirit. Which of these resonates with you, and why? Pray for God to vitalize His indwelling qualities in you. Pray also for patience while you wait.

Stepping Out: Each day this week, pray for your church to be Jesus-focused and Spirit-driven above all.

Abiding

> Then he said to them, "Give to Caesar what is Caesar's and give to
> God what is God's."
>
> —Matthew 22:21 (Mt 22:15–22)

Jesus spent the last part of His ministry in and around Jerusalem. The majority of His time was spent teaching in the temple courts. Among the crowd of listeners were the religious leaders who questioned Jesus' authority and were increasingly threatened by His influence. In fact, after being put to shame twice in one sermon, the Pharisees were set on trapping Jesus in His words. They sent their own disciples as well as an enemy faction, the Herodians, to do so.

A united group of enemies approached Jesus, hoping to force Him into choosing between loyalty to God or loyalty to Caesar. After flattering Jesus, they laid their trap, asking whether it was "right [for Jews] to pay taxes to Caesar or not." From their perspective, they figured that either way Jesus answered the question, He would make Himself look bad. If He said yes, it was right to pay taxes to the occupying government, the people would consider Him disloyal to the Jewish nation. If He said no, He would be admitting treason, a crime punishable by death.

Regardless of their smooth approach, Jesus knew what they were trying to do. Instead of simply answering the question, He asked them for a coin. Turning the question back on His opponents, He asked them whose name and inscription were on the coin. "Caesar's," they replied. With that, they had their answer. Jesus then told His foes where their loyalty should abide.

Benjamin Franklin has been credited with the quip "Nothing in life is certain except for death and taxes." But long before Franklin, Jesus was speaking wisdom about such topics. Clearly, since their inception, taxes have been a burdensome obligation for most. One might say that they are a necessary evil, as they pay for many things needed to make our society functional. In ancient times, and even now in some parts of the world, taxes collected by an oppressive governing body are often exorbitant and mismanaged. Whether we like it or not, however, we are obliged to pay our taxes or pay a penalty.

Jesus wants us to be law-abiding citizens *and* to be generous with God. In today's passage, Jesus plainly states that our civic responsibility and abiding love for God are not in opposition, but should work in tandem.

Stepping In: Read Malachi 3:8-10; Romans 11:35-12:1 and 13:4-7. How do these verses encourage you to be more generous with God? How can your love for God be more abiding? Pray for wisdom about what pleases God, and ask for a willingness to do those things more diligently.

Stepping Out: Commit to living according to the Malachi 3:10 credo. Also, look for ways to be generous to God in other ways as well. Oh yeah, and don't forget to pay your taxes too!

Advised

> "He answered, 'Then I beg you, father, send Lazarus to my father's
> house, for I have five brothers. Let him warn them, so that they will
> not also come to this place of torment.'"
> —Luke 16:27–28 (Lk 16:19–31)

Perhaps hardened by past false prophets, the Pharisees and teachers of the Law failed to heed the calls of Jesus and of John the Baptist before Him. Disbelieving the validity of their claims that the kingdom of heaven was near, and discrediting the authority of the messengers, the religious elite saw both men as blasphemous nuisances. The elite believed that they were righteous before God because of their pure Jewish bloodline and adherence to the laws of Moses. Jesus' repeated references to forgiveness and repentance only aggravated them further. With the rise in Jesus' popularity and influence, the Pharisees' annoyance turned to murderous anger.

Knowing He was being watched by seething opponents, Jesus advised His disciples and devoted followers about many "religious" follies while speaking in parables. On one such occasion, after a candid lesson on trustworthy stewardship, Jesus told another parable about a rich man and a poor leper. The rich man led a luxurious life and the poor man a miserable one, and in time they both died. The poor leper went to heaven and the rich man to a "place of torment" (aka "hell" or "Hades"). Though told as a parable, the insinuation that the rich man represented the Jewish elite could not have been clearer. Begging for mercy, the rich man finally thought of someone other than himself. By then, it was too late.

It is stunning to think how lightly people can speak about heaven and hell. Some flatly deny the existence of either place. Others like the idea of heaven but dismiss the notion of a place of eternal torment. Of those who agree that heaven and hell are real, many have only a cursory interest in learning more about them.

The truth is, one day we will all find out for ourselves who is right. The Bible tells us that the human soul will go to one of two nonnegotiable places after death: a place with God or a place apart from God. Those who believe that Jesus is the way, the truth, and the life will be in paradise with Him forever. Those who reject Him will have chosen an eternity apart from Him, where there is "weeping and gnashing of teeth" (and worse) forever.

Jesus wants us to be advised about our choices, as He wants us to advise others. And though monetary wealth is not the issue here, Jesus used this illustration to remind us of the seductive and destructive allure of worldly comforts. Sadly, many will prefer to enjoy their rewards now rather than later.

Stepping In: Read Ezekiel 16:49–50; Matthew 6:2–4, 13:41–42; Mark 16:15–16; John 14:6; 2 Peter 2:4–13. Do these verses convict you of the need for all to hear God's truth? Pray for the courage to advise others of the truth.

Stepping Out: This week, heed the rich man's plea; bring the saving news of Jesus to your "brothers." Make it a goal to reach out to five people and let them know about their two choices.

Beholden

"Behold, I am coming soon! Blessed is he who keeps the words of
prophesy in this book."
                                                    —Revelation 22:7 (Rv 22:1–21)

When the apostle John wound up in prison on the Greek island of Patmos, he could never have
imagined the supernatural odyssey God was going to take him on. Employed to record God's end-
time revelation, John was given the task of writing a letter of encouragement and warning to the seven
churches in Asia Minor. After being transported "in the Spirit" into the very throne room of God,
John scribed all he saw and heard. He carefully quoted Jesus' words throughout this letter.

In this final scene, after God's judgment was complete and Satan vanquished, John recorded
the wonder and brilliance of the New Jerusalem "coming down out of heaven." John was shown the
Eternal City, with its streets of gold, and the River of Life pouring out from God's throne. The beauty
and splendor were almost too much to behold. Proof of God's promised redemption was before him,
and the words of angels confirmed that prophecy had been perfectly fulfilled.

Then John heard Jesus say the words in the above verse, calling for His listeners to pay attention;
His arrival was imminent. Jesus wanted the recipients of John's letter to know that upon His return,
all who beheld and heeded its warnings would be happy they did. Indeed, this apocalyptic message
would serve to excite and to warn generations of believers to come. Such believers have wondered if
they will see Jesus' return.

Because Jesus is completely faithful and trustworthy, we have no reason to doubt that, when
He says He is "coming soon," that is exactly what He means. Yet from our human perspective, two
thousand or more years is not "soon." In our world of high-speed internet and instant messaging,
having to wait more than five minutes for a mere text response is unacceptably slow. In the case of
God's coming wrath and judgment, however, not many of us are in a big hurry.

The truth is, though many have attempted to predict it, no one knows the time or day when Jesus
will come back. It could be tomorrow. Jesus wants us to be ready. He has given us His words through
the scripture to teach us His ways, correct our errors, and guide us toward the life He has planned
for us since the beginning of time. He has told us what must happen and has given each of us the
opportunity to choose Him, to choose Life. To behold Him and to keep His Word is to participate in
the Great Commission—to let others know how the story ends before it is too late.

Stepping In: Read Matthew 7:24-27, 16:27-28, 24:44, 28:18-21; John 8:51, 14:15, 15:9-11; 1 Thessalonians
5:1–6; and Revelation 1:3. How do these verses inspire you to share with others what Jesus has shown
you? Pray that others may become as beholden of Christ's truth as you are—and be ready for His
return.

Stepping Out: Take some time this week, in a small group or with a friend, to review the prophecies
in the Bible, especially in Revelation, and determine if you are heeding them. If you are not, plan to
do so soon.

Grateful

"Don't I have the right to do what I want with my own money? Or are you envious because I am generous? So the last will be first, and the first will be last."

—Matthew 20:15–16 (Mt 20:1–16)

While on His final journey to Jerusalem, Jesus taught his disciples about the dangers of self-reliance and love of worldly wealth. He referred to the sacrifices one must make to follow Him, and emphasized the backward nature of the kingdom of heaven, where those who seek first place will come in last and those who serve others will be first.

Jesus restated this same contrary conclusion in a parable about a generous vineyard owner and his envious employees. Jesus knew that the disciples were still having their own inner struggles regarding human versus spiritual values. He explained that generosity is the prerogative of the giver, especially if the giver is God. In this story, the master paid all his employees the same wage, regardless of how long they had been in the field. The disciples could easily recognize their own desire for favor and status, if not compensation. They would have grasped the warning about not allowing bitter competition to tarnish the joy of being heaven-bound. Only later would they comprehend how this lesson was also a foreshadow of potential jealousy that long-suffering believers might feel about those who had done far less for the kingdom, yet still received the same reward. What Jesus hoped they would come away with was a deep sense of gratitude for what their generous Father had blessed them with, regardless of what anyone else was given.

One of the core philosophies of twelve-step recovery programs today is that an "attitude of gratitude" is necessary for success. People today can become dependent on any number of things: sex, drugs, gambling, pornography, shopping, video-gaming, you name it. A core similarity that has persisted since Jesus' time is a dependence on self rather than on God. In an attempt to control our lives and our futures, we lean on our own strengths, knowledge, and efforts to create a sense of security.

Even Christians falsely believe in the illusion of earthly security, sometimes above our confidence in the omnipotent power of God. And, like the disciples, we keep a mental tally of our spiritual credits, thinking that we are somehow earning a higher position in the heavenly realms. In today's passage, Jesus puts that theory to rest.

Furthermore, jealousy has no place among believers. This is a test for those of us still anchored to a merit-based ideology. Instead of keeping score, we ought to be celebrating each wage earner, regardless of how or when those wages were earned. Our attitude should always be one of gratitude.

Stepping In: Read Psalm 136:1; Proverbs 27:4; Ecclesiastes 4:4; Philippians 2:3; Colossians 3:15; James 4:11–12; and 1 Peter 2:9–10. Meditate on the difference between jealousy and gratitude. Praise God for adopting you and all He will call.

Stepping Out: This week be grateful for God's generosity by accepting all believers for where they are in their journeys. Instead of being critical, be an encouragement.

January 10
Inclusive

"Do not stop him," Jesus said. "No one who does a miracle in my name can in the next moment say anything bad about me, for whoever is not against us is for us."

—Mark 9:39–40 (Mk 9:38–41)

On the outskirts of Galilee, away from throngs of needy followers, Jesus set about teaching His disciples many things regarding the coming kingdom of God. He began by informing them of the hard truth of His impending death and resurrection. The disciples, as yet spiritually immature, could not fully grasp their Master's meaning. They started to postulate about things to come, wondering who would be the greatest among them in the kingdom of which Jesus spoke.

Quickly correcting their wrong thinking, Jesus explained the nature of the servant/master relationship in His kingdom. They still did not discern the role of believers in God's hierarchy. Some of the disciples scolded and discouraged a man, who was not one of the Twelve, from doing miracles in Jesus' name. Jesus capitalized on the teachable moment once again by instructing His disciples to allow such kingdom work to happen, and moreover to encourage it. Clearly, the disciples had much to learn. The sooner they could exchange their limited and exclusive view of God's plan and Jesus' power for an infinite and inclusive view, the better.

Throughout the generations, there have been many false prophets who have abused verses like today's for their personal gain. This should not come as a surprise to anyone; Jesus Himself predicted this. However, Jesus is referring to *true believers* in these verses, not just anyone claiming to have power through affiliation.

Thankfully, Jesus provides a litmus test to determine authenticity. Anyone who performs a miracle in Jesus' name is an honest proponent of His authority and mission. Conversely, anyone who uses Jesus' name in vain or claims some other source of power (namely their own) for their wondrous acts, but doesn't give credit to God or name Jesus as Lord, is not an authentic disciple. Clearly, the former represents those who are *for* Jesus, while the latter represent those who are *against* Him.

This may seem somewhat obvious, but Jesus often reminds us to beware of Satan's deceit. To be on the safe side, we are wise to employ Jesus' method for determining the motives behind wowing displays of seeming altruism before deciding what camp the apparent miracle-worker falls into. On the flip side, we should encourage and include all who are the real deal.

Stepping In: Read Numbers 11:27–29; Matthew 12:30; and Philippians 1:15–18. What do these verses tell you about the importance of proper motives in effective ministry? What is your opinion of various approaches to healing and evangelizing? Are you inclusive or exclusive of those who do things differently, and why? Pray for discernment to distinguish Spirit-driven acts from false ones. Pray for unity among authentic believers.

Stepping Out: This week, be an encouragement to those doing miraculous kingdom work in Jesus' name, regardless of whether you approve of their status or methods. Be inclusive.

Straightforward

> Jesus answered, "Do you think these Galileans were worse sinners
> than all the other Galileans because they suffered this way? I tell you,
> no! But unless you repent, you too will all perish."
> —Luke 13:2–3 (Lk 13:1–9)

In His third and final year of ministry, Jesus' teachings and healings drew great crowds. So large were some that people's safety was jeopardized by the pressing throng. On one such occasion, Jesus was questioned by a riled group about an incident that had taken place in the temple in Jerusalem. Pilate's officials had killed some worshippers for allegedly failing to adhere to certain Roman sacrificial regulations.

To dispel the common Jewish belief that calamities of this sort were caused by some great sin, Jesus asked the question everyone was thinking. He followed it up with His emphatic "No!" With His public ministry soon to come to an end, Jesus began to speak in the most straightforward of manners. He wanted everyone to know what was at stake. He urgently encouraged His audience to understand their personal responsibility in pursuing a right relationship with God and in recognizing that all sin, big or small, must be atoned for. Rather than worrying about who was to blame, Jesus implored His listeners to repent—to turn to the One who would forgive them. Bringing the conversation from God's wrath to His mercy, Jesus then told a parable about an impatient vineyard owner, a fruitless tree, and the hopeful gardener who interceded on the tree's behalf. These stories helped to illustrate that God is just, abundantly forbearing, and kind.

Like the Israelites, all people have tried to understand the causes and effects of sin. Human beings were created by God with a moral compass. Most acknowledge that sin (going against God's laws) is something best to avoid—or perhaps just the consequences thereof.

God doesn't see sin like we do. Where we justify it, explain it, minimize it, ignore it, or blame it on someone else, God just sees it for what it is: sin. Sin separates us from God. And though sin will always get in the way of one's relationship with God, those who believe in Jesus' atonement need not fear permanent separation.

This theology is straightforward enough, yet misconceptions about God, Jesus, sin, and forgiveness abound. As Christians, it is our duty to lead others to truth. It is nevertheless the case that some take the straightforward approach too far, carrying signs and shouting through bullhorns, "Repent or die!" The parable in today's passage indicates that Jesus would like us to be more like the gardener than the vineyard owner: straightforward, yet caring.

In addition to gently speaking truth, it is also our responsibility to intercede on behalf of the hurting, confused, fearful, angry, and hopeless people in our midst. Yes, we live in a fallen world, where unexplainably terrible things happen. Jesus offers hope to those who look forward to the sinless eternity He promises. Let us lead others toward our Merciful Lord.

Stepping In: Read Job 4:7–9; Jeremiah 15:19; Ezekiel 18:30; Matthew 3:1–3; Acts 3:19; and Romans 3:22–24. What did these verses teach you about sin and repentance? What sin is God leading you to repent of? This week, confess it, receive Jesus' forgiveness, and do not return to it.

Stepping Out: This week, be brave and straightforward, yet humble and love-filled as you speak truth about sin, forgiveness, and repentance to someone who is still unclear about God's redemptive plan.

Found

> "For whoever wants to save his life will lose it, but whoever loses his life for me will find it. What good will it be for a man if he gains the whole world, yet forfeits his soul? Or what can a man give in exchange for his soul?"
>
> —Matthew 16:25–26 (Mt 16:21–28)

During His three-year ministry, many people came to faith in Jesus because of His mercy, teaching, and miracles. Aside from bringing spiritual enlightenment to as many of the "lost sheep of Israel" as would receive Him, Jesus focused on training His disciples for their future ministry of bringing the gospel to the entire world. Jesus spoke plainly with them about His imminent departure and the glorious reason for it.

Because of the disciples' limited spiritual perspective, the prediction of their Master's death was devastating to them. Though they had promised unwavering allegiance to Jesus, and Peter had rightly proclaimed Him the "Christ, the Son of the living God," they each silently grieved the loss of hope that Jesus was also their earthly king. They could not yet perceive that Jesus was the King of kings, the Redeemer of not just Israel, but the world.

And so, in another example of the backward laws of His kingdom, where the first is last and the greatest least, Jesus explained that to lose one's life *for Him* is to find it. The reassurance likely brought little comfort to the disciples in the moment, only more grief and confusion. No one voiced concern, but they certainly had to have been thinking, "How can giving up everything gain us anything?" Perhaps they were even wondering, "How can Jesus save our souls if He is dead?"

Thankfully, Christians today have the help of the Holy Spirit to understand the meaning behind Jesus' statements. Indeed, the entire Bible was written so that God's people would not be lost in their ignorance and sin. When we open of the pages of scripture and begin to place ourselves in the story, we suddenly go from lost to found, captive to free, dead to alive, doomed to saved. We see that God has a plan and a provision for every aspect of a believer's life, including what comes at the end of physical life.

The Bible makes it clear that our souls are not our own. They belong either to God or to Satan. Jesus purchases the souls of everyone who puts their faith in Him. All others will perish. Today's passage reminds us that this is a choice every person makes. With eternity at stake, it is nothing to take lightly. People who see no value in the life Jesus offers, preferring to live for the worldly things they can acquire and achieve, will ultimately lose everything. Sadly, many choose to be the so-called masters of their own destinies, not really knowing where that dire path leads.

Stepping In: Read John 12:25–26. Pray and earnestly seek God's will for your life. Do His wants and plans match up with yours? What are you claiming ownership of that you need to give over to Jesus? Pray for a willingness to yield to Him more.

Stepping Out: This week, pray for those who are not yet found in Jesus, that they will wisely choose life in Him. Pray for them by name, asking God to give them to Jesus as His own.

January 13

Exemplary

"Anyone who breaks one of the least of these commandments and teaches others to do the same will be called least in the kingdom of heaven, but whoever practices and teaches these commands will be called great in the kingdom of heaven."

—Matthew 5:19 (Skim Mt 5)

Speaking to a large and mostly Jewish audience on a hillside near Capernaum, Jesus was both encouraging and challenging over the course of the multiday Sermon on the Mount. In His second year in public ministry, Jesus had a reputation for being a miracle worker and bold teacher. Among the throng of onlookers were the faithful, the curious, the needy, and the cynical. Jesus promised them blessings for godly character and perseverance, and urged action in response to God's love.

Then He transitioned to the topic of Jewish law. Referring not only to the Ten Commandments, but also the law of the Prophets and the law yet to be established by Himself, Jesus boldly professed His intent—not to abolish, but to fulfill the law's every letter. This statement would have certainly aroused His listeners' attention. The Pharisees in the crowd would have been outraged by these seemingly blasphemous words. Targeting the pride, arrogance, legalism, and hypocrisy of these Jewish leaders, who imposed unattainable religious regulation on the people (and did not comply with such regulation themselves), Jesus explained the eternal consequences of their attitudes and actions. His words hit their mark, fueling the fire of the Pharisees' anger and setting in motion the plot to end His life. It is no wonder that the next topic in Jesus' speech was murder.

Though the world calls Christianity a religion, Christians often refer to it as a relationship. Today, believers in Christ are free from the burdens of unattainable laws and unresolvable sin. All the commands in the Old and New Testaments, every letter of the Law and the Prophets, and every prophecy ever written was or will be fulfilled by Jesus' life, death, resurrection, ascension, and return.

Yet, even in our freedom, we are obliged to obey God's commandments. Instead of the heavy burden and awkward yoke of endless rules and requirements, Jesus simplifies them for us with one command in two parts: to love the Lord your God, and to love others as you would like to be loved. With a cynical world watching, Christians must set an example of this command lived out in everything we do and say. Our words and actions must be sincere and from the heart. Otherwise, we run the risk of being no better than the image-driven, hypocritical Pharisees.

Stepping In: Read Exodus 20:1–17 and Matthew 22:36–40. Considering that loving God and others are the first and second greatest commandments, how exemplary is your life in these areas? Ask Jesus to direct your heart toward joyful obedience in these two essential Christian commands.

Stepping Out: This week, love your neighbor as yourself. Do something to improve your relationship with the people who live near you, even if it is a small gesture of kindness, helpfulness, or grace. Treat those closest to you with the utmost care—as you may need the favor returned one day.

Audible

> So they took away the stone. Then Jesus looked up and said, "Father,
> I thank you that you have heard me. I knew that you always hear me,
> but I said this for the benefit of the people standing here, that they may
> believe that you sent me."
>
> —John 11:41–42 (Jn 11:17–44)

Toward the end of His earthly ministry, Jesus briefly sought a respite from the persecution He faced in Judea. He spent some time in the less religiously volatile region of Perea, east of the Jordan. While He and His disciples were there, they received the news that Jesus' good friend Lazarus had fallen gravely ill. Regardless of the danger He was likely to encounter, Jesus decided He would go to Bethany and attend to His friend. However, seeing an opportunity to reveal His ultimate power, Jesus strategically allowed two days to pass before heading there.

He was met on the road by Martha, one of Lazarus' sisters. She informed Him that His friend had been entombed for four days. All hope of his restoration to health had long been lost. Speaking comforting words about being "the resurrection and the life," Jesus gave her a glimpse of His intended plan, not only to raise her brother but also Himself at the right time (Jn 11:25). Martha thought that He was referring to the end of the age, and her hopes were lifted only a little.

When Mary and the other mourners found Jesus, He could see their extreme grief—and their lack of understanding of His power over death. He was Himself moved to tears. However, He did not tarry in the moment; He asked to be shown Lazarus' tomb. Once there, He ordered the stone to be removed. Disregarding Martha's concern over the stench that would pour out of the cave, Jesus reminded the gathering to have faith. The stunned crowd watched as Lazarus responded to the Lord's audible voice. Lazarus emerged still wrapped in his graveclothes, but very much alive.

Without Jesus, death is a permanent state of misery and regret. According to scripture, hell is far worse than we could ever imagine. More than just a place of perpetual agony and torment, it is a devastatingly hopeless place of separation from God. The hunger and thirst people try to satisfy with things of this world are only a foretaste of the constant longing that those who do not choose Jesus' saving grace will experience eternally.

By contrast, Jesus is all we need to satisfy both physical and spiritual needs forever. He is our food (the Bread of Life), and our drink (the Living Water). We are His sheep and He is our Shepherd. He is the Gate that keeps us safe within the fold and shuts out the evildoers.

These are the words Jesus spoke while on earth. Today, Christians are blessed to hear God's voice in the written words of the Bible and through the whispers of the Holy Spirit. As with Jesus and the Father, communication between God and His children is reciprocal, conversational. Lovingly, our heavenly Father hears and responds to our cries. Respectfully, we listen to and obey His commands. Those who have trained their ears to His "still small voice" are given ample words to live fully by.

Stepping In: Read 1 Kings 19:11–13; Psalm 86:5-7, 116:1-2; Jeremiah 29:11-12, 33:3; Matthew 7:7–8; Luke 11:28; and James 4:2–3. How do these verses encourage you to call on *and* listen to God? If there is anything holding you back from bringing your prayers, praises, and petitions to God, ask Him now to relieve you of this burden.

Stepping Out: This week, have conversations with God, actively talking *and* listening.

Prayerful

"This, then, is how you should pray: 'Our Father in heaven, hallowed be your name, your kingdom come, your will be done on earth as it is in heaven. Give us today our daily bread. Forgive us our debts, as we forgive our debtors. And lead us not into temptation, but deliver us from the evil one.'"

—Matthew 6:9–13 (Mt 6:5–15)

In the middle of His earthly ministry, Jesus taught large crowds that gathered wherever He went. The Sermon on the Mount was one such occasion. After telling His audience that they should stop praying like babbling pagans, Jesus gave them instructions on how to pray instead.

Those hearing Jesus' instructions would have reacted to them in several ways. Some would have been encouraged to learn that God could be so approachable. Others may have been offended by being told exactly what to pray. The Jews in attendance, especially the religious leaders, may have thought this was a blasphemous statement, as only the chosen ones could call the one true God "Father." They had to have thought, "How can Jesus suggest that *all* may pray to God in such a personal and familiar way?" Even they, who had been praying to God for centuries, would never think to commune with Him in such a candid and direct way. Only the priests could speak plainly with God, sometimes at risk of offending Him with an improper approach.

For Jesus' disciples, however, this new way of praying brought the closeness that Jesus experienced with His Father into their own prayer lives as well.

Today, we take the Lord's Prayer for granted. Many of us memorized the Catholic version as children, and can still quote it with ease. Unfortunately, the rote nature of this recitation leaves us devoid of the spiritual impact this prayer was intended to have. We forget who first spoke it and why. We forget the power that this prayer can have when uttered with reverence and sincerity.

Jesus didn't have to help us learn how to pray, but He wanted to. He could have let us continue to ramble on ad nauseam, but He spared us (and Himself) the waste of time and energy. This prayer is an invitation for all to speak directly to our heavenly Father: acknowledge Him, center ourselves in His will, seek forgiveness, and place our requests at His feet. God is expecting our call. It is up to us to initiate a clutter-free line of communication with the Master of the Universe, the Lover of our souls, our Daddy.

Stepping In: Read several different versions or translations of this passage. Choose the one you like best and meditate on it using the Say It method.[1] Which word or phrase impacted your thinking most, and why?

Stepping Out: Read Matthew 6:5–15. Consider to what extent God has forgiven you. This week, forgive others *as* God has forgiven you (in the same way and to the same degree). Give unto others and it will be given to you as well.

---

[1] For more information about the Say It method and other methods I recommend in the Stepping In sections throughout this book, please see the appendix.

January 16
Vocal

> One night the Lord spoke to Paul in a vision: "Do not be afraid; keep
> on speaking, do not be silent."
>
> —Acts 18:9 (Acts 18:1–17)

After his life-changing experience with the resurrected Lord on the road to Damascus, Saul's (Paul's) days of persecuting and killing Jesus followers were over. Having been given back his physical sight, in addition to receiving spiritual insight, Paul was completely convinced that Jesus was the Christ. At Jesus' command, Paul made it his life's mission to share this news with the world.

And so, shortly after his conversion to Christianity, Paul joined the other apostles in their missionary work. Along with various companions, including Luke—the author of the gospel by the same name, as well as the book of Acts—Paul set out to bring the good news of God's kingdom in Christ to regions beyond Israel. By his third missionary voyage, Paul had seen many come to faith and be saved; those were the joyous successes which spurred him on. However, he had also faced plenty of rejection as well as violent opposition. He was harassed, beaten, chased out of towns, and imprisoned, all in the name of the Lord Jesus.

In Athens, his discouragement reached an all-time high. The city was full of idol-worshippers and confused people of God who seemed to have lost their way. Speaking boldly at every opportunity, Paul professed the truth of the resurrected Lord, and the hope and salvation found only in Him. But Athenians were hard-hearted, so Paul left and went to Corinth instead. There, he met a similarly oppositional and abusive crowd.

But Jesus did not leave Paul alone in fear. Through a vision, Jesus put fresh wind in Paul's sails. After that, Paul became all the more vocal in His proclamation of Christ.

God communicates with His people in a variety of ways. Before there was the written Word of God, the Bible, He spoke by way of angelic messengers, prophets, rabbis, visions, and dreams. Today, it is more common for us to receive encouragement, warnings, and instructions through scripture, sermons, godly friends, and direct communication with God through prayer.

Especially in times of need, worry, fear, and discouragement, it is a comfort that we as believers can call on Jesus personally, and that He will hear us and respond. Through this relationship of trust, we learn that we can confidently pursue the work He has given us, despite the hardships we face in doing so.

Contrary to how it may look or feel, the safest place for us to be is in the middle of God's will. Whether our calling takes us to a local homeless shelter to serve a hot meal to the less fortunate, or to a war-torn mission field on the other side of the planet, Jesus goes with us. With His indwelling Spirit working in and through us, we are empowered to act in love and truth. Today's verse is a command to speak up for Jesus.

Stepping In: Read Exodus 9:16; Deuteronomy 31:6, 32:3; Psalm 118:17; Matthew 28:19–20; Mark 16:15–16; and Acts 4:29. How do these verses encourage, embolden, or even challenge you to be a vocal proponent of Christ? Ask Jesus to reassure you of His power and provision as you walk in faith and speak and act in love.

Stepping Out: This week, be a vocal ambassador of Christ. Insert truth about Jesus into every conversation.

January 17

Peace-Giving

"When you enter a house, first say, 'Peace to this house.' If a man of
peace is there, your peace will rest on him; if not, it will return to you."
—Luke 10:5–6 (Lk 10:1–16)

In the final year of His ministry, Jesus' reputation as a prominent rabbi and powerful healer was at its height. He was in high demand wherever He went. After training and gifting His twelve disciples, Jesus appointed them apostles and sent them out to promote the kingdom of God to the nation of Israel. As a result, many people were healed and saved. His followers grew in numbers daily.

Unfortunately, because of His popularity and influence, the number of Jewish leaders who opposed Jesus and His followers was also increasing at an alarming rate. With His time quickly running out, Jesus commissioned seventy (some manuscripts say seventy-two) of His devoted followers to go out, two by two, into the countryside to offer the good news of His saving grace. As He had done with the Twelve, Jesus instructed them to take nothing with them for their journey, to rely on the hospitality of strangers, and to trust in God's provision.

In the above passage, Jesus gave them further instruction regarding how to approach the people they would encounter. The culture of the time highly valued hospitality, and hosting those who came with a word from God was an honor. To be deemed unworthy of the privilege would have been a shaming experience—one they would likely take to heart.

This is the first example in the Bible of average citizens evangelizing. It is an important lesson for Christians throughout history regarding proper gospel-sharing etiquette. Today, the buddy system is still used in many outreach programs as a matter of best practice, if not safety.

For those of us not sent out to evangelize, sharing God's Word is most effectively done through authentic interpersonal relationships, in which familiarity and trust are well established. We intentionally come alongside our friends, neighbors, coworkers, classmates, and family members who could use spiritual encouragement. By meeting them in their own homes or in neutral territory, we allow them to feel comfortable and in control of their environment. By offering peace and open-mindedness before anything else, we set the stage for a positive encounter. By bringing our own personal witness to the conversation, we show how Christianity is a relationship instead of a religion. By interspersing scripture passages that have been helpful to us in our walk with Christ, we plant powerful seeds of hope. Through the Spirit's guidance and prayer, our peace-giving will come to rest on many.

Stepping In: Read Numbers 6:24–27; 1 Kings 2:33; Psalm 29:10-11, 37:37-38; and John 14:27. God has a lot to say about peace. What is He saying to you about the amount of peace you have in your life, and how much you offer to those around you? Pray for the Spirit to give you enough peace to share with others.

Stepping Out: This week, put this verse into practice. Build authentic relationships based on peace-giving interactions. From that standpoint, you can then share the good news of your Savior, Jesus.

January 18

Unadulterated

"Listen and understand. What goes into a man's mouth does not make him 'unclean,' but what comes out of his mouth, that is what makes him 'unclean.'"

—Matthew 15:10–11 (Mt 15:1–20)

During His time ministering to the people in Galilee, Jesus encountered seekers of all kinds. Most who sought Him out needed physical and spiritual healing; Jesus met their needs. Many came out to experience His authoritative teaching, and perhaps hoping to witness a miracle or two; Jesus never disappointed. Some showed up to gain evidence of His unlawful and blasphemous ways; Jesus always left them stumped.

In one such instance, some Pharisees and teachers of the Law journeyed all the way from Jerusalem to confront Jesus and His disciples about disobeying Jewish traditions regarding cleanliness. Apparently, word had reached the ears of this pious group that Jesus and His disciples were not in the habit of performing ceremonial hand-washing prior to eating. Armed with self-righteous indignation and hoping to discredit Jesus, these men hurled their accusation at Him in front of a crowd—only to have the accusing finger pointed back at them. Jesus revealed the Pharisees' hypocrisy and emphasized their misguided beliefs by quoting the words of God's prophet, Isaiah. Then Jesus got to the heart of the matter: the origins of evil are not from without, but from within. All the ceremonial washing in the world will not cleanse stained souls.

It is important to remember that today's verses are not actually talking about food choice or sanitation. By "unclean," the Pharisees meant that because Jesus and His disciples had not complied with their religious code of conduct (i.e., man-made rules), they were considered contaminated and unworthy of participating in further religious activities until the appropriate purifying steps were taken. Essentially, the Pharisees were telling Jesus that His rabbinical status was void until proven otherwise. That would have been true had Jesus been merely a human teacher.

This passage points out the tendency of the self-righteous to project their notion of what is godly onto others, including God Himself. Though we tend to look down on the Pharisees for their closed-mindedness, Christians today are sometimes guilty of the same hypocrisy—which boils down to a "do as I say, not as I do" mentality. These verses are a reminder that an unadulterated faith begins with a pure heart.

Stepping In: Read Luke 6:45 and Acts 10:9–16. How do these verses help you better understand where religious purity originated? How do they stir your awareness of your own faulty theology? Pray that the Spirit of God gives you a heart of compassion and a mind of discernment.

Stepping Out: This week, think before you speak! Put every word you are about to say through the filter of spiritual wisdom. Does it communicate what is truly in your heart? Is it based on unadulterated biblical truth? Does it honor God? And, is it useful for building others, and yourself, up? If not, it is probably best left unsaid.

Confident

"And when you pray, do not keep on babbling like the pagans, for they think they will be heard because of their many words. Do not be like them, for your Father knows what you need before you ask Him."

—Matthew 6:7–8 (Mt 6:5-15)

During His Sermon on the Mount, Jesus spoke directly to the heart of His listeners. With the Pharisees and religious leaders in mind, He spoke candidly about proper prayer etiquette. After lambasting those who were in the habit of standing on the street corners pontificating for all to hear, Jesus reiterated that all the pomp and circumstance, and all the flowery language and excess words were unnecessary. Indeed, their attempts to sound ultra-godly sounded more like babbling pagans to God. Jesus' comments, though embarrassing to the pagans, would have been infuriating to the religious elite. Because He had said, "your *Father* knows what you need before you ask Him," the Jews understood that the lesson of this passage was meant for them. Jesus was not only instructing His audience about prayer, but He was teaching about pride. More than anything, Jesus wanted the people to be confident in God and not themselves– especially when it came to prayer.

Jesus knew how His words would affect His audience. He chose to bring an element of tension to His teaching because it would stir people to action. The pagans in the crowd likely considered their tendency toward lengthy diatribes and quietly committed to toning them down in the future. The Jews, mortified to be compared to heathens, likely seethed in anger, but doubtlessly vowed to make the necessary changes never to put in that camp again.

Prayer has always been a sacred and beautiful privilege. It is our way of communicating with the Creator and Master of the universe. It is a holy lifeline to our heavenly Father. Because of this, Jesus teaches us how to pray. He does not want us to make the same mistakes the priests and the Pharisees did: caring more about being heard by others than by God. He also does not want us to be ignorant about the God we are praying to, as the pagans were.

To ensure that we are never left to flounder in our pursuit of God, Jesus gives believers the Holy Spirit. Even so, the influence of the dominant culture can blur a Christian's spiritual vision when it comes to proper prayer etiquette. With skeptical eyes watching, a Christian may feel compelled to use many churchy words, in the hope of sounding credible. Knowing that the ears of the yet unsaved are listening, a Christian may find herself or himself preaching instead of praying for God's will.

Jesus reminds us to keep it simple and to focus on God. Today's verse is a wonderful reminder that prayer is more about what we offer to God than what we seek from Him. Confident that He already knows our requests, we can use our words to praise Him instead.

Stepping In: Each time you pray this week, imagine that you are sitting on your heavenly Father's lap. Let the closeness and intimacy of your relationship do the speaking for you. Seek His will, ask Him what pleases Him, and thank Him for knowing and loving you so well.

Stepping Out: Be an example of praying with confident simplicity this week. Exude the peace and comfort that comes from knowing that your Father is aware of your need and is already working for your good in all situations you bring before Him.

Clement

"Be merciful, just as your Father is merciful."
—Luke 6:36 (Lk 6:12–36)

Once Jesus had assembled His twelve disciples, He concentrated His efforts on training them to carry on His ministry, preparing them to be the first missionaries of the Way. He often spoke very candidly about contrasting attitudes and behavior among those truly devoted to God and His causes versus those who only claimed such allegiance.

After a night of prayer, Jesus gathered His disciples to teach them many moral lessons in His Sermon on the Mount. He began with a series of blessings and warnings. In extremely clear terms, He pointed out the reward for faithful perseverance and the consequences for greedy and gluttonous behavior.

Jesus was not suggesting His disciples avoid evildoers. In fact, His commands dictated the opposite approach: loving one's enemies. Knowing this would stir a thoughtful response among those with a heart for God, and a resentful resistance among those whose hearts were far from God, Jesus concluded with His injunction for mercy. Though the whole audience benefited from the teaching, the deeper message was for Jesus' disciples. Jesus gave them a glimpse into their future work of offering reconciliation to the Gentiles, and reminded them that their heavenly Father had first extended clemency to them.

To a non-Christian, today's verse would mean very little. Truly, the word "Father" may conjure up a host of emotions, many of them not good. The notion of mercy is rather foreign in our me-centric world. In the context of loving one's enemies—in and of itself a crazy idea—showing grace, forgiveness, and kindness to those who mistreat us just doesn't make sense.

From a strictly human perspective, all this is quite true. For Christians, however, each word in this verse should bring about a happy realization of our blessed state. Because we have been shown undeserved mercy, to the extent that our lives have been saved now and for eternity, we can extend that same gift to others. Our loving Father has shown us how. Jesus gave this command to His apostles so that we, who were once enemies of God, could experience grace, mercy, and hope. Out of our gratitude, we are to be equally clement to others.

Stepping In: Read Micah 6:8; Romans 5:10, 8:15; Colossians 1:21–23; James 2:12–13; and 1 John 3:1. Look up verses about God's mercy as well. Take some time to meditate on today's verse using the Emphasize It method (See appendix). Thank Jesus for His mercy toward you, and ask Him for a merciful heart toward others.

Stepping Out: Choose an area in which God has been especially clement to you, and extend that same kindness to someone (maybe even someone you are not particularly fond of) this week. In following Jesus' command, give to another just as God has given to you.

Yielding

"But the one who received the seed that fell on good soil is the man who hears the word and understands it. He produces a crop, yielding a hundred, sixty or thirty times what is sown."

—Matthew 13:23 (Mt 13:1–23)

Jesus entered His ministry fully aware that His message would be received in a variety of ways. Many people were attracted to His message of hope and redemption. When He began performing miracles, healing the sick and demon-possessed, and even reviving the dead, people flocked to see what He might do next. By the middle of His ministry, vast numbers of people followed Jesus, all wanting something different from Him, each able to accept Him in his or her own way.

A large crowd gathered on the shores of the Sea of Galilee and Jesus began to teach them from a boat. He told a story about a farmer sowing seeds on different types of soil. When His disciples asked Him why He spoke in figures of speech, Jesus explained that only those to whom He gave the ability to understand His parables would gain the wisdom they contained. All others would receive only generic advice.

In the parable of the sower, Jesus was informing His disciples that, like Him, they would be casting their seed of truth among all kinds of people: those who would receive it quickly, then fall away at the first sign of adversity; those who would receive it and begin to grow in their faith until worldly worries became all they could see; and those who would refuse to accept it at all. One group, however, would be those whose hearts were full of faith, but to varying degrees. The moral of His teaching was that the better the soil (the listener's heart), the greater the yield of the heavenly crop.

Because Jesus wanted His disciples and us to understand the meaning of this parable, He went on to explain it in detail. The message for all Christians is clear. We are to share God's truth generously, broadcasting its seeds widely, in the knowledge that not all of it will be well received.

Jesus does not tell us this so that we can be absolved of any further gardening duties. To the contrary, it should be our goal to improve the growing conditions in any way we can, starting with our own soil! As we build relationships with unbelievers, we begin to clear the field of rocks and roots by laying the topsoil of biblical truth. Once some seeds have been planted, we must fertilize the soil with our example and testimony. When we see new growth emerging, it is essential that we weed and water. The choking vines of worldly deception must be kept down. The heat of scrutiny must be quenched with the water of biblical truth spoken in love. Even the rich soil of born-again believers must be stirred and amended with regular infusions of spiritual nourishment. Beyond the obedience of sharing God's love and truth, we too must continually assess and improve our own soil.

Today's verse is a reminder that spiritual maturity is like a garden. Left unattended, things may grow, but to yield a fruitful crop one must mindfully and repeatedly address the condition of the soil. A pliable heart is the rich soil God can use in His garden. And it will yield an eternal crop!

Stepping In: Take some time to recall what your soil was like when you first put your faith in Christ. What is the condition of your heart now? Pray for an increasing yield in your faith life.

Stepping Out: This week, while nurturing your own heart, work at amending the soil of those in whom you have planted seeds. Liberally share the richness of knowledge God is teaching you.

Prudent

> "Settle matters quickly with your adversary who is taking you to court. Do it while you are still on your way, or he may hand you over to the judge, and the judge will hand you over to the officer, and you may be thrown into prison."
>
> —Matthew 5:25 (Mt 5:17-26)

While speaking about murder during His Sermon on the Mount, Jesus expressed the necessity of expediting resolution with those with whom one has a dispute. Knowing that crowd would understand that, whenever possible, it was best to avoid the cost, hassle, and consequences of involving a judge in one's personal affairs, Jesus suggested a more prudent approach.

Still, some might have puzzled over the emphatic nature of this warning. Jesus wanted His statement to cause His listeners to consider many things. Who is one's adversary, and what does that adversary have against one? Is it better to invite slander and extortion, rather than defend oneself in court and prove one's innocence? Is it truly better to cut one's losses and seek resolution, rather than pursue justification? The answers to these queries reveal one's heart, whether one's motives are pure or full of pride and greed. By prompting the questions, Jesus hoped to stir more than His audience's moral conscience. His greater desire was to awaken a spiritual perception of the true accuser—Satan—who would attempt to lead all of God's people toward eternal judgment.

Legally speaking, Jesus' advice in this verse is good. However, Christians (with the help of scripture and the aid of the Holy Spirit) can also ascertain a deeper meaning and heed the eternal warning therein: seek justice not retribution. The New Testament makes it clear that the adversary is the Devil himself, the judge is God, and the officers are most likely angels (employed by whose side is uncertain).

Even with all the biblical knowledge in the world, we must first recognize our opponent to resist him. Then we must weigh the costs of taking him on. Jesus says, "Don't even go there." Stop the proceedings before they start. Cut your losses if necessary. From a strictly legal standpoint, settling out of court is almost always the safer and more cost-effective means of putting an end to a potentially ugly mud-slinging session. From a spiritual perspective, it is by far the preferred way to avoid entanglement with the Enemy—especially considering the costly consequences.

Stepping In: Read Matthew 5:21–26 and 1 Peter 5:8–9. Considering these passages, which refer to the battle for your soul, what steps will you take to "meet your adversary on the road"? Pray for the Holy Spirit to fortify you and give you discernment for who to be on guard against, and how to deal with them prudently.

Stepping Out: Make every effort not to be adversarial yourself. If you have an outstanding matter with someone, seek a peaceful and fair resolution this week—out of court if possible, for everyone's best interest.

January 23
Assenting

"Follow me."
—Matthew 9:9 (Mt 9:1–12)

While walking through the streets of Capernaum, early in His earthly ministry, Jesus issued this abrupt command to a young man named Matthew, also known as Levi. From the other side of his tax-collecting booth, a wide-eyed Matthew could not believe his ears. "Why is this influential rabbi talking to me?" he must have thought. "Doesn't He see who I am?" Instead of disregarding or despising this young fellow for being a greedy and corrupt Roman sympathizer, Jesus saw him as a potential recruit, full of initiative and potential.

Matthew, who had no doubt heard about Jesus, was left with a choice: stay in his lucrative but socially abhorrent job, or make a fresh start with this charismatic stranger? The command to follow was more than a spontaneous invitation from Jesus. It was an intentional selection on His part. It was a summons that required wholehearted commitment and absolute devotion.

Nonetheless, Matthew's response was immediate. Without hesitation, he quit his job and assented to His new rabbi's request. With that decision, Matthew's life would forever be changed, starting with his vocation and his name. A special note about this Matthew's two names: Levi, his Hebrew name, means "attached" or "to take." Jesus called him by the Greek translation of his name, Matthew, meaning "a gift of Yahweh."

Today, most of our lives are ruled by our jam-packed schedules. We have jobs, homes, kids, friends, and hobbies, all clamoring for our attention. Most of us have responsibilities galore and inescapable debt to attend to. Our cell phones and day-planners are our constant companions. The thought of just dropping everything at a moment's notice to pursue the will of our unseen Savior defies logic. From a human perspective, that choice would be impulsive, foolish, and totally irresponsible.

Yet deep in a Christian's soul is a place that knows assenting to Jesus' commands is always the best move. With the discernment of the Holy Spirit, we can look beyond the immediate and into eternity. From that perspective, we can confidently follow Jesus whenever and wherever He leads us. Jesus chooses us, as He chose Matthew, not for our knowledge, abilities, or righteousness, but for our willingness to obey His call and trust Him with the outcome. That knowledge should spur us to a similarly rapid response.

Stepping In: Take some time to think about the names or titles you go by. Who gave these to you? Do you agree with them? Ask God to whisper the name He calls you by, what it means, and why He chose it for you. Thank Him for this special endearment.

Stepping Out: This week, be willing to promptly and joyfully assent to Jesus' requests.

Attuned

"He who has an ear, let him hear what the Spirit says to the churches.
To him who overcomes, I will give the right to eat from the tree of life,
which is in the paradise of God."

—Revelation 2:7 (Rv 2:1–7)

The apostle John, who was known by the affectionate title of "the disciple whom Jesus loved," experienced many joys and hardships in his time as a missionary for Christ. Both the Jewish leaders and the Roman officials constantly opposed those who worked for the promotion of the Christian effort, so John and his colleagues regularly faced fierce persecution. In fact, many were martyred for the cause. John himself narrowly and miraculously escaped being boiled alive in hot oil, only to be imprisoned on the small Greek island of Patmos, where he spent a year in relative isolation.

God used this time to His advantage. Away from the distraction of the world and the demands of apostleship, John gave his undivided attention to the Lord, especially on the Lord's Day (Sunday—a day of rest, even for prisoners). During these quiet times, the Lord supernaturally transported John into His presence. God gave John specific words to write as an encouragement and a warning to the seven churches in Asia Minor.

In His address to the church in Ephesus, Jesus first commended its leaders for their virtuous deeds. Then He rebuked them for having forsaken Him, their "first love." Calling them to repent and return to the devotion they once had, Jesus encouraged them to refrain from spiritual compromise and to attune their hearts to Him instead. Jesus offered the Ephesians an opportunity and a promise: listen, hear, and enjoy the "fruit" of the victorious.

In our stimulus-rich world, we can hardly escape the daily bombardment of sights and sounds that are always around us. We may be listening to the radio, talking with a friend, glancing at our Facebook page, reading emails, or texting—and all while walking or driving (though not safely). This shows that, while we may appear to be paying attention to the things going on around us, we are only able to process some of it. We hear a great deal, but listen to very little.

Throughout scripture, God repeatedly calls on His people to hear His words, listen to what they say, and heed them. But this requires us to face the speaker and tune in only to Him—a tall order in our frenzied lives. This is where Christians must be different. With the world watching us, we must set the example of how to attune our focus to Jesus. We are called to be light to those living in darkness, to bring hope to the hopeless, and to share truth with those trapped in lies. We cannot do this from behind our electronic devices. All of us who are blessed to be called "overcomers" came to be so by listening to someone who shared the gospel. It is now time for us to return the favor.

Stepping In: Read Genesis 2:9, 3; Proverbs 16:20; Jeremiah 29:12, 33:3; John 16:33; Romans 8:34–37; James 1:22; and 1 John 5:1–5. Take some time to thank God for forgiving your sins and inviting you to His heavenly banquet.

Stepping Out: This week, attune your ear to God's words and commands. Ask the Spirit to direct you toward obedient action. If nothing else comes to you, hand out "tree fruit" in the name of Jesus.

January 25
Believing

"Do you believe that I am able to do this?"
—Matthew 9:28 (Mt 9:27–34)

At the height of His ministry, while Jesus and His disciples were teaching and healing in Galilee, two blind men groped their way into the crowd that surrounded Jesus. Shouting through the assembly, "Have mercy on us, Son of David," these two would not be dissuaded in their pursuit of the One they had heard was a healer sent by God—the rumored Messiah.

Later, after Jesus had gone indoors, away from the pressing throng, the two men continued their unrelenting pursuit of Him. They made their way into the house and came before Jesus, steeped in hope that their request would be granted. To be sure of their faith, Jesus asked them, "Do you believe?"

The men replied emphatically, "Yes, Lord!"

Filled with compassion, Jesus not only spoke words of healing to these two new believers, but did what no other rabbi would consider doing: He touched the untouchables.

The days of agreements being settled with a word and a handshake seem to be a thing of the past. The unfortunate truth of our world today is that little credibility is given to the spoken word. Now, it seems, we do not make any deal without a signed contract in triplicate. We are skeptical, believing only what we have seen for ourselves.

So, what happens if we too no longer have the use of our eyes to validate truth? In many ways, this is the spiritual situation for all of us. We cannot see Jesus performing miracles per se, but does that make those miracles any less real? No. We take Jesus at His word, and we recognize miracles for what they are—or better yet, where they came from. With the indwelling Holy Spirit, our Bible, and wise and trusted fellow servants of God to help us discern the truth, Christians can point others to the healing wonders and faithful promises of our Savior. Together, we can help to eradicate spiritual blindness, as we touch the lives of others for eternity. Following Jesus' example, we too must establish contact with the blind to open their eyes.

Stepping In: Read Isaiah 35:5–6; Also, skim the references to the word "believe" in your Bible's concordance. There is a lot to be said about belief. Now look at Genesis 15:4–5. What promises of God do you struggle to believe? Pray and ask Him to give you blind faith.

Stepping Out: This week, ask the Spirit to lead you toward those whom Jesus wants you to lay your hands upon and pray for healing. This gift of the Spirit is given only to those Jesus chooses for His purposes and in His timing. That said, it is good to pray for the awareness of God's leading, and to be ready to act faithfully if and when the time arises.

January 26
Protective

"Do not give to dogs what is sacred; do not throw your pearls to pigs. If you do, they may trample them under their feet, and then turn to tear you to pieces."

—Matthew 7:6 (Mt 7:1–8)

When Jesus concluded His thoughts on judgment with this statement, the listening crowd no doubt struggled to find meaning in His odd and incongruent suggestion. They may have wondered, "What do pearls, dogs, and pigs have to do with judging?"

In the culture of Jesus' day, dogs and pigs were considered unclean and valueless. Neither were good for food nor sacrifice. They were not allowed in homes or temples. Clearly, no one would be so careless as to give them table scraps, let alone treasured possessions.

But Jesus gave His listeners a grammatical clue as to the true meaning of this passage when He stated that "sacred" things treated carelessly would be trampled under "feet," not paws or trotters. Even if the cleverest of listeners figured out that the dogs and pigs of which Jesus spoke were actually vile and dangerous people, only the most discerning would decipher "what is sacred" to mean the Word of God. Jesus was imploring the faithful to be protective of God's precious treasures – His wisdom and truth.

Even theologians of our day struggle to unlock the mysteries of Holy Scripture. Many passages are still shrouded in uncertainty—on purpose. Our finite minds are limited for our own good. Some truths become revealed in time, and some never do. God decides.

What this verse says is that what we are allowed to know is a precious gift for believers. Once we receive this knowledge, we are to protect it from harm. Jesus tells us to be careful not to share this special treasure with those who will misuse or abuse it. If we do, we stand to do both our physical bodies and our church body irreparable harm. Though there is a fine line between judging someone and accurately discerning their character, Jesus has decided that it is a lesson worth learning. Today's verse should remind Christians of the extreme importance of protecting the sacredness of God's Holy Word, both Jesus and His truth.

Stepping In: Read Galatians 5:22–23; Colossians 3:12–15; 1 John 4:8; and Proverbs 28:6. Meditate on the characteristics that distinguish Christians from non-Christians. Pray that God will develop these more fully in you and in others. Pray for truth and salvation to come to unbelievers.

Stepping Out: This week, do more asking than telling. Build relationships. As stewards of God's priceless message, share it carefully. Be aware and protective not to carelessly toss Jesus' name around, or draw negative attention through inappropriate preaching or oversharing. Pray for the Spirit's discernment for when to share gospel truths and when to keep quiet.

Observant

> "Why were you searching for me?" He asked. "Didn't you know that
> I had to be in my Father's house?"
>
> —Luke 2:49 (Lk 2:1–52)

Each year, according to Jewish custom, Jesus' father Joseph went down to Jerusalem from Nazareth to partake in the Passover festivities. When Jesus was twelve years old, both Jesus and His mother Mary accompanied Joseph on this pilgrimage. While they were there, Jesus went with His parents to the temple to worship God. When the celebrations ended, Mary and Joseph joined the caravan heading back toward Nazareth. After a day of travel, however, they realized that Jesus was not with them.

In a panic, Mary and Joseph hurried back to Jerusalem. For three days they searched the city, only to eventually find Jesus right where they had left Him—in the temple. Relieved yet hurt, Mary asked Jesus why He had put her and His father through such an ordeal, to which He gave the above reply.

At that time, neither of Jesus' parents fully understood what He meant, nor could they grasp the significance of His seemingly defiant act. However, all who had heard Jesus' discerning remarks and wise questions to the rabbis reported to His parents their amazement over the boy's spiritual insight. Filled with pride and joy, Mary treasured this knowledge, and said no more about the incident. She knew in her heart that Jesus had done what was right before God. Jesus went back home with His parents and remained obedient to them thereafter.

Parents in every generation most likely relate to this story all too well, at least the part about Mary and Joseph experiencing panic over thinking they had lost their child. Instantly, an image is conjured up of not seeing your own son or daughter in a crowd, or of a toddler wandering off when you thought the child was right beside you. Parents feel the need to keep extremely close tabs on their children for fear of abduction or other evil acts befalling them. It is a parent's instinct to protect their offspring from harm.

Though these are legitimate concerns, these are not the main point of this story. Instead, this passage teaches us to be observant of the spiritual needs of the next generation. Jesus needed to spend time with His heavenly Father, but His earthly parents were unaware of that need. So unaware were they, in fact, that they did not even notice He had stayed in the temple after they left.

As people of all ages grow in the maturity of their faith, their spiritual needs change. Those of us who can support them in this journey should do so. The best support is to encourage others to do as Jesus does—stay with the Father, seeking His will and His ways.

Stepping In: Read Genesis 28:16–17; Jeremiah 29:12–13; and Luke 4:16. How observant are you of those seeking Jesus? How are you helping them to find Him? Pray for insight for whom to come alongside and how.

Stepping Out: This week, offer encouragement to someone who is seeking God or growing in faith.

January 28
Trusting

"Which of you, if your son asks for bread, will give him a stone? Or if he asks for a fish, will give him a snake? If you then, though you are evil, know how to give good gifts to your children, how much more will your Father in heaven give good gifts to those who ask him!"
—Matthew 7:9–11 (Mt 7:1–12)

At the root of all Jesus' teaching was a theology of restoration. In the Sermon on the Mount, Jesus emphasized the importance of seeking a right relationship with God and then with others, based on love and trust. After encouraging the people to persistently pursue God and bring their requests directly to Him, Jesus promised that the doors of heaven would open for them.

While the idea of an accessible God would have thrilled the general population, it would have been a threat to those who controlled the current religious system. Jesus reiterated His point with an ironic comparison: if human parents were to be trusted to lovingly provide for their children, "how much more" would the Father of all provide? Jesus is suggesting that not only is the heavenly Father an approachable and trustworthy God, but He is generous and practical as well.

Unlike the Jews of Jesus' day, Christians today enjoy direct access to our heavenly Father. This is not something we should ever take for granted. Jesus bought this route to God with His own blood. By trusting that Jesus' sacrifice on the cross was sufficient to atone for the sin of the world, the evil that once separated us from God's grace has been removed.

Yet, saved as Christians may be, it is still up to us to pursue God. (Ask, seek, knock.) We are blessed to have God's Word in its entirety at our disposal. We can easily read and reread His Sermon on the Mount whenever we choose. The disadvantage of this is that familiarity often breeds complacency. With too many things vying for our attention, it is easy to simply graze on scripture, and not take it in. When we do this, we miss out on the richness of His Word and the depth of His teaching.

When we trust God with our time and our lives, He rewards us with nourishing bread (truth), and gives us opportunities to fish for lost souls and to removal "stone" barriers that hinder godly pursuits. At the same time, He protects us against the serpent and his deception. All this is available to those who ask.

Stepping In: Read Genesis 3:15; Matthew 4:1–4, 6:7–8, and 28:1–2; John 6:1-13, 11:38-44; and Revelation 12:9, 20:2. Reflect on the richness of today's passage. Thank God for His sovereign plan. Consider the things you ask God for. Are they wants or needs? Ask Him to show you how He has already rewarded you for trusting Him. Praise Him.

Stepping Out: This week, be a good gift giver. Anticipate and act on the needs of others before they ask—or better yet, without them even knowing who gave to them.

Mindful

> "You have heard it was said to the people long ago, 'Do not murder, and anyone who murders will be subject to judgment.' But I tell you that anyone who is angry with his brother or sister will be subject to judgment."
>
> —Matthew 5:21–22 (Mt 5:21–26)

The mostly Jewish crowd gathered to hear Jesus' teaching would have recognized His reference to the sixth commandment. Of the ten sins to avoid, this one was an obvious moral and legal offense, justifying severe repercussions. Upon hearing the first part of Jesus' statement, the knowing crowd no doubt nodded their heads in agreement. However, the second half would have left most confused, if not miffed. What was Jesus talking about? Was He saying that anger deserved the same punishment as murder? This was a hard teaching. No one would contest a harsh punishment for the taking of a person's life. But, according to this young rabbi, even thoughts of rage would result in judgment. If this was true, could anyone escape God's wrath?

Some may have decided to discredit Jesus' theology thereafter. Those who decided to have an open and mindful approach came to realize that Jesus was saying that judgment is the result of an unmerciful heart attitude, more than just a person's actions.

Murder is usually viewed as an unforgivable offense. Even in our day and age, when our sources of entertainment seem to glorify violence and distort our sense of accountability, most of us innately know that taking a human life is wrong.

Jesus takes this notion to a deeper level, reminding us that we have a moral and social responsibility to harness our thoughts, words, and actions, and to be mindful of the effect we have on others. True to Jesus' teaching, today's lesson focuses on the heart of the matter—our love for God and others. It is a reminder that, though our behavior may be above reproach in the eyes of the watching world, we cannot hide our beliefs and attitudes from God.

And, truthfully, we are probably not fooling anyone else either. While we might not run someone off the road for cutting us off in traffic, we often don't hesitate to post snarky comments about others on our Facebook pages. Though we might not literally murder someone, our thoughtless words and actions have the power to end a friendship, harm a marriage, damage a reputation, or ruin a person's livelihood. Jesus calls us to be thoughtful, self-controlled, and considerate. Mark Jesus' words: anger and other strong emotions, left unchecked and unaccounted for, lead to myriad consequences both now and eternally.

Stepping In: Read Exodus 20:13; Proverbs 29:11; Ecclesiastes 7:9; and James 1:19–20, along with other verses about anger. How would you rate your mindfulness and self-control when frustrated or angry? How would God rate you? Pray for a calm, mindful, and self-controlled spirit.

Stepping Out: Each time you start to get angry this week, close your eyes and slowly count to ten. If necessary, take a walk and have a talk with Jesus until your anger subsides. Remember, you are in control of your thoughts, words, and actions. Ask the Holy Spirit to guide your heart.

January 30
Guilty

"If any of you is without sin, let him be the first to throw a stone at her."
—John 8:7 (Jn 8:1–11)

With each seemingly blasphemous claim and unauthorized healing, Jesus incited His enemies to greater murderous rage. While He was in Jerusalem for the Feast of Tabernacles, Jesus was confronted by many Jews who contended that the prophet they were waiting for would not come from Galilee. Apparently, they had forgotten that Jesus was born in the Judean town of Bethlehem, which irrefutably coincided with the scripture they tried to use against Him. Undeterred by their ignorance, Jesus continued to reiterate His purpose in doing the Father's will, and stated that soon He would be returning to the One who sent Him.

And so it went. Every attempt at disprove Jesus' Christ-claim was answered emphatically with physical and scriptural proof. Because of His audacity, the Pharisees became obsessed with incriminating Jesus. They brought before Him a woman caught in adultery, so that they could frame Him for opposing the law. Instead of condoning or condemning her, Jesus simply asked these men the above question. No one dared to respond. No stones were thrown that day, but at least one soul was saved.

Sins are crimes against God. We are all guilty of them, regardless of whether they are the result of our behavior or our private thoughts. Since Jesus is the only One given the right to judge, it is a sin when we judge others unduly. That said, society has laws which, if broken, result in a commensurate punishment as deemed by a court of law. Without this structure, our society would likely be deplorably uncivilized.

Though most of us do not contest the implementation of social laws, we, like the Pharisees, add to them needlessly. According to our own sets of moral values, we judge not only the actions but also the character of others. Silently or otherwise, we condemn those whose sins we perceive as greater than our own. It is as if we believe that if we can prove another's guilt, we will divert the attention of the authorities away from our own. Or worse, we may falsely believe that we are above reproach, as did the Pharisees.

These tactics do not work with God. Today's verse is a perfect example of how Jesus calls our bluff. Then and now, a person is innocent until proven guilty, by law or God. If Jesus declares a person guilt-free, then on them no condemnation remains.

Stepping In: Read Deuteronomy 17:6–7; Proverbs 6:16–19; John 8:1, 36; and Romans 2:1, 22–23; 3:22–24; 6:1–2, 23, and 8:1. Take some time to meditate on the seriousness of sin. Praise God that through Jesus, we are no longer guilty in His eyes. Pray that you too will view others this same way.

Stepping Out: This week, take to heart Jesus' words in John 8:7. Refrain from judging and condemning others. If necessary, humbly speak to others who are unjustly accusing or slandering.

Radiant

"In the same way, let your light shine before men, that they may see
your good deeds, and praise your Father in heaven."
—Matthew 5:16 (Mt 5:1–16)

Jesus began His Sermon on the Mount with promised blessings for the weary, burdened, and needy who exhibited godly character and faithfully persevered. Looking out at the multitude who had come seeking relief from their difficult lives, and perhaps a glimpse of a miraculous sign, Jesus addressed their greater need for spiritual healing, wisdom, and truth. Along with the things He promised God would give them, Jesus explained what would be expected of them in return. The above verse was a reminder and a command never to let the flame of love for God and others be allowed to grow dim.

As children of the one true God, the Jewish people were to be "salt" and "light." They were to display their faith in bold and appealing ways. Jesus prompted the faithful to let their godly lives and generosity be a radiant example for all to see, to the glory and praise of God. Perhaps He hoped to remind His fellow Jews that, as God led them out of the darkness of slavery and into the Promised Land by His own light, they too should guide others into the safety of God's arms.

More than two thousand years after Jesus spoke these words, His audiences are still encouraged and challenged by them. As Christians, we are called to live lives that project God's truth and love to the world around us. This means that we need to step outside the walls of our homes and churches and be a positive presence wherever we go.

Jesus knows that this will not always be easy. He warned that the faithful would be scrutinized for both their theology and approach. But, focused on heavenly rewards, we persevere in casting a radiant light of truth that is attractive and biblically sound. Like the warm glow of candle in a dark room, our witness and our deeds should illuminate truth and guide others to Jesus. We need to take our love-lights into the dark places of this world, where they are needed most. Led by the Holy Spirit, believers must put aside fear, doubt, personal agendas, and pride to be effective bringers of light for God's purposes and glory. We must let our light to be seen.

Stepping In: Read Psalm 19:8; Matthew 5:13–16; and John 8:12. Take some time to contemplate the importance of being a light in a dark world. Thank Jesus for being the radiant source of truth, hope, and light. Ask Him to bring you opportunities to reflect His light to those who need it most.

Stepping Out: With Matthew 6:2 in mind, set a goal this week to be a joyful yet humble giver. Take the grocery cart back each time you are at the store. Hold the door open and allow others to go first. Be gracious in traffic—with a smile. Jesus is smiling too.

February 1
True

Then Peter remembered the word Jesus had spoken: "Before the rooster crows, you will disown me three times." And he went outside and wept bitterly.

—Matthew 26:75 (Mt 26:31–35, 69–75)

During the Last Supper with His disciples, Jesus spoke of the difficult reality they would soon face. Even His three closest companions struggled to accept that their Master would be leaving them and that one of their own would betray Him. After washing His student's feet, Jesus prepared to leave the upper room and begin the march toward His destiny – the cross. Seeing his opportunity to duck out and commence his evil plan, Judas Iscariot slipped out first.

After leading the remaining apostles to the garden of Gethsemane, Jesus took Peter, James, and John further into the olive grove so they could keep watch while He prayed. But even Peter, who confessed loyalty to Jesus to the end, could not manage to stay awake. Completely alone, Jesus petitioned His Father for relief from the "cup" He would soon partake of. Sweating drops of blood, Jesus resolved to commit His will and His life into the Father's hands.

Jesus then walked out to meet His betrayer. Judas and a lynch mob had arrived to take Him away. True to form, Peter impulsively reached for his sword and severed the ear of the high priest's servant. Rebuking Peter and repairing the injured ear, Jesus reassured everyone that, though He could easily summon angels to defend Himself, He intended to put up no resistance. His devotees scattered in terror, Peter among them.

As Jesus was questioned and beaten, Peter stood at a distance, filled with confusion and fear. He huddled next to a small fire in the high priest's courtyard as Friday morning dawned. There, Peter denied knowing Jesus—not to anyone of importance, but to servants, and not once, but three times. As the rooster crowed, Peter realized just how true Jesus' words had always been.

People familiar with the gospels tend to have strong views about the various disciples. Didymus, although he surely possessed many redeeming qualities, will be forever pegged as "Doubting Thomas." Similarly, for obvious reasons, Judas Iscariot is seen as the villainous traitor. Peter is often remembered for his quick temper and impetuous nature, and probably rightly so. However, he was also one of Jesus' closest friends. Sadly though, when the going got tough, the not-so-tough got going. In the heat of the moment, chaos and fear won out over resolve and devotion.

Before we judge Peter or the others too harshly, let us consider how quickly our own allegiance fades in times of trouble. Even staunch Christians may waver in their faith when disaster strikes close to home. Instead of being true to Jesus in our troubles, we simply react, abandoning Jesus and our trust in Him.

Thankfully, with the help of the Holy Spirit, Christians today can stand firm in true faith when we choose to take Jesus at His word: "In this world you will have trouble. But take heart! I have overcome the world" (Jn 16:33).

Stepping In: Read Psalm 119:160-161; John 16:31-33, 17:17; Ephesians 1:13–14; and James 1:18. How do these verses encourage you to believe that Jesus' words are true? When have you allowed fear or insecurity to diminish your faith or alter your witness? Pray for the strength to remain true to Jesus always.

Stepping Out: This week, demonstrate your true faith and devotion to Jesus by speaking out for Him at every opportunity. Resolve to *never* disown Him!

Self-Aware

> "Why do you look at a speck of sawdust in your brother's eye and pay no attention to the plank in your own eye? How can you say to your brother, 'Let me take the speck out of your eye,' when all the time there is a plank in your own eye? You hypocrite, first take the plank out of your own eye, and then you will see clearly to remove the speck from your brother's eye."
>
> —Matthew 7:3–5 (Mt 7:1–6)

The sizable crowd gathered to hear Jesus speak probably let out a roar of laughter at the absurdity of this statement. Maybe after the seriousness of His teaching so far, they thought, "Finally, some comic relief."

But Jesus was not joking. He used an extreme example, not to lighten the mood, but rather to emphasize the ridiculous nature of misplaced righteousness. Though anyone hearing these words could relate to the fact that they, at some point or another, were guilt of pointing out another's folly while ignoring their own, this message was most likely directed at the religious leaders in attendance. Jesus knew of these pious men's tendency to critique everyone else's performance in following the Levitical laws and cultural regulations, while they themselves did not meet the same requirements. He called them what they were—hypocrites (actors, performers, deceivers). In so doing, Jesus brought awareness of the tendency to highlight another's faults into everyone's clear focus.

Today's Bible readers might easily find fault in the arrogance and spiritual blindness of the Pharisees. After all, Jesus spent a considerable amount of time lambasting them for their ungodly attitudes and behaviors. Yet it would serve the modern Christian well to realize that the world views us in much the same way: judgmental, closed-minded, exclusionary, and self-righteous. Jesus spoke these words as much for us as for the religious men of His day.

As Christ's ambassadors, it is extremely important for us to practice the kind of self-awareness Jesus wants us to learn. Because the skeptical world is watching, and because we will be judged by the same measure we use to judge others, Christians must be extra careful to examine ourselves first—our faults, our motives, our sin. Before we make a thoughtless, side-angled comment about so-and-so's weekend behavior, before we offer unsolicited parenting advice, before we even playfully criticize someone for questionable driving abilities, we should first take note of our own imperfections in these and other areas. If we do, we might not be so quick to fuss over the specks in other people's eyes.

Stepping In: Read 1 John 2:15–16. What do these verses reveal about potential planks you may have in your eyes? Ask God to help you remove them and give you clear vision to see yourself and others in a proper light. Thank Him for restoring your sight so that you can be humbly self-aware!

Stepping Out: This week, when you are tempted to inwardly or outwardly offer your helpful opinion about someone's appearance, beliefs, or behavior—stop. Ask God to give you eyes to see others as He sees them. Also, while focusing on what you can fix in yourself, remember that each of us is a cherished creation, even with our imperfections.

Reassigned

"You are Simon son of John. You will be called Cephas" (which, when translated, is Peter).

—John 1:42 (Jn 1:29–34)

In the years leading up the Jesus' public ministry, His cousin, John the Baptist, was preparing the way for Him by preaching the news of the coming kingdom of heaven. The nation of Israel, having looked forward to the fulfillment of prophecies regarding this event, was anxious to receive their new king—the one who would redeem them from the yoke of Roman oppression. Eager to learn more, many flocked to the wilderness to hear John's message of repentance and to be baptized in the river Jordan. Jesus Himself went out to be baptized by John, and in so doing revealed His divine nature to those present. Then, led by the Spirit, Jesus went into the desert to be tempted by Satan.

After this, Jesus began to preach the gospel and teach the Word of God throughout Galilee, effectively superseding John's ministry. In fact, many of John's former disciples left him to follow Jesus instead. One of them was Andrew, who ran to tell his brother Simon that he had found the Messiah. From then on, Andrew and Simon were Jesus' devoted disciples. Jesus, seeing something special in Simon, changed his name from a common Hebrew name to the Aramaic name Cephas (Greek for Peter), meaning "rock." Knowing that Peter would one day be pivotal in building the foundation of His church, the body of believers, Jesus reassigned His new apprentice both in name and purpose.

Names are important. They represent not just who we are, but what we are. A name is a person's title and a reflection of character. This was especially so in ancient Jewish culture. When a child was born, he or she was given a strong and meaningful name that would announce to the world that this person was truly a blessing from God. Simon was given a common name, meaning "listen."

Yet that was not what Jesus knew about Simon. Jesus saw a solid young man with the potential to be one of Christianity's founding fathers. This is how Jesus sees each of us today. We may live behind the names and titles we've been given, or have given ourselves, but Jesus gives each of us a new name and a new purpose in His kingdom. Often, because of the bad things we have done in our lives, we personify the labels we've been assigned. However, when we become children of God, Jesus changes our names from ordinary to extraordinary, simple to stunning, unworthy to undeniable, lost to longed-for. He reassigns us from orphaned to adopted.

Stepping In: Read 2 Samuel 7:8–9; 2 Corinthians 5:17–19; Ephesians 4:22–24; and Revelation 2:17 and 3:11–12. What are some names or labels you identify with? What is the name Jesus calls you by? Ask Him to show you the significance of the title and purpose He gave you.

Stepping Out: This week, look at each person the way Jesus sees that person. In your mind (or aloud if appropriate), give everyone a title worthy of the Christ-like characteristics you see in them. For example, "John" may become "John the Generous." While you are at it, give one to yourself as well.

Submissive

Jesus answered, "It says: 'Do not put the Lord your God to the test.'"
—Luke 4:12 (Lk 4:1–13)

During his time in the wilderness, John the Baptist boldly proclaimed the coming Messiah, calling the faithful to repent of sins and turn back to God. Many were baptized into the faith Jesus would Himself soon promote. Not out of need, but to set an example of obedience to God, Jesus was also baptized by John in the Jordan River. At that time, God spoke His blessing on His Son from heaven, for all present to witness.

Jesus was then swept away into the desert to be tempted by Satan. He endured both physical and spiritual testing for forty days and forty nights, completely submissive to His Father's will. During that time of fasting and isolation, Jesus relied entirely on His Father for strength, wisdom, and courage. Meanwhile, Satan bombarded Him with temptations. Jesus, fortified by the Spirit, resisted the Devil at every turn. Using the Word of God as His defensive weapon, He triumphed over Satan's attempts to cause Him to sin. He plainly told His foe that all ploys were useless. God cannot be tempted nor tested by any of His created beings—not even a fallen angel.

Satan is still very much at work in our world today, and temptation is still one of his favorite schemes. The lure of getting what we don't have or attaining something more or better constantly assails us. If our own desires don't cause us to lust, then media and advertisements certainly will. Satan knows this all too well. As he did with Jesus, he capitalizes on the opportunity to harass those who are alone and vulnerable.

Jesus shows us how to overcome temptation. Even in His humanness, He did not succumb to the pressure to give in and take the easier way. Neither did He flex His muscles and bring down angels to fend off His assailant. Instead, He called on the wisdom of His Father; going right to the Word of God for His help. Christians today can learn a lesson from Jesus' example here. Not only are we to recognize and resist Satan's crafty deceptions, but we are also to employ the power of God's Word in our defense against all kinds of temptation. In this way, we too can be submissive to God and not to Satan.

Stepping In: Read Deuteronomy 6:16–17; Psalm 78:17–19; 1 Corinthians 10:13; Ephesians 6:17; and Hebrews 4:15. How do you put God to the test? When have you been submissive to Satan's temptations rather than remaining obedient to God? Ask Him to reveal any ways that you do so. Pray that you do not test God or succumb to temptation.

Stepping Out: This week, using a topical reference or Bible concordance, find and memorize scripture passages that will help you combat temptation in your life.

Anticipatory

"I tell you the truth, this generation will certainly not pass away until all these things have happened. Heaven and earth will pass away, but my words will never pass away."

—Matthew 24:34–35 (Mt 24:1–35)

Jesus did everything according to the will of the Father. Sitting on the Mount of Olives just outside of Jerusalem, He explained in stark detail the devastation that would take place, not only in Jerusalem, but worldwide. Interwoven among this terrifying news was a clear message of hope: Jesus would return and restore peace after all these events took place. Jesus wanted His men to be prepared for and to anticipate His second coming. Regardless of what they would face, He needed them to stay strong and stand firm in their faith.

When they heard the above words, the disciples' confidence most likely turned to confusion. So many questions may have flooded their minds. Was "this generation" a time frame or a people group? Would heaven and earth pass away in the disciples' lifetime? Full of anticipation and fear, the disciples had to trust Jesus while they waited to see how His prophecies played out.

Bible readers throughout the generations have also puzzled over these verses. Like the disciples, we too wonder what Jesus had meant by the word *generation*. Obviously, the world did not come to an end in the thirty to forty years after these words were spoken. However, the Jewish world as they knew it most certainly did. Inside the time frame that Jesus predicted, the temple and most of Jerusalem were besieged and then destroyed in AD 70.

The Jews continue to struggle to reclaim their identity and sense of place, while Christianity spreads like wildfire across the globe. To this day, Israel and its neighbors live in contentious instability, and will continue to until the end of the age.

That said, Jesus' words inform us *what* to expect, not *when* to expect it. Though many of us believe that the birthing pains have already begun, Jesus tells us that when He returns, we won't be able to miss Him. Since we know not the time or day, we, like the apostles, must press on in our kingdom work with determination and anticipation. As the days become more wicked and the earth more degraded, sad as these conditions may be, Christians can view these scenarios with acceptance and eager hope, looking forward to when all things are renewed.

Stepping In: Read Jeremiah 8:1–3 and Revelation 1:7, 21:1-4. Do you look forward to Jesus' second coming with fear or with anticipation? Why do you think you feel the way you do? Pray and ask for comfort and peace as we live each day as if it were our last on this fallen earth.

Stepping Out: This week, memorize a verse, so that Jesus' words do not "pass away" in your mind.

Crowned

"I know your afflictions and your poverty—yet you are rich!"
—Revelation 2:9 (Rv 2:8–11)

As Christ's apostles crusaded throughout the Asian subcontinent, planting churches and promoting Christianity among resistant Jews and polytheists, they certainly experienced their fair share of poverty and affliction. All of them endured extreme hatred and threats of violence. The apostle John, though persecuted, miraculously escaped an early death. During a time of fervent prayer, he was supernaturally transported into God's presence, where Jesus gave him specific instructions to record the revelation he was about to receive and send it to the seven churches in Asia Minor.

In the section of the letter addressed to the "angel" (pastor) of the church in Smyrna, Jesus gave the above acknowledgment. He went on to encourage the believers in Smyrna to stay pure in their faith among slandering Jews and others who were agents of Satan. He forewarned them about persecution and imprisonment, and implored them to keep the faith, even to the point of death. To bless them, Jesus reminded them that their perseverance would be rewarded with the "crown of life." He promised them eternal royalty regardless of their earthly status.

Many things are backward in the kingdom of heaven, including this notion of wealth. Jesus talked frequently about how opposed worldly perspectives are to spiritual ones. The first will be last and vice versa. The blind will see and vice versa. Those who give up their lives will live and vice versa. Those who cling to the things of this world will see no other reward, whereas those who cherish heavenly treasure shall receive the crown of glory in the end.

More than ever, modern people equate success and happiness with the amount of money and possessions they have. Certainly, advertising and media play a key role in promoting the maxim that more is better. Scripture speaks clearly to the contrary. In fact, Jesus told a rich young ruler that "it is hard for a rich man to enter the kingdom of heaven … it is easier for a camel to go through the eye of a needle" (Mt 19:23, 24). Jesus also said, "For where your treasure is, there your heart will be also" (Lk 12:34).

Clearly, God wants us to know that money does not buy true riches, nor does it purchase access to heaven. Regardless of how much wealth, health, notoriety, comfort, or perceived security one has, without a saving faith in Jesus, these things will amount to nothing in the end. Those who faithfully persevere in this life will be crowned in glory in eternity.

Stepping In: Read Matthew 10:22; 1 Corinthians 9:24–27; 2 Corinthians 6:3–10; 2 Timothy 4:8; James 1:12, 2:5; and 1 Peter 5:4. How do these verses influence your perspective on worldly versus heavenly wealth? Pray for a right perspective and a willingness to change your mind, heart, and habits to align with Jesus' attitude.

Stepping Out: For one day this week, give up one worldly comfort (car, pillow, cell phone, latte) so that you can focus on what truly matters—Jesus and the promise of the crown you shall receive.

Loving

> "You have heard that it was said, 'Love your neighbor and hate your enemy.' But I tell you: Love your enemies and pray for those who persecute you, that you may be sons and daughters of your Father in heaven."
>
> —Matthew 5:43–45 (Mt 5:43–48)

Here, Jesus bestowed on His listeners His sixth and final "You have heard it said, but I tell you …" statement. Each time, He was reminding the Jews of their commitment to follow the Levitical laws of their forefathers. He then followed that reminder with a new command, one He knew would challenge those attending His multi-day Sermon on the Mount.

This statement summarized the essence of Jesus' teaching throughout this early-ministry event, and encapsulated Jesus' ultimate command to love God and others above all else. These words might have sounded like nice platitudes to those hearing them. However, they were meant to be more than good advice. They were an admonition and a warning to love everyone regardless of their perceived worthiness, *so that* "you may be sons and daughters of your Father in heaven." As is typical with Jesus' teaching, the statement implies that the converse is also true: without love, a person cannot be related to God. Both of these implications would have riled the religious leaders in attendance.

Moreover, Jesus wasn't just telling His audience to pray for their persecutors so that the persecution would end. He was saying that believers should pray for persecutors as they would for a loved one. In that way, they would show that they were true and loving children of God.

This command isn't any easier for us today than it was for Jesus' first-century followers. But a command it is. In fact, in three of the four gospels, Jesus restates the words of Moses, saying, "Love the Lord your God with all your heart (soul, mind, and strength), and love your neighbor as yourself," as the first and second greatest commandments. This is very old and very wise advice, and an imperative for Christians living according to Jesus.

However, in our overscheduled lives, we barely have time to love and pray for our own families, let alone people who don't like us. As with all the difficult commands He gives us, Jesus wants us to trust Him on this. Praying for people who mistreat you may not be easy or even make sense, but we are to be obedient children nonetheless. We will never know the blessings our Father has for us unless we trust Him with all things. We are to think, act, and love differently—as disciples.

Stepping In: Read Matthew 5:43–48. Pray to your Father in heaven that as a child of God, you will act accordingly, being willing to love and pray for the unlovable.

Stepping Out: In addition to praying for them, show those not-so-favorite people in your life that you love them. It can be as simple as sharing a smile, opening a door, or saying a kind word.

Sharp

> "Are you still so dull?"
> —Matthew 15:16 (Mt 15:1–20)

This rhetorical question was a stinging rebuke aimed at Peter and the other disciples, meant to stir their emotions. With His opponents becoming increasingly persistent and vehement, Jesus needed His apprentices to be sharp. After nearly two years by Jesus' side, taking in all the wisdom they could glean from Him, the depth and complexity of His message still eluded them at times, especially when Jesus began teaching exclusively by parables. These stories were intended to baffle the untrained listener but reveal hidden spiritual truth to His discerning followers.

His followers were still human, however, and often tried to understand Jesus' message with their heads rather than their hearts. When Jesus concluded His explanation of what God considered "clean" and "unclean" with a parable about uprooted plants and blind guides, the disciples were as mystified as anyone in the audience. Peter voiced what the others were wondering, and Jesus was clearly disappointed. He no doubt hoped that His disciples would remember that all His teachings were anchored in the core truth that a heart guided by love for God and others is a heart that sees clearly, is rooted in faith, and is "clean."

Jesus' harsh rebuke caused its recipients to wince. Many people now think the words unduly critical and even mean. Did Jesus really think Peter was "dull"—stupid, dim-witted, inept? When today's Bible students struggle with scriptural understanding, does Jesus also consider them unintelligent?

The answer to these questions is unequivocally, no. In fact, Jesus is not commenting on mental aptitude at all. By "dull," He means a lack of spiritual sharpness and focus. This is often the result of an incomplete understanding of scripture stemming from lackluster faith. It can also be a consequence of allowing worldly influences to dumb down one's spiritual perspective. If one of Jesus' most zealous supporters could be rendered "dull" by the difficulty of his circumstances, how much more susceptible are we?

In a world that has effectively replaced Jesus' authority with a theology of self-determination, it is unsurprising how spiritually desensitized our culture has become. Jesus expects all His disciples, past, present, and future, to mature in our faith and to hone our discerning spirits.

Stepping In: Read Hebrews 4:12. Now, reread Matthew 15:1–20 and reflect on this passage using the Character method (See appendix). Who did you identify with and why? How does Jesus' rebuke make you feel? Pray for understanding and a sharp mind to discern and apply His teaching.

Stepping Out: This week, employ the "iron sharpens iron" philosophy (Prv 27:17) with grace and humility. Be willing to be "sharpened" by others as well. Thank God for this spiritual gift.

Seeing

> "Can a blind man lead a blind man? Will they not both fall into a pit?"
> —Luke 6:39 (Lk 6:12–20, 37–42)

After Jesus was baptized by His cousin and tempted by Satan, He went to Galilee, calling godly men to be His disciples. He appointed twelve of them as His first gospel missionaries: the apostles. Leading by example, Jesus taught His apprentices how to offer God's love to the physically and spiritually needy. Jesus focused on teaching His men moral lessons, interspersed with times of teaching in the synagogues and healing the infirm.

During one public teaching, known now as the Sermon on the Mount, Jesus explained that God's people would be known by their words and their actions. They would speak kindly, give freely, reserve judgment, and care even for their enemies. Though many who listened were amazed at His teaching, some were offended. Answering the thoughts of the spiritually blind, Jesus posed His famous question about the blind leading the blind. Though the scenario was comical to imagine, Jesus' inquiry was meant in all seriousness. Folly would certainly befall anyone who followed a false leader or faulty doctrine.

Jesus, who called Himself the Good Shepherd, knows how weak and vulnerable humans are. Like sheep, people seek safety, security, love, acceptance, and belonging. We look to the ones who appear to be smart, strong, and in charge. We are quick to put our hope in those who meet all these criteria, regardless of whether they pass a spiritual (or criminal, for that matter) background check. It is a perfect recipe for the blind to lead the blind. Our world has seen plenty of extreme examples of this in its history: Hitler, Jim Jones, and Saddam Hussein, just to name a few. The confidence, persuasive words, and charismatic demeanor of such leaders blind us to the truth of who they are and who they aren't.

There is only one person who should have our whole hearts' devotion: Jesus. Even our trustworthy pastors and honest community leaders are only regular people at the end of the day. The best way to identify misleaders and avoid pitfalls is to pass everything through prayer and scripture. We need to employ our brains, our eyes, and our spirits to fend off the Enemy's deception. If Jesus Himself is not leading you, don't go!

Stepping In: Read Matthew 23:23–24; John 14:15–20; Romans 2:17–24; 2 Corinthians 4:1–4; and 1 John 2:9–11. How do these verses help you understand more about spiritual blindness? Ask God to help you become one who sees.

Stepping Out: This week, practice seeing things for what they really are. Be careful not to lead or be led away from the righteous path of Jesus. Cling to the truth of His Word and resist the Devil's temptation to compromise.

Potent

> "The kingdom of heaven is like a mustard seed, which a man took and planted in his field. Though it is the smallest of all your seeds, yet when it grows, it is the largest of the garden plants and becomes a tree, so that the birds of the air come and perch in its branches."
>
> —Matthew 13:31–32 (Mt 13:24–32)

Those who had been with Jesus from the beginning of His ministry would have heard Him mention "the kingdom" and "heaven" many times before. The parable of the mustard seed was delivered during Jesus' impromptu floating sermon to a massive shoreside crowd. He preached a series of parables beginning with "the kingdom of heaven is like …" He segued from a parable about weeds among wheat to another agricultural parable regarding the small yet potent mustard seed. The crowd might have deduced that Jesus was describing heaven as a lovely garden with sheltering trees in which birds could rest. They could not have known that the kingdom of which Jesus spoke was much larger and more far-reaching. His disciples, meanwhile, would have been contemplating the vastness of the gospel's reach, and how many would find safety under the canopy of salvation.

From Genesis to Revelation, we find the story of humanity's struggle to reestablish a right standing with God, so that we may once again dwell in His presence. The kingdom of God, or heaven, is a central theme throughout the pages of scripture, though it is defined as a believer's eternal dwelling place only in the New Testament. At the center of this eternal home stands the Tree of Life. All hope for humanity lies in gaining access to that tree.

It is not surprising, then, that Jesus spoke of a tree when referring to the kingdom of heaven. The words in today's verse remind us that eternal hope should be the focus of our faith. Even when we feel that our efforts are paltry and insignificant, we are to remember that "faith as small as a mustard seed" can become a path to paradise. Something as small as a single word can deliver a potent remedy to the ills of this world. That word is "Jesus." Throughout the generations, the small seeds of faith that Christians have been planting have indeed grown into the worldwide influence that Christianity has now. As Christ's representatives, our fruit is what makes us attractive to an unbelieving world. Yet it is not enough to simply admire the orchard from a distance. Those who wish to eat of the eternal fruit must enter the garden by its only gate. Jesus is that gate.

Stepping In: Read Genesis 2:8-9, 3:22-24; Matthew 5:43-48, 17:20; John 14:13, 16:25-27; Acts 4:12; Romans 10:13; and Galatians 5:22–23. Do you trust in the potency of Jesus' name and your witness? Pray for the confidence to faithfully plant seeds and develop lasting fruit for God's kingdom.

Stepping Out: This week, talk about your Savior. Speak His name aloud. Call on His name as you seek His will, and respond in obedience.

February 11
Rejoicing

"However, do not rejoice that the spirits submit to you, but rejoice that your names are written in heaven."

—Luke 10:20 (Lk 10:1–24)

At the height of His public ministry, Jesus traveled widely, spreading His gospel message, healing many ailments, and casting out demons. From Bethlehem in the south to Caesarea Philippi in the north, Jesus covered great distances to reach the spiritually lost. Jesus also commissioned seventy (some documents say seventy-two) devotees to go out two by two into the country to practice what they had seen their Master do. When the seventy returned, they gave Jesus a jubilant report of their successes, even in expelling demons. However, before these men rejoiced too greatly over their power, Jesus reminded them to focus on what was more important.

Today's disciples have been given the apostles' same commission by our Lord Jesus: go out into the world and prepare the people for the coming kingdom of heaven. Though not many of us will receive the gift of miraculous healing abilities, we who have the Holy Spirit are gifted with a capacity to share God's love and truth in many ways and with all kinds of people. We have the powerful Word of God at our disposal, the Sword of Truth.

Because of the wonderful work of Jesus' apostles and those who came after, most Christians are free to worship the one true God. In many parts of the world, people can read for themselves the very words of God found in the Holy Bible. Those of us who read about the saving grace of God and put our faith in Jesus as our Lord and Savior can know without a doubt that our names are written in the Lamb's Book of Life. Those early missionaries may not have known what that was at the time, but they had their Lord's word on it—and that was good enough.

Today, all Christians must carry the torch of the apostles, bringing the light of truth and love into our dark world. With all the saints throughout time, we too will be found rejoicing in the end.

Stepping In: Read Luke 15:8–10; Ephesians 6:17; Hebrews 4:12; and Revelation 13:8 and 21:9–27. How do these verses paint a more complete picture of what Jesus is talking about in the Luke passage? Ask God where you fit into His plan for discipleship. Are you one of the inner Twelve, the seventy, or the followers? Seek God's will for your personal ministry as you rejoice in your salvation.

Stepping Out: This week, be contagiously joyful about your eternal security. Heed the words of 1 Peter 3:15 as you share the reason for your happiness and hope with those who are interested.

42

February 12
Bright

"I am the light of the world. Whoever follows me will never walk in darkness, but will have the light of life."

—John 8:12 (Jn 8:12–30)

Throughout His earthly ministry, Jesus boldly preached the word of God to illuminate the truth of His Father's loving plan to redeem His people through the coming Messiah. Though Jewish religious leaders knew the scripture well, they could not understand that Jesus was the fulfillment of the messianic prophecies. Similarly, those who witnessed Jesus' spiritually superior teaching and miraculous deeds failed to recognize the source of His knowledge and power. They continued to view Jesus merely as a prophet, an astonishing healer, a wise rabbi, or an earthly king. Moreover, with every hard teaching, many of His followers fell away. Yet Jesus persisted in informing all who would listen that He was the Son of Man and the Son of God the Father, causing the Jewish leaders to become increasingly driven to put an end to His ministry and life.

Only months before going to the cross, Jesus covertly went to Jerusalem for the Feast of Tabernacles, despite intense opposition there. He went to the temple and began to teach about the redemptive work He and the Father were doing, warning His audience to pay attention. Using the ceremonial elements of water and fire as illustrations of God's Spirit manifest in Himself, Jesus offered His audience yet another opportunity to put their faith in Him. Jesus identified Himself as God's guiding light. The bright truth of His words caused some to draw near and others to flee.

Our world is a darkening place. Satan, prince of this world, prefers it that way. Light exposes things as they really are. Lies and deception may be hidden in the shadows, but light reveals the truth. Shame, guilt, hatred, envy, greed, and corruption live in the dark places in our lives, our hearts, and our world. This is why the dark is a fearful place. In the shadows, one cannot see clearly; one cannot tell if one is being deceived. When we cannot see well, we wind up listening to the voices around us, telling us which way to go. In the dark, we follow blind leaders who tell us what we want to hear.

Jesus came into the world to shine His bright light of truth. But the world preferred darkness, and it still does. Yet for those who are tired of stumbling, tired of groping, tired of confusion and fear, Jesus offers the solution. Look to Him for light, truth, and guidance, and there you will also find hope for a bright future.

Stepping In: Read Exodus 13:21–22; Psalm 27:1, 119:105; Proverbs 4:18-19, 6:23; John 1:1-13, 3:19-21, 14:28-31. How do these verses encourage and convict you about light and darkness, good and evil? Pray that God reveals and removes any darkness in and around you, exchanging shadowy deception with bright clarity.

Stepping Out: This week, live out 2 Corinthians 3:18. Reflect God's light and glory with an unveiled face to a dark world. Do not hide your light; shine brightly for Jesus.

February 13
Insightful

"So do not be afraid of them. There is nothing concealed that will not
be disclosed, or hidden that will not be made known."
—Matthew 10:26 (Mt 10:1–26)

After two years of teaching, training, and leading by example, Jesus sat His disciples down for a lengthy talk on what they could expect, both good and bad, in the mission fields He was about to send them to. He promised miraculous powers to heal and to save, and predicted many hardships they would surely face along the way. Aside from going into the unknown without so much as an extra cloak, they would be at the mercy of strangers and subject to all manner of resistance and opposition. They were likely to deal with physical harm and incarceration. Nevertheless, Jesus meant to comfort and remind His men of what their mission was and whom they were to proclaim. Jesus encouraged them not to be afraid, reminding His newly appointed apostles that nothing they experienced would blindside them or Him.

Christians today often fall into two camps: the holy-huddle type and the fearless evangelist. People in the second group are usually the ones to hear and quickly obey God's call to mission work and outreach ministries. Armed with Bibles and pastoral instructions, these religious go-getters bound fearlessly into the harvest fields, committed to spreading the gospel come Hades or high water. Some succeed. Many more falter as the waves of rejection and hateful opposition wash over them. The world's negative reaction to the truth should not come as a surprise to anyone who has studied the scripture.

As today's passage clearly points out, faithfully obeying the call to leave our comfort zones and proclaim Jesus as Lord and Savior will come at a cost. It pays to be both obedient and insightful. Jesus does not want us to step blindly into the unknown, nor does He want us to go it alone. Those who are wise look to the Light of the World to illuminate the path before them.

Stepping In: Read Isaiah 65:1; Romans 10:20-21, 16:25-27; and 1 Corinthians 2:7–10. How do these verses help you be comforted in your Christian walk, even when you feel ill-equipped? Pray for the Spirit to reveal what you need to know each day, then trust. Thank Him for the insight.

Stepping Out: This week, share an insight or a revelation that God has given to you. Remember to use "I" statements. Your testimony is a powerful tool for spreading the good news of how Jesus changes lives.

Loved

"For God so loved the world that he gave his one and only Son, that whoever believes in him shall not perish but have eternal life."
—John 3:16 (Jn 3:1–21)

From the beginning of humanity, God desired a close relationship with His people. After the fall, however, it was obvious that humanity needed clear rules and boundaries to live within so that they did not stray too far from Him. Consequently, God gave His people the Law through Moses. From then on, certain men were given the task of teaching these rules to the people.

Among these were an elite class of scripturally learned men called Pharisees. Having memorized the entire Pentateuch, these men were revered for their knowledge and piety. Many of them became so self-absorbed and arrogant that they honored themselves above God. They believed that because of their lineage and their careful observance of the Law, they would automatically inherit eternal life. When Jesus testified otherwise, they heartily rejected Him and His message. Then, inflamed with jealousy, they plotted to kill Him.

One Pharisee, a man called Nicodemus, let his curiosity get the better of him. He went to see Jesus under cover of night. Jesus, knowing Nicodemus' deep need for true life, taught how he must be "born again." Jesus then made the emphatic statement above. Aware that by the word "Son," Jesus meant Himself, Nicodemus was faced with a life-changing choice: remain stubborn and lost, or bravely agree to be loved.

The story of Jesus and Nicodemus was rich with meaning then and remains so now. Most importantly, it is a story of God's great love for all His people. When He created us, He set in motion a plan for redeeming His children. The old system could never lead to salvation, so God sent Jesus to atone for sin, once and for all. But God knows that pride, prejudice, and stubbornness can easily lead to spiritual blindness.

Jesus always meets us right where we are, mentally and spiritually, speaking to us in a language we can understand. As He did with Nicodemus, Jesus uses our intellects, temperaments, and areas of expertise to point out truths about Himself. In fact, He created these qualities in us for this very reason. When we are ready for true answers, Jesus always supplies them. Because He loves us, He tells us what we need to hear, when we need to hear it, and in a manner we can understand. Equipped with this truth, we can let others know that they too are loved.

Stepping In: Read Numbers 21:8–9; Isaiah 9:6–7; John 4:13–14; Acts 13:39; Romans 5:8, 8:32; and Ephesians 2:4–5. Praise God for loving you so much that He sent His Son to die for you.

Stepping Out: This week, use your God-given strengths to proclaim the truth about Jesus and to share God's amazing love with those who don't yet know Him. Because you are loved, love others well.

February 15
Faithful

"You have heard it said, 'Do not commit adultery.' But I tell you that anyone who looks at a woman lustfully has already committed adultery with her in his heart."

—Matthew 5:27-28 (Mt 5:27–30)

During His Sermon on the Mount, Jesus offered new definitions for old and familiar commandments of God. His statement about adultery no doubt caused a stir. Some listeners would have instantly felt the sting of guilt and shame at these words. Others would have been provoked to indignation at the thought. Surely Jesus was exaggerating; everyone knew that committing adultery was an act, not merely a thought in one's head.

Jesus, however, told His listeners plainly that a wandering eye was equal to a wandering heart. All rationalizations aside, an unfaithful heart was at the root of an unfaithful eye. Left unchecked and unaccounted for, the lustful eye would lead the body astray. Jesus wanted His audience to know that faithfulness, whether it was to a spouse or to God, was a matter of the heart. Therefore, each person would be held accountable for their impure thoughts as well as their ungodly acts, according to Jesus' new theology.

More so today than ever, this command would be viewed as one of the 'lesser laws.' Unless you live in a very sheltered community, where sexual purity is taught and somehow enforced, the second half of Jesus' statement is hard to take seriously. In our morally depraved world, the sanctity of marriage is losing ground and sexuality is flaunted shamelessly. It is everywhere, on display for all to see. It is impossible to ignore, even for Christians.

For those of us who profess faith in Jesus, this verse is a sobering reminder that God expects more from us. Moreover, He wants more *for* us. With the world watching, Christians must believe and live differently. Our thoughts and actions must prove that our hearts belong to God. When we keep our focus on Him, we draw strength to be honorable and faithful in everything we do. If we allow our eyes to wander, soon our hearts will follow. Jesus reminds us to shield our eyes, guard our hearts, and remain faithful.

Stepping In: Search your heart for any physical and/or emotional infidelity. Where have you let your eye wander? Pray for strength to resist temptation. Ask God to help you execute a plan for staying on a virtuous path.

Stepping Out: Impose a day, or better yet a week, of self-censorship from sexually suggestive or explicit input. Since it is not safe to walk around with your eyes closed, nor practical to stay home in a dark room, you need to ask God for the willpower to avert your gaze from all sources of sexual provocation. Each time you do, whisper to yourself, "I am faithful."

February 16
Prolific

"I tell you the truth, unless a kernel of wheat falls to the ground and dies, it remains only a single seed. But if it dies, it produces many seeds."

—John 12:24 (Jn 12:20–28)

Just days before going to the cross, Jesus made His triumphal entry into Jerusalem. Some Greek Jewish converts who were also in the city began asking where they could find Jesus. When the disciples reported this to Him, Jesus stated that the hour had come for Him to be glorified. He had spent most of His ministry preaching to the Jews who would reject Him. Now the conversion of the Gentiles would signify that the world was ready for spiritual change. This was as prophecy had predicted; it was the sign that the time was right for His atoning work to be done.

Jesus summarized the purpose of His upcoming death in the analogy of the kernel of wheat. Though His apostles did not know it at the time, the legacy of Jesus would be a prolific and enduring movement brought to the world by themselves. As Jesus also predicted, many of the men hearing His words would be immortalized by martyrs' deaths.

Throughout history, this analogy has been proven true time and again. Certainly, Jesus' death, resurrection, and ascension spurred the most prolific results of any movement known to man. Because He died and rose again, the truth of who He is and what He did has been perpetuated throughout the world. That one Man, Jesus, changed the lives and eternities of millions of believers, and His work is not finished yet. The seed of faith continues to produce devoted followers who become inspired leaders who become planters, cultivators, and harvesters of a great harvest. The crop is still growing, and there is still a great need for field workers.

We are those workers! Like the apostles, we must take this message of life to a bleak and desperate world, planting seeds of hope along the way. God willing, we will not meet a martyr's end. But if we do, glory be to God, and may our legacy live on.

As today's passage indicates, a death does have to occur for a Christian to be a productive member of Jesus' crew: a death to self. We must cast off our old lives, ways, prejudices, stigmas, bad habits, self-centeredness, and rebelliousness to "pick up [our] cross (daily) and follow [Him]." In Christ, we are new creations, born again to be prolific sowers of seeds.

Stepping In: Read Genesis 8:22; Matthew 9:37–38; Mark 4:3–8; Luke 9:23; and 2 Corinthians 5:17, 9:6-10. How do these verses encourage or challenge you? Pray for a fully yielded life and prolific discipleship that will produce a lasting legacy.

Stepping Out: This week, according to the Spirit's prompting, choose an area of your life you have not fully yielded to Jesus, one in which you need to "die to self." Take a first step in doing that. In addition, as a small group, with a friend, or alone, hand out sunflower seeds snack packs to people in your community. Offer "seeds of hope"—and a tasty treat—as a conversation starter.

Informed

Jesus replied, "You are in error because you do not know the Scriptures
or the power of God."

—Matthew 22:29 (Mt 22:23–33)

After His final and triumphal entry into Jerusalem, Jesus spent much of His remaining time teaching in the temple courts. Not everyone was pleased. The chief priests, Pharisee, Herodians, and teachers of the Law were unwilling to accept His divine authority, and tried repeatedly to prove Him false. The Sadducees were part of this opposition. Hoping to catch Him in a misinterpretation of Levitical law, some of these so-called experts asked Jesus about marriage in the resurrection. Sadducees did not believe in resurrection. Jesus knew they were trying to pit His Word against that of their patriarch, Moses. Jesus responded by pointing out their lack of understanding of scripture. Quoting Exodus, He highlighted their misunderstanding of the living God, past and present.

Today, New Testament readers have access to a more complete picture of life after death than anyone would have had in the first century. In Jesus' day, the Jews' spiritual knowledge was based solely on early scriptural writings and oral traditions. Depending on their sect, their interpretation of these teachings varied greatly.

When Jesus entered the scene, He taught about God from an historical, scripture-based perspective, but also added His own interpretations. For Christians, His commands are the new law. In today's passage, Jesus shows that He is the authority on the Word of God because He *is* the Word of God. Today's verse presents a twofold challenge. First, to speak truth, we must be informed on scripture. Second, we are never to underestimate the power of God or His Word. In fact, our very faith is built on firm belief in the resurrection power. Nothing is outside of God's abilities; it says so right in the inerrant Good Book.

Stepping In: Read Exodus 3:6; Deuteronomy 25:5–10; Acts 26:6–8; Romans 8:11; 1 Corinthians 15:22; and Philippians 3:10–11. Meditate on these scripture passages. Thank God for the resurrection power that is in you.

Stepping Out: Commit to being informed by memorizing scripture. Set a goal of learning one verse per week, starting now. Jesus is the Word; put Him in your heart and mind!

February 18
Bold

"Whatever town or village you enter, search for some worthy person there and stay at his house until you leave. As you enter the home, give it your greeting. If the home is deserving, let your peace rest on it; if it is not, let your peace return to you."
—Matthew 10:11–13 (Mt 10:1–14)

After Jesus had tasked His disciples with their first solo missionary duties, He gave His newly appointed apostles the above instructions. The success of their mission would depend on complete reliance on God. They were instructed not to bring along so much as an extra coat or a few coins in their belts. It must have been a relief to learn that Jesus had at least considered their need for shelter. Since their culture dictated the hospitable treatment of strangers, the disciples perhaps may not have been overly concerned about their physical needs being met. However, finding "worthy" persons in homes "deserving" of the peace they would bestow might have seemed complicated. But Jesus informed His men of the miraculous power and authority He planned to give each of them. Assured of their Master's abilities and encouraged by His confidence in them, the disciples could be bold and effective agents for God. They looked to Him and not to the difficulty of their circumstances as they set out on their journeys.

The type of hospitality known in ancient times can still be found in certain regions of the world. Jesus, however, was and is directing His missionaries toward people who do more than simply welcome them and offer them food and shelter. The people whom Jesus wanted His disciples to dwell among also welcomed the gospel message the disciples brought. Missionaries today must find similarly deserving people with whom to trade hospitality for God's life-saving Word.

Unlike Jesus' first missionaries, Christians today are aware of the urgency to get His salvation message out to all who welcome it. Because lives and souls are at stake, and because there is no way of knowing when Jesus will return, we must boldly proclaim truth to those who have open ears, hearts, and homes.

Stepping In: Read Mark 6:7–11; Genesis 12:1–9; and Exodus 3. What do these verses say about the calling of God? Put yourself in the shoes of one of these men who were told to leave everything behind and *go*. Is God telling you to go somewhere? Pray for a receptive and responsive spirit.

Stepping Out: This week, look for opportunities to visit with folks with whom you can share your faith and hope. Be bold but humble in your approach. Gratefully accept kindness and generosity in exchange for your hope-filled message of God's saving grace and love.

Cleansed

"Was no one found to return and praise God except this foreigner?"
Then he said to him, "Rise and go; your faith has made you well."
—Luke 17:18–19 (Lk 17:11–19)

After raising His friend Lazarus from the dead in Bethany, Jesus began the journey back to Galilee. Along the way, He gathered His remaining faithful followers to make a final trek to Jerusalem in time for the Passover and the Passion. The path He chose took Him through Samaria. He had several reasons for this. One was to avoid hostile Jews, who were not likely to be in such a religiously abhorrent region. Another was to bring healing to some who would have otherwise missed it.

Outside of a border town, Jesus encountered ten lepers who called to Him for mercy. Nine of them were Jews, and one was a Samaritan. Instead of healing them instantly, Jesus told them to show themselves to the priests in the village. Obediently, they set out to do so. As they went, they were cured of their disease. The Samaritan man, overwhelmed with gratitude for the Lord's gift of healing, ran back to Jesus and threw himself at His feet. Jesus then commented on the vast difference in attitude between the Samaritan and the Jews. The Samaritan was made wholly new, cleansed both physically and spiritually, and would forever be beholden to Jesus. However, as soon as the others had been transformed they forgot about their healer entirely.

Jesus' stories and parables have much to teach us today. They speak to the human condition that has endured the test of time. Knowing we are fickle creatures, Jesus uses a variety of ways to reach us. When we are healthy and secure, He teaches us about pride and complacency. When we are weak and discouraged, He strengthens us with His unfailing peace. When we are desperate and needy, He allows us to learn lessons of faith, trust, and gratitude. Jesus has a way of leveling the playing field for all who seek Him.

Like the ten lepers, when faced with a crisis or calamity, we tend to look past our differences and pool our resources in an effort to make it through. Once the storm passes, we drift back to our separate corners and resume our old attitudes and behaviors. Jesus knew this about the nine Jewish lepers, and he knows this about us.

The beautiful truth remains that Jesus willingly steps across all our barriers to offer us whatever our faith requires, including tangible results. Instead of shunning the outcast and the diseased, Jesus seeks them out. As we see in this example, people respond in many ways to Jesus' cleansing work: some recognize and appreciate it, while others do not. For the nine, the healing was only skin-deep. For the Samaritan, Jesus' healing was from the inside out.

Stepping In: Read Leviticus 13:2–3, 46; Matthew 8:1–4; and Ephesians 2:11-16 Take some time to think about the barriers you face. How has Jesus helped you to navigate them? Praise Him for meeting you where you are and building your faith uniquely. Thank Him for cleansing you inside and out!

Stepping Out: This week, choose a barrier from above list and help Jesus break it down with love.

February 20
Centered

"Blessed are the pure in heart, for they will see God."
—Matthew 5:8 (Mt 5:1–12)

At the time when Jesus began His ministry, the people of Israel were desperate for relief from their difficult lives. More than that, they were in great need of spiritual revival. Living under political, economic, and religious oppression had left many weary and heavy-hearted. When they learned about the wonderful teaching of this new rabbi, Jesus, and the miraculous deeds He was performing, they sought Him out in droves.

Jesus and His first disciples encountered one such group in Capernaum. Leading them to a nearby mountain, Jesus began the Sermon on the Mount with a list of blessings meant to encourage and challenge His audience. In each of these blessings, which we now call the Beatitudes, Jesus addressed the spiritual condition of the crowd.

In blessing the pure of heart, Jesus not only challenged His listeners to examine their own hearts for signs of disease or corruption, but also inspired them to contemplate the blessing of seeing God. The humble masses, knowing full well that their hearts could never be truly pure, may have considered themselves unworthy of such a blessing. Yet, in their desire to know and please God, they sought His face nonetheless. On the other hand, the religious leadership falsely believed that this blessing was automatically theirs. It was the first group who understood that a blessed life was one centered on God, not self.

Anatomy books and Hallmark cards aside, there is no disputing the fact that our hearts represent the place where we feel love and other emotions. In a perfect world, the emotional center of our beings would remain safe from and unaffected by harmful external influences such as fear, anger, jealousy, hatred, greed, bitterness, and grief. However, life is messy. Our hearts may experience feelings of joy, peace, contentment, faith, comfort, security, and love, but the negative emotions we feel tend to linger and scar.

It is foolhardy to trust in our own ability to handle the onslaught of confusing and hurtful feelings our hearts musts process in our lifetimes. Thinking we can keep our hearts pure on our own leads to stubbornness and pride. Today's verse is a wonderful reminder that Jesus is standing right in front of us, waiting for us to offer Him our whole hearts. Once our eyes are on Him, our hearts can release the things that clutter and clog them, leaving us open to God's blessings.

Stepping In: What clutters your heart? What are the things that you love and focus your attention on? Are these things in God's will for you? Take time this week to look inside your heart. If God is not at the center, invite him in, knowing you may have to make room for Him. Pray for a willingness to make God the center of your heart and life.

Stepping Out: This week, look for God all around you: in nature, in the faces of loved ones, in random acts of kindness, in beauty, in music, and so on. Go for a walk and count the many miraculous signs of a loving Creator. Invite a friend to join you so you can discuss the way each of you experiences Jesus every day. Focus on the positive, and let your heart be filled with pure joy.

Rational

"You don't know what you are asking," Jesus said to them. "Can you drink the cup I am going to drink?"

—Matthew 20:23 (Mt 20:17–28)

As Jesus made His way to Jerusalem to complete His earthly mission on the cross, a large group of followers went with Him. Among the caravan were His twelve disciples and other family members, including the mother of the brothers James and John. Like so many of His early devotees, this woman believed that Jesus was to be Israel's new earthly king. She wanted to secure her sons good positions in His royal entourage, so she asked Jesus for His favor on them.

Jesus let her know that she didn't understand what she was asking for. Then, turning to the brothers, He asked them whether they could drink of the cup ordained for Him. Being two of Jesus' most loyal disciples and closest friends, they eagerly answered, "We can."

Though James and John may have rightly understood the word "cup" as a reference to sharing in their Master's suffering, they did not realize the extent of the pain and hardship they and the other disciples would endure because of their devotion and obedience to Christ. Nor did they know the anguish Jesus would soon endure for their sakes. Truly, their rational minds could not yet comprehend the plans God the Father had for His Son and the rest of His children, both in the near and distant future.

Today, a Christian's repertoire of rational thoughts includes biblical wisdom and experiential knowledge of God's power, promise, and provision. We are blessed to know how the story of the cross plays out. And while most of us strive to be obedient to Jesus' commands, few are as quick as James and John to accept the cup of suffering that obedience often entails.

Unless we live in isolation from the unbelieving world, we as Christians will eventually deal with negativity because of our beliefs. Most of us have likely experienced some measure of persecution already. This resistance to truth can range from mild mockery to social rejection to imprisonment to torture and death. Thankfully, most of us are not asked to pay the ultimate price for following our Lord. But some are. James was among the first of the disciples to do so. Others followed.

Given the choice, most of us would rather take the easier, less costly path. Though the cup we drink in this life may be bitter and hard to swallow, our rational minds know that Jesus has turned that poison to wine.

Stepping In: Read Isaiah 51:22; Matthew 26:37–39; John 16:33; and 2 Corinthians 5:16–21. What are your thoughts about Jesus suffering for you? How do you feel about suffering for Him? Do you think that what you can see and demonstrate is more rational than what you believe in your heart? Ask Jesus to make His thoughts yours.

Stepping Out: This week, use biblically rational thinking to direct your attitude and your actions. Be willing to defend Jesus regardless of the cup you may have to drink because if it.

February 22

Heartened

"I have told you these things, so that in me you may have peace. In this world you will have trouble. But take heart! I have overcome the world."

—John 16:33 (Jn 16:17–33)

On the night Jesus was to be betrayed, arrested, falsely tried, beaten, and abandoned, He shared one last Passover meal with His disciples. Over the course of the evening, Jesus spoke of and did many things that left the disciples confused and troubled. Using the unleavened bread to represent His body and the wine to represent His blood, He asked His men to eat and drink in remembrance of Him. He washed their feet to teach them about humble servanthood and brotherly love. He predicted that one of them would become a traitor and another would deny even knowing Him.

To leave them heartened rather than discouraged, Jesus reminded them that the love of the Father would be with them as He had been with them. Knowing they did not yet understand why He had to leave, He told them again that He would return. In the meantime, they would receive the Spirit of Truth to guide them and connect them to Himself. Finally, seeing the confusion that still plagued His men, Jesus urged them to take heart. "In a little while," the disciples' grief would indeed turn to joy.

From the moment Adam and Eve disobeyed God in the garden of Eden, pain, death, and struggle entered the world. As the world population continues to explode, the demand for the resources we need to live also increases. Battles for land, food, and power put societies at odds with one another. Though some of us live in relative peace and abundance, many more experience the effects of a troubled and dying planet. We can only expect this to worsen if current trends continue. Even Christians, who understand that this is to be expected, struggle to be at peace with it.

Jesus tells us to persevere in faith. He encourages us to look beyond the now to the trouble-free future He has promised us. But He knows that remaining heartened in trying times is no easy task. Today's verse serves as a reminder that we must focus on Jesus—what He has done, what He will do, and who we are in Him. We must remember to engage the indwelling Holy Spirit and be assured that we are literally never alone. When the world pushes us away, rejects our ideals, treats us poorly, and tries to convince us we are wrong, we can be heartened by the peace that comes directly from the throne of God. There, we find One who knows us, understands us, is there for us in body, mind, and spirit, and loves us even when no one else does. With the help of the Spirit, we too can overcome troubles in the world and look forward to an eternal, carefree life to come.

Stepping In: Read Psalm 85:8; Isaiah 9:6; John 14:27, 15:18-21; Romans 8:33–37; 1 John 4:1-4; and Revelation 2:7, 11, 17. How do these verses encourage and hearten you? Pray that you may have peace in your troubles.

Stepping Out: Each day this week, pray for peaceful resolutions to specific world problems, and that God receives the glory for these wondrous and merciful acts.

February 23
Committed

"Follow me, and let the dead bury their own dead."
—Matthew 8:22 (Mt 8:18–22)

In the middle of His ministry, Jesus was gaining new followers daily. Many men came to Him with promises of faithful devotion. Likely they had heard of or witnessed His Sermon on the Mount. Word of His authoritative teaching and miraculous healing powers preceded Him everywhere He went. Some of these eager believers stayed the course, while many more did not. The same authoritative teaching that drew seekers to Him also delivered hard truths only a few were willing to fully accept.

During one of His teachings, Jesus addressed a Jewish teacher of the Law who had professed his devotion. Jesus explained that to be a disciple required sacrificing worldly comfort and security. Hearing this, another disciple said that he would like to follow Jesus, but that he had to go and bury his father first. It is important to note that, in Jewish culture, this young man was bound by the Law and by custom to perform certain duties for his dead father. If his father was dead, or nearly so, the young man would likely have been consumed with burial preparations and not out following a young, new rabbi around. Jesus sensed his disingenuousness, knowing that this young man's interest in being His follower was contingent on convenience.

Jesus called his bluff. The statement above no doubt left His listeners dumbfounded. How could someone who was dead bury another dead person? This talk seemed like pure nonsense. Few, if any, understood that Jesus was referring to being spiritually dead. One who was spiritually alive would be committed to following the Lord and nothing else.

Spiritual vitality is as much a relevant topic today as it ever has been, if not more. Consider the myriad books, videos, sermons, and seminars on this topic being promoted, not all of them based on Christian ideals.

Jesus makes the path to spiritual wholeness simple: follow Him. Simple this may be, but easy it is not. There are many implied requirements involved in being a true disciple. Among them are: wholehearted love for God and others, steadfast commitment to keeping His commandments, and willingness to sacrifice one's personal pleasures and pursuits for Christ's causes. To the worldly, this lifestyle seems restrictive and boring. Christians know that it is a life that leads to satisfaction, the opposite of the dead-end pursuits of the world.

The good news is that God has made a way for us to live a vibrant life in Christ, one step of obedience at a time. Like following a firefighter out of a burning building, one must stay close enough to hear His instructions, do what He does, and never let Him out of your sight! Once saved, a spiritually alive person can show others how never to have to face the threat of death again.

Stepping In: Read Exodus 23:2; Leviticus 18:4–5; John 10:3–5; and 1 Peter 2:21. Meditate on these verses. How is God leading you to follow Him, and where are you putting up resistance? Pray for a willingness to commit to faithful obedience, without reservation.

Stepping Out: This week, be committed to repenting of one dead-end pursuit. Ask the Holy Spirit to guide you away from a bad habit or attitude and toward Christ.

Accorded

> "Behold, I am coming soon! My reward is with me, and I will give to everyone according to what he has done."
>
> —Revelation 22:12 (Rv 22:1–21)

At the end of his supernatural odyssey, the apostle John fell at the feet of his angel-guide in reverent worship. The angel quickly reprimanded John, reminding him to "Worship God!"

John had been given an inside view of the throne room of God, visions of ghastly beasts and horrific evil, and glimpses of the spectacular beauty of the New Jerusalem. He had stood in the presence of the glorified Lord Jesus. From the beginning to the end of this experience, John received the instructions of the Lamb, proclaiming the truth He wished His churches to know and heed.

After the final judgments were issued and God's justice enacted, John relished the picture of the redeemed earth and the promised salvation of God's children. John could see into the future, when all will be set right. All sin and evil were abolished, and the righteous walked in the light of the Lord. Jesus again promised John that He is "coming soon." Jesus' reward will be perfect peace achieved through His victory over Satan. All who put their faith in Him will be at His side. Those who reject Jesus to the end will forever be banished from His presence.

Christians, by definition, are Christ's disciples, or students under the tutelage of the Lord Jesus. As we mature in our faith, we are increasingly compelled to express our love for our Savior in more outward ways. It is at this point that the Christian becomes a modern-day apostle instead of merely an apprentice.

Throughout the pages of scripture are the Lord's commands. They were given to us, not just to know and appreciate, but to do. In the last chapter of the book of Revelation, the apostle John was instructed by an angel of the Lord, to "not seal up the words of the prophesy, because the time is near." If the time was near then, it is even closer now. God gave us His revelation so that we could be encouraged to stay faithful and strong as the days grow increasingly evil, and to proclaim the truth of this letter to all who are perishing, before it is too late.

Only God knows whose names are in the Lamb's Book of Life. When Jesus returns, those whose names are not found in it will not be accorded another chance to change their minds. Now is the time to give our friends, neighbors, loved ones, coworkers, acquaintances, and even those whom we don't know or love so well the information found in the book we *do* have access to: the Bible. One's eternity depends on knowing the whole story and deciding for oneself where one wants to be when Jesus returns.

Stepping In: Read Isaiah 40:10, 62:11-12; Ezekiel 3:27; Daniel 8:15-26, 12:9-10; Matthew 16:27–28; Romans 13:11–12; and Galatians 6:7–8. Knowing you have been accorded knowledge of the gospel truth, how do these verses inspire you to step up your evangelical game? Pray for power to act.

Stepping Out: This week, between you and Jesus, take an honest look at what you have done either for or against the Lord. Make the necessary adjustments.

Merciful

"Blessed are the merciful, for they will be shown mercy."
—Matthew 5:7 (Mt 5:1–12)

Jesus began His Sermon on the Mount with a list of encouraging beatitudes. In each, Jesus promised a blessing for those who, by God's grace, persevered through the difficult realities of life. For the needy masses gathered there, Jesus' words brought the promise of comfort and mercy. For the religious leaders in attendance, His message cut to the heart of their arrogance, pride, and spiritual depravity. Jesus' words reminded His audience that mercy required both attitude and action. Mercy was to be freely given and received. This was good news to those who had been denied such treatment, and a poignant jab to the religious authorities who repeatedly failed to demonstrate this godly trait.

Mercy is always an undeserved gift, a pardon instead of a deserved punishment. Though God readily bestows it on those who seek it, humans are not always as generous in doling out mercy to others. We all know what it is like to wait in torment as a parent decides whether to exact a punishment commensurate to our offense, or to grant us leniency instead. Some of us have experienced similar anxiety before a judge, police officer, teacher, coach, or priest. We often forget all this when we are on the other side of the table. Regrettably, most of us can recall enjoying the scene as we drew out the agony of, say, a younger sibling who longed to return to our good graces.

Why is human nature so contrary and cruel? Jesus makes our task simple for us. Show mercy *as* (in the same way and to the same degree) we have been shown mercy. Everyone is blessed when mercy is given and received.

Stepping In: Read Lamentations 3:22–23; Matthew 18:21–35; Luke 1:50; and James 2:12–13. What do these verses teach you about mercy? When was the last time someone extended mercy to you and vice versa? What it easier: to give mercy or to receive it? Thank God for the mercies He offers to you every morning. Ask Him to give you a more merciful heart.

Stepping Out: Offer mercy to others this week. Make it a goal to extend mercy to someone each day. Challenge yourself to be merciful even to those who don't deserve it. Be the blessing you want to receive.

February 26
Rewarded

"For the Son of Man is going to come in his Father's glory with his angels, and then he is going to reward each person according to what he has done. I tell you the truth, some who are standing here will not taste death before they see the Son of Man coming in his kingdom."
—Matthew 16:27–28 (Mt 16:21–28)

From the beginning of His earthly ministry, Jesus knew that He would one day return to His rightful place beside His heavenly Father. He had been given a task—to save humanity from sin's destruction. Jesus wasted no time in training His disciples for their own mission to inform the world of Jesus' triumph over death. In the years they spent with Jesus, the Twelve came to love and trust their Master. These men devoted their lives to promoting His ministry. Over time, they began to comprehend that He was no ordinary rabbi, but, as John the Baptist had proclaimed, the "Lamb of God, who takes away the sin of the world."

Yet, dismay over Jesus' imminent departure left His followers feeling anything but hopeful. Even knowing that He would return was not enough to allay their fears. With the words above, Jesus hoped to bring encouragement and shift their focus from the physical reality to the spiritual truth. Though He knew that His overwhelmed apprentices could not fully understand what He was saying, Jesus hoped that they understood enough to trust Him nonetheless. He hoped they could look beyond their imminent loss to the reward of His glorious return.

As we wait for His return, these promises of Jesus to His disciples two thousand years ago take on a richer meaning. The truth of the complete scripture is such a blessing. Unlike the first disciples, we know that this story has a happy ending, at least for those who believe. We have the benefit of seeing prophecies fulfilled. We can see the unfolding of prophesied events. We know that Jesus can be taken at His word; He is trustworthy and reliable. His promise to come with His angels and reward each person for what they have done will be realized. Some of us may even not "taste death" before that time comes. Like the first disciples (who did die before Jesus' second coming), many of us also have experienced the Spirit of God moving in power and have witnessed examples of His kingdom here on earth in many tangible ways. The best is yet to come. What an awesome truth. What an awesome God. What an awesome reward.

Stepping In: Read Job 34:10–11; Psalm 62:11–12; Luke 17:30–35; John 1:29, 14:1-3; and Acts 1:11. Are you comforted or concerned about Jesus' return? How do these verses help you understand a believer's role in kingdom work? Pray for peace and understanding about how to prepare for our Lord's return.

Stepping Out: Knowing that judgment is coming, and time may be short, live as an example of this expectant hope. This week, have a conversation with someone about your hope in the ultimate reward.

February 27

Pursuant

"Ask and it will be given to you; seek and you will find; knock and the door will be opened to you. For everyone who asks receives; he who seeks finds; and to him who knocks, the door will be opened."

—Matthew 7:7–8 (Mt 7:1–12)

During the Sermon on the Mount, Jesus repeatedly emphasized the importance of aligning one's heart with God by seeking a right relationship with Him and with others. He called the place where such people reside "the kingdom of heaven." Jesus revealed shockingly simple steps one can take to gain entry to this place, where every heart's desire is met. In contrast to the rigorous religious practices all Jews were expected to observe, Jesus' teaching placed the emphasis on a person's persistent and pursuant heart.

Who was this young rabbi to make such a claim? Could believers' every desire be theirs for the asking? Could anyone but God promise such a blessing? These questions, among others, no doubt rippled through the crowd. Excited by the prospect of so easily receiving what they desired, some may have clamored for Jesus to put His promise to the test. Others, like the religious leaders in attendance, likely wanted to confront Jesus about His blasphemous claim. Regardless of their reactions, all hearing this new theology would have had their interest in Jesus piqued.

What a beautiful privilege it is to be able to bring our requests directly to God, knowing that He promises that the pursuant seeker will find reward. However, Christians who know Jesus understand that this does not give us carte blanche to ask for and receive our every desire. As is always the case with Jesus' teaching, the blessed are those who love God above all else—those who prioritize His will before their own. Jesus tells us, "Seek first the kingdom and His righteousness, and all these things (wants and needs) will be given to you as well" (Mt 6:33).

God knows what we want and need before we ask Him. When Jesus tells us to ask, seek, and knock, He wants us to search for the heart of God. There, we will find all the best things we could possibly hope for, because those things are what God wants for us. To do this, we must shift away from our causal and expectant approach with God, and intentionally and actively pursue Him and His will for us. Then, lo and behold, the door to blessings will fly open!

Stepping In: Read Psalm 20:1-5, 37:4; Jeremiah 29:13; Matthew 6:7-8, and 1 John 5:14–15. How closely do your requests align with God's will? Do you seek His kingdom first? Pray for God to make the desires of your heart His. Praise Jesus for promising you wonderful things when you ask Him with a pure heart.

Stepping Out: This week, write down and share the ways God has answered your requests when they have aligned with His will for you. Think about times when you were glad your requests did not get answered your way.

February 28
Wanting

"What do you want me to do for you?"
—Mark 10:51 (Mk 10:46–52)

As Jesus made His final trek to Jerusalem, He passed through the town of Jericho. He and His entourage were met by a large and eager crowd. Among them were two blind beggars wondering what all the excitement was about. Overhearing murmurs that Jesus was coming, the two blind men began shouting, "Son of David, have mercy on us!" As Jesus drew near, the crowd tried to hush the two beggars, to no avail.

One of the two was named Bartimaeus. Having been born blind, he knew no other life than sitting on the road, asking for handouts. Hope was not something that people in his position could afford to waste energy on. Yet something in Bartimaeus shifted as Jesus approached. If what he had heard about this amazing young rabbi from Nazareth was true, perhaps he too could receive healing—if only Bartimaeus could get His attention.

Undeterred by the crowd's reprimands, Bartimaeus shouted louder. Jesus heard his plea and had compassion on him and his companion. Calling them over, Jesus asked Bartimaeus what he wanted. Though it seems obvious that these men sought a cure for their blindness, Jesus' question required them to think about what they truly wanted. Jesus knew Bartimaeus' heart and could see that this man wanted to receive both physical sight and spiritual insight.

Some might find today's verse a bit puzzling. At face value, the question seems rhetorical. However, there are two important things to remember about this subject. One, it cannot be assumed that the blind actually want to deal with the responsibility of such an abrupt life change. Two, it was not just anyone asking the question. When we consider the possibility of have a wish granted as if by some magical genie, most of us automatically think of a malady we would like cured or a physical feature we would like improved. We wish that our circumstances would become worry-free, most commonly by obtaining more money. In our finite minds, these temporal fixes equate to an easier life and therefore more happiness.

Though God cares about our needs and desires, He is more concerned with our characters. Jesus knows that we have a hard time thinking things through. He knows that if we could see our lives from His perspective, our priorities would change. When Jesus asks us this same question, He wants us to think about the ramifications of our request. He wants us to think beyond what we think we want. He wants us to consider our spirits, not just our bodies. He wants us to consider the motives behind our wanting.

Stepping In: Read Psalm 146:8; Isaiah 35:1–5; Luke 4:18–19; John 9:39–41; 2 Corinthians 4:4; and Ephesians 1:18 and 5:8. After considering these verses, what reply would you give to Jesus if He asked you what you want from Him? Pray that your priorities shift from immediate and temporal to spiritual and eternal.

Stepping Out: This week, ask Jesus what He wants from you. With the Spirit's help, take first steps toward obeying His request. (PS: accountability partners increase success.)

February 29
Peaceful

"Blessed are the peacemakers, for they will be called the sons of God."
—Matthew 5:9 (Mt 5:1–12)

Jesus began His Sermon on the Mount with a list of blessings for those possessing certain godly character traits. These blessings were more than mere platitudes. Each blessing was meant to challenge listeners to evaluate the condition of their hearts and their relationships with God and others.

The mostly Jewish audience may have taken Jesus' blessing of the peacemakers as a simple reminder that God's chosen people should strive for a more peaceable lifestyle. However, Jesus was informing them that the title "sons of God," and the position of heir in His kingdom, was available to *all* who worked according to God's plan for peace. Though many in His audience would not have realized it, Jesus was personally promising to honor the words of this statement. He was letting His listeners know that He possessed the authority to bless and adopt God's peaceful heirs.

To say that it is a blessing to be called a child of God is an extreme understatement. Christians today understand that this is a priceless gift. Though all who are saved by grace through faith in Jesus as Lord can rest assured that their position in the royal family is secure, Jesus reminds us that we are truly fortunate to also be known as peacemakers.

Christians are Christ's representatives. Because we enjoy a blessed title and position in His kingdom, we should also claim the role of bringing peace to the world in which we live. As a troubled and deeply divided world watches, we have an opportunity and a responsibility to offer a peaceful contribution to every situation we are in. When we strive to create peaceful environments in our homes, workplaces, communities, and churches, as well as in places we travel, we exhibit a godly character that does not go unnoticed. In time, people will associate our peaceful nature, cooperative spirit, joyful presence, and positive attitude with our faith. We can smile and know that Jesus' words have always been true.

Stepping In: Fill in your name and your gender pronoun to personalize this statement: "Blessed is_____, a peacemaker, for _____ will be called a child of God." Read it several times and let the reality of this sink in. You are both a peacemaker at heart *and* a beloved heir to God's kingdom. Let the weight of this blessing and responsibility of it wash over you. Praise God for blessing you with the ability to bless others with acts of peace and love.

Stepping Out: Look up Romans 12:18. Because peace does not happen by accident, it will take an effort on your part to make it happen. Start today by being quick to forgive, slow to anger, and flexible whenever possible. Instead of adding fuel to the fire of a disagreement, offer a solution. When all else fails, agree to disagree and walk away. Peace begins with you.

Reliant

"Do not take along any gold or silver or copper in your belts; take no bag for the journey, or extra tunic, or sandals or a staff; for the worker is worth his keep."

—Matthew 10:9–10 (Mt 10:1–10)

After Jesus had called, taught, trained, and given power and authority to His twelve disciples, He commissioned them to go out and preach the gospel to the "lost sheep of Israel." His newly appointed apostles were told to cure illnesses, bring the dead to life, cast out evil spirits, and profess that the "kingdom of heaven is near." Then Jesus added the above instructions.

Suddenly their Master's command did not sound so promising. How could they be expected to set out on an indeterminate journey without so much as a loaf of bread? Some probably shook their heads in doubt. Others, still riding high on the news of receiving miraculous abilities, were ready to set out regardless of the situation's uncertainty. The only thing any of them knew for sure was that they would soon be completely reliant on God, each other, and the mercy of strangers. As they discovered in the days to come, their trust in the Lord was tested and proven—for their good and His glory. These men learned to rely on Jesus' strength and not their own to make it through.

For most of us today, the thought of living without basic amenities and creature comforts for an undisclosed period of time is absurd. Honestly, being without our cell phones for even a day throws most of us into a panic. Rarely if ever are we asked to leave on a journey without taking money and provisions along. That would be foolhardy at best.

Missionaries throughout history, though they often faced plenty of uncertainty and deprivation, would be the first to tell of how richly the Lord provides. It is often under extreme circumstances, when people are forced to depend solely on God for sustenance and safety, that miracles are displayed. This principle holds true for the average Christian as well.

The problem for most of us is that we do not like to be reliant on others for anything. We don't trust anyone else to meet our needs or have our best interests in mind. Humanly speaking, this may well be true. But God is not a limited mortal. He is the omnipotent, omniscient, omnipresent, sovereign Creator of the universe. Moreover, He is altogether good and completely trustworthy. Missionary or not, when God sends us on an errand, He supplies us with what we need for the task. Our obedience and faithful reliance on Him allows for His miraculous work to be done in and through us.

Stepping In: Imagine yourself in this story using the Envision It method (See appendix). Put yourself into the shoes of one of the apostles. What would your attitude be? Is God calling you to the mission field or into a challenging ministry? Bravely pray for an opportunity to be fully reliant on Him.

Stepping Out: This week, pray for, join, and/or contribute to a missionary cause.

March 2
Anointed

> "The Spirit of the Lord is on me, because he has anointed me to preach good news to the poor. He has sent me to proclaim freedom for the prisoners and recovery of sight for the blind, to release the oppressed, to proclaim the year of the Lord's favor."
>
> —Luke 4:18–19 (Lk 4:14–30)

After His time in the desert, being tempted be Satan, Jesus, filled with the Spirit, returned to Galilee. Boldly, He taught in the synagogues of that region and was welcomed by many. People were happy to hear the good news of which He spoke.

Wanting also to share the gospel with His family and former neighbors, Jesus left Galilee and went to His hometown of Nazareth. As was His custom, He went to the synagogue. After He had read from the scroll of Isaiah, He sat and began to teach. What He said astonished His listeners. Though the crowd spoke kindly to Jesus' face, many questioned the authority by which the son of a carpenter could speak of fulfilling prophecy.

Knowing their thoughts, Jesus observed aloud, "Only in his hometown and in his own house is a prophet without honor" (Mt 13:57). He compared His audience to those who had rejected God's prophets, Elisha and Elijah. The infuriated crowd drove Him out of town with the intent of throwing Him off a cliff. But it was not His time to die, and He eluded them. In the end, the anointing Jesus wanted to share with the people of His hometown became the dust He shook off His sandals instead.

Unlike Jesus' early audiences, Christians today have the Spirit of the Lord dwelling within them. With the Spirit's help, we can comprehend scripture and understand how prophecy points to Jesus. Yet, even with godly wisdom and discernment in our favor, some of us still struggle to acknowledge and accept God at work in those closest to us. Like the Nazarenes, we have a hard time believing that God would choose one of our own to be His instrument. Suddenly, prior knowledge, history, and bias cloud our perception of this person's potentially valid witness. We would likely be just as skeptical about a neighbor, someone we knew as the son or daughter of a blue-collar worker, who suddenly became a famous religious figure with many followers worldwide.

Regardless of who a person is or where that person comes from, if God calls them and anoints them with His Spirit, they will succeed. All Christians are called to spread the good news of Jesus. God doesn't care about our credentials; in fact, He often chooses the most unlikely sorts to do His work, so that He gets the glory for doing what only He can do. Jesus started the kingdom work of proclaiming freedom, restoring sight to the blind, releasing the oppressed, and initiating "the year of the Lord's favor." Until He returns, it is our job to continue this mission.

Stepping In: Read Leviticus 25:8–17; Psalm 102:18–20, 103:1-6; Isaiah 42:6–7, 61; and Luke 9:5. Are you being obedient to God's call to share His gospel? Why or why not? Pray for the Spirit's anointing to do so.

Stepping Out: This week, share with someone in spiritual bondage the freedoms you have found in Christ. Humbly express the hope you have in your Savior because He has restored your sight.

Empowered

"It is not for you to know the times or dates the Father has set by his own authority. But you will receive power when the Holy Spirit comes on you; and you will be my witnesses in Jerusalem, and in all Judea and Samaria, and to the ends of the earth."

—Acts 1:7–8 (Acts 1:1–11)

Luke, a companion of Paul, wrote the gospel of Luke and the book of Acts (also called the Acts of the Apostles). A physician by trade, Luke used his inquiring mind, literary skills, and eye for detail to write an accurate historical account of Christianity's first missionaries.

Luke began his second letter to his friend and publisher, Theophilus, by chronicling the transition period between Jesus' ascension to heaven and the initial movements of the first apostles. Basing his facts on the personal accounts of those who had known Jesus and had experienced His miraculous displays of power firsthand, Luke was able to quote many of Jesus' own words. Today's verses were likely quoted from a disciple reporting one of their last encounters with the Lord before He ascended. Someone had asked Jesus if He intended to restore the earthly kingdom of Israel. Refocusing their attention on the spiritual purpose for His and their mission, Jesus reminded them that He would empower them to bring about a kingdom more vast and significant than they could yet fathom. Then He was taken up to heaven right before their eyes.

These refrains have been an enduring reminder for Christians throughout the ages that it is not our business to know the details of God's plans. Our task is to go forth in His name. Blessed with the indwelling Holy Spirit, modern-day apostles of Christ must continue the work the first missionaries began two millennia ago. Because of their bravery and unshakable faith, the gospel is now known in nearly every nation of the world. But there is still much work yet to be done. There are still many dark places where the light of Jesus needs to be brought—places where people either willful deny truth, or are simply lost in the shadows of their ignorance. Regardless, everyone deserves to know what their options are: continuing in sinful rebellion that leads to death, or choosing faith in a Savior and life eternal.

In a world where most people do not believe they need the forgiveness of a savior, this is no small task. People believe this lie that Satan works very hard to perpetuate. As truth-bearers, Christians must heed the words of today's passage posthaste. Thankfully, Jesus has empowered us with wisdom and abilities to do the work of aiding in the restoration of His kingdom. Until Jesus returns, the earth and its inhabitants are all we have. They are worth saving.

Stepping In: Read Psalm 102:12–13; Matthew 24:14, 28:16-20; Luke 10:19–20; Romans 10:12–15; Philippians 4:13; and 1 John 4:2–4. How is the Spirit challenging you to trust in God's ways and timing in your life and ministry? Ask the Holy Spirit to empower you to obey God's commands and to reveal His power at work in you.

Stepping Out: With whom is the Spirit prompting you to share the gospel? Do so this week.

Truthful

"I tell you the truth, you shall see heaven open up, and the angels of
God ascending and descending on the Son of Man."
—John 1:51 (Jn 1:35–51)

During the time when John the Baptist was preaching the coming kingdom of God and baptizing people in the Jordan River, east of Jerusalem, Jesus Himself came to be immersed in the waters. John, knowing that His cousin Jesus was a far superior man of God, reluctantly agreed to the task. As John lifted Jesus up from below the surface, his cousin's divinity was revealed. The prophecy of Jacob's ladder was fulfilled as the clouds parted, a dove descended from heaven and landed on Jesus, and the audible voice of God was heard praising His Son. From then on, John pointed to Jesus as the Lamb of God, the Messiah.

Thereafter, many of John's disciples left him to follow Jesus. Among them were Andrew and his brother Simon (Peter). Together they traveled up to the town of Bethsaida in Galilee, where Jesus called Philip (Bartholomew) to follow Him. Philip went to tell his friend Nathanael that he had found the one Moses and the prophets had written about—Jesus of Nazareth. Bluntly, Nathanael questioned how anything good could come from that place.

Curious, though, Nathanael went to see Jesus for himself. Before they had been formally introduced, Jesus (knowing what Nathanael had said) offered him a compliment on his truthful character. By revealing His omniscience, Jesus also offered His new disciple proof that something great had indeed come from Nazareth. At that, Nathanael believed. Jesus let His fledgling followers know that what they had witnessed was only the beginning of how He intended to bring God's kingdom to earth.

Jesus always chooses His words carefully. He presents the truth in ways each of us can receive personally. For His Jewish disciples, new to the gospel, Jesus' references to the prophecies and scripture would have been a useful tool in building their faith. Additionally, Jesus allowed His disciples to experience the fulfilment of many such prophecies.

Though we might not ever witness such grand miracles as our first-century counterparts, Christians today can point to many proofs of Jesus' power in our lives and world. When we are truthful, we acknowledge the glory of creation, the many answered prayers and fulfilled promises, and the positive impact of God's written Word. Even so, He knows that some of us need more reassurance than words on a page. Many of us are like Nathanael, bringing doubts and questions.

Jesus not only welcomes these, He encourages us to honestly bring our concerns to Him. He is happy to reward truthful character with spiritual wisdom and insight. Though Jesus knows our thoughts before we speak them, He delights in us when we voice them honestly.

Stepping In: Read Genesis 28:10–12; Psalm 32:2, 139:4; Isaiah 64:1–4; and Matthew 3:13–17. In what way has Jesus assured you that He is the promised Savior? In what areas do you still have reservations? Ask Him for peace and confidence to take Him at His Word and trust His promises.

Stepping Out: This week, encourage your skeptical friends to bring their honest questions about Jesus to you. With the help of the Holy Spirit and your Bible, demonstrate how you seek truthful answers. Remember, the Word of God never returns void (Is 55:11).

Ready

"I will go and heal him."
—Matthew 8:7 (See also Luke 7:1–10)

Shortly after giving His Sermon on the Mount, Jesus entered the town of Capernaum, His ministry base in Galilee. There, He spent extended periods of time teaching and healing the people. As word of His wisdom and miraculous abilities spread, many from that region and beyond came to faith. Among them was a God-fearing centurion, a Roman soldier of high rank. The centurion's valued servant had fallen gravely ill. Having most likely exhausted all other means of saving his servant, the centurion turned to the Jewish elders in hopes that they could help him find Jesus. The Jewish leaders were typically not quick to help a Roman soldier, nor did they acknowledge Jesus' authority to heal. But they acquiesced because of their appreciation for this man's contribution to the building of their temple.

When the centurion approached Jesus with his request, Jesus readily responded. Aware not only of the man's faith, but also of the social risks this man was willing to take to save a servant, Jesus' heart was filled with compassion. Jesus agreed to help without hesitation. The centurion, overwhelmed by his personal unworthiness to be in the presence of the Lord, humbly suggested that Jesus need not go; He could simply heal the servant with a word. The centurion's great faith was revealed, leading to his servant's restoration to health and to his household's salvation.

Now more than ever, time is the most precious of all commodities. Most of us feel that we cannot manage one more demand on our time. That said, we all make time for what it truly important to us. As Christians, what is important to Jesus should also be important to us.

During His time on earth, Jesus prioritized people over agendas. Do we? He was willing to stop what He was doing to help someone in need, regardless of the cultural, religious, or political awkwardness of the situation. How often do we do this? Jesus was ready to show His love for both the centurion and his servant with action. Is this our typical response?

Jesus recognized a potential believer and went out of His way to acknowledge the centurion's humility and faith. This is something we should all make time to do. We must be ready to step out in faith to bring healing to others, expectant of our Lord's ability and willingness to intervene on their and our behalf.

Stepping In: Read Proverbs 16:9; Matthew 6:31–33; Ephesians 5:15-17, 6:14-15; and Colossians 4:5–6. How do you prioritize your time? Do you put off kingdom work for a more convenient moment? How ready are you to uphold Jesus' causes, even when they interfere with your plans? Talk to God about this. Ask for a faithful and ready Spirit.

Stepping Out: Each time you pray this week, ask God for an ability to see others' need for help, and for a willingness to do something about it. Call on Jesus' power and step close enough to touch others with the same healing love that Jesus uses to heal the hurting. Combine prayer and physical touch (when appropriate) for maximum effect.

Expectant

"To be sure, Elijah comes and will restore all things. But I tell you, Elijah has already come, and they did not recognize him, but have done to him everything they wished. In the same way the Son of Man is going to suffer at their hands."

—Matthew 17:11–12 (Mt 17:1–13)

Before entering the last phase of His earthly mission, Jesus shared a special moment with three of His disciples. Taking Peter, James, and John to a remote mountain location, Jesus underwent a transfiguration, allowing them to see His holy, radiant presence. Jesus' unearthly brightness, coupled with the appearance of their long-dead prophet Elijah, and forefather Moses, inspired Peter to want to stay and worship there indefinitely. However, when the three disciples heard the audible voice of God praising His Son and instructing them to heed His word, they fell facedown in mortal fear. Jesus comforted the three and instructed them to keep quiet about what they had seen and heard.

Peter, with his characteristically unbridled curiosity, asked Jesus to clarify the prophecy about Elijah coming "first." Jesus explained that, as the people had rejected previous prophets and their words, those who came after could expect the same treatment. By this He was referring to Himself, the disciples, and all who would proclaim the name of the Lord.

Evidence of God's glory has always been present in the world. All of creation endlessly declares His power and authority—except for fickle humans. We humans use the minds God gave us to analyze what we know by what we see and comprehend. To make sense of our world, we try to fit everything we experience into tangible parameters. Things outside the scope of our understanding are too far-fetched to be real. For many, God and His ability to affect our lives today fall into this category. Like the apostle Peter, even those of us who believe often need reassurance and clarification at every turn.

Jesus knows that we need help in remaining convinced of what we think we know. When we pay attention, we will see the many signs and proofs of promises, prayers, and prophecies being fulfilled. When we look for Him expectantly, we see that He "is able to do immeasurably more than we can ask or imagine, according to His power that is at work within us" (Eph 3:20–21). While looking for signs of God at work in our world, we mustn't miss the signs that are right in front of us. God's glory is evident everywhere. Today's verses are a reminder for all generations to look expectantly for signs of God's revelation, which He gives to us every day. Look forward to the day when the faithful, along with Elijah, will be present when Jesus restores all things!

Stepping In: Read Psalm 19, 78:1-4; Malachi 4:4–6; and Revelation 11:3. Take some time to consider the miraculous events you have experienced in your life. Did you recognize them as such at the time? Praise Jesus for His marvelous power and sovereignty, past, present and future. Pray for an expectant faith and insightful vision.

Stepping Out: This week, reflect Jesus' radiance by lovingly sharing personal miracle stories and fulfilled promises. Talk about the prophecies you are still eagerly expecting.

Overjoyed

Suddenly Jesus met them. "Greetings," he said. They came to him, clasped his feet and worshipped him. Then Jesus said to them, "Do not be afraid. Go and tell my brothers to go to Galilee; there they will see me."

—Matthew 28:9–10 (Mt 27:45–56; 28:1–10)

Many of the events Jesus had predicted and had tried to prepare His disciples for had come true. Some were still yet to be realized. Jesus had been betrayed by one of His own men, Judas Iscariot, who later took his own life. Jesus had been beaten, mocked, falsely accused, and hung on a cross. Jesus had died and been buried. Jesus would return.

Yet when Jesus arose from the dead after three days in the grave, just as He had said He would, the disciples were completely unaware of what had transpired. They had no doubt felt the earthquake, but they would not have known about the graves releasing resurrected saints. Because they had not stayed with Jesus to His end nor kept a vigil at His grave, they were not there to witness the angel moving the stone away from the tomb. Only a faithful group of women knew that the Lord was alive.

Obeying the angel's command, the women ran to tell the disciples that Jesus was risen. They hadn't gone far before Jesus Himself appeared. Completely overcome by joy and relief, the women fell at the Lord's feet. Jesus casually greeted them and offered them tender reassurance before sending them to finish the task the angel had given them.

Generations of Christians have been brought up with the resurrection story. It is what we base our faith upon. However, aside from Easter Sunday, few of us regularly feel overjoyed about it. Some believers have a regrettably lackadaisical attitude about Jesus' suffering and sacrifice. Though we may love Jesus and be truly grateful for our salvation, many of us fail to fully appreciate the magnitude of the miracle that took place on that Sunday morning all those centuries ago. Nor do we generally muster an adequately heartfelt response to the amazing blessing it is for us. Because Jesus lives, we have life in the Spirit now and eternal life forever. That is no small deal! We ought to take a lesson from the vigilant women in today's passage and fall overjoyed at Jesus' feet every day, grateful and relieved that He has conquered death and is with us and in us. Then, following their example, we ought to run to tell others the good news.

Stepping In: Read Matthew 12:48–50; John 20:11–17; Romans 8:29; and Hebrews 2:11–12, 17. How do you feel about Jesus' resurrection from the dead? Do you believe that He lives? Pray for an appropriately joyful response to this amazing news, and thank Him for dying and coming back for you.

Stepping Out: This week, either privately or corporately, express your overflowing joy for the beautiful truth that Jesus lives! Sing praises to the Lord. The louder, the better.

Restored

"Do you want to get well?"

—John 5:6 (Jn 5:1–15)

Early in the second year of His public ministry, Jesus went to Jerusalem for a religious feast, as was His custom. While He was there, He visited a pool by the Sheep Gate, near the northern wall of the city. Many sick and lame people lay waiting by the pool, hoping to be brought into the healing waters when those waters were "stirred." Jesus saw desperation on the faces of those wanting to be first into the pool when the waters mysteriously moved.

Saddened by their misguided faith, He sought out the man whom He had come to heal. For thirty-eight years, this man had lain by the pool, crippled and unable to reach the waters in time. Jesus asked the man a seemingly obvious question: "Do you want to get well?" Instead of answering with an immediate yes, this man made an excuse for not being able to get to the water; he blamed others for their neglect. Though the Bible does not say what his condition was, he clearly had been an invalid for such a long time that he could not imagine a different life. The reality of having to reengage with society and be responsible for himself was probably a frightening prospect. He had become resigned and complacent over the decades and was faced with a hard choice.

Jesus did not allow this man's barriers to get in the way of his restoration. He healed him and told him to, "Get up! Pick up your mat and walk … [S]top sinning or something worst may happen to you" (Jn 5:8). His body restored, it was time for the invalid's days of resentment and bitter inaction to be over.

In our modern world, with a myriad of social services and patient treatment options available, the hopeless and pathetic scene depicted in this story should not still exist—but it does. For a variety of reasons, people still fall through the cracks. There are plenty of marginalized, rejected, and forgotten people today quickly losing hope in finding a cure for their social, mental, and physical ills. Many have become similarly discouraged, cynical, distrusting, resigned and angry. They defensively blame others for their plight. Some have been in their situation for so long that they simply have become comfortable in their misery, believing they do not have what it takes to be a responsible, contributing member of society. Some may believe that they are incapable of being fixed or, worse, unworthy.

Jesus does not take any of these factors for granted. That is why He asks us if we really want to be fully restored. Because God gives us free will, we must choose to either continue in our diseased ways or accept the spiritual healing that He offers. Though He may not fix all the physical conditions that we have, if we truly desire to be well, He will restore our souls, spirits, and relationship with Himself.

Stepping In: Read Psalm 103:1–5; John 10:7–10; Acts 10:37–38; James 5:13–16; and 1 Peter 2:24–25 and 5:7. What is your response when Jesus asks you the question in today's verse? What is keeping you from trusting Jesus with your troubles and illnesses? Pray for pure faith and courage to make the better choice. Be restored.

Stepping Out: This week, come alongside someone who is still lying by the pool. Lead them to Jesus.

March 9
Watched-Over

"These are the words of him who has the sharp, double-edged sword.
I know where you live—where Satan has his throne. Yet you remain
true to my name."

—Revelation 2:12–13 (Rv 2:12–17)

During the preparation of His disciples for their coming ministries, Jesus warned them that He would be sending them out "like sheep among wolves" (Mt 10:16). Jesus sent His men to bring the gospel to fellow Israelites, and indeed they were met with ferocious cultural and religious resistance. This continued after Jesus' ascension to heaven, when His apostles stepped out into completely unknown territory—bringing the good news of salvation through Jesus to the Gentiles and pagans.

In his missionary journeys, the apostle John fearlessly promoted Christianity throughout Asia Minor, successfully planting many churches amid the predominantly polytheistic cultures there and taking great risks to do so. In captivity, John was taken "in the Spirit" from his Patmos prison cell into the presence of God, where Jesus Himself gave him the task of scribing God's end-times revelation.

Jesus began His message with the above words. Aware of the culture of evil the leaders of the church in Pergamum were dealing with, Jesus wanted them to be encouraged. He was aware and watching over them. He went on to commend them for remaining strong even as friends were being martyred. Jesus also noted an attitude of complacency developing regarding idol worship among some of the congregants. He warned them to repent, or the sword in His mouth would be used against them.

Jesus knows where we live. We are being watched over by His protective gaze. This reality can cause believers to experience a deep sense of comfort and safety. He sees our difficulties and is closely monitoring our circumstances. However, this same truth may feel like an invasion of privacy for those who have something to hide. Those who prefer that their shady dealings and defiant attitudes not be revealed, find the thought of God watching everything on His spiritual surveillance camera anything but comforting. Nothing goes unnoticed by God.

A true test of our Christian character is what kind of person we are when we believe no one is looking. Because Satan is the ruler of this world, we live in an evil place. Lies, distractions, and temptations bombard us every day. Without the armor of God to shield us, we can easily fall prey to the Devil's schemes. Though most of the armor we mentally and spiritually put on is defensive in nature, there is one piece of offensive attire we must use to combat Satan—the sword, which is the Word of God. If it is good enough for Jesus to use to vanquish the Enemy, it should work for us in our battle to remain true to His name.

Stepping In: Read Psalm 139:1–4; Ephesians 2:1–2, 6:17; 2 Timothy 3:1–5; Hebrews 4:12–13; and Revelation 1:16. From the 2 Timothy passage, what "idols" do you need to confess and repent of? Praise God for watching over you while you cling to the truth in 1 Corinthians 10:13. Pray that God's protective Spirit encapsulates you.

Stepping Out: This week, fortify your artillery by memorizing scripture that will help you ward off evil and fight temptation. Let your life be a testimony that remains true to Jesus' name.

Unrelenting

"Woman, you have great faith! Your request is granted."
—Matthew 15:28 (Mt 15:21–28)

After spending considerable time and energy ministering to the people of Galilee, Jesus and His disciples left that area and made their way toward the town of Tyre on the Mediterranean Sea. A Canaanite (Greek-born, non-Jewish) woman came to Jesus, pleading with Him to heal her demon-possessed daughter. Jesus did not respond. The woman persisted. The disciples finally asked Jesus if they should send her away. Speaking so that the woman could hear, He stated that He had come only to heal His own people.

Unrelenting, the desperate woman fell at Jesus' feet, begging, "Lord, help me." He responded by telling her that she was less worthy than a dog to receive a blessing from Him. Even this curt and offensive comment did not dissuade her. In faith and humility, she acknowledged her lowly and undeserving position. Still, she asked for whatever mercy He was willing to part with.

Jesus saw this woman's true heart. He recognized her unwavering belief in His ability to help her, and appreciated her shamelessness in asking. Seeing her love for her daughter and her belief in His love for all people, Jesus acquiesced.

In American society, it is hard for us to understand the cultural and social divisions that segmented the ancient world. However, even today these divisions exist and are vehemently defended. Many of us are stunned by how Jesus treated the woman in today's passage, but in His day and in that culture, He was acting in accordance with common social and religious mores. He was also staying on task with His mission of saving the "lost sheep of Israel." Though Jesus certainly saved many who were not of Jewish descent, it is important to remember that, according to scripture, His personal ministry was to bring salvation to God's chosen people. Later, His apostles would bring salvation to the Gentiles.

This passage is included in the Bible as a reminder that Jesus has always been a God of love and compassion, regardless of the barriers He must cross. He offers the dogs more than mere scraps, giving His sons and daughters riches beyond compare. Those who defy cultural odds, remain steadfast in faith regardless of opposition, and pursue Jesus with unrelenting determination will have their requests granted.

Stepping In: Reread Matthew 15:21–28. How does Jesus' initial treatment of this woman make you feel? Have you ever experienced Jesus' silence in your desperate need? How does the woman's unrelenting faith and humility motivate you to pursue Jesus, regardless of perceived barriers? Praise Him for an increased faith through perseverance.

Stepping Out: This week, partner with at least one other person to be unrelenting prayer warriors. Continue the work of bringing the lost sheep from all nations to Jesus.

March 11
Overflowing

"The good man brings good things out of the good stored up in his heart, and the evil man brings evil things out of the evil stored up in his heart. For out of the overflow of the heart his mouth speaks."
—Luke 6:45 (Lk 6:12–20, 43–45)

Throughout His public ministry, Jesus combined the work of teaching and healing the needy masses with the important job of instructing His twelve disciples. As an example to His men and as a key source of spiritual strength for Himself, Jesus prioritized His prayer life with His heavenly Father.

In the second year of His ministry, after a night of fervent prayer, Jesus gathered His men on a Galilean hillside to teach them many things, including the two types of hearts they were likely to encounter in their own ministries: the heart set on pleasing God, and the heart set on pleasing self. A large crowd gathered around to hear what the young rabbi had to say. While the audience certainly gained knowledge about right behaviors before God, the disciples learned how to discern God's spiritual truth. Using an agrarian example, Jesus pointed out that people, like plants, either bear good and useful fruit or that which is useless or harmful. It was easy to determine a good person from a bad one; their mouths would overflow with ample proof.

To this day, there are still only two heart conditions. Those who are devoted to God tend to wear their hearts on their sleeves; their words match their deeds and are, for the most part, good. By contrast, those who are far from God tend to prefer to live in the shadows, and the things they say and do reflect that shadiness.

To the naked eye or ear, as it were, it is sometimes hard to distinguish between the godly and the ungodly. Because Jesus' return gets a little bit closer with each passing day, the prince of this world, Satan, must resort to increasingly deceptive measures. Anyone who is not secure in their future with Christ is susceptible to Satan's ploys. Instead of speaking of hope and acting in love, Satan's minions tout the virtues of personal success, power, and independence. God's children work toward inclusion and acceptance, rejoicing over each new saved soul. Those who put their trust in anything or anyone other than God are busy building walls and stockpiling weapons, never satisfied until they have achieved dominance and control.

Jesus wants us to be aware of one simple fact: if you want to be on the winning team, listen to and follow those who are overflowing with praise for Jesus and whose fruit is good. Accept no substitutes.

Stepping In: Read Deuteronomy 4:9–10; Proverbs 4:20–24; Matthew 12:34; and Galatians 5:22–23. Is God calling you to bring out the good that is in your heart? Ask Him to help you speak and listen to His truth alone.

Stepping Out: This week, let your words reflect a heart that is overflowing with the hope and security you have in Jesus.

Connected

"Many will say to me on that day, 'Lord, Lord, did we not prophecy in your name, and drive out demons and perform many miracles?' Then I will tell them plainly, 'I never knew you. Away from me, you evildoers!'"

—Matthew 7:22–23 (Mt 7:15–23)

Jesus concluded His Sermon on the Mount by explaining that the way to God was a narrow gate that many would miss. Some would not find their way to into God's eternal presence because of their own hardened hearts, others because they had been led astray by evildoers. Jesus pointed out that even some who professed Him as Lord would turn out to be false witnesses.

His Jewish listeners would have been familiar with warnings about false prophets. However, Jesus' proclamation that He was the Lord, the One by whose name people would prophesy, would have seemed an outlandish claim to most, and a blasphemous statement to the religious elite. The crowd was left to wonder, "Can Jesus really be the Messiah, or is He one of the charismatic phonies He's warning us against?" Only those who had taken to heart the words of His teachings would have known that Jesus was as genuine as they come. His message: stay connected to Him through faith, love, and trust, and "on that day," the Lord will welcome you home.

Jesus has always been God, the One who saves and judges. This will never change. He is still in the business of miracles, even if they are not on such a grand scale as they were when He walked the earth. Today, prophecy is unnecessary because we have the Holy Scripture to tell us what is to come. As believers, we still have the power to perform miracles in Jesus' name, mostly through prayer.

Today's message should not be a discouragement to those who stay faithfully connected to Jesus and seek His will in everything. It should, however, be a stern warning to those who *perform* wondrous deeds for the sake of being seen. On the day Jesus returns, each person will either be rewarded for faithfully upholding love and truth, or judged for loving and serving only themselves. This latter group of actors, though they claim to do good works, will be left wanting—forever.

Stepping In: Read Matthew 6:1–4; Luke 13:24; 2 Thessalonians 2:9–12; and Revelation 13:11–15. What do these verses say about being genuine? Does the power of deception surprise you? Why or why not? Pray for a strong connection with the Spirit of God so that you can recognize falseness in yourself as well as in others.

Stepping Out: This week, guard yourself against pride. Pray that you will value a strong relationship with Jesus more than accolades for your biblical knowledge or righteous acts. Then behave accordingly. As you claim the power of Jesus, do so with confidence and humility. Seek first God's will in everything.

Elevated

"When you have lifted up the Son of Man, then you will know that I am the one I claim to be and that I do nothing on my own but speak just what the Father has taught me."

—John 8:28 (Jn 8:1–30)

Over the course of His first two years in public ministry, Jesus taught God's Word authoritatively and poured out His compassion on the people through a variety of miracles. This earned Him a substantial following. However, as He entered His third and final year as an earthly prophet and healer, His teachings became too difficult for many to accept. Scores of followers turned away.

At the same time, opposition against Him, especially in Judea, was fierce. With that in mind, Jesus waited until everyone was distracted by the Feast of Tabernacles before entering Jerusalem. Then He went to temple and began teaching about the prophesied work He and the Father were doing in preparation for His coming kingdom.

His audience questioned the validity of His claim, stating that it did not meet the requirements of the Law, which called for two or more witnesses as proof. Jesus pointed out that His Father was the second witness. Still confused, the people asked where His Father was. From there, the conversation shifted. Jesus went on to talk about His death and that He was going to a place "above," where they could not go. Because of the validity of His witness, He would be right to judge all who did not believe Him. Finally, He gave them a glimpse of what was to come by assuring them He would be "lifted up," to which some responded with faith.

For Christians, this notion of lifting Jesus up is both wonderfully positive and incredibly solemn and humbling. First, we lift our eyes to view Jesus hanging there on the cross, and we cannot help but be brought to our knees in grief and gratitude. Then, as we focus our gaze heavenward, we are transported into a state of glorious exaltation: Jesus is risen, and no longer do we need to fear what is below.

Many of the mysteries of Jesus' teachings are clear to Christians. We can read and know that Jesus is the Son of God, the Son of Man, and the Savior of the world. Likewise, we understand that God is the Father and Creator of all. By the grace of the Holy Spirit, all these truths have been made known to us.

This was not the case for Jesus' first-century audience. Time and again, Jesus tried to explain that all the prophecies and scripture passages pointed to and would be fulfilled by Him. Still, there were those who either could not or would not agree. Just as there were Israelites in Moses' day who doubted the healing power of the snake on the pole in the desert, many doubted and today continue to doubt the power of Jesus' work on the cross—to their peril. Those who have trusted in His healing powers have been elevated with Christ, now and forever.

Stepping In: Read Numbers 21:4–9; Psalm 121:1–2; Isaiah 40:25–26; 2 Corinthians 4:4; Ephesians 2:1–7; and Hebrews 10:26–31. What do these verses teach you about elevating Jesus in all that you do? What are the consequences for failing to believe in and honor God? Praise God above, and pray for those who will sink to the depths without Him if they continue in their stubborn disobedience.

Stepping Out: This week, prioritize kingdom work above your own. Let your life point to the exalted Son.

March 14
Prepared

"Therefore keep watch, because you do not know on what day your Lord will come. But understand this: If the owner of the house had known at what time the thief was coming, he would have kept watch and would not have let his house be broken into. So you must also be ready, because the Son of Man will come at an hour when you do not expect him."

—Matthew 24:42–44 (Mt 24:1–51)

With only days until Jesus would be led as a criminal to the cross, He concentrated His efforts into one last intensive teaching for His disciples. He took them to the Mount of Olives outside Jerusalem to regroup. His teaching explained in some detail the near and future events of judgment that would take place. He warned them not to be fooled by false Christs and phony prophets, but to stand firm in their faith until He returned—an event no one would fail to notice.

Jesus' predictions, though frightening to hear, prepared His apostles for what was to come and encouraged His men to step confidently into their missionary duties, knowing that His "words never pass away." In today's passage, Jesus reiterated the importance of being ever watchful for His second coming. He equated His reappearance with that of a thief in the night, and emphasized the unexpected nature of this cataclysmic event. So unknown is the timing that neither He nor the angels are privy to this part of the Father's plan. Jesus implored his disciples to be prepared and to wait expectantly while keeping a vigilant watch.

One thing we can say for certain is that Jesus' return gets nearer every day. Though the scripture tells us that no one knows when the day of judgment will come, many have foolishly tried to predict it. Today's Bible reader can very easily get swept away in the description of events that precede Jesus' return and agree that we are most likely in the throes of "birthing pains." Then again, haven't we been in these throes for quite some time already? With each atrocious act of human wickedness, with every catastrophic natural disaster, with every charismatic egomaniac promising the way to prosperity and eternal life, our world inches closer to the end.

Yet none of these episodes even comes close to the day of reckoning Jesus speaks of. For all we know, it could happen tomorrow. Jesus wants His followers to be prepared. He wants us to help Him fulfill the prophecy of spreading the gospel worldwide, starting right where we are. Remember, a small rock in a pond can create a large ripple effect; a single candle in a dark room can be bright enough to see by.

Stepping In: Read Isaiah 13:6–13; Micah 5:2–4; 1 Thessalonians 5:1–3; and Revelation 12:1–5. How prepared do you feel for Christ's return? Are you fearful or excited? Pray for an alert mind and eager heart.

Stepping Out: This week, act on the prompting God is giving you to help spread the good news.

Tractable

At that time Jesus, full of joy through the Holy Spirit, said, "I praise you Father, Lord of heaven and earth, because you have hidden these things from the wise and learned, and revealed it to little children. Yes, Father, for this was your good pleasure."

—Luke 10:21 (Lk 10:1–24)

Jesus traveled widely during the height of His ministry, healing and teaching in the regions from the Salt Sea to the Sea of Galilee, on both sides of the river Jordan. His authoritative work as a rabbi, as well as His skill as a healer, brought Him fame throughout the land. Many of his followers thought Him a prophet, and perhaps a mystic, but a man nonetheless. Even His own disciples failed to fully grasp His divinity. Jesus regularly said and proved that He had authority *from* God, but it was necessary that His true identity be kept secret until the time was right. That time would come all too quickly.

Thus, Jesus sent His missionaries into all of Israel, spreading the good news of the gospel and caring for the needs of the people: first the Twelve, then seventy more. All were filled with joy over their successful ventures—especially Jesus, as the above verse shows. Though His words may have sounded belittling, Jesus was truly rejoicing that these uneducated, common, yet tractable men had been used by God in mighty ways. Anyone who encountered the miraculous work they had done surely noticed this as well. To Jesus' delight, God the Father would get all the glory.

Today's passage offers good news for all Christians now. As was the case in the days when Jesus walked the earth, His true identity is revealed only to those with open hearts and minds. Proof of intelligent design is literally all around us, but some still refuse to believe in a loving creator God. The Bible tells us plainly that people "are without excuse" for their unbelief. (Ro 1:20). For those who prefer to rely on the powers of the human mind, science, technology, and myriad theories to explain our existence, the mysteries of God will remain hidden.

That is the way God would like it to be. In simple terms, He would rather entrust His secrets to those with the innocence, humility, trust, acceptance, acquiescence, and tractability of little children. He is joyful that the deserving will receive blessings from the Almighty. He is also painfully aware that the arrogant and worldly-wise will receive what they deserve as well: an eternity apart from God. Those of us who are not among the "learned" should be encouraged by this passage, which gives us plenty to celebrate. Perhaps our joy will soften hearts of the hardened.

Stepping In: Read Romans 1:18–20 and 1 Corinthians 1:26–31. How do these verses help you understand the type of person God delights in using for His purposes? Do they describe you? Take some time to thank God by praying today's verse back to Him. Pray that He make you more tractable.

Stepping Out: This week, look for ways to bring "good pleasure" to your heavenly Father, then do them!

Clothed

"Behold, I come like a thief! Blessed is he who stays awake and keeps his clothes with him, so that he may not go naked and be shamefully exposed."

—Revelation 16:15 (Rv 16:1–21)

In three years as Jesus' disciple and forty-plus years as His apostle, John experienced many wondrous spectacles and miraculous occurrences. But nothing could have prepared him for what he saw and heard while "in the Spirit" on the prison island of Patmos. Trying his best to put it into words—some of it utterly beautiful and some of it devastatingly frightening—John occasionally received some helpful advice from Jesus. Jesus inserted today's beatitude in the middle of the Armageddon scene. While the "bowls of wrath" were being poured out, ushering in the worst of the judgments which were to befall the earth and its inhabitants, the Savior gave this wake-up call to those who had an ear to hear His warning.

Today, very few people read the book of Revelation. Even those who esteem the Bible as God's living Word tend to avoid creation's final chapter. It is difficult to interpret and frightening to comprehend. Nevertheless, it remains Jesus' letter of encouragement and warning to His church.

Jesus calls for our attention. He implores us to stay alert and be on the lookout for His appearance, which will come when we least expect it. Christians will be startled, though not surprised, by His sudden appearance. Those who have been otherwise distracted will be completely caught off guard.

Jesus tells us to be prepared, to have our garments of salvation ready to put on. When the time of final judgment is upon the earth, all who are saved by grace through faith in Jesus will be clothed in gleaming white robes of righteousness. They will be spared the worst of the wrath that will envelop the earth. Those who have chosen to disregard the cleansing blood of the Savior will be left "naked and shamefully exposed."

Many are stunned by this truth. Could this be the plan of a loving God? Though we love the idea of justice, we often reject the notion of God's justice in the form of wrath and judgment. These are two sides of the same coin; we cannot have one without the other. Christians must not water down this message, but instead proclaim it to all who will hear.

Stepping In: Read Genesis 3; Psalm 51; Isaiah 61:10, 64:6-9; Luke 12:37–40; Hebrews 9:11–14; 1 John 1:7; and Revelation 3:17–18. Skim chapters 5 through 16 of Revelation. What is God teaching you about the cost of your salvation? What is your response?

Stepping Out: One day this week, wear all white in preparation for the robes you will one day don forever.

Sacrificial

> "If your right eye causes you to sin, gouge it out and throw it away. It is better for you to lose one part of your body than to have your whole body thrown into hell. And if your right hand causes you to sin, cut it off and throw it away. It is better for you to lose one part of your body than for your whole body to be thrown into hell."
>
> —Matthew 5:29-30 (Mt 5:27-30)

Those attending Jesus' multiday sermon on a hillside outside of Capernaum in Galilee expected to be awed by His bold, authoritative teaching. They were not prepared to hear unthinkable suggestions about self-mutilation. The notion that sin invoked God's wrath was nothing new. But that anyone should consider taking such extreme measures against it was preposterous.

This exhortation comes after Jesus' explanation of adultery as a matter of the heart rather than the body. He hoped that truth would transfer to this one. He knew that His words were shocking and hard to accept. Still, He chose these strong statements to impress upon His listeners the importance of taking every possible precaution against sin. Clearly, He wanted the people to internalize their responsibility for keeping their hearts pure, their eyes fixed on holy things, and their actions above reproach. He wanted them to understand that giving up some worldly pleasures for the sake of saving one's soul was worth the cost.

These verses were never meant to be taken literally. But there have been some throughout history who have done so—to an unfortunate end. These zealots were not only foolhardy, but completely off base. The message for believers in every generation is that we, as individuals and as a collective body, must aggressively and proactively identify and eradicate sin in our lives.

Sin means intentionally breaking God's commands. It manifests in causing division or dissension among believers, engaging in unrepentant misbehavior, or leading others astray in any fashion. Jesus makes clear that the dire consequence of sin is death—eternal separation from God. Regardless of the eternal security we enjoy through faith in Jesus, Christians are still responsible for the condition of their hearts.

In the context of His earlier teaching on adultery, Jesus' plea for prudence could not be more relevant for the lust-crazed and sexually uninhibited culture in which many of us live. We as Christ's ambassadors are called to resist, turn away from, or remove anything that hinders our own or others' relationships with God, including our private lives and behaviors. Following Jesus' example, we must model a sacrificial and faithful life joyfully.

Stepping In: Read Genesis 2:22–25; Mark 10:1–9; Luke 22:40; Romans 6:12–14; and 1 Corinthians 12:12–14. Ask the Spirit to reveal any sin in you that you need to get rid of. Pray for strength to sacrifice old habits so that you do not succumb to temptation or cause others to stumble on your account. Consider your body holy unto God.

Stepping Out: This week, take a first step toward becoming a healthier member of your church body. Be a catalyst for change in your home, work, church, and community as you demonstrate faithfulness to God in every area of your life. Model sacrificial living joyfully.

Awake

> "The kingdom of heaven is like a man who sowed good seed in his field. But while everyone was sleeping, his enemy came and sowed weeds among the wheat, and went away."
> —Matthew 13:24–26 (Mt 13:1–30)

As the most talk-about public figure of His day, Jesus was rarely afforded any privacy away from His adversaries' ears to impart the hidden truths of God to His chosen men. Thus, Jesus began to teach His disciples in parabolic terms.

On one such occasion, Jesus told a parable about a farmer sowing seeds onto different types of soil. He explained that the seed was God's Word, and the soil was the heart of the receiver. Jesus told them another parable about weeds, equating the sower of good seed to "the kingdom of heaven." He alluded to the heavenly reward they should expect for generously and conscientiously sharing the gospel. However, they would need to stay awake to guard against the enemy's crafty attempts to corrupt the harvest by planting bad seeds among the good.

Though the agricultural analogy may not strike a chord with every Christian today, this parable is simple enough to interpret. The world is one big mission field, and we who call ourselves Christians should consider ourselves Jesus' garden assistants. We sow the good seed, help to enrich the soil of receptive hearts, and we do not sleep on duty. If we are ever vigilant to spot and uproot weeds (lies about God) as they come up, we can help the Master Gardener in His work.

As Jesus tells us in verses 29 and 30 of this chapter, those helping to tend the garden must know which weeds to pull up and which to leave alone. Practically speaking, if the act of exposing wrong thinking will in any way cause others to lose faith, then the wrong thinking is better left for Jesus to deal with at the time of harvest. With a measure of tolerance and a watchful eye, we are to work the fields that slope upward toward heaven.

In a world with shocking amounts of evil hedging in from all sides, any measure of tolerance can be difficult to muster. As servants of our Lord, we must trust Him with the eternal outcome of all His crops, good and bad.

Stepping In: Consider the characters in this parable. Who is the man, the servant, and the enemy? Who are those sleeping? Where do you fit into this story? Now read Matthew 13:37–43. How close were you in your summation? Pray for an alertness to the Evil One's tricks and deception, and the fortitude to fend off his attacks.

Stepping Out: This week, confront any look-alike beliefs you have allowed to grow alongside the truth by testing them against scripture. Awake, rise, and shine the light of God's Word on your weeds.

March 19

Persistent

> "Make every effort to enter through the narrow door, because many,
> I tell you, will try to enter and not be able to."
> —Luke 13:24 (Lk 13:22–30)

Before His final march to Jerusalem, where His true identity would be revealed, Jesus crossed over the Jordan River to enjoy a bit of relative calm. In one of the villages there, Jesus was asked how many would be saved when the day of the Lord arrived. Jesus gave an elusive reply. True to form, He did not directly answer the question, but rather gave a response that would necessitate further contemplation on the part of the audience. Jesus wanted His followers to know that persistence in faith would soon become even more difficult, causing many to lose their way. Those who stayed true to Jesus, though they would be in the minority, would gain access to heaven through Him, its only "narrow door."

From the beginning of human history, people have tried to manipulate God. Adam and Eve, though they had it as good as it gets, were seduced into believing they could be as powerful as God. They tested Him and failed. Humanity has been suffering the consequences of their lack of faith and obedience ever since.

We still attempt to control our lives and destinies. Based on what we believe about God and eternity, we each choose a path by which to walk through life. Most people choose the path of least resistance; they simply go with the flow. In the Western world, Christians are often viewed as exclusionary, judgmental, intolerant, hypocritical, and narrow-minded because of our singular focus. All these negative buzzwords go against the grain of the dominant culture's belief that everyone should be free to express their beliefs in any way they wish. The fact remains that most will choose the broad path that does not lead toward God because they do not want to be told what to do or be held accountable for their actions.

Christians know that there is one God, one truth. There is only one way to an eternity in heaven: Jesus. The path is narrow, the door is small, and only the persistently faithful will choose it.

Stepping In: Read Matthew 7:13–14; John 6:53–66, 14:6; and Ephesians 2:8–10. Do you feel the societal pressures to accept all viewpoints and philosophies? Pray that God undergirds your faith against worldly wisdom and enticements. Focus on Jesus and the prize that awaits you, and persist in your convictions.

Stepping Out: This week, as the Spirit leads, be a persistent proponent of truth.

Holistic

Jesus replied, "'Love the Lord your God with all your heart and with all your soul and with all your mind.' This is the first and greatest commandment. And the second is like it: 'Love your neighbor as yourself.' All the Law and the Prophets hang on these two commandments."

—Matthew 22:37–40 (Mt 22:34–40)

Jesus spent the last week of His earthly ministry in and around Jerusalem, teaching in the temple courts. The large crowds that gathered there were amazed by His wisdom and authority, and His numbers increased daily. However, there were some who were not impressed. In fact, with each interaction they had with Jesus, the Pharisees became increasingly incensed. They actively plotted to have Jesus arrested on charges of heresy.

Hearing that Jesus had silenced the Sadducees, a Pharisee who was an expert in the Law asked Jesus which of the commandments should be considered the greatest. The Pharisee was trying to trick Jesus into naming just one, when Jews regarded all the commandments as equally important. This man was sure he would finally get the evidence needed to convict Jesus of blasphemy. But he and his compatriots were wrong. Not only did Jesus give them a perfectly acceptable answer, He also skillfully revealed His opponent's weak spots.

Many Christians today can quote these verses from Matthew with ease. One could say that these make up the Christian credo, if you will. Yet many of us struggle to live out these commandments on a regular basis. In fact, these commandments are nearly impossible to obey fully without divine intervention. We might be fairly decent at loving God with our whole minds, memorizing scripture and learning all we can about our Lord, but we might be rather poor at loving Him with all our hearts. And how exactly does someone love God with one's soul, anyway? As for loving our neighbors … well, that is a tall order any way you look at it.

Jesus does want us to approach our relationship with Him holistically. It all is contingent on love. The more we understand how wonderful our Savior is, what He has done for us, and what He promises to do in and through us, the more we ought to be head over heels for Him. However, we first must shift our focus from the temporal to the eternal; maintaining a heaven-focused view while living in our temporary home. We need to be willing to put other loves aside and give Jesus our full attention. Then we will be able to follow these commands—even the second one.

Stepping In: Read Leviticus 19:18 and Deuteronomy 6:4–9. Do you love Jesus holistically—with your whole heart, mind, soul, and strength? Is your love for Jesus evident to others? What needs to change so that these commands are possible? Thank God now, and ask Him for help to love Him with your whole being.

Stepping Out: This week, invite a neighbor or someone you don't normally spend time with over for coffee, or offer to help them in some way.

Peace-Filled

"Peace be with you."
—Luke 24:36 (Luke 24:1–49)

Toward the end of His life, Jesus repeatedly reminded His disciples that, though He had to go away, He would return. Seeing that His chosen apostles did not understand what He was saying, He told them plainly that He had to die, be buried, and on the third day be raised. Though they trusted Jesus and were well-aware of His miraculous powers, they could not accept the truth of this message. Even considering that they had grown up learning the prophecies of the coming Messiah, their desire for an earthly king blinded them to the spiritual truth of who Jesus was and what He had to do to redeem Israel and the world.

And so, as Jesus hung on the cross, His devoted followers fled in fear and confusion. Only after He had been taken down and buried did the apostles (minus one: Judas Iscariot, who had committed suicide) dare to regroup. Together, they mourned and puzzled over their future.

But not for long. Some of the women who had seen the empty tomb came to report that Jesus was alive. However, it was not until two of Jesus' other followers brought the same news that the apostles began to believe. To remove all doubt, Jesus Himself appeared among them in their locked room. Knowing that they would be shocked and possibly frightened, Jesus offered the calming greeting, "Peace be with you." Then He talked with them, showed them His hands and His feet, and ate with them. Stunned yet peace-filled, the disciples relished the joy of being reunited with their Lord.

In times of grief, words of comfort are sometimes hard to accept. For people mourning the loss of dearly beloved friends or family members, even Christian platitudes fall short. In the days following Jesus' crucifixion, guilt and shame compounded the disciples' deep sense of loss. Not only had they lost their Lord, who had been rabbi, companion, and friend, but they had lost the hope of being rescued from the oppressive Roman rule under which they lived.

In more recent history, the loss of Martin Luther King Jr. and John F. Kennedy were similarly devastating blows to the hope many Americans placed in the early civil rights movement. Without leaders to champion our causes, we feel utterly lost and hopeless. And though Jesus never promised a carefree and harmonious life—actually, quite the contrary—He did promise that His followers would never have to worry about their eternity. Everything that He did and said is proof that He is able to fulfill His promises. This is the peace with which we are filled.

Stepping In: Read Numbers 6:24–26, Psalm 29:11, Isaiah 9:6, John 16:33, Philippians 4:7, Colossians 3:15, Hebrews 12:14, and 1 Peter 5:7. Meditate on these verses; let God's peace fill your spirit. Praise Jesus for bringing peace to earth.

Stepping Out: This week, make every effort to bring peace into your home and community. Let your words and actions reflect the peace that lives in you.

Philanthropic

> "In everything I did, I showed you that by this kind of hard work we must help the weak, remembering the words the Lord Jesus himself said: 'It is more blessed to give than to receive.'"
>
> —Acts 20:35 (Acts 20:7–38)

During his third missionary journey, the apostle Paul sailed around the Mediterranean region, bringing encouragement to new Christians along his route. Then he was called by God to return to Jerusalem, regardless of the opposition he was sure to face there. Paul stopped on the island of Mitylene and sent for the elders of the new church of God in Ephesus to join him. Knowing he would not see these fellow servants in Christ again, he made a heart-wrenching plea for them to stay strong in the Way. He urged them to continue the hard work of building unity in the body of believers, and to follow his example of philanthropic giving. Pointing out the example he had set for perseverance and selfless service, he encouraged the Ephesian leaders to carry it on.

By turning giving into a beatitude, Paul brought the Ephesian's focus back to Jesus and away from worry about what the future might hold and their grief of losing a friend and mentor. He reminded them that their obedience and mercy would bring blessings to themselves and others. Though the task of remaining rooted in the values of Jesus were difficult in a polytheistic culture, these faithful leaders' resolve was greatly refreshed by the words Paul gave them.

Since the fall of man, humans have been plagued by the deeply rooted condition of selfishness. More than ever, it is not only accepted but expected that one's happiness is contingent on having as much as possible. In Jesus' upside-down kingdom, this notion is disproved time and again. Today's verse reminds us of this.

Paul did not shy away from hardship, nor did he make light of it. Neither should today's apostles— us. Instead, we ought to take notice of how Paul let his life be an example of walking by faith, regardless of the difficulties. We, like the Ephesian leaders, need a refresher course on godly values from time to time.

Like all apostles of Christ living in a cultural and religious melting pot, we are sure to face resistance and opposition. To bring blessing to ourselves and others, and more importantly to honor God, we must continue to meet the needs of the lost and hurting in the world, embracing our philanthropic duties. It is because of our keen awareness of how truly blessed we are that our hearts overflow with compassion for those who are lacking. To give this priceless gift away is the joy of a true believer's heart. The rewards far outweigh the costs.

Stepping In: Read Deuteronomy 15:7-11, 16:17; Proverbs 3:27, 11:24-25; Malachi 3:10; Luke 6:38; and 2 Corinthians 9:6–8. How do these verses inspire or challenge you? What philanthropic activities is Jesus calling you to? Pray for courage to give freely and generously, regardless of the cost.

Stepping Out: In the same way and measure that God has given to you, joyfully give to others this week.

Meek

"Blessed are the meek, for they shall inherit the earth."
—Matthew 5:5 (Mt 5:1–12)

Jewish society in Jesus' day was very class-driven. Society was divided into distinct socioeconomic, political, and religious groups, separated by real, albeit often invisible barriers. Aside from the apparatus of the Roman government, Jewish leaders held the highest, most influential positions in society. Because of this, they were filled with arrogance and pride. These supposed men of God enjoyed their power and privilege by exerting control over the religious and cultural lives of the Jewish people. Those under their authority were mostly uneducated and poor, with no say or rights.

Speaking to both groups during His Sermon on the Mount, Jesus tested the conventional wisdom of His audience. To the religious elite, the beatitude for the meek would have been an insult. These men expected to inherit God's kingdom, including the earth. The thought of the voiceless masses taking the elite's portion would have been ludicrous, if not maddening. For the general population, who quietly accepted their second-class status, this blessing would have come as a surprise. In Jesus' backward kingdom, the meek wield far more power than do those who would wrest control by force.

Most of us think that to be meek is to be weak, passive, fragile, and ineffectual. It is hard to imagine how meekness could be of any use to the kingdom of God or a blessing to His people. That is where our thinking needs to shift. Instead of the bold, powerful, cunning, charismatic, dominant, arrogant, and prideful types taking over the promised kingdom, Jesus tells us that it will be the gentle, kind-hearted, humble, self-controlled, sacrificial, and peace-seeking who will possess it.

The earth in its current state is ruled by corrupt forces. It will one day be replaced by the New Jerusalem and become our home forever. Until then, Jesus has entrusted those He knows will have the right attitude and caring approach to steward the earth. These same gentle-spirited caregivers will enjoy a privileged role in the new earth to come. Suddenly, meekness does not seem like such a negative personality trait after all.

Stepping In: Is pride something you struggle with? Think of the things you have done and the things you have acquired that you are proud of. Make a mental or physical list if necessary. Now, consider God's part in these accomplishments. Humbling, isn't it? Stop right now and thank God for blessing you with your abilities. Pray to Him to reveal hidden pride. Ask Him for a humble heart and attitude. Embrace your meekness, looking forward to your reward!

Stepping Out: Give credit where credit is due—to God! This week, catch yourself every time you start to say "I." Consider if what you are about to say is indeed true *and* if it will benefit your listener. Try instead to praise God for the blessings and gifts He has given you. Practice humility with your thoughts, words, and actions.

Salted

"Everyone will be salted with fire."
—Mark 9:49 (Mk 9:38–50)

From a remote location outside of Galilee, Jesus talked with His disciples about the grand and serious nature of God's plan for His coming kingdom, emphasizing the importance of His apostles' commitment to holiness and virtue. As devout Jews, the disciples had no doubt experienced the shaming consequences of disobedience of the Law. They were familiar with the seriousness of sin.

In describing the fire, Jesus conveyed His need for them to know the extreme eternal consequences that would befall the unrepentant at the time of judgment. He had already given them the draconic example of self-mutilation being preferable to sin. But He didn't stop there. He went on the describe the dreaded destination reserved for unrepentant souls. It is a place where worms never die or stop burrowing into the flesh. The flames never go out, but continue to scorch the body endlessly. Though some would be spared the worst of sin's effects, all will experience its sting to some extent. All will be seasoned with fire. While salt may preserve the body from permanent damage, fire will bring about the necessary purification for a mature faith.

To say you are a Christian is to believe that Jesus is who He says He is. It is to believe He has done and will do what He said He would. Jesus is at the center of the Christian faith. Those who believe take Him at His Word.

That being true, we cannot ignore the inclusivity of this verse. *All* will experience fire and salt. A look into scripture reveals the different applications for which God uses each. Both have positive and negative implications. For instance, salt can be a purifying and preserving agent, and it can also represent additional pain being applied to an already agonizing situation, like salt in a wound. Likewise, fire is often referred to as a cleansing and refining agent, but can represent overwhelming destruction or condemnation.

Jesus tells us that no one can avoid being affected by these two elements. The Bible is clear about how each will be applied, why, and to whom. Though Christians will feel the sting of the purifying salt and fire, it is nothing compared to the relentless and unending torment of the salt and fire of judgment. Much more than mere discomfort and potential humiliation, this picture of eternal judgment is nothing to be taken lightly. Jesus wants all generations of Christians to fully grasp God's mercy *and* His justice. Simply put, Jesus tells us to be warned and "Have salt in yourselves, and be at peace with each other" (Mk 9:50).

Stepping In: Read Isaiah 33:14; Matthew 3:11-12, 5:13; 1 Corinthians 3:11–14; Colossians 4:6; and 1 Peter 1:7. What did you learn from these verses about how fire and salt are symbolized in the Bible? How do you respond to being "salted with fire"? Ask God to help you understand the good and bad aspects of salt and fire.

Stepping Out: Be salt and light. Humbly guide others toward Jesus for the forgiveness and repentance of sins. Testify to God's mercy and justice.

March 25

Cordial

"You know that the rulers of the Gentiles lord it over them, and their high officials exercise authority over them. Not so with you. Instead, whoever wants to become great among you must be your servant, and whoever wants to be first must be your slave—just as the Son of Man did not come to be served, but to serve, and to give his life as a ransom for many."

—Matthew 20:25–28 (Mt 20:20–28)

As Jesus traveled to Jerusalem for the last time, many people accompanied Him, including His twelve disciples. Among the crowd was the mother of James and John. She asked Jesus for a special favor: for her sons to receive preferential placement in His kingdom. Clearly, she did not know what she was asking, and Jesus told her so. Once word got out to the rest of the disciples that the brothers were vying for position in Jesus' court, animosity threatened their unity.

Jesus knew that His men were only reacting to the uncertainty of their circumstances. They were afraid of what the future would hold. Their self-preservation instincts manifested in displays of jealousy and pride. Jesus refocused them with a call to service. Not only were they to refrain from slighting each other and gloating, but they were to remember His example of servitude. As brothers in Christ, Jesus expected them to be cordial, forgiving, helpful, and genuinely loving to one another—and to the world.

Those in positions of authority have a choice as to how they treat those who are under them. Be they presidents, military generals, or royalty, each must decide whether they lord their power and superiority over their subjects, or act with decency and humility, as one human to another.

More than that, Jesus reminds us time and again about the importance of servitude. These verses clearly show just how opposed the ranking system of heaven is to that of the world. Yet Christians still struggle with putting this theology into practice.

Jesus tells us in no uncertain terms that the world's way is not our way. As Christ's ambassadors, we are to be, at the very least, cordial with believers and nonbelievers alike. Better, we should be kind, considerate, patient, giving, generous, selfless, sacrificial, and loving. If we are not compelled to serve for the simple reason that service ensures a good position in eternity, then we should to do it because Jesus Himself did so for us—even to the point of death.

Stepping In: Read Exodus 30:12; Isaiah 42:1–4; Luke 22:24–30; John 13:13–17; and Philippians 2:5–8. Pray in humble gratitude for the ransom Jesus paid for you, rescuing you from your former hopeless state. Ask for a servant's heart and the ability to be cordial to all.

Stepping Out: This week, go beyond being cordial. Be the opposite of those who lord their authority over others. Be the one who humbly goes out of your way to help others, simply because you can.

Embedded

"My prayer is not that you take them out of the world but that you
protect them from the evil one."

—John 17:15 (Jn 17:1–19)

For three years, Jesus taught and trained His disciples in preparation for the moment that was quickly approaching. Everything Jesus said and did was to serve two purposes: to do the will of the One who sent Him, and to instill an unshakable faith in His chosen disciples. With the moment to bring glory to Himself and the Father at hand, Jesus offered His men a final lesson. In all circumstances, they were to look to the Father and pray.

After praying for Himself, Jesus prayed for His disciples. Soon they would be without their leader, scattered and lost, frantic and hopeless, even if briefly. As the eleven remaining apostles listened intently, Jesus prayed for those the Father had given Him. He prayed for their unwavering faith in Him and in God, and for them to continue to do the will of the Father. Jesus asked the Father to protect His apostles, even as they remained embedded in a fallen world. Knowing His disciples would live with fear and uncertainty, Jesus offered words of hope and encouragement. Believers are never alone, but are safe under the watchful eye and attentive ear of God.

Today, we don't use the term "sanctification" very often in conversation. Ultimately, however, that is the crux of Jesus' prayer for His disciples. It was very important for them, as they stepped into their permanent roles as apostles of Christ, to know that they were covered by God's divine holiness. They were no longer ordinary citizens; they were set apart for saintly duties. It would have been very encouraging to hear Jesus' prayer for protection. Jesus Himself was interceding on their behalf, asking His Father to keep them safe as they courageously embedded themselves in hostile territory.

Jesus prayed this prayer aloud for His disciples to hear. He prays it still for all His children. He wants us to be encouraged by His words. He wants us to be confident remaining in Him while in the world. Instead of enjoying the shelter of our holy huddles, Jesus tells His devoted followers to go out "and make disciples of all nations." (Mt 28:19). That means venturing into potentially dangerous places and into the Evil One's line of fire. Since there is much kingdom work to be done before Jesus returns, we all must bear fruit right where God has placed us, trusting Him to keep us safe in the process.

Stepping In: Read Numbers 6:24–26; Psalm 46:1; Proverbs 2:11, 4:6; Isaiah 41:10; Matthew 28:20; Romans 8:28–30; and 2 Thessalonians 3:1–3. What worldly troubles are you currently dealing with? Pray that your confidence in Jesus increases, so that you can bravely be a representative of Christ, embedded wherever He places you.

Stepping Out: This week, serve in a new ministry to stretch your faith and prove God's provision.

Responsive

"Come, follow me, and I will make you fishers of men."
—Matthew 4:19 (Mt 4:1–19)

Early in His ministry, Jesus called his first disciples. He didn't seek out the strongest, smartest, or most religious men he could find. He didn't look for the most respected, honest, or humble sort of fellow either. Instead, He chose men who were responsive and moldable.

The first He summoned to follow Him were two men fishing from their father's boat in the Sea of Galilee: Simon (Peter) and his brother Andrew. As disciples of John the Baptist, these brothers had learned that Jesus was believed to be the Messiah. They were casting their nets when Jesus called out to them, and the invitation instantly presented them with a crucial choice. Would they walk away from everything they had known, or would they refuse the request of the Christ? Weighing their options in a moment, the two men responded without hesitation. In faith, Peter and Andrew set out to follow Jesus. No longer would their lives be ordinary, simple, or predictable. No longer would they merely cast their nets for a day's worth of fish. From then on, their catch would include something far more valuable: souls won for eternity.

In this day and age, we might consider Peter and Andrew's responsiveness impulsive or reckless. Some might even view it as negligent or irresponsible. We can only imagine what Andrew and Peter's family thought of their decision. Most of us prefer the perceived security of a structured and predictable existence. Sudden changes unsettle us. We like to plan for and pursue our own interests, believing that we can control the outcome by careful implementation. We like to believe that we are the masters of our own destinies, that we know best how to manage our affairs. It would take an extremely special opportunity to get most of us to make a sudden and drastic change.

The calling of our Lord certainly qualifies as such a special opportunity. Yet how often do we dismiss His call as nonsense when it arises? The criteria for being a disciple of Jesus has not changed. He is still recruiting those who are responsive to His call.

Stepping In: Read Mark 1:14–20; Luke 5:1–11; and John 1:35–42. Train your ear to hear Jesus' voice. Spend time with your Teacher, Friend, and Savior. Pay attention to what He is saying to you. Ask Him to soften your heart and make it more receptive to the hard truths you don't like to hear. Be responsive to His commands.

Stepping Out: Is Jesus asking you to join Him? If you are uncertain, pray that He will make it clear. All His followers are called to be His hands and feet while on this planet. What are your heart and your gut telling you to do? Who has God placed in your life that Jesus is prompting you to cast a net to? Today, heed His command. Step out in faith. Be a fisher of men. Go!

Relieved

"Come to me all you who are weary and burdened, and I will give you rest. Take my yoke upon you and learn from me, for I am gentle and humble in heart, and you will find rest for your souls. For my yoke is easy and my burden is light."

—Matthew 11:28–30 (Mt 11:1–30)

By the end of His second year in public ministry, Jesus' influence was widespread, affecting the cultural, religious, and political climates. Knowing that taking Jesus out of the picture too soon would likely cause a revolt, the Jewish leaders, aided by the Roman government, had John the Baptist arrested instead.

Jesus, rather than succumbing to the opposition's threat by going into hiding, opted to expand His efforts by sending His twelve disciples further into the mission fields of Israel. John, who had heard reports of the miraculous deeds performed by Jesus' disciples among the people, sent his own disciples to ask Him if He was indeed the Christ.

Jesus could see the confusion, worry, and perhaps jealousy in these men's eyes. He knew that they were feeling lost and insecure without their master. So, before Jesus sent them back to report that He was who He claimed to be—verified by their own eye-witness of miracles—He spoke encouraging words to them and to the crowd that had gathered. He affirmed that their faith in Him and in John had not been misplaced. He encouraged His listeners to trust in Him. He offered them rest from their burdens. John's disciples then could complete their task with a new sense of peace, purpose, and lightness.

How many times throughout history have God's children questioned His plan and puzzled over His distribution of power? In a world of confusion and chaos, even Christians can find themselves doubting the wisdom of God and wondering if Jesus really does have everything under control. Not unlike John the Baptist's forlorn disciples, we, the faithful today, sometimes feel like our efforts are all for naught, that others are reaping the benefits of devotion while we are reaping only burnout. Today's passage reminds us that not only has God always been with us through our struggles, but He is acutely aware of our need for rest and rejuvenation. We need look no further than to Jesus for relief. When we stay close to the Father in prayer, replenishing our minds with scripture and yielding to the gentle guidance of the Holy Spirit, Jesus takes the burden off our shoulders and puts it onto His own, where it can easily be carried.

Stepping In: Read Exodus 33:14; Isaiah 40:28-31; John 7:37–39; and Galatians 5:1. What burdens are wearing you down? Are the pressures of this world making you weary? Bring them to Jesus. Trust that He will help you. Maybe He will relieve them physically, or perhaps He will give you the strength to bear them. Trust. Ask. Wait. And be relieved.

Stepping Out: This week, help lighten a friend's spiritual load by sharing encouraging accounts of times when Jesus relieved you of your spiritual and physical burdens through answered prayers.

Unceasing

"And will God not bring about justice for his chosen ones, who cry out to him day and night? Will he keep putting them off? I tell you, he will see that they get justice, and quickly. However, when the Son of Man comes, will he find faith on the earth?"

—Luke 18:7–8 (Lk 18:1–8)

Before heading to Jerusalem for the last time, Jesus made His way through much of Israel, gathering the last of His devoted followers for some final important teachings. In addition to continuing to spread the gospel and perform many miraculous signs and healings, Jesus spoke of the dire consequences for ambivalence about or rejection of the Messiah.

On one such occasion, Jesus told a parable about a wicked judge and a persistent widow. Many times, this woman came to the judge, pleading for justice in her case. Her repeated appearances finally wore the judge down. She got the justice she was seeking. Those who heard this parable learned that persistence pays off. For the more spiritually minded, the lesson was about how much more merciful God is to those who pray unceasingly than to those whose faith is not as enduring.

From a cursory reading of this passage, one could easily misinterpret the text to imply that God is represented by the judge in this story. Jesus is relying on a certain amount of spiritual discernment to peel back the layers of truth. Jesus is indicating that God is the opposite of the wicked judge in every way. Whereas the judge continued to reject this woman's case, refusing to do the job he was employed to do, God hears and considers each and every supplication that reaches His ears. Whereas the judge decided to do what was right under duress, God is eager to award justice to the righteous plaintiff. The key, Jesus tells us, is unceasing prayer. This is the link between God and His people, a lifeline.

Simple as this sounds, Jesus knows that in the times ahead, faith will be tested and prayer will become increasingly rare. Regardless of the declining popularity of faith-filled prayer, Jesus tells us to never stop clinging to this invisible thread of hope.

Stepping In: Read Psalm 88:1–2; Isaiah 40:30; Matthew 6:9-13, 7:7; Ephesians 6:18; Philippians 4:6–7; and Colossians 4:2. Ask God for a heart devoted to prayer. Thank Him for hearing and responding with grace and mercy.

Stepping Out: This week, be an unceasing, intercessory pray-er. Also, prayerfully look for opportunities to promote justice in your community.

Enthusiastic

"What I tell you in the dark, speak it in the daylight; what is whispered
in your ear, proclaim it from the rooftops."

—Matthew 10:27 (Mt 10:1–27)

From the time Jesus called His disciples to the time He sent them to spread the gospel among the Israelites, He was preparing them for the work ahead. Today's verse comes in the middle of a speech to His newly appointed apostles, in between promises and predictions, warnings and admonitions. He had just warned them, and was about to warn them again, of the dire pitfalls of attempting to change unyielding people's hearts and minds. He sprinkled this teaching with enthusiastic commands such as the one above. In the power He had promised them, and with the training they had already received, Jesus wanted them to go bravely into the den of wolves with the message of truth and love. The time had come for private disclosures to be made public, regardless of the cost.

Today, there are all manner of evangelistic approaches. Some of them are mild and some of them intense. Some are attractive and some obnoxious. From a human perspective, the effectiveness of any given tactic for sharing the gospel is debatable. But, though people may not agree on any one method for reaching the lost, God can use all types. He equips each of us differently for this task—on purpose. No two ways are identical. We need only trust and obey when we are led by the Spirit to speak God's truth.

Today's passage should remind us all that Jesus is aware of the difficulties of bringing the truth out into the light. In an enthusiastic but not foolhardy manner, we should confidently proclaim God's whole truth: the convicting words of judgment, the hope-filled words of salvation, and the irrefutable message of our own changed lives. These are not secrets to be kept but pronouncements to be shared.

Stepping In: Read Isaiah 61:1; Luke 4:18–19; and Colossians 4:2–4. Pray for God to guide and equip you to follow His command to bring the truth into the light. Look for opportunities to do so this week.

Stepping Out: Read 1 Peter 3:15. What is God whispering in your ear? Who is He putting in your path for you to share your hope with? This week, take that step of obedience in following His command.

Reasonable

"If your brother sins against you, go and show him his fault, just between the two of you. If he listens to you, you have won your brother over. But if he will not listen, take one or two others along, so that 'every matter may be established by the testimony of two or three witnesses.' If he refuses to listen to them, tell it to the church; and if he refuses to listen even to the church, treat him as you would a pagan or a tax collector."

—Matthew 18:15–17 (Mt 18:15–20)

After nearly three years of training alongside their Lord and Master, Jesus' apprentices were encouraged to carry out portions of His ministry. As His commissioned apostles, they brought the gospel to the "lost sheep of Israel," hence gaining somewhat of a following themselves. However, their powers were still limited by a lack of faith.

Some of the disciples failed to cast out a demon from a young boy, and Jesus felt that His men needed more help to understand some fundamental truths. Jesus knew that their worldly perspective and their inability to accept the necessity of the cross were stunting their spiritual growth. They had even argued about who would be the greatest in the kingdom, demonstrating their lack of understanding about heavenly versus worldly values.

Since they were acting like children, Jesus used a "little one" as an example of who would truly be the greatest in the kingdom of heaven. He instructed them to change their heart posture from one of seeking control to one of full reliance on God. A true disciple was one who trusted in God's power and plan and was obedient to His will. In answer to the pride-filled grumbling of the Twelve, Jesus laid out steps for reconciliation. He reminded them of their allegiance not only to Him, but to each other as well. He called for them to be kind, loving, and reasonable in all their dealings.

What a lesson for people to learn today, especially Christians! In our world of selfish ambition and constant striving for more, better, and best, we suffer from the same worldly limitations that the first Christians did. Preferring to focus on our own interests, we often fail to notice things of eternal value. We still want to be "greatest in the kingdom."

Unfortunately, we wind up in the same plight as the apostles: unable to effectively help others, even in the name of Jesus. Like all disciples throughout history, the root of our evangelistic failures is a lack of humble submission, coupled with unreasonable expectations we project onto others, and pride. In these verses, we are reminded to keep our feelings—and the gossip that goes with them—in check. We are to put our agendas aside as we seek unity above personal gain.

Imagine a world where we all had this goal in mind. This is the kind of heaven-focused society all Christians should strive for. It is how we are to live and the example we should set.

Stepping In: Read Leviticus 19:17–18; Deuteronomy 19:15; Romans 16:17–18; Galatians 6:1; and James 5:19–20. How do these verses impress upon you the need for Christian unity based on a proper posture before God? Ask the Spirit to instruct you in your approach to dealing with difficult situations and personalities.

Stepping Out: This week, be reasonable and fair with everyone, and especially grace-filled and helpful with your brethren. Strive for unity, and set an example of Christ-like decency through protocol.

April 1
Adaptable

"Foxes have holes and birds of the air have nests, but the Son of Man has no place to lay his head."

—Matthew 8:20 (Mt 8:18–22)

At the time Jesus spoke these words, He was hitting His stride in His ministry. His popularity was skyrocketing, and His following was getting quite large. Word was spreading fast throughout Israel of the powerful sermon He had given on the hillside near Capernaum, the healing He was doing, and the miraculous ways He could cast out demons. He certainly had the attention of everyone around—those who believed in His divine authority and those who did not.

Sometime after casting a fever out of His disciple Peter's mother-in-law with the touch of His hand, Jesus was approached by a teacher of the Law, who promised to follow Him wherever He went. Jesus responded with the observation that He had "no place to lay his head." In simple terms, His words were a warning about the cost of becoming a disciple. A commitment to follow Christ involved a willingness to give up the comforts of home. Some hearing those words may have nodded their heads in agreement, as Jesus was indeed a nomad, never staying in one place for long.

That was only part of the equation. On a deeper level, Jesus was informing His followers of their new citizenship. Children of God should look forward to resting in their heavenly home and not be attached to their earthly dwelling place. Using the messianic term "Son of Man," Jesus sought to both identify with humanity and to reveal in-part His heavenly origins. Those who would choose the sacrifices involved in following, could be assured of a share in His reward. Clearly, believers would have to be adaptable to their changing circumstances as they walked toward their eternal home.

For some, the notion of home conjures up a Hallmark image of a happy family in a lovely house. For others, this idea of a place of safety and belonging is more elusive, or perhaps disappointing. As the industrial revolution swept the nations, the once nomadic peoples of the vast prairies soon sought their livelihoods in cities rather than fields. A stationary society developed a sense of permanence and place.

Now, at least for most of us, identity and security are very much wrapped up in the place we call home. We invest hugely in it. Most of us do not stray too far from it and the comforts it provides—even Christians. We look at homeless people with pity. We view missionaries with wide-eyed wonder. Why would people choose to live that way?

Maybe the missionaries are the ones who have it right. If we take Jesus at His word, we risk shattering our cozy, safe concept of home—for good. As hard as it may be, Christians should know better than to get too comfortable in this temporary dwelling place. We ought to learn the art of living a life of Spirit-led adaptability, always ready to leave the nest when called.

Stepping In: Read 1 Chronicles 17:9–10; Psalm 127:1–2; Isaiah 32:18–20; Mark 10:29–30; and Luke 4:24. Pray and ask God to reveal your misconceptions of "home." Ask Him for the mental flexibility to be adaptable wherever He leads you.

Stepping Out: This week, pray for missionaries around the world. If the Spirit moves you, commit to initiating a relationship with one—writing to them, providing financial support, visiting. Pray for a willingness to be moved by God and for His purposes.

April 2

Revived

"I tell you the truth, no one can see the kingdom of God unless he is born again."

—John 3:3 (Jn 3:1–21)

As had been the case with the ministry of His predecessor and cousin, John the Baptist, Jesus' ministry was also wrought with controversy. People, especially the Jews, received the message of the imminent arrival of God's new kingdom in a variety of ways. Some accepted it readily, either because they were excited about the fulfillment of prophecies or because they were eager for the promised relief from the oppressive Roman rule under which they lived. Others were skeptical, thinking that John and Jesus might be false prophets. Another group—the Pharisees and teachers of the Law—adamantly opposed John and Jesus, thinking them blasphemous fools and a direct threat to religious authority.

One of the prominent Jewish leaders, however, recognized that Jesus' power was of God and wanted to see for himself who this young rabbi was. Worried about his reputation but too curious to stay away, this man, Nicodemus, came to speak with Jesus under the cover of night. Nicodemus was awed by the miraculous signs Jesus was becoming known for. He pondered aloud about the source of Jesus' power.

Rather than responding directly, Jesus gave a strange reply about being born again. Seeing Nicodemus' confusion, Jesus corrected the man's literal interpretation of His words and steered the conversation toward a spiritual explanation of eternal life instead. Thus, Jesus established, or perhaps revived, Nicodemus' hope for an eternal future.

The parallels between Nicodemus and the modern-day seeker are many. Let's explore each in turn, and how they apply to us today:

- Nicodemus came to Jesus with a long list of religious *biases*, meaning preconceived notions and prior experiences. Our biases become the filter through which we see Jesus.
- Nicodemus was wowed by the spectacle of miraculous signs. Modern worship can easily become entertainment.
- Nicodemus sought to satisfy his curiosity rather than to seek true counsel. Seekers today are often self-serving and not genuinely interested in truth-filled answers.
- Nicodemus was ashamed to be associated with Jesus. Christians today sometimes shy away from proclaiming His name.

Nevertheless, Nicodemus made the first move, and Jesus took him the rest of the way. This is a big lesson for us to learn today. Even when we come with mere curiosity or an arsenal of questions, Jesus welcomes us in. Jesus looks beyond our prejudices and superficial wonderings to address our deepest needs. He revives our souls.

Like Nicodemus, those of us who seek truth will find it. We too learn that Jesus is the only way to be cleansed of sin and born into His royal family.

Stepping In: Read Isaiah 44:3, 55:1–3; Jeremiah 2:13; Ezekiel 36:24–27; John 4:14; and Revelation 22:1. How do these verses help you to understand the process of being born again? How has your own baptism into faith revived your soul? Praise Jesus for offering you His life-giving water, the Spirit by which to live anew.

Stepping Out: This week, greet Jesus in the full light of day, proudly proclaiming His name and power. If you have not proclaimed your allegiance to Jesus through baptism, talk to your pastor about doing so.

Subtle

> "The kingdom of heaven is like yeast that a woman took and mixed
> into a large amount of flour until it worked all through the dough."
> —Matthew 13:33 (Mt 13:24–35)

Entering the second half of His ministry, Jesus began teaching almost exclusively by way of parables. He had several reasons for doing this. One was to fulfill the words of the psalmist Asaph. Another was to shield the truth from His persecutors, while developing the skill of spiritual discernment in His faithful followers, especially His twelve disciples.

During one of His sermons, Jesus used several analogies to help His audience understand what the kingdom of heaven is like. After describing heaven to be like "a man sowing good seeds in his garden," and describing how a tiny "mustard seed ... becomes a tree [for] the birds of the air," Jesus then likened the kingdom to yeast. Yeast, which often represented the infiltration of evil in the world, in this instance referred to the positive influence of this reactive and potent substance. His discerning disciples understood that this yeast was gospel's subtle influence, which would indeed lead to a massive expansion of faith. Jesus' message: a small and subtle amount of well-placed gospel truth, like yeast, will go far.

What a wonderful and accurate illustration Jesus gives us of the effectiveness of using a subtle approach when sharing the gospel. Because of the potency of Jesus' Word, Christians needn't pour it on too thick to get the message across. Like too much yeast added to dough, too many overzealous attempts to win someone over will not lead to the desired effect. We need not heap on the good deeds and dole out heavy doses of scripture to every unbeliever we come across. Today's verse encourages us to let a sprinkling of love and hope sink in before we add any other ingredient.

Like baking a good loaf, changing the hearts and minds of unbelievers takes patience, measured efforts, and (God's) timing. The key ingredient to expansion in both instances is the yeast—the gospel. As Jesus' bakery assistants, we are called to humbly and conscientiously stir God's potent Word into our daily interactions. Then we step back and allow the Master Baker to shape the dough and bring it to the oven. Though we are to sweeten the recipe with our kindness and genuine care, it is up to the Holy Trinity to produce the finished product. We can mix the dough, but God is the Baker.

Stepping In: Read Psalm 96:2–3; Matthew 6:1–4; Luke 12:11-12; John 6:44, 65; Galatians 5:22; Philippians 2:3–4; and 1 Peter 3:15–16. How does your life proclaim the good things that God has done for you? Is your testimony a subtle but effective example of your changed life in Christ? Pray for wisdom about how and when to sprinkle yeast.

Stepping Out: This week, share with someone the words of Jesus that have been helpful to you lately. Let this personal approach be a subtle entry point for a spiritual conversation.

April 4
Accepting

"Surely you will quote this proverb to me: 'Physician, heal yourself! Do here in your hometown what we have heard that you did in Capernaum.'"

—Luke 4:23 (Lk 4:1–30)

Jesus' ministry started with two substantial events: His baptism in the river Jordan, and His temptation in the desert at the hands of Satan himself. In each instance, the presence of God in the form of the Holy Spirit was with Jesus, offering Him comfort, strength, and guidance. After enduring forty days and nights of isolation, hunger, and testing (physical, emotional, and spiritual), Jesus commenced His missionary duties. From a home base in Capernaum on the Sea of Galilee, Jesus traveled throughout Israel, revealing God's truth wherever He went. He quickly gained a reputation for being a wise and honorable teacher.

In His hometown of Nazareth, however, Jesus was only initially received warmly. He read from the scroll of Isaiah, and the people gathered were awed at His authoritative manner. When He told them plainly that He was the fulfillment of the prophet's words, the crowd became indignant. Jesus then exposed the closed-mindedness of His former neighbors and relatives, quoting a commonplace saying to highlight the skeptical nature of their thinking. The irate crowd attempted but failed to throw Him off a cliff.

We have a modern proverb of our own that restates Jesus' saying in this scripture: "I'll believe it when I see it." Like His first-century audience, most of us are skeptical about things that seem too good to be true. We want proof.

Jesus had returned to His hometown to share His good news with the people He grew up with. Because of familiarity and bias, they refused to accept His deity at face value. This type of cynical attitude prevails even today. It seems to be a human tendency to question the credentials of our successful friends and neighbors. Whether from jealousy or just pure skepticism over extraordinary achievements, we mentally dictate the level of advancement we feel those closest to us ought to attain. Apparently, this type of reverse nepotism has been going on for millennia. The unfortunate side effect is that we can easily miss the real deal when it is right in front of us. Many missed Jesus when He was on earth. Many still do.

Stepping In: Read Isaiah 61. Are you accepting of Jesus' power and authority over you? Have you ever demanded proof of His abilities to heal or to exact change? Confess your fears and doubts. Ask for forgiveness now. Pray for a deeper level of faith, trust, and acceptance of Jesus' authority.

Stepping Out: This week, evaluate your own skepticism or jealousy of others who have "unwarranted" successes (spiritual or otherwise). As the Spirit leads you, ask for forgiveness from those you may have hurt because you withheld acceptance and belief in them.

April 5

Inspired

> Then Jesus came to them and said, "All authority in heaven and on earth has been given to me. Therefore, go and make disciples of all nations, baptizing them in the name of the Father and of the Son and of the Holy Spirit, and teaching them to obey everything I have commanded you."
>
> —Matthew 28:18–20 (Mt 28:1–20)

Three days after Jesus had been laid in Joseph of Arimathea's tomb, an angel of the Lord appeared on the stone blocking the entrance. Along with the blazing white angel came a violent earthquake that caused the graves of long-dead saints to be opened, releasing many resurrected souls. Behind the stone lay empty graveclothes—Jesus was not there.

The angel, after moving the stone away, gave two vigilant women friends of Jesus the news that their Lord was alive, and told them to go and tell the disciples. When the disciples heard the news and received their instructions, they quickly set out for Galilee and went to the mountain where Jesus had said He would meet them. As soon as they saw Him, most of the remaining eleven disciples joyfully worshipped Jesus, though some doubted. Jesus, after reassured His men of His supremacy, commissioned them to carry the good news of His victory over death to "all nations." Though some disciples may have initially resisted His command, the world now has them to thank for faithfully carrying out their inspired mission.

This commission was not just for Jesus' first disciples. It is a command for disciples of Christ in all generations, including us. From the day Jesus spoke these words near Galilee until He returns, Jesus' followers are to continue to "go and make disciples of all nations."

But there are a few qualifiers we should not overlook. For one, it is only under Jesus' authority that we can do this work for Him, or any kingdom work for that matter. He must be our guide. Two, it is important to note that by "nations," Jesus meant "people groups." Our task is to tell people from all walks of life about Jesus, wherever they may be—even next door. Three, since Jesus did not go it alone, neither should we. Not only should we join other faithful believers in this monumental effort, but we must also take along the Holy Trinity. Jesus equipped His apostles with the "resurrection power" they would need to bring His kingdom to all the earth, He also supplies every believer with this same life force – His Spirit.

Last, we are not to simply tell others *about* Jesus. We are to let our witness inspire those around us to want what we have. We have our marching orders—now let's get to it!

Stepping In: Read Psalm 2:7–8; Daniel 7:13–14; Matthew 18:19–20; Mark 16:15–16; Luke 10:22; Romans 8:11–17; and Ephesians 1:18–23. Take some time to ponder Jesus' authority over all the nations. How much do you submit to His authority over you and utilize the power He has entrusted you with? Pray that God inspires you to inspire others.

Stepping Out: This week, inspire others by example to obey what Jesus has commanded. Showing love and kindness to your neighbors is always a good place to start.

April 6
Considerate

"So in everything, do to others what you would have them do to you,
for this sums up the Law and the Prophets."
—Matthew 7:12 (Mt 7:1–12)

Following up His teaching on appreciating God's generosity and encouraging the audience of His Sermon on the Mount to personally seek God with a pursuant and expectant faith, Jesus concluded that this same intentionality should carry over into one's personal life as well. Jesus continually emphasized the importance of God-honoring relationships. In the above verse, He went so far as to boldly state that of all the rules one must live by in order to please God, the one that summarizes them all is that of treating others with consideration and respect.

For the Jews in the audience, this suggestion may have seemed too simple to be true. For the Pharisees, this assertion would have seemed blasphemous, causing them to think, "Who is this man Jesus to tell us the meaning of the Law?" More than to all the rest, it was to these pious men that Jesus directed His statement. Jesus wanted the crowd to understand that knowing and loving God involved more than just following a list of rules. As important as seeking God's approval and obeying His commands were, Jesus was saying that it was equally vital to demonstrate godly love in everything and with everyone. This new take on the Law may have sounded simple, but shifting one's focus from mindlessly performing religious duties to prioritizing the consideration of others proved a difficult task for some.

Today, we call this commandment "the Golden Rule." Most of us today are familiar with the concept of "do unto others as you would have them do unto you," but in Jesus' time, such an injunction was in stark contrast with the Old Testament "eye for an eye" ideology.

Modern readers of the Old Testament may marvel at the strict regulations for righteous living imposed on the Jews before the time of Jesus. It is hard for us to fathom the complexity of this ancient religion and culture. It is especially difficult for us to understand the severe personal and social repercussions for unorthodox behavior or noncompliance with the Law.

Though we don't have the long list of dos and don'ts the first century Jews did, we do not find it any easier to obey the Golden Rule we do have. Jesus tells us to treat others with consideration "in everything," not just the things we find convenient or socially acceptable. It goes without saying that this implies using respectful words, kind actions, and sensitivity in all our dealing with others. It also implies that there is a universal standard of decency by which we live.

But is there? The answer is yes: our Bible.

Stepping In: Review the Ten Commandments this week (Dt 5:1–21). Also read Deuteronomy 18:14–22 to better understand the nature of the true Prophet. Meditate on these scripture passages. Take to heart their message. Listen to what God is saying to you specifically. Pray for a heart of awareness and obedience.

Stepping Out: This week, apply today's verse to your life. In each interaction with others, consider how you would want to be treated if you were standing in their shoes; then act accordingly.

April 7
Open-Handed

Calling his disciples to him, Jesus said, "I tell you the truth, this poor widow has put more into the treasury than all the others. They gave out of their wealth; but she, out of her poverty, put in everything—all that she had to live on."

—Mark 12:43–44 (Mk 11:1–11; 12:35–44)

In preparation for the final phase of His earthly ministry, Jesus, His disciples, and His followers left the region of Galilee and went to Jerusalem. There, Jesus devoted His time to completing His disciples' training and preaching the good news.

One day in the temple courts, Jesus was asked about whose son is the Christ. Trying to force Jesus into an admission of what they perceived to be false deity, they expected proof of their allegations to ensue. However, quoting the psalmist David, Jesus cleverly turned the question back on them.

He then went on to warn the attentive audience of God worshippers to be on guard against corrupt teachers of the Law, who tout their positions and "devour widows." On the coattails of this speech, Jesus capitalized on the opportunity to give His disciples a true example of humble and open-handed living. He showed them what a heart for God really looks like.

A strange phenomenon seems to plague all generations on this planet: the richer people get, the stingier they become. Statistics show that, proportionately speaking, the higher the income, the smaller the proportionate charitable giving. The converse seems also to be true: the poorer the people, the more generous they tend to be.

This is, of course, a generalization; there are exceptions to the rule. However, given that Jesus Himself brought it up all those years ago, it is clearly a real issue. Sadly, it is this sort of greed and closed-handedness that narrows the gate of heaven for many. In our world of self-reliance and financial security, a true heart for God is hard to come by. Our views of ownership and entitlement are absurdly skewed.

Jesus wants us to get this right. Not only did God give us all that He had—His Son—He also gives us all we have. Our response should be a willingness to share some of this wealth.

Stepping In: Read Deuteronomy 15:7-8; Matthew 7:13-14, 19:23-24; and 2 Corinthians 8:1–12. What is your relationship with money? Do you hold it loosely or do you hold it fast? How generous are you toward God with your finances? Pray for a better understanding about what is yours and what is God's. Ask Him to help you rest in His care, secure in His ways.

Stepping Out: Sometime this week, maybe at church, give all you have in your wallet to a God-worthy cause. Be as open-handed as you are open-hearted.

April 8
Magnanimous

"If you had known what these words mean, 'I desire mercy, not sacrifice,' you would not have condemned the innocent. For the Son of Man is the Lord of the Sabbath."

—Matthew 12:7–8 (Mt 12:1–8)

Upon their return from their first apostolic mission to preach the gospel of truth to the nation of Israel, Jesus' disciples rejoined their Master as He traveled throughout Galilee. One Sabbath afternoon, while walking through a field of wheat, the group became hungry. Hearing no protest from Jesus, the men broke off some heads of wheat and ate.

The unlawfulness of collecting food on the religious day of rest did not escape the notice of some local Pharisees. Consequently, Jesus was questioned about His disciples' sacrilegious behavior. Jesus responded by pointing out how God, on several notable occasions, mercifully allowed His servants to eat what ordinarily would have been restricted by the Law. Jesus rebuked His adversaries' lack of scriptural understanding and their inability to put people's needs above staunch legalism. His reference to the prophet Hosea's warnings about being a hard-hearted and rebellious people no doubt further angered the religious authorities.

Jesus' message was clear. As the Son of Man and the Lord of the Sabbath, He was certainly within His rights to choose "mercy, not sacrifice." God's favor was on the magnanimous above the lawful.

Today, very few people still observe the Sabbath in its strictest sense. We certainly do not follow it to the extent of the ancient Jews, who observed thirty-nine "shall nots" on their day of rest, including selecting, tearing, and reaping. What the Lord intended for our good, religious zealots turned into a nearly impossible list of requirements.

Unsurprisingly, many people have moved to the far end of the spectrum regarding setting aside a day that is holy unto the Lord. Yes, most us enjoy having a day off from work, and many of us go to church on Sunday. But to say that we truly honor God with a whole day may be a stretch.

As Christians, we mustn't be so fast to dismiss the importance of keeping the Sabbath holy. Jesus, who is Lord of the Sabbath, set a keen example of what constitutes a proper use of time on one's day of rest. As we learn from today's passage, more vital to Jesus than restricting one's activities is the intentionality with which one stays in step with the Lord. While church, worship, spending time in God's Word, enjoying fellowship with other believers, and physically taking it easy are important, so too is being available for magnanimous acts of mercy. These things please the Lord and bring us the joy and rejuvenation we need to start a new week.

Stepping In: Read Hosea 6; Micah 6:8 and Matthew 9:9-13. On what side of the religious strictness spectrum do you fall? Pray that God guides you to a happy middle ground, where Jesus is at the true center.

Stepping Out: This week, show mercy instead of rigidity in all your dealings. Be magnanimous, generous, kind, and forgiving in all your dealings. Use God's holy day to please the Lord.

April 9
Heartfelt

When the Lord saw her, his heart went out to her and he said, "Don't cry."

—Luke 7:13 (Lk 7:1–17)

After spending time among the people of Capernaum, near the Sea of Galilee, Jesus and His disciples went down to a town called Nain, near Nazareth. Because of His impressive teaching in the temple and works of compassionate healing performed everywhere He went, a sizable crowd accompanied Jesus on His journey. As they arrived at the town gate, a funeral procession was coming out. Jesus, knowing that the dead person was the only son of a widow, felt extreme empathy for the dead boy's grieving mother. Without prompting or reservation, Jesus extended His heartfelt mercy to an individual so caught up in her own pain that she did not even notice the Lord and His assembly. But He didn't stop with kind words alone. To the shock of those standing there, Jesus touched the dead boy's coffin (making Himself—a rabbi—ceremonially unclean) and called the young man back to life. All who witnessed this miracle were awestruck.

This side of heaven, most of us will likely never know how many times Jesus has rescued us or a loved one from death or near-death. With the advance of modern medicine, technology, and at-the-ready response teams, we are often quick to credit these lifesaving methods above those of a more intangible nature: God's divine intervention. How many moments of unprovoked and undeserved compassion from our Lord have we missed because we had been so absorbed in our own distress?

The truth is, none of that matters to God. He will have compassion on whomever He pleases, whether we ask for it or not. That said, Jesus most certainly hears and answers us when we do cry out to Him. In fact, in the verses preceding today's passage, a desperate man, feeling very unworthy of having Jesus come into his presence, sent some Jewish leaders to summon Him. This man knew that all Jesus needed to do was say a word and his servant would be healed. This man's faith inspired Jesus' healing response. If we are ever in doubt of our Savior's heartfelt love for us, just examine nearly any page in the New Testament. You will see plenty of examples in black and white and red.

Stepping In: Read 1 Kings 17:17–24; 2 Kings 4:32–37; Matthew 9:20–22 and Revelation 21:4. Have you ever felt unworthy of God's compassion or mercy? Can you think of a time when Jesus cared for you without you asking? Thank Him for His sacrifice, caring, healing, and grace.

Stepping Out: This week, extend heartfelt care to someone who is hurting. Encourage them to take heart in Jesus. Share how He has comforted and cared for you in your times of need. Explain how He is always available to those who cry out to Him, even those who don't understand why, how, or who.

Trustworthy

"Who then is the faithful and wise servant, whom the master has put in charge of the servants in his household to give them their food at the proper time?"

—Matthew 24:45 (Mt 24:1–51)

Though Jesus traveled throughout Israel during His three-year ministry, at God's appointed time, He went to Jerusalem for the final fulfillment of His earthly duties. According to the plan that was laid out before the formation of the world, Jesus provoked His opponents, the Pharisees and teachers of the Law, to a murderous rage by pointing out their wickedness and hypocrisy, sealing His own fate. In absolute submission to His Father's authority, Jesus walked boldly to the cross, willing to be a sacrificial atonement for all.

After leaving the temple, Jesus sat down on the Mount of Olives to teach His disciples about the events that would soon take place. He also spelled out the eventuality of the final judgement at the time of His return. He warned them not to be fooled by false Christs and phony prophets.

Then Jesus told them a parable about wise and wicked servants. At that point in their education and experience with Jesus, the disciples would certainly have guessed that the long awaited "master" was Him, and that they would be "faithful and wise" if they properly managed the charges they were entrusted with. The disciples understood the plight of the impatient and evil servants who did not manage well what they were given. The disciples recognized the importance Jesus placed on their trustworthiness.

These words of Jesus still speak a loud and clear message to those in positions of authority, in the church or otherwise. Jesus still expects those He has entrusted to lead to do so in an upright fashion. Not only should these leaders always keep their focus on Jesus and prioritize the Father's will, but they should provide for the needs of those under them.

Today's verse communicates the importance of conscientious administration. In the instance of a pastor "feeding his flock," he or she would be wise to pace messages wisely so as not to choke listeners with too much information too fast. At the same time, the flock should not be starved. The unwise and unfaithful pastor who loses sight of Jesus altogether will tend to forget his or her privileged position and the responsibility entrusted to him or her.

In any arena, leaders who lead others away from Christ rather than toward Him are the ones Jesus calls "wicked." Jesus tells us that there is a place for such people, and it is not good. He cautions us to be trustworthy ourselves, while being aware of those who are not.

Stepping In: Read Matthew 25:21; 1 Corinthians 3:1–3; 2 Timothy 2:15; Hebrews 5:7–14; and 1 Peter 2:1–3. What or who has God entrusted you with? How trustworthy are you in fulfilling your calling? Pray for wisdom and faith.

Stepping Out: This week, make any necessary adjustments to your current ministry so that you remain in God's will and ways. Be a good and trustworthy servant.

Nonjudgmental

"Do not judge, or you too will be judged. For in the same way you judge others, you will be judged, and with the same measure you use, it will be measured to you."

—Matthew 7:1–2 (Mt 7:1–6)

Over the course of His multi-day Sermon on the Mount, Jesus imparted both practical and spiritual truths to His audience. He spoke directly into the psyche of each person present, calling them to examine their thoughts, behaviors, and motives. More than anything, Jesus wanted His listeners to take to heart His teachings so that they could apply them to their relationship with God and others. Each topic Jesus expounded on was meant to elicit a thoughtful response, causing His listeners to consider how well or poorly they dealt with each.

Directing His comments to the religious leaders in the assembly, Jesus delved into the subject of judgment. In the Jewish culture, it was well understood that only God or those appointed by God could rightfully judge others. The Jewish elite did so without reservation, feeling well within their rights to issue moral, ethical, and even civil judgments. Jesus, the only true and fair Judge, was not about to let the hypocrisy and pride of these men go unnoticed. He explained that turnabout was fair play when it came to judgment. These words would have caused all to rethink their positions on passing judgment—none more so than the self-righteous religious men hearing them.

Most of us would like to think of ourselves as nonjudgmental. Yet, when we really consider how often we think snide thoughts, make offhand comments, or post snarky observations on social media, we suddenly realize that we are more critical than we think. As private as we believe our inner dialogues to be, God is completely aware of every spoken and unspoken word.

Just from a practical standpoint, the knowledge that each hurtful thought, snide comment, snicker of superiority, and disdainful glare is tallied up and will be doled back to us in kind should make us more conscientious. However, this is a deeply rooted issue of the heart, with pride at the very core. Jesus is saying that when we believe we are somehow better than others, we will be humbled. We will be served what we have been dishing out—a taste of our own medicine. Many will eat humble pie as a result.

Stepping In: Read 2 Corinthians 10; Philippians 2:1–4; and James 4. Ask God to reveal what measures of comparison you use regarding others. Pray that He replaces your boastful or critical thoughts with a genuinely humble and nonjudgmental attitude.

Stepping Out: This week, hold every thought captive in obedience to Christ's call to humility. When negative thoughts about others enter your mind, replace them with positive ones. Thank God that He made each of us uniquely in His image. Go out of your way to point out the good you see in others all week.

April 12
Tireless

"My Father is always at work to this very day, and I, too, am working."
—John 5:17 (Jn 5:16–30)

In the middle of His earthly ministry, Jesus went to Jerusalem to celebrate a religious holiday. He spent time among the people, sharing His gospel message and healing those in need. As was also His custom, Jesus prioritized times of worship and scriptural teaching in the temple. Knowing that he was being watched by the Jewish leadership, He addressed them directly with His claim about His Father's work. Stunned by what they perceived as blatant blasphemy, the Jewish leaders resolved to find a way to bring Jesus' ministry and life to an end. Instead of backing down, Jesus continued to emphasize His inseparable and reciprocal relationship with His Father, God. He and the Father were tirelessly working to bring salvation to Israel.

In our fast-paced and overstimulated culture, it is easy to forget that God is still hard at work. The rapidly declining state of the world, the dysfunction of society, and the tentativeness of peace seem to indicate the opposite. There is simply no denying that we live in a fallen world.

Yet when we take the time to look around, there is also plenty of evidence of God's handiwork. All of nature sings out God's praises. Is anyone listening? Our bodies, minds, and emotions replicate those of God Himself. More importantly, we were created as spiritual beings, designed to be in a loving relationship with our Creator, and to worship Him above all else.

Jesus has always set, and still does set, the perfect example of living this relationship out. Because He does what the Father does, we should follow suit. Jesus knows this is easier said than done. Just as Jesus faced persecution for His undeniable affiliation with the Father, we should also expect resistance. And, just as Jesus kept His eyes focused above, we must tirelessly keep our eyes on Him.

Stepping In: Read Psalm 19:1-6, 90:17; Proverbs 16:3; Matthew 6:10; John 15:5; Ephesians 2:10; Philippians 2:13; and Colossians 3:23. What do these verses teach you about working with and for God? To what work is the Spirit leading you? Pray for guidance and courage to step out and faithfully obey His call. Seek tireless strength to do His will.

Stepping Out: This week, identify a work God is already doing and join Him.

April 13
Perceptive

"Do not be afraid of those who kill the body but cannot kill the soul. Rather, be afraid of the One who can destroy both body and soul in hell."

—Matthew 10:28 (Mt 10:1–28)

In preparation for sending the Twelve out to bring the good news of the gospel to the nation of Israel, Jesus informed His men of the many types of danger they were certain to encounter during their missionary journeys. He also told His beloved disciples not to worry.

During this long speech, His newly appointed apostles may have forgotten the preface: Jesus was going to give them miraculous powers to heal and save many, and as freely as they had been given blessings from their Master, they should likewise give. With this knowledge and the many practical pieces of advice they were given in this teaching, Jesus was attempting to prepare them for every possible scenario.

But Jesus knew that they would still face real human fear. Though most of the Focus of His oration was on how the physical world would influence their experiences, Jesus brought them back to spiritual truths in the above verse. In so doing, Jesus highlighted the need for His apostles to cling to their faith, while at the same time remaining perceptive of the dangers they would likely face.

Not many people, then or now, can say that they do not fear the threat of violent danger. Missionaries throughout history and even today have faced the same potentially lethal outcomes that Jesus warned His original crusaders about. Many have been martyred for proclaiming Jesus as Lord and refusing to deny the gospel.

But those who are called to bring the good news of God's saving grace through His Son Jesus are also equipped to do so. Like the apostles, modern-day missionaries are given the ability to reach people where they are. They are cloaked with God's spiritual, and often physical, protection. Those who do lose their lives in the name of Christ are brought home in His timing, having not succumbed to the fear of Satan nor death. Their lives brought change even when those lives were taken from them.

Though not all of us are called to the mission field, we all are called to take on ministries in the service of Christ. Wherever our callings lead us, we must be perceptive of God's provision. In so doing, we can go forth without fear, knowing God is with us, in us, and for us.

Stepping In: Meditate on Romans 8:28-39 this week. Pray for a yielded heart and a spiritually perceptive mind.

Stepping Out: This week, maybe as a small group activity, watch "The End of the Spear," directed by Jim Hanon. Discuss your thoughts on mission work and how God works in all circumstances.

Attentive

"Martha, Martha," the Lord answered, "you are worried and upset about many things, but only one thing is needed. Mary has chosen what is better, and it will not be taken away from her."
—Luke 10:41–42 (Lk 10:38–42)

During the height of His ministry, when Jesus' teaching and healing services were in great demand, He still found time to visit friends and family. In the town of Bethany, just outside of Jerusalem, Jesus took a break to enjoy the company of some hospitable new acquaintances: the sisters Mary and Martha, whose brother was Lazarus. Martha, the older sister, complained to Jesus that Mary was not helping her with the tasks of serving their guests. In a tone of patient compassion, Jesus refocused Martha's attention. Martha felt the societal pressure to lavishly accommodate an honored guest, and hardly noticed that the Lord was sharing heavenly wisdom. Mary, on the other hand, was keenly aware of who was in her presence, and remained attentive to Jesus' every word. Where Martha saw her sister's inactivity, Mary only saw Jesus. She had chosen to give her full attention to what was best.

In our hustle-bustle world, it is easy to relate to Martha's frustration in these verses. We have so many things vying for our attention. Most of us believe that if we do not keep up, we will surely fall hopelessly behind. Advances in technology have only added to the constant demand for immediacy. We are always plugged in and on the go.

This is true even in our Christian walk. Being a service-oriented people, we often feel the pressure to say yes to everything except that all-important quiet time of sitting at the feet of Jesus. Truthfully speaking, we get to decide to what we devote our attention. Jesus knows that we are busy. He understands that we are responsible for many things. But when He has something to say, He wants us to be attentive—not because of anything He gains by it, but because, in that moment, it is the best possible use of our time. These verses remind us that Jesus does not want us to miss what is best.

Stepping In: Read Deuteronomy 30:19–20; Nehemiah 8:3; Psalm 23; Proverbs 18:13–15; Matthew 6:25–27; and James 1:22. How did the Lord speak to you about attentive listening through these verses? Thank Him for blessing you with His words of wisdom. If you listen closely, you will hear Him whisper your name (maybe even twice).

Stepping Out: This week, fight the temptation to hurry and scurry about. Take noticeable time to just be with Jesus through prayer and listening, reading your Bible, and reflecting on scripture. Be an example of an attentive Christian to others.

Erudite

"What do you think about the Christ? Whose son is he?"
—Matthew 22:42 (Mt 22:41–46)

During the final days of His earthly ministry, Jesus spent much of His time teaching in the temple courts in Jerusalem. Among the crowds of eager listeners were His most ardent opponents: the Pharisees. In this rare instance, Jesus initiated a conversation with them by asking them the above questions. They replied assuredly, "The son of David."

Though they were erudite about the scripture passages pertaining to messianic prophecy, the Pharisees' ignorance of their spiritual meaning was soon revealed. Jesus quoted a psalm of David to show their profound ineptitude. While "in the Spirit," David had written, "The Lord said to my Lord: 'Sit at my right hand until I put your enemies under your feet.'" Jesus asked the Pharisees to explain how the one they referred to as the "son of David" could also have been called "Lord" by David. Jesus let the implications of this quandary sink in. He watched as their faces registered the truth of what this meant: Christ was both God and the son of David—Son of Man. Much to the Pharisees' dismay, this explained Jesus' claim to deity. Trying to save face, the Pharisees gave Jesus no answer. From that day on, they vowed to make no more inquiries of Him.

There are many alive today who continue to deny that Jesus, who was a man, is also God. Few, though, refuse to believe that Jesus existed. Historical evidence proves that He lived an extraordinary life as a teacher and a healer, and that He died a criminal's death on the cross. For some, this is where the story gets a little fuzzy. For faithful Christians, however, this is where the story of our redemption becomes crystal clear. First-century critics of Jesus saw a delusional rabbi with a messiah complex. We, in light of the full scripture, see that everything God said and did points to the cross and the salvation it brings believers. What was a dashed hope for an earthly restoration of the kingdom of Israel is a fulfilled plan for an eternal kingdom.

Jews of today still await the coming messiah. Christians look forward to the second coming of our Lord Jesus, when the whole earth will be judged and renewed. The world believes only what it sees. Erudite disciples of Christ understand that there is far more to life than meets the eye.

Stepping In: Read 1 Kings 5:1–5; Psalm 89, 110:1; Acts 2:34–36; and Hebrews 10:11–14. How do these verses help you to better understand God's sovereign plan for a Savior from the beginning of time? How does this eternal story bring you comfort? Pray for clarity about who Jesus is to you, and what you should do about it.

Stepping Out: Become an erudite scholar of scripture by linking Old Testament prophecies to their New Testament fulfillment in Christ. Look for opportunities this week to profess who you know Jesus, the Messiah, to be.

Reborn

> "I am the resurrection and the life. He who believes in me will live, even though he dies; and whoever lives and believes in me will never die. Do you believe this?"
>
> —John 11:25–26 (Jn 11:1–37)

In the middle of His third year of ministry, with the inevitability of the cross quickly approaching, Jesus used every opportunity to reach His people with the truth of His gospel. Yet most of the Jews still stubbornly denied His claim to deity. In fact, an active plot against Him was underway in Jerusalem. Leaving Judea for the less hostile region of Perea, Jesus and His disciples ministered to the people there until they received word of their friend Lazarus' critical illness. Martha, one of Lazarus' sisters, heard that Jesus was on His way and ran to meet Him on the road. Jesus consoled Martha with a reminder of His power to restore life. Then He made Lazarus one of many to be reborn in body and in spirit.

The significance of this miracle cannot be stressed enough. Christianity is based on the conviction that Jesus has the power to overcome final death for Himself and for all who believe. Jesus needed His followers, and all who would come after, to fully grasp this reality. But Jesus knows that people need proof.

The fact that Lazarus had been in the tomb for four days is key. The simple, morbid truth was that His friend would have already begun to decompose; all hope of him having simply fallen into a coma was completely ruled out. Lazarus was irrefutably dead. This was the exact scenario Jesus had planned for. Before going to the cross, He needed to demonstrate His power to restore faith, hope, and even life.

As Jesus asked Martha, He also asks us: "Do you believe this?" When we face trials, illness, and tragedy, what is our faith response? Do we waver, or do we trust that Jesus knows what He is doing? Are we tempted to believe that Jesus *can* do anything, but question if He *will*? Do we still love Him when the answer to our prayers is "No" or "Not yet"? Those of us who have been reborn must never forget our eternal hope. We must live in that hope and faith each day, regardless of our circumstances.

Stepping In: Read Psalm 30:3; Daniel 12:1–3; John 5:28-29, 6:38-39; Romans 8:11; and Ephesians 2:1–5. How do these verses help increase your confidence in the Lord's resurrection power for your life, now and forever? Does your life reflect the fact that you are reborn, a new creation in Christ? If not, will you start today?

Stepping Out: This week, listen to and reflect on the song "Resurrecting" by Elevation Worship. Then, because you have been reborn, smile at everyone you see. If they ask, tell them why you are so happy.

Flexible

"If anyone will not welcome you or listen to your words, shake the dust
off your feet when you leave that home or town."
—Matthew 10:14 (Mt 10:1–14)

From the time Jesus called each of His disciples, they were in training for their missional lives ahead. Jesus commissioned the Twelve to share the good news that the "kingdom of heaven is near" with the "lost sheep of Israel." He gave them some specific instructions to follow: avoid the Gentiles and their land; perform miracles of healing and restoration; take nothing with you; find someone worthy to board you, and stay with them until you leave that town. Jesus also explained what they were to do if they found no one willing to offer them hospitality. Their plans had to be flexible to accommodate whatever types of people they faced.

The act of shaking the dust off one's sandals would have been familiar to these men, being a common Jewish practice. It was an indignant gesture meant to signify the removal of something unworthy or unholy from what belonged to God. It was like saying, "I will have nothing to do with this place, nor will I take any of it with me." Symbolically, it implied that even a speck of unholy dust must not be allowed to contaminate God's holy instruments.

Jesus did not want His apostles to waste their time evangelizing to an unreceptive or hostile audience. Nor does He not want His current-day disciples to wander down fruitless or dangerous paths. As He instructed His first-century missionaries to shake off the minute particles of negativity from such encounters, He also tells today's bringers of good news to rid themselves of influences that threaten to corrupt their faith or hinder their ministries.

This is easier said than done. The fact is, sharing the truth is not a "one size fits all" proposition. Christians who have a heart for the unsaved must be flexible and compliant with the Spirit's leading, even if it means walking away from a potential believer. Only God knows who He is drawing to Himself. Only He knows the time, place, and people involved in that process. With an open heart and an open mind, each of God's children will be given opportunities to participate in bringing His kingdom to earth. In the meantime, we must be alert, ready, patient, and flexible.

Stepping In: Read Genesis 12 verses 1 & 4 with Matthew 5:23-24. What do these verses say about flexibility? Is God leading you into an uncertain situation, or away from something that is hard for you to give up? Pray and ask God for the discernment and mental flexibility to adapt to His changing plans.

Stepping Out: This week, really check your motives in your ministries. Pray and ask God to reveal those whom you should walk toward and those better to leave to Him. Be willing to take a step back if that is what the Spirit requires.

Purposed

"Neither this man nor his parents sinned," said Jesus, "but this happened so that the work of God might be displayed in his life."
—John 9:3 (Jn 8:48–9:12)

With the end of His ministry in sight, Jesus took calculated risks to reach all who would hear and accept His message of salvation. On one such occasion, Jesus, faithful Jew that He was, went to the epicenter of His persecution—Jerusalem—to attend the Feast of Dedications. After arousing the religious leaders anger over His claim to deity, Jesus left the temple before his opponents could seize Him; His time to be glorified had not yet come.

As Jesus and His disciples walked along, they came upon a man born blind. The disciples asked Jesus whose sin had caused the man's blindness, his own or his parents. Jesus did not refute the commonly held belief that sin (personal or generational) could lead to such calamity. Instead, He suggested that it could have come about for an entirely different reason: purposed to bring glory to God. This would have been a stunning revelation.

To show them what He meant, and without the blind man having asked for healing, Jesus spit in the dust and applied the mud to the man's eyes. Then He said to the man, "Go, wash in Pool of Siloam" (Jn 9:7). The man did as he was told, and returned to his village with his sight fully restored. His astonished neighbors took him to the Pharisees to show them the miracle and to report who had performed it. Confidently, the man proclaimed his healing could only have been done by a "man of God," and not a "sinner" as the Pharisees contended. Clearly, unlike those of the Pharisees, the blind man's physical and spiritual eyes had been opened.

God created each of us just the way we are, on purpose. This is a hard truth for many of us to accept. For those born with or who have developed debilitating conditions, it is difficult, even maddening, to imagine that this situation could be a part of God's plan.

Today's verse makes it clear that Jesus has purposed even our pain and suffering. Regardless of our trouble's cause, Jesus can redeem it and use it for good. As in the case of the man born blind, any time Jesus touches our lives, physical and spiritual healing are possible.

However, we have certain responsibilities in this arrangement. First, we must have an open mind. Jesus might need to use some unconventional methods (like spit-mud, for instance). Second, we need to let Jesus into our personal space. Barriers must come down, and we need to get out of His way. Third, when Jesus says "Go," we need to move. Obedience is key, regardless of the complexity or absurdity of the command. Last, we must allow the work of God to be displayed in our lives thereafter, proclaiming our healer by name and bringing glory to God.

Stepping In: Read Genesis 2:7; Psalm 146:8; Isaiah 35:3-5, 61:1; Jeremiah 29:11; Matthew 11:4–5; John 11:4; and 2 Corinthians 12:8–10. How do these verses encourage you in your current situation? Ask Jesus to reveal how He has purposed your pain for your good and His glory. Praise God for the work He is doing in and through you.

Stepping Out: This week, compare with your small group or some friends the way Jesus has healed you. Discuss the ways you are displaying His miraculous work in your life. If you are not displaying His grace, plan to begin doing so.

Unassuming

"What do you want me to do for you?"
—Matthew 20:32 (Mt 20:29–34)

On Jesus' final journey from Galilee to Jerusalem, He and His disciples stopped in the town of Jericho. As they were readying to leave that place, two blind men began shouting to Jesus, "Lord, Son of David, have mercy on us!" Pausing in front of them, Jesus asked what they wanted. He did not ask this question because He did not know the answer, He asked it so that others would learn from His unassuming example. He chose to establish a personal connection. Though Jesus and His disciples were delayed by this distraction for a brief time, the impact would be felt for generations to come. All who witnessed this miracle saw Jesus' power and love—not least among them being His two new followers.

Our world is still full of need. The homeless need shelter. The poor need provision. The sick need doctors. The lost need a Savior. Jesus Himself tells us that the poor we will always have with us; it is what we do about poverty that counts.

Today's short verse gives us some important clues. First, we are to take time to talk with people. In our hectic, me-centered society, this is a tall order. Of all our resources, time seems to be the one in the highest demand and the shortest supply. Jesus sets a perfect example for us here. He was on His way out of town, en route to a very significant event. He could have easily deemed Himself too busy or distracted to stop. But He didn't.

Second, we should not assume we know what people need before we ask them. Even with the best of intentions, we often fail here. Jesus, who knew the request before it was asked, valued the voice of those He served. So should we.

Last, if we are to demonstrate the true love of Christ, we must move in closer to the people we serve. Too often, our society creates invisible barriers between the haves and the have-nots. As Christians, we must not let our sight determine the worthiness of a soul needing saving. Jesus touched the untouchables. This is the example He sets for us as well.

Stepping In: Reread Matthew 20:29–34. Take some time to think about these verses and how they show the way Jesus cares for and values the whole person. How has He met your unrequested needs? Thank Him and ask Him for the things you may be assuming He already knows. He wants to hear from you.

Stepping Out: This week, demonstrate your love for others by moving in closer to those in need. Sit beside them and unassumingly ask them what they need. Really listen. Don't be afraid to touch.

Rooted

> "Every plant that my heavenly Father has not planted will be pulled up
> by its roots. Leave them; they are blind guides. If a blind man leads a
> blind man, both will fall into a pit."
>
> —Matthew 15:13–14 (Mt 15:1–20)

When word of Jesus' offenses reached the Pharisees in Jerusalem, some of them decided to journey to Galilee to confront Him personally. Jesus addressed the concerns of these self-righteous men about His disregard for some Jewish traditions by presented them with examples of their own transgressions, backed up by scripture. Jesus explained to His disciples that they needn't worry about these "blind guides"; their spiritual blindness would eventually lead them to irreversible consequences. Indeed, all who were not rooted in truth would suffer.

Apparently, misguided religious fanatics are not a new phenomenon. Even God's first chosen people were known to zealously (if unknowingly) promote faulty theology. The Bible gives us numerous examples of the Jews' struggle to fully understand and follow God's commands over the course of recorded history. At times they recognized their need for God and were attentive to His will. At other times they were rebellious and shortsighted, exercising their independence and creating their own rules.

Failure to recognize Jesus as the Christ, and rejection of the proofs He gives, continues to this day. There are more religions now than ever before, with more cults emerging every day. Each sect believes that their way is right, and all the others are wrong. When belief-based hatred and violence rule the international scene, Christians must heed Jesus' warning. Though retaliation sometimes seems appropriate, we must remain rooted in faith and trust that God has a plan for every person on this planet. Blind guides do not need our help finding their way to the pit. But those who abide in Jesus can lead many out of harm's way.

Stepping In: Read Isaiah 11:1–5, 53; 60:1–3, 21; and 61:1–3. How do these foreshadows of Jesus help you to be more rooted in your faith? Pray for strength to wait on the Lord's judgment for the wicked. Pray to know when to engage the opposition, and when to leave them.

Stepping Out: This week, tend to your own garden. Take time to nurture the ones who are planted by God as an act of worship toward our Lord of Justice.

Intolerant

"I know your deeds, your love and faith, your service and perseverance, and that you are now doing more than you did at first. Nevertheless, I have this against you: You tolerate that woman Jezebel, who calls herself a prophetess."

—Revelation 2:19–20 (Rv 2:18–29)

Having been supernaturally transported into the presence of God, the apostle John was given words to write to each of the seven Christian churches in the Asian provinces. In His salutation to the church in Thyatira, Jesus invoked an image of Himself as "the Son of God," whose features proved His power and authority. He issued them a warning about Jezebel. Jezebel, though not likely an actual person, represented one who is evil, corrupt, and seductive. Though the church was faithful in some ways, their tolerance of false teachings in their midst could not be ignored. Jesus meant to highlight the dangers that such an influence would cause. What the church leaders may have seen as slight compromises to accommodate the dominant culture would become signs of moral degradation and spiritual depravity if left unchecked. Jesus made it clear: tolerate no evil!

In America, this issue of tolerance is one of our culture's hot buttons. Many see Christians as intolerant because they choose to uphold the moral laws of the Bible above cultural norms. Upon closer examination, we see a double standard emerge. Most people agree that harmful people or influences should not be allowed into our homes, communities, and schools. Many people label this same protective behavior "intolerant" when it has to do with religion, especially Christianity. Most people would not question a parent's right to monitor their children's social activities, but many balk at Jesus' commands for sanctity.

Today's passage is a reminder that our heavenly Father has the right to oversee His children's moral and spiritual well-being. Like a lovingly strict parent, Jesus models how we should be intolerant of things that can harm our loved ones: greed, pride, sexual immorality, lack of self-control, and exposure to lies and corruption. Christians must work together to stop the infiltration of evil. Evil threatens the moral and ethical foundation of the body of Christ—the Church Jesus bought and paid for with His own shed blood. Though this is not a culturally popular notion, Christians must uphold truth by filtering out the acceptable from the unacceptable, as any good parent would.

Stepping In: Read Habakkuk 1:13; Romans 12:1–2; 1 Corinthians 6:12-20, 10:31-33; Ephesians 5:1–7; Philippians 4:8–9; and 1 John 1:9–10. Are you currently tolerating or participating in any morally questionable practices? Repent today, and praise God for His forgiveness and strength to do what is right.

Stepping Out: This week, up your Christian game. Do more than you did at first to increase your faith. Start by being intolerant of anyone or anything that draws you or others away from God.

April 22
Loyal

"It has been said, 'Anyone who divorces his wife must give her a certificate of divorce.' But I tell you that anyone who divorces his wife, except for marital unfaithfulness, causes her to become an adulteress, and anyone who marries the divorced woman commits adultery."

—Matthew 5:31–32

The above statement was one of Jesus' many references to the teachings God gave Moses for instructing the Jewish nation in righteous living. Most who heard Him would have been familiar with the doctrine that clearly defined marriage as a lasting bond between a man and a woman. They would also have known the permissible exceptions to this rule. Men were allowed to have more than one wife, but not vice versa. Though divorce was not viewed kindly, men were free to issue a divorce at their discretion. Women held no such authority; loyalty was one-sided. Furthermore, without a husband or proper divorce papers, a woman became a disgraced outcast.

Jesus challenged these norms by adding His own working definition of what constituted a rightful divorce. The husband and the wife would share responsibility for their marriage's dissolution, as well as the social repercussions. In so doing, He established a level playing field where one had never been before. This new notion would have stunned many in His audience, especially the men. Suddenly, loyalty took on a whole new meaning.

The sanctity of marriage is as important to Jesus today as it has always been. The distortion and abuse of this sacred union must still grieve Him greatly. In a society where over half of all marriages end in divorce and with an absurd number of them due to infidelity, this teaching could not be more relevant.

Though it may have looked like God once endorsed polygamy and allowed for inequality to persist between husbands and wives, it was man's interpretation of God's laws that resulted in these skewed marital practices. Jesus' aim was to set the record straight—on marriage and many other topics. Then and now, accountability for divorce rests on both parties. However, it is clear in the greater context of Jesus' teachings that He wants us to look beyond the "you play, you pay" philosophy. Intentions are at the heart of the matter, as are virtue, commitment, and loyalty, regardless of which gender you are. Marriage will always be a holy, enduring union in God's eyes.

Stepping In: What does loyalty mean you? Have you been on either end of relational unfaithfulness or betrayal? Pray for healing in your heart and in your relationships. Meditate on the notion that God's people are the bride of Christ, a union of utmost importance.

Stepping Out: After praying to God to give you a virtuous, loyal, and committed heart, make every effort to live this out. Check your intentions and motivations for selfishness or deceit. Repent of these attitudes and behavior and return to the right path ASAP.

April 23
Excused

"As for the person who hears my words but does not keep them, I do
not judge him. For I did not come to judge the world, but to save it."
—John 12:47 (Jn 12:37–50)

While in Jerusalem, just days before His natural life ended, Jesus spoke plainly to His disciples about His impending death. He told them He would be "lifted up" (on the cross) to fulfill God's plan for the redemption of His people. Jesus stated that the time for the Father's name to be glorified had come. Then "a voice from heaven" was heard affirming that indeed His name would be glorified, and glorified again.

Despite this undeniable confirmation of Jesus' authority, some people remained skeptical. They commented that the Law stated that the Christ should not die, but be eternal. Had they remembered Isaiah's prophecies regarding the Messiah, they would have realized that Jesus was the One they had been expecting. But their hardened hearts would not allow it. Even the religious leaders who did believe that Jesus was the Christ would not admit it, for fear of losing their positions in the synagogue.

As much as Jesus wanted to gather the "lost sheep of Israel" to Himself, He knew that arrogance and pride would prevent many from accepting Him as the Christ. He had no illusions about even the most pious being able to keep His commands fully, as perfection was not a human quality. Nonetheless, out of love for His creation, Jesus would offer salvation to all, whether they chose to receive it or not. Jesus would eventually judge humanity, but not until His saving work was accomplished.

Someone reading today's verse may think that it is a contradiction of the verses that state that Jesus will be the judge of humanity (Mt 19:28; Jn 5:22; Acts 10:42; 2 Cor 5:10; Jas 5:9; Rv 19:11). Though Jesus is the ultimate Judge, He will refrain from issuing His final verdict until the "end of the age." When He returns, the people's faith (or lack thereof) will be all the evidence He needs to convict or exonerate them.

Jesus is patient and righteous, giving each of us innumerable chances to prove our devotion. Jesus knows that none of us is perfect. Even the most faithful can never obey every one of His commands. Like the first-century Jews, some today falsely believe that by religious affiliation, genetic inheritance, or works, they will be found faultless before our Lord and Judge. This simply is not the case.

Jesus reminds us in today's verse that He does not hold us accountable for what we cannot do. But He will hold us accountable for what we believe. As Christians, we are to try to do as Jesus says, but He knows and accepts our shoddy success rate. In the end, what is in our hearts will either render us excused of guilt or worthy of judgment.

Stepping In: Read John 3:18; Romans 1:20, 6:22-23, 8:1-2; and 1 Corinthians 4:5. How do these verses help explain the time of judgment and who will be judged? Do you use your salvation as an excuse to give Jesus only minimal effort? Ask Jesus for forgiveness and for the strength to do His will.

Stepping Out: This week, dedicate yourself to obeying Jesus' greatest commandments: love the Lord your God with everything you have, and love your neighbor as yourself. Find tangible ways to do both.

Restrained

"See to it no one knows about this."
—Matthew 9:30 (Mt 9:27–34)

During the height of His ministry, nothing Jesus did or said went unnoticed—except that which He chose to conceal. After restoring the sight to two blind beggars, Jesus issued them the above command. But even if the two healed men managed to contain their exuberance, their new condition would undoubtedly be noticed in their hometown. Indeed, it is contrary and absurd to think that they could keep from revealing how they were healed and by whom.

Jesus, of course, knew this. He knew also that eventually His name would be mentioned in association with the blind men's restored sight. Possibly to test their obedience, Jesus asked the men to keep quiet about the miracle anyway. He did not want to draw attention to His miraculous abilities, giving the Pharisees more evidence in their case against Him before the time was right. Inasmuch as it was humanly possible, He was asking for all the help He could get in keeping His identity quiet for the time being.

Now that Jesus has been glorified and is risen, one might feel that believers should always boldly proclaim the restorative powers of our Lord. The more unrestrained witnesses, the better—right?

Though it may be true that Jesus' identity no longer need be kept secret for fear of inciting the rage of jealous Pharisees, Christians must still employ self-control for a different reason. Today, rather than avoiding the attention of the *wrong* people, exuberant believers must use intentional tactics that attract *all people*. In our excitement to share the good news, we sometimes forget that not everyone we encounter is ready for a salvation sermon.

God draws those He will call. It is our duty, as modern-day disciples, to utilize the discerning power of the Holy Spirit as we watch for people He puts in our path. After we have established a relationship, we wait for a sign of receptivity to Jesus' message. Only then should we—with gentleness and humility—tell of all the wonderful things God has done for us. When it comes to attracting or repelling people, a measure of restraint goes a long way. The right word, at right time, said in the right way, will never return void.

Stepping In: Read Proverbs 10:19, 12:18; Isaiah 55:10-11; and James 1:26, 3:3-6. Meditate on these verses. What is God whispering to you about the words you chose to use or not use? Pray that God gives you wisdom about when to speak and when to keep quiet.

Stepping Out: This week, apply the "less is more" approach to your sharing of the gospel. Remember, action always will speak louder than words.

April 25
Compensated

"But when you give a banquet, invite the poor, the crippled, the lame,
the blind, and you will be blessed. Although they cannot repay you,
you will be repaid at the resurrection of the righteous."
—Luke 14:13–14 (Lk 14:1–24)

Nearing the end of Jesus' earthly ministry, His most staunch opponents, the Pharisees, kept a very close eye on His every move. As a means of establishing a good vantage point, one of the Pharisees invited Jesus to dinner at his house. Underneath this act of kindness was the ulterior motive to lead Jesus into speaking incriminating words, or blaspheming, in the presence of many witnesses.

Jesus beat His opponents to a topic of much debate by asking those at the table if it was lawful to heal on the Sabbath. No one answered. Jesus then asked about rescuing a son or a valued animal if they fell into a well on the Sabbath. Again, silence.

To further highlight their blatant hypocrisy, Jesus mentioned another sacrilegious behavior that was all too common among these pious men: self-aggrandizement. As a commentary on what He saw before Him, Jesus told a parable about banquet invitation etiquette, proper seating arrangements, and expected compensation. His descriptions exposed the dinner guests' obvious abuse of these social mores, as well as pointing out their disregard of Jewish edicts dealing with the care of the less fortunate. The Pharisees' plan was foiled: instead of finding fault in Jesus, they themselves were found guilty.

Modern readers of this text know that Jesus was alluding to the kingdom of heaven in this parable. Gaining access to the wedding feast is a high honor. It is not necessarily the rich and famous who wind up on the guest list. The main teaching point of this passage is that those who claim to love God and follow Christ must invite others to the banquet and hold the doors open for even the most unlikely guests.

Jesus reminds us time and again that there are only two eternal destinations: heaven, with God, and hell, apart from God. He encourages us to make the most of every opportunity to humbly serve and lead others in truth—not with reciprocation in mind, but heavenly treasures. Those who obey this command will be more than adequately compensated.

Stepping In: Read Proverbs 25:6–7; Daniel 12:2–3; Matthew 6:19–21; Luke 18:18–23; 1 Corinthians 15:12–19; and 1 Thessalonians 4:16–18. How do these verses help you to understand your responsibility to prioritize others' needs above your own? Are you excited about your heavenly compensation for obediently leading others to Jesus? If not, pray for God to soften your heart toward the "uninvited."

Stepping Out: This week, invite someone to church, regardless of how different from you they might be.

Embodied

"Again, I tell you that if two of you on earth agree about anything you ask for, it will be done for you by my Father in heaven. For where two or more come together in my name, there am I with them."
—Matthew 18:19–20 (Mt 18:15–20)

Jesus knew His time on earth was short. He knew that the task of preparing His disciples for their monumental missions would be laborious and intense, for Him and for them. In their training, Jesus tried to instill in His men many spiritual truths. He needed them to know that He and His Father were one; Jesus was indeed God incarnate. His wisdom, His compassion, and His powers were constantly on display as proof of His divinity. Above all, it was His own humble submission to the will of the Father that He needed His apostles to fully grasp and to emulate. This included the plan for salvation through His sacrificial death.

As much as they revered Him as Messiah, the disciples struggled to relinquish their grip on an earthly perspective—that their king should reign, not perish. They could only envision a temporal kingdom, and argued about who would be the greatest in that place. Jesus explained to them that their heart posture was all wrong. Instead of fantasizing about the power and prestige they might be granted as heirs to the throne, their attitude should embody that of a servant to God, submitting every thought and effort to the Father's will.

Unity was essential: as with the Father and Son, so too with believers. This unity was to start with them. Through unity, they might quickly resolve disputes, encourage others to be unified, and accomplish anything they agreed upon in the Spirit. Together they embodied the Spirit of God and could bring about much positive change.

Throughout history, these verses have been an anchor of hope for those with pure intent. Surely, God has honored Jesus' promises in many wondrous ways. He has provided His personal attention and provision for those who gather around a humble request, seeking the Father's will.

There have been those who misused this pledge to meet less virtuous goals. Sadly, some claim that God has supported many an unjust cause because of this vow. However, true believers know that this is not the way God operates. One cannot take the first half of this promise without the second. Though God does answer personal prayers, these verses remind us that a unified gathering is a powerful force. As those who embody the Spirit, calling on God *in the name of Jesus*, we can achieve great things for His kingdom. Because all members of the Trinity are screening each call, it is impossible for this promise to fail or be abused. Christians today are wise to utilize this infallible cosmic helpline. With Jesus in our midst, our Father in heaven is ready to receive His children's collective requests.

Stepping In: Read Matthew 7:7–8 and 17:14-21. Have you tested God's promise to answer prayers? What was the result? Have you thanked Him, even when the answer came in unexpected ways? If not, do so now.

Stepping Out: This week, gather with other believers to raise your humble requests to God in Jesus' name. Watch and listen expectantly for His reply.

April 27
Peaceable

"Therefore, if you are offering your gift at the altar and there remember that your brother has something against you, leave your gift there in front of the altar. First go and be reconciled to your brother; then come and offer your gift."

—Matthew 5:23–24 (Mt 5:21–26)

Throughout His multi-day Sermon on the Mount, Jesus expounded on the theme of loving God and others. Jesus offered His audience a new and controversial definition of murder as more than the physical act of taking another's life. Murder included the mental practice of harboring hatred.

In today's verses, Jesus referred to a common Jewish ritual to illustrate His point about approaching God and man with a pure heart. Most people, hearing these words, would not have considered their personal conflicts to have any bearing on their religious obligations, Jesus implied that having reconciled affairs was a prerequisite for a sufficiently humble posture before God.

As is evident throughout scripture, the condition of one's heart is of first importance to God. Essentially, Jesus was saying that one cannot have a heart for God if one does not have a genuine heart for others. Prioritizing the work necessary for maintaining peaceable relationships ensures that one is on the right track and precludes even one's religious duties.

In a fast-paced world, we rely heavily on muscle memory. For most of us, going through the motions is how we get through our day. The days, weeks, and years blur together. Even our worship becomes routine. If we are not careful, we can mindlessly allow our negative emotions to accompany us into everything we do—including our spiritual practices.

Today's verses remind us that we must consciously and intentionally strive for a peaceable life, both inside and outside of church. Though the days of ritual offerings may be gone, the necessity for an appropriate heart posture before our holy God will never change. We may not be held to rigid standard of dress or behavior when we attend a church, but that should not translate into casualness of devotion. God is still God, worthy of our heartfelt and sincere worship.

Obedience to the commands given in these verses is for our benefit, not just for God's honor. When we approach God free from the mental and emotional burden of strained relations, we can give God the gift of our unencumbered adoration. Undistracted, we are ready to receive His blessing of peace with us and in us.

Stepping In: What baggage do you carry into worship with you each week? Is your heart too burdened to freely worship God with all you have? Ask God to relieve you of this heaviness. Ask Him to reveal who you need to be reconciled with before approaching His altar. Then ask the Holy Spirit to empower you to seek reconciliation with your adversaries.

Stepping Out: This week, follow the Holy Spirit's promptings for taking next steps toward healing relationships by living out the following verses: Romans 12:18; 1 Thessalonians 5:15; and Hebrews 12:14. Own your part. Be responsible and respectable in word and deed. Be peaceable.

April 28

Nonviolent

"Put your sword away! Shall I not drink the cup the Father has given me?"
—John 18:11 (Jn 18:1–11)

On the last night of Jesus' human life, He partook of one final Passover meal with His disciples. Jesus prayed for Himself, His apostles, and all believers. Then He led His men toward the place of His betrayal. His disciples, wrought with confusion and overwhelmed by conflicting emotions, accompanied their Master, bringing with them the items He had instructed them to take (their money purses and two swords). Slowly, they made their way out of Jerusalem, across the Kidron Valley, and into the garden of Gethsemane.

Once there, Jesus told eight of His men to wait at a distance and took Peter, James, and John farther into the olive grove. He told these three to stay alert and stand watch while He prayed. However, three times during His anguished prayer, Jesus found His exhausted companions sleeping. Then, as a small militia of armed guards, chief priests, Pharisees, and Judas Iscariot stormed toward Jesus, His men sprang to their feet.

Jesus addressed the mob by asking them whom they sought. "Jesus of Nazareth," they replied.

"I am He," Jesus said (Jn 18:6).

His riled accusers eyed the disciples. Jesus reminded them that they had come to take only Him. Peter reacted impulsively to the threat by drawing his sword and cutting off the ear of an arresting officer. Quickly, Jesus put an end to the violent outburst and commanded that the sword be put away. He was ready to be "numbered with [His] transgressors." Jesus healed the man's ear and explained that no force was necessary. He, after all, had never presented any threat in the years they had known Him. However, to His distressed disciples, especially Peter, the nonviolent response to danger made no sense—at least not yet.

The reference to the cup Jesus was to drink is unfamiliar to many Bible readers today. The Jewish disciples would have recognized it as referring to God's wrath. They did not understand why Jesus would willingly accept the suffering that drinking of this cup would involve.

We know how this story plays out. We know who Jesus is and the significance of His words and actions. Though we do not like the fact that such evil had to be a part of the process, we understand that God had a plan to turn it to good. Jesus conquered evil and death!

Yet, like Peter, we often jump to the defense of our faith with more force than is necessary or right. Some may cite Jesus' zealous behavior at times as an example. When Jesus forcibly drove the money changers from the temple, He overturned tables and used a whip to scare the corrupt rabble from His Father's house (Jn 2:12–17). But there is no mention of Jesus harming anyone, ever. Those who know and love Jesus will follow His example of pacifism, avoiding conflict and violence as a matter of course. As Christians, the only sword we will ever need is His Word.

Stepping In: Read Psalm 75:8; Isaiah 51:17, 53; Jeremiah 25:15–16; Luke 22:35–38; Ephesians 6:17; and Revelation 14:9–10. How do these verses help you to better understand the way in which the cup Jesus drank saves us from God's wrath and judgment? Take some time to praise Him for His love and sacrifice so that you could be spared.

Stepping Out: This week, sharpen your sword by memorizing a passage of scripture, ready to give an answer for the hope you have in Jesus—without throwing the Bible at anyone.

April 29

Unwavering

"I tell you the truth, if you have faith as small as a mustard seed, you can say to this mountain, 'Move from here to there' and it will move. Nothing will be impossible for you."

—Matthew 17:20–21 (Mt 17:14–23)

Returning triumphant from their first apostolic mission, the Twelve reported to Jesus the miraculous ways they had healed and ministered to the people. Even so, the disciples' faith was far from unwavering, causing their ministry efforts to be ineffectual at times. On one occasion, they were unable to heal a demon-possessed boy. Clearly frustrated, Jesus had the afflicted child brought to Him and cast the demon out Himself. His rebuke about the size of his disciples' faith was not intended to shame them, but to remind them of the lessons they had already learned about faith, prayer, and unwavering belief. Jesus' power was not just *with* them, but *in* them. Soon, He would be passing the ministry to these men; the work of the kingdom would be in their hands. With time running out, this lesson was one that Jesus needed His missionaries to fully understand.

Sadly, Christ followers still struggle with the same issues that tripped up the disciples: fear, doubt, and pride. Our own spiritual effectiveness becomes limited when we fail to fully believe in God's omnipotence and trust in Jesus' faithfulness. We fail because—even with the Holy Spirit's help—we try to do things by our own strength, not God's.

This passage reminds us to trust Jesus unwaveringly to meet us in our moments of need, and not to rely on our own ability to do or say the right thing. Jesus' words should cause the believer to recall what we know about Him and how He has proven His power in our lives thus far. Fear, doubt, and selfish ambition have no place in true faith. Jesus calls us to an unwavering conviction based on mountains we have seen moved, and mustard-seed sized faith we have seen grow beyond what is humanly possible. The only limitation to us realizing our full kingdom potential are our finite minds. With Jesus, nothing is impossible.

Stepping In: Read Isaiah 54:10; Matthew 19:26; Luke 1:37, 17:5–6; and 1 Corinthians 13:1–3. Take some time to consider the mountains that are currently in your path. Is your perception of these problems influenced by your own ability to resolve them? Ask Jesus to give you an unwavering faith to trust in *His* power within you. Pray that He corrects your perspective on what is insurmountable.

Stepping Out: Make a list of mountains you have moved by faith. Thank God each time you look at it this week.

Converted

"Today salvation has come to this house, because this man, too, is a son of Abraham. For the Son of Man came to seek and save what was lost."

—Luke 19:9–10 (Lk 19:1–10)

During Jesus' three-year ministry, He and His disciples traveled widely, spreading the gospel, teaching in synagogues, and performing miraculous signs and healings. When the time came for Him to finish the work He had started, Jesus made a final circuit of the region, gathering the faithful to accompany Him on His journey to Jerusalem.

As Jesus passed through Jericho, a large crowd lined the streets, hoping to catch a glimpse of Him. Many came to see this miracle-working man for themselves, a notorious Jewish tax collector named Zacchaeus among them. Zacchaeus was anxious to lay eyes on Jesus, but too short to see above the crowds. So he set aside his dignity and climbed a tree for a better view.

As Jesus passed under the tree, He ordered Zacchaeus down and invited Himself to stay at his house. Stunned but thrilled, Zacchaeus quickly agreed. Apparently, just being in Jesus' presence caused a true conversion within Zacchaeus. Convicted of his crimes against the people as well as his sin against God, he told Jesus his plan to make amends.

Jesus, knowing that this wealthy but despised man's change of heart was genuine, reinstated Zacchaeus to a place of honor in His kingdom. Zacchaeus was converted from sinner to saved, lost to found.

Today, the world is full of Zacchaeuses. Most cultures in the world not only accept but glorify those who rise above their humble circumstance to gain wealth, power, and success—even if it is at the expense of others. Some say, "That's just the price of doing business." For those whose ultimate goals are affluence and worldly comfort, how they come by these things is relatively unimportant, certainly worth the social and relational costs involved.

From time to time, however, one of these driven and self-satisfied individuals becomes curious about the things they're missing out on. Looking at the way others conduct themselves, these Zacchaeuses begin to recognize where they are lacking: authentic relationships, true purpose, joy. As God draws them to Himself, they realize their loneliness and depravity. When they see the life that Jesus offers, it suddenly becomes clear that they have been doing it all wrong, and it is time to start doing it right.

As we see in today's passage, it is not uncommon for those who have experienced a personal interaction with Jesus to respond with abundant gratitude, spilling over to those around them. The impact of these gratefully converted Zacchaeuses is far greater than all their money could buy by far!

Stepping In: Read Leviticus 6:1–5; Isaiah 30:15, 43:18-19; Ezekiel 34:12–16; Luke 3:8-9, 15:2, 18:22; and Romans 12:3. What was your attitude about getting ahead in worldly terms before you were converted to Christianity? Praise God for drawing you to Himself, for opening your eyes to the error of your ways, and for offering you a new life.

Stepping Out: Is Jesus calling you out of your tree? This week, move from being a spectator to a participant. Also, look for ways repay people above and beyond what you owe them.

Obliging

"But so that we may not offend them, go to the lake and throw out your line. Take the first fish you catch; open its mouth and you will find a four-drachma coin. Take it and give it to them for my tax and yours."
—Matthew 17:27 (Mt 17:24–27)

After ministering to the whole region of Galilee, Jesus and His disciples arrived back in Capernaum, perhaps for a time of rest by the lake. On his way into the house where they were staying, Peter was stopped by some tax collectors who wanted to know if Jesus was in the habit of paying the required temple tax. Peter instinctively answered, "Yes, He does."

Once Peter returned to the house, Jesus broached the subject before Peter had a chance to. Jesus asked if kings collected taxes from their sons or from others. "Others," Peter replied. Referring to Himself, Jesus explained that "sons are exempt" from the king's taxation. He then instructed Peter to go and collect the required tax in a most unusual way. Jesus creatively paid off potential troublemakers, leaving neither Roman nor Jew with grounds for taking offense. The tax collectors were none the wiser about the fishy source of revenue.

A famous saying today is "Nothing is certain except death and taxes." Christians cannot avoid paying taxes, but we are certainly exempt from final death. As comical as the thought of pulling a coin from the mouth of a fish may be, the implications of this verse are profound.

First, we should not ignore Jesus' goal. He was concerned about not offending others, even the dreaded tax collectors. Jesus didn't want His status to attract undue attention or cause friction, and neither should we.

Second, Jesus wanted Peter to acquire the money they needed in a humble and honest way. Jesus instructed Peter to do what he already knew how to do: fish. Obviously, this applies to us as well.

Third, because the money Peter found was more than enough, he paid two fees, not keeping the surplus for himself. This lesson of generosity, even in the context of obligation, should be observed. Jesus is our example for behavior. Essentially, He is showing us how good citizenship on earth is practice for good citizenship in heaven.

Stepping In: Read Acts 16:3-5; Romans 12:16, 13:1-2, 14:19; and Ephesians 4:1–3. What do these verses say about striving for harmonious living, and why it is important? What is your current attitude about obligations to your church and government? Thank Jesus for modeling the best way to live. Pray for the strength to oblige.

Stepping Out: This week, go out of your way to be graciously obliging to the requirements of this earthy existence. Remember, according to 2 Corinthians 9:6–9, God loves a cheerful giver, even when you are only giving what you owe.

Arrested

"Who are you, Lord?" Saul asked. "I am Jesus, whom you are persecuting." He replied. "Now get up and go into the city, and you will be told what you must do."

—Acts 9:5–6 (Acts 9:1–19)

Saul, an industrious Jewish tentmaker from the northern Galilean town of Tarsus, spent considerable time in Jerusalem, a hub of commerce and his religion's epicenter. Saul enjoyed the liberties his Roman citizenship afforded him, and soon became a well-respected and successful businessman. He was also a zealous Pharisee and one of Christianity's more aggressive opponents. He violently persecuted Jesus' followers after Jesus' death. He sought to hunt down, arrest, and even kill those who promoted the new faith.

He was on this Christian manhunt when the conversation in today's passage occurred. Saul had been on his way to Damascus, and his progress was arrested by the blinding light and audible voice of the glorified Jesus. Falling to the ground in fear, Saul asked his question. He was led away and told to wait for instructions. For three days, his life was arrested. He was unable to see, forced to look inward at the person he had become. In those dark and lonesome hours, Jesus worked on Saul's heart, beginning the conversion to come.

In our hurried and harried existences, we are frustrated by interruptions to our plans. Sometimes, however, as was the case with Saul of Tarsus, these interruptions are meant to slow us down enough to allow us time to reflect on the meaning or futility of our lives. Not all calamities are caused by Jesus to teach us necessary life lessons, but many times that does wind up being the end result. In other words, even if Jesus did not bring about the cessation of activity, He can and often does use it to His advantage.

In those moments of arrested progress, we are given the opportunity to seek the Lord's guidance, inquiring what He wants from us and for us. It is not uncommon for Jesus to have some questions of His own He would like us to consider. He may want to know why we are avoiding, ignoring, rebelling against, denying, opposing, or rejecting Him. He may want us to examine our beliefs, motives, and attitudes. When we humbly and honestly confess our desperate need for Him, He brings about restoration—of spiritual sight and of our relationship with Him. When we obey His commands, we are no longer bound by fear and isolation. Instead of being arrested, we become truly free.

Stepping In: Read Isaiah 61:1; Ezekiel 3:22–27; and Luke 10:3. After rereading Acts 9:1–6, rewrite and ponder Jesus' question in verse 4. Replace Saul's name with yours. Replace "persecute" with an appropriate verb. Pray for Jesus to release you from your spiritual shackles, so you can be free to follow Him.

Stepping Out: This week, do the thing you know Jesus is asking you to do. Follow His instructions.

Worthy

"Are not two sparrows sold for a penny? Yet not one of them will fall to the ground apart from the will of your Father. And even the very hairs on your head are numbered. So don't be afraid; you are worth more than many sparrows."

—Matthew 10:29–31 (Mt 10:1–31)

Before sending His apostles into the mission fields of Israel, Jesus gave His men some much-needed advice and instruction. He wanted His newly appointed apostles to be well-aware of the power they possessed to minister and heal, so they would use it appropriately. He also wanted them to be prepared for the hardships they would face. Jesus advised them that both He and the Father would attend to every detail of their mission. Therefore, there was nothing to fear. Jesus infused His men with a deep sense of value, worth, and safety. He needed them to go out in confidence, assured that they were not going alone—that the very Person who made them and knew each of them intimately would be right there with them.

Among the Jews, sparrows were the smallest of the animals sacrificed at the temple. Jesus used this example to illustrate how seemingly worthless creatures were indeed valuable in God's sight. Not only were sparrows purposefully made by God, but the sacrificial atonement they provided for sin was priceless. Ordinary Jews could not approach the holiness of God in their shameful state. Only the blood of an innocent animal could cover their unworthiness.

Today, Christians are made pure by Jesus' blood. We are blameless in God's sight and may approach Him with confidence. We are worthy new creations and no longer live in fear of condemnation. Because of this, it should be our joy to proclaim the hope and freedom we have in Christ to all whom the Spirit puts in our path. We are valued by our heavenly Father. This knowledge gives us strength to endure even the painful and difficult sacrifices we make for His kingdom. Not one tear will be shed without His notice and concern.

Stepping In: Read 1 Samuel 14:45; Acts 27:34; and Romans 8:1. After rereading today's verse, reflect on it using the Own It method (See appendix). Thank God for the way He knows you and loves you so well. Pray that He will help you overcome any feelings of doubt or worthlessness you may have.

Stepping Out: This week, considering today's verse, view others as possessors of intrinsic value. Remind yourself that no one, regardless of how they look or behave, is any less valuable than anyone else—including you.

Gushing

"Whoever believes in me, as the Scripture has said, streams of living water will flow from within him."

—John 7:38 (Jn 7:14–44)

Three times a year, Jewish men who lived within a reasonable distance from, and were physically able to travel, made their way to Jerusalem for significant feasts. As the men of Capernaum readied themselves to make the pilgrimage south for the Feast of Tabernacles, Jesus' brothers implored Him to do the same. But for the time being, Jesus was neither interested in making a public spectacle of His powers, nor willing to attract the attention of His persecutors there. To avoid detection, He waited until midway through the festival before quietly slipping into the city.

Once in the temple, Jesus began to teach. He stated that His teaching was from the Father, and that He, unlike the religious leaders, sought only to honor God and not Himself. The crowd was amazed at His wisdom and scriptural knowledge. Some questioned if He could be the Messiah. Others accused Him of being a deceiver. Most could not envision Him as more than the carpenter's son from Galilee. Jesus assured them that they did not know who He was or where He was from.

During the seven days of the feast, the celebrants commemorated God's provision of water and manna during their time of wandering in the wilderness. They poured out a cup of water gathered from the Pool of Siloam, thought of as the pool of salvation, on the altar each day. On the eighth day, they rested and worshipped in the temple all day. Jesus then proclaimed that He was the source of all life-giving water. He explained that all who would take and drink of it would gush with spiritual and eternal life.

Jesus always has an answer for our questions. As He did with the Jews—taking their knowledge of God and the scripture to the next level—He also does for us today. He knows the barriers that keep us from fully trusting Him, and He knocks each of them down with the power of His mighty Word.

Today's Christians can approach the challenges of life, including coming to know who this man Jesus is, by reading His complete story in the Bible. By comparing the Old and New Testaments, Christians can discover God's plan for redemption. They can learn about our Savior's humanity and holiness, His merciful and just nature, and how patient, loving, and generous He is. When we learn that He gave up everything to save us, and that He offers us abundant life freely, we ought to be gushing over with joy and gratitude.

However, we must drink in His Word and trust in His power to save to receive His endless supply of quenching water. Christians today know that to partake of the living Water is to be eternally satisfied, having God's indwelling Holy Spirit forever flowing through us. What a blessing it is to believe in Jesus!

Stepping In: Read Exodus 23:16–17; Deuteronomy 31:10–13; Isaiah 12:1-6, 58:11, Joel 2:21-28; and John 3:10-15, 4:10-14. Are streams of living water gushing in your life? Who are you blessing with this quenching refreshment? Pray for your heart to soften to the Spirit's leading, and that evidence of God within you overflows to the world around you.

Stepping Out: This week, let random acts of love and compassion flow freely from you to everyone.

Untroubled

"And surely I am with you always, to the very end of the age."
—Matthew 28:20 (Mt 28:1–20)

Jesus' disciples experienced extreme emotional distress during the time of His arrest and crucifixion. One of them didn't make it out alive. After Judas Iscariot betrayed Jesus in the garden of Gethsemane, he was overcome by guilt and remorse. A failed attempt to return the bribe he had received from the chief priests and elders led to him hanging himself in despair.

The other disciples—even Peter, who had vowed unwavering devotion to Jesus—scattered when their Master was bound and hauled off to face the Sanhedrin. Fear of reprisal kept them from venturing too close as Jesus was tried, beaten, and hung on a cross to die. Earthquakes and unearthly darkness drove the disciples (and likely others) into hiding. Because they had not stayed with Jesus through His ordeal, the disciples remained unaware of Jesus' resurrection until the women who had kept vigil came to tell them. They did not learn for some time that they had been implicated in a cover-up story to explain Jesus' missing corpse.

When they got the news that Jesus was alive and requesting their presence, however, they were quick to respond. They went to Galilee, as they had been instructed, and met a very much alive Jesus. His men were overwhelmed and relieved, though some were also skeptical. The skepticism did not stop Jesus from commissioning His apostles to spread His gospel to all the peoples of the world. He sent them off with powerful words of encouragement. Assured of their Master's continued spiritual presence, they went forth untroubled.

There is no less power in Jesus' words now then there was at the time they were spoken. What an amazingly beautiful and comforting fact this is for all who believe. Everywhere His followers go, Jesus is there. He promises to be *with* us and *in* us—forever! Even in a chaotic and uncertain world, Christians can live untroubled lives. Jesus will guide, help, and protect all who obey His command. Those who have embraced the Great Commission as their own can do so with confidence. The command to "go and make disciples of all nations" is for every Christian throughout time (Mt 18:19). Jesus promises that those He calls, He will also equip. He reminds us that the power of the resurrection is *in* us. He assures us that we are never alone. Simply put, we have no excuse for not doing the work we have been called to do for our Savior. We need only step out in faith and obedience, and He will lead the way.

Stepping In: Read Deuteronomy 31:6; 1 Kings 8:57–58; Matthew 18:19–20; Romans 8:11, 30; Ephesians 1:18-21; and Hebrews 13:20–21. Praise God for these blessed assurances. Pray for strength and courage to carry His message to the world, and for the clear guidance to do so. Ask Him to trade your obedience for an untroubled heart.

Stepping Out: Whatever you do this week, do it knowing that Jesus is *with* you and *in* you.

High-Spirited

"I tell you," he replied, "if they keep quiet, the stones will cry out."
—Luke 19:40 (Lk 19:28–44)

As Jesus entered Jerusalem on His way toward betrayal, arrest, trial, torture, and death on the cross, He was greeted by an exuberant crowd. The people of the city lined the streets, laying their cloaks on the road and waving palm branches, shouting praises to their king. Many had witnessed Jesus' miraculous signs. Some had been personally healed by Him. Even the religious leaders who were plotting to kill Him gathered to see the grand procession. These self-righteous men were not enthusiastic about the high-spirited display they witnessed, and told Jesus to rebuke His followers for causing a public disturbance. Jesus' reply to His adversaries was, for them, just another example of His blasphemous arrogance. They were unaware of how, in just a few days, Jesus' death would cause nature to respond with more than mere cries.

There is nothing new about cheering masses enthusiastically welcoming an idolized figure. In the case of Jesus, it is an entirely appropriate response, reflecting the overwhelming gratitude and respect we have for our Lord and Savior. These days, however, in all but a minority of charismatic churches, we are more likely to experience a joyful noise at a sporting event or rock concert than we are at church. Somewhere along the line, high-spirited, outward expressions of worship have become uncouth or passé, at least compared to the practices of the early church.

Today's verse is a reminder that unrestrained praise is the natural response to being in the presence of the Lord. It is a bit sad to think that of all of God's creations, human beings—the ones He made in His own image—are the ones who purposefully stifle our praise of Him. Though this verse is not meant to be taken literally, it is a clear allusion to how even the silent voices of nature scream, "Hosanna—great are you, Lord!"

Stepping In: Read Psalm 19:1-4, 66:4; Habakkuk 2:11; Romans 8:18–21; and Revelation 5:13–14. How do these verses encourage and help you to understand the nature of worship? Pray for inspiration to pour out your praise to our worthy God in a high-spirited display of adoration and gratitude.

Stepping Out: This week, with a small group or some friends, listen to "Great Are You Lord," (the All Sons and Daughters or Casting Crowns version). Sing it out, raise your hands, fall down and worship—whatever the Spirit leads you to do in response to the Lord's greatness. Then practice this freedom at church.

May 7
Deferential

"I tell you the truth, it will be more bearable for Sodom and Gomorrah
on the day of judgment than for that town."
—Matthew 10:15 (Mt 10:1–16)

After two years spent teaching and training His disciples, Jesus prepared to send them out into the mission field to minister to the physical and spiritual needs of the "lost sheep of Israel." In His commissioning speech, Jesus told the disciples that they should have nothing to do with those who rejected them or their message. The comparison He made to the destroyed cities of Sodom and Gomorrah emphasize the seriousness of such a refusal.

The apostles, having been raised in good Jewish homes, would have heard the lore of these two evil places, and no doubt thought the cities deserving of their punishment. But to say that anyone would be worse off than these famously corrupt towns, simply for not offering hospitality or a listening ear, may have seemed a bit harsh.

However, Jesus was not warning His men about people who were merely stubborn or rude. He was referring to those who would refuse to accept the good news because of spiritual blindness ---those whose hearts were hardened against God's truth. This group would suffer dire consequence because of their failure to accept the gospel and its messengers. Indeed, their fate would be worse than anything anyone had heard of or could imagine: an eternity apart from God.

There are still many ungodly places on this planet. As the world's population explodes, the number of people who choose a spiritual path other than Christianity rises right along with it. To the optimistic Christian, this can mean that there are bountiful fields in which to harvest new believers. To perhaps the more realistic, this means that there may be more places where darkness reigns than we can reach. Unfortunately, with the naked eye, it is impossible to know which is true.

That is where the Holy Spirit comes in. The more we seek spiritual discernment, the more able we are to determine where God is leading us and whom He would like us to reach out to. The more deferential a perspective we have on God's sovereignty, the fewer dead-end paths we are likely to take. Until Jesus returns, Christians are to shine light into the dark places of our world, beginning with the hearts and minds of those who don't yet know about Jesus' saving grace. In these places, a little light goes a long way; its warmth and illumination are attractive, drawing people in. Sadly, though, in the places where Satan has a stronghold, darkness is preferred. Faulty beliefs shadow minds against love's penetrating rays. There, Satan and his devotees will perish.

Jesus tells us to avoid such places. We must defer to His omniscient judgment by allowing the Spirit to lead us away from fruitless fields.

Stepping In: Read Genesis 19. Is it hard to imagine such despicable wickedness? Now, read the newspaper and you will find more of the same—and that is only what is getting printed. Pray earnestly for the salvation of souls caught in dark despair all around the world.

Stepping Out: This week, demonstrate a deferential attitude toward God's plan for judgment by obeying His command to speak truth in love. Reach those you can, and leave those you can't to God.

Perceiving

"You are not far from the kingdom of God."
—Mark 12:34 (Mk 11:1–11, 27–33; 12:28–34)

The teachers of the Law started a debate with Jesus about which of God's commandments He considered to be the greatest. They hoped to corner Jesus into blasphemy under Jewish law. After Jesus had quoted the Shema – a prayer which commands Israel to love God, He added a second commandment requiring one to love one's neighbor as oneself. One brave and perceptive man responded, praising Jesus for the correctness of His answer and agreeing that indeed love is far better than sacrifice in the eyes of God. Jesus affirmed that this man was close to the kingdom of God, angering His opponents further.

We live in a complicated world and a confusing time. Even with Jesus as our anchor, we are often tossed about by the storms of this life. At times our faith is rock solid, and at other times we feel like we could easily be blown off course by the next strong wind of adversity. For those who perceive Christianity as a religion rather than a relationship, staying on a positive track can seem like walking a gauntlet of rules and requirements.

Jesus never wanted us to live that way. He came to offer us a new way, free from the bondage of man-made laws. True Christianity is about having a love relationship with our Savior and Friend. Out of the overflow of adoration for Jesus comes a natural outpouring of affection for others. That is the way God designed it to be. This is why Jesus often quoted scripture and followed it up with His new covenant addendums. It is about turning faith into action, bringing the kingdom of heaven to the world around us. Those who understand can indeed perceive the closeness of God's kingdom.

Stepping In: Read Exodus 19:5–6; Deuteronomy 6:4–5; Matthew 3:1-2, 13:10-14; and Colossians 1:3–14. How do these verses help you understand who perceives the nearness the kingdom of God and who does not? Praise Jesus, who chose you to be one who understands His truth and gave you a heart to share it.

Stepping Out: This week, invite someone into a conversation about the kingdom of God. Lovingly and humbly share your testimony of hope in Christ.

Empathetic

"I have compassion for these people; they have already been with me for three days and have nothing to eat. I do not want to send them away hungry, or they may collapse on the way."

—Matthew 15:32 (Mt 15:29–39)

After returning from the towns of Tyre and Sidon on the Mediterranean Sea, Jesus climbed up a large hill near the Sea of Galilee, and sat down to teach and heal. For days, people brought Him their sick, lame, blind, and mute to be made well by His healing touch and word. These people, many of whom struggled merely to subsist, were worn down by the religious demands placed on them as well as the oppressed political climate in which they lived. Full of compassion, Jesus sought to meet as many needs as time allowed.

With nightfall approaching on the third day of this massive gathering, Jesus became concerned about the people's need for physical nourishment. In today's verse, His practical and empathetic nature was again revealed. Though they had experienced Jesus' miraculous abilities to feed more than five thousand with a boy's small lunch, His disciples questioned where they could find enough bread for a similarly large group. Jesus asked His men how much bread they had. They told Him, "Seven (loaves) and a few small fish." Recognizing their Lord's merciful Spirit, and remembering His supernatural powers, the disciples were quick to bring Him their paltry resources. These were soon multiplied beyond comprehension. With pride and joy, the disciples passed out ample baskets of food to the awestruck crowd. That day, many bodies, minds, and spirits were rejuvenated.

Jesus' mission is our mission today. We continue His work of meeting the physical and spiritual needs of the sick and hungry among us. Following in the footsteps of the Twelve, Christians today are obliged to search out the lost, marginalized, and desperate, offering them love, hope, and sustenance. To do this, we must do more than silently sympathize. As Jesus' compassion led to tangible action, so must our empathy spur us to active response.

As modern-day disciples, we must also learn the lesson of trusting Jesus to provide. Jesus looked to His Father in thankful expectation; we must do the same. This takes awareness and intentionality on our part, seeing people as Jesus sees them. Instead of seeing an inconvenience, see an opportunity. Instead of making an excuse, make an effort. Instead of turning to avoid an uncomfortable situation, step toward it in faith. Each time you venture out of your house, drape the servant's towel over your arm. Look to the Father, pray in the Spirit, and walk beside Jesus in service.

Stepping In: Read Mark 14:7; John 13:1-5, 21:17-18; and 1 Peter 4:10. How closely do you follow Jesus' example to love and serve others? Is the Spirit whispering to your heart to consider taking a next step? Pray for an empathetic heart, the desire to help others, and a willingness to act.

Stepping Out: With eyes that see all people as children of God, and a heart filled with empathy for the hurting, look for and respond to a specific need in your community. Remember, actions speak louder than words, especially when they are motivated by love!

May 10
Awakened

"Wake up! Strengthen what remains and is about to die, for I have not found your deeds complete in the sight of God."
—Revelation 3:2 (Rv 3:1–6)

In the vision that John received from God while imprisoned on the Greek island of Patmos, Jesus commissioned His faithful apostle to be the first recipient of God's end-times revelation. To begin, Jesus told John to write to the seven churches in Asia Minor, conveying His words of encouragement and warning so they could be prepared for what was to take place. In His fifth address, to the church in Sardis, Jesus had no comforting salutations to give. Instead, He called the church leaders out on their false reputation for being a vibrant, Spirit-filled church. As the One who holds together all churches in His name, and the only One capable of distributing the Spirit of God and telling it where it should go, Jesus told the leaders in Sardis that their church was nearly dead. Then Jesus issued a serious warning. Not mincing any words, He said that their deeds were empty gestures, meant only for show and to gain approval from men. As beautiful and lavish as the church looked, in God's eyes it resembled a rotting corpse. The time for revival had come; the church at Sardis had to awaken from its spiritual coma or be pronounced dead.

It would be easy to misinterpret Jesus' warning. At first glance, it appears that the church leaders were at risk of losing their salvation unless they woke up and quit pretending to practice vibrant faith. Yet this is not the case. There are two factors at play in this scenario: spiritual apathy and spiritual distraction. Both are sadly all too common in our world today.

As in Sardis, many modern Christians live with an abundance of wealth. Money and comforts are not bad in and of themselves, but they can easily lead to a false sense of security and the illusion of self-sufficiency. With all our needs met, we are lulled into complacency, which, if left unchecked, leads to apathy. Unless we exercise the heart muscle of our faith, we lose it.

Similarly, in our me-centric lives, we are easily distracted by all the things we fill our time with: family, work, agendas, entertainment, computers, cell phones, even volunteer and church activities. Rarely do we slow down to listen to the Spirit or to seek God's will for us.

So, like the Sardisians, Christians today must hear Jesus' wake-up call. We must consciously invite the Spirit to move from our heads to our hearts, thus allowing an awakened Spirit to direct our thoughts and actions.

Stepping In: Read Proverbs 11:28, 28:11; Matthew 6:24, 19:21-26; Luke 8:14; Romans 15:13; Galatians 5:22–25; and 1 Timothy 6:10. How do these verses awaken your Spirit to pursue God's will rather than self-satisfaction? Pray for strength to adjust your thoughts and actions to accommodate the Spirit's leadings.

Stepping Out: Each day this week, awaken an hour early so that you can align your day with God's will. Allow the Holy Spirit to lead your prayers and illuminate the scripture passages He has for you that day.

Vigilant

"At that time the kingdom of heaven will be like ten virgins who took
their lamps and went out to meet the bridegroom."
—Matthew 25:1 (Mt 24:1–3; 25:1–13)

Speaking to His disciples during a private teaching on the Mount of Olives outside of Jerusalem, Jesus explained many things about near and distant future events. Jesus prepared His disciples for the difficulties ahead—including His imminent death. He reiterated that the time of His return and the consequent unfolding of the time of judgment were unknown even to Him. Because of this fact, He implored His men to remain faithful and keep watch for signs of the "end of the age."

Speaking in parables, Jesus first told them about a faithful and wise servant and one who was wicked and foolish. Then Jesus told a parable about ten virgin bridesmaids, awaiting the groom's arrival. Five of these girls were prepared with oil for their lamps and trimmed wicks; they stayed alert and waited vigilantly. The other five girls were lazy and did not take the things they needed to be helpful to the bride. In their impatience, they fell asleep and missed the groom's announcement. In a panic, they begged the wise virgins for some oil, but were denied. While they were shopping for more supplies, the door to the banquet was shut. They had missed the party and were left out in the cold.

The nuance of this parable is often lost on the modern reader. It is easy to pick up the meaning of this passage—it is wise to be prepared for Jesus' return—but we can miss the relevance of the virgin bridesmaids. In biblical Jewish culture, the consummation of a marriage took place in the evening. While the bride awaited her groom in a house or tent, her young friends waited outside with lamps lit, ready to lead him to his new wife.

In the context of Christianity, the implications are vast. Jesus is the groom, and the bride is His church, the worldwide body of believers. The virgin bridesmaids, pure and blameless souls, are all who will be ready to respond when He returns. That's us!

As our Lord has told us time and again, He will return when we least expect it. He not only wants us to be prepared ourselves for that day, but He expects us to assist the body of Christ—His bride the church—to be in a place of alert anticipation. It is our job to continue the vigilant and hope-filled night watch, and to let the unprepared know about the wedding they might miss.

Stepping In: Read Matthew 26:40; Luke 12:35–38; 1 Thessalonians 5:4–6; and Revelation 4:5, 19:7–8, and 21:2. How do these verses help you to understand your role in preparing yourself and others for Jesus' return? How vigilant are you in keeping watch? Pray for clarity on how you can assist the body of Christ in this task.

Stepping Out: This week, talk with other Christians about specific ways you all are preparing for Jesus' return. Share ideas and try something new.

May 12
Invited

"At the time of the banquet he sent his servant to tell those who had
been invited, 'Come, for everything is now ready.'"
—Luke 14:17 (Lk 14:1–24)

During the final year of Jesus' public ministry, the number of his followers began to drop off, while the number of His opponents rose. This was partly due to the increasing bluntness with which Jesus spoke of the depravity of human nature, and the hypocrisy of those claiming to represent God. Another reason people started to turn away from the gospel was that it was becoming clear that Jesus was not the new king of Israel they had hoped He would be—not if He was slated to die a martyr's death, that is.

Though some were losing interest in Jesus, the Pharisees still felt it wise to keep a close watch on Him. One of the Pharisees invited Jesus to share a meal with him and several other Jewish leaders. One of them revealed his misinterpretation of Jesus' wedding feast parable by boasting of his joy at being one of the invited guests. Using a different parable about a great banquet, Jesus effectively refuted the notion that the Jewish leaders would automatically be included in God's glorious feast simply because of their bloodlines or religiosity. The message was clear enough: though the Jews had been the first to be invited into the kingdom of God, many would lose their position due to lack of true faith, selfish ambition, dishonesty, pride, and ignorance. In their place would be those who realized the value of such an invitation and accepted it humbly and without qualms.

Most of us are equally guilty of offering lame excuses for not appropriately responding to God's invitations over the course of our lives. As the Pharisees surely did, we tend to respond by further attempting to defend ourselves or indignantly denying fault. We think we can somehow hide our disingenuousness. We offer our reasons for not obeying God's requests and commands. Banking on God's forgiving nature, believers tend to push the boundaries of grace.

Today's verse speaks of a much weightier topic than correcting bad behavior. It pertains to the eternal consequence for refusing to accept Jesus' invitation for salvation. Many people alive today say that they believe in a god, and are therefore heaven-bound. As Christians, we know that Jesus is the only way to salvation. This parable exposes the deadly downfall of the Pharisees and everyone else who follows in their footsteps. God wants a full banquet table. Christians must invite all the guests we can.

Stepping In: Read Hosea 2:23; Luke 13:29–30; John 1:11-13, 14:6 Romans 15:11; 2 Peter 3:9; and Revelation 19:9. Do you know people who do not know about heaven, or who wrongly believe that they will be going there? Pray for opportunities to share the wonderful, life-saving news with them that Jesus is the way, the truth, and the life—forever.

Stepping Out: This week, invite someone you suspect to be unsaved into a conversation about heaven. Graciously speak truth into their life, ask questions, and shine the Spirit's light on false theologies. Invite them to church, and agree to pick them up and take them yourself.

Able

> "The harvest is plentiful but the workers are few."
> —Matthew 9:37 (Mt 9:35–10:1)

With His ministry hitting stride, Jesus and His disciples made their way through the towns and villages around the Sea of Galilee, preaching the good news of the coming kingdom of God and healing the diseased. Before sending the Twelve alone into the missionary field, where they would gain firsthand experience ministering in His name, Jesus summarized the enormity of their task. In agricultural terminology, Jesus compared kingdom work to the collection of a bountiful crop. Soon the disciples would have the opportunity to touch the lives of countless people in need of truth and healing—far too many for so few to adequately reach. Jesus didn't tell His disciples this to discourage them. His words were meant to inspire His men to go out and gather additional workers for the gospel cause. Considering the workload set before them, such recruitment would be to their benefit. Moreover, Jesus needed them to know that it would His power, not their own, that would enable them to carry out their heavenly task.

The harvest work of Christians is still a seemingly endless task, yet perhaps more daunting. Not only are there far more people on the planet today, but the crop is also more diverse than it once was. The ratio of workers to workload remains dismally low. Though those of us who call ourselves Christians make up the largest religious group worldwide at 31.5 percent of all peoples who claim a religious affiliation, according to a 2010 Pew research poll, we may not want to toot our horns just yet. The other 68.5 percent of the population claims allegiance to a faith other than Christianity.

The harvest field is indeed remarkably vast. As Jesus did with His first-century disciples, He also does for us: by His Spirit He makes the impossible possible. He makes those who feel inadequate to the task more than able—He makes them victorious.

Stepping In: Read Joel 3:12–13; Ephesians 3:20–21; and Revelation 14:14–16. Take some time to consider the two types of harvests mentioned in scripture. Keep in mind that, until Jesus returns, we are the workers He is sending into the fields. Pray that God gives you a heart for the lost and for opportunities to share His good news with someone. Thank Him for the confidence that, by His strength, you are able to do more than you can imagine.

Stepping Out: This week, use your God-given abilities to work for His kingdom. Put your knowledge and skills to work in the missionary fields of life—work, home, school, and community. Join the workforce and encourage others to do the same.

May 14
Called

> "Come," he said.
> —Matthew 14:29 (Mt 14:22–36)

Entering His third year of ministry, Jesus was at the height of His popularity, partly because He consistently met the needs of the people with bold acts of love and mercy. One of these displays was the miraculous feeding of five thousand near the northern shore of the Sea of Galilee. After the satisfied multitude had been sent back to their homes, the exhausted disciples set off by boat to their own home port of Capernaum. As they rowed into the night, the disciples were unaware they were heading into a storm.

Jesus had not gone with His men; He had retreated up a nearby mountain for a time of solitude and prayer. As morning approached, Jesus set out to join the disciples. Walking on the water into the violent squall that had picked up, Jesus came upon the wave-tossed boat and its terrified crew. The disciples saw Jesus standing on the turbulent waters and thought He was a ghost. They cried out in mortal fear.

Jesus calmed them (as well as the storm) with His reassuring words and presence. He then invited a skeptical Peter to join Him outside the boat with one word: "Come." Peter, the one on whom Jesus' church would be built, made the choice to trust His Master and step out in faith. However, the reality of his situation hit him, and he started to sink. When his eyes were fixed on Jesus, he did the impossible. When his focus went to the storm around him, he faltered.

Today, each believer must decide how she or he will respond to this same simple command. From the time Jesus first calls any of His followers, there is a crucial choice that must be made: to trust and obey, or to refuse His invitation. Devotion to Jesus means sacrifices of time, attention, resources, emotional energies, and one's very heart. This may seem like an exorbitant price to pay to be a follower of Jesus. But, as any of us who have taken that step of faith know, it is well worth it.

Each of us has a unique approach to stepping out of the boat when called by our Lord. Some are like Peter, leaping out without thinking. When reality hits, their focus goes from Jesus to their circumstances, causing a crisis of faith. Others take a more tentative approach, but once they commit, they are all in. Jesus can and does use all types. What He wants us to learn from today's passage is that when He invites us to join Him, He will supply all we need to succeed—*if* we keep our focus on Him.

Let us learn from Peter's mistake. Trust what you know in your heart and not what your eyes are telling you. When called, step out in faith and follow Jesus.

Stepping In: Read Matthew 16:24–25; Romans 14:7–8; 1 Corinthians 6:19–20; and 2 Corinthians 4:17. Using the Envision It method, reflect on the Matthew 14 passage. How would you have responded if you were Peter? How would you respond if it were you in that boat? Pray that your commitment to Jesus is evident in your actions.

Stepping Out: This week, respond to Jesus when you are called. With your small group or with some friends, listen to "Oceans," by Hillsong United. Discuss the ways Jesus is calling each of you out upon the waters, and what you plan to do in response.

May 15

Assertive

"I tell you, though he will not get up and give the bread because he is
his friend, yet because of the man's boldness he will get up and give
him as much as he needs."

—Luke 11:8 (Lk 11:1–13)

Sometime after visiting with His friends Mary and Martha in Bethany, Jesus and His disciples prepared to go into Jerusalem to continue their work. As was His custom, Jesus spent time alone with His Father, praying and seeking guidance. When He had rejoined His men, the disciples asked Jesus to teach them to pray. They were not asking Him about the mechanics of praying necessarily—the disciples were good Jewish men who had grown up praying to God. What they were asking for was how to pray in the personal and intimate way Jesus did.

Because they asked, Jesus taught them how to pray directly to their Father in heaven, using a concise mix of praise and petition to seek God's will and favor. He equated this lesson to a man who called on his friend late at night for some bread. Like a desperately hungry person, God's friends seek His provision. In this way, Jesus taught His men to seek God's will boldly, for those who ask insistently shall receive.

Christians live in the glorious truth that we can confidently appeal to our loving, heavenly Father in our times of spiritual need, regardless of the hour. God wants to give to us more than we can ask for or imagine. This is possible when we seek His will above all, engaging the Spirit that lives in us.

Jesus knew His disciples were on the right track when they asked Him to teach them to pray. He showed them and us how to draw nearer to God by addressing Him respectfully and personally. Jesus made it clear that no matter what time of the day or night, a true seeker should never shy away from pursuing the good things that God has for His friends. In the case of those praying in the Holy Spirit, pleading for the nourishing Word of God, assertiveness is highly rewarded. God offers daily bread and so much more to those who ask Him.

Stepping In: Read Proverbs 30:7–8; Isaiah 55:1–2; Matthew 6:9–13; Ephesians 3:20-21; and James 4:2–3. What truths about prayer and petition is the Spirit teaching you? Pray that God reveal and remove any faulty motives you bring into your prayer life, so that you can approach God humbly and with confident assertiveness.

Stepping Out: This week, look for opportunities to be on both sides of the door. Be assertive in your approach to seeking God's will and wisdom, *and* be willing to serve those who bravely ask you for help.

Faith-Filled

"I tell you the truth, I have not found anyone in Israel with such great faith."
—Matthew 8:10 (Mt 8:5–13)

In the town of Capernaum, near where Jesus had issued the Sermon on the Mount, a large crowd of followers surrounded Jesus and His disciples, hoping to receive further teaching and healing. A Roman centurion was among those who heard the gospel message and believed. He understood that, beyond any human authority he himself might possess, Jesus had the ultimate authority to heal and to save. Therefore, the centurion humbled himself in public, professing His faith in a man many still did not believe in, to try to save the life of a mere servant. So hopeful and faith-filled was this man that he willingly forfeited his pride to call on the healing power of Jesus. This was an extraordinary act of faith from a very unlikely person.

A modern example of this would be if the owner of a multinational chemical company decided to seek the help of a local doctor who was known to have successfully treated poisoned citizens, in order to save the life of one of the factory's workers. The truth is, we do not see this sort of thing happening very often. Too much is at stake for both parties. Plus, most people do not have the kind of faith needed to disregard the barriers and potential repercussions and see their request through. Even in so-called religious arenas, it is difficult to find someone who has such an unwavering faith—someone who completely trusts in the power and authority of the Word of Jesus, especially under the pressure of scrutiny. Yet faith-filled people like the centurion are still making the biggest impact in our jaded world. They are a light that shines hope into the darkness of disillusionment.

Stepping In: Read and meditate on Matthew 17:20 and Hebrews 11:1–3. In what areas of your life do you lack faith? Pray that God will increase your confidence in His authority and abilities. Pray that you will trust Jesus in all circumstances. Ask the Spirit to fill you to overflowing with love, hope, and faith (Romans 15:13).

Stepping Out: This week, look for opportunities to be an example of one living a faith-filled life. Commit to doing whatever it takes to save the life of a friend, in the name of Jesus.

Yearning

He who testifies to these things says, "Yes, I am coming soon." Amen.
Come, Lord Jesus.

—Revelation 22:20 (Revelation 22:1–21)

At the end of the fantastic spiritual odyssey the apostle John had been taken on, these words of Jesus would have come as a welcome testimony—not only because they were a definitive proclamation of Jesus' imminent return, but because they meant that the whole whirlwind adventure had not been merely the product of his own imagination.

The whole affair must have been overwhelming and disconcerting from the outset. Thinking that he would be relegated to a lonely existence of hard labor and isolation on the island of Patmos, John could not have known of the plans God had for him. Commissioned to write God's end-times revelation, he witnessed as justice was served to those who remained faithful, while the wicked were sent to their doom along with the dragon—Satan. An angel-guide showed John the final fulfillment of the prophecies: "the New Jerusalem coming down out of heaven." As the magnificence and beauty of the scene unfolded before his eyes, the terror of the apocalyptic drama he had just observed faded into a perfect peace. God's Word was trustworthy and true; His plan would come to fruition just as He had said it would, rendering every spiritual yearning satisfied. Jesus Himself testified to this fact.

Some translations of the Bible interpret the word "soon" in today's verse as "quickly." Though this doesn't make sense to those who perceive two thousand plus years as anything but "soon," it is possible that both definitions of Jesus' statement are true. For one thing, it is important to remember that God does not view time in the same way humans do. For God, "a day is a like a thousand years, and a thousand years like a day." (2 Peter 3:8). In other words, time is relative. God is not bound by our constructs of clock or calendar.

That said, "soon" might be tomorrow—or it might be in another millennium. On a more hopeful note, to say that Jesus will come "quickly" is certainly good news for those of us who are yearning for His return. Jesus promises believers that, when judgment comes, the end of suffering, pain, evil, hatred, corruption, deception, and uncertainty will be "quick." We will receive our new blemish-free bodies, sinless souls, and worry-free minds, and walk in the light of God's love and glory forever. This is something Christians greatly yearn for. Who can blame us?

However, the promise of Jesus' return does not thrill everyone. The thought of the wrath and judgment that must take place seems a harsh sentence to some. As yearners, we must lovingly warn people of the fact: Jesus is coming. Amen—may it be so.

Stepping In: Read Matthew 24; John 18:37; and Revelation 1:1–3, 7 and 22:7, 12, 20. Are you yearning for Jesus' return, or does this fact frighten or worry you? Why or why not? Pray that you can reach those who are perishing before that wonderful day arrives.

Stepping Out: Each day this week, proclaim Jesus as if it were the last day on earth. It just might be.

Smart

> "The kingdom of heaven is like treasure hidden in a field. When a man found it, he hid it again, and then in his joy went and sold all he had and bought that field."
>
> —Matthew 13:44 (Mt 13:24–44)

Because spiritual discernment was the key to unlocking the mystery of His teaching, Jesus chose to impart knowledge to His disciples using parables. In this way, Jesus challenged His devoted followers to ponder the deeper spiritual context of His words. To the undiscerning listener, His message would be received merely as common-sense advice.

In His teaching, Jesus used several parabolic comparisons beginning with the phrase, "The kingdom of heaven is like …" In today's verse, He equated the riches of heavenly knowledge to a hidden treasure. Banks were, at that time, nonexistent, and the practice of burying valuables for safekeeping was common. To the undiscerning, this parable could be interpreted as a tale of someone's lucky happenstance—a story of a person stumbling upon a "king's ransom" and quietly cashing in his life savings to purchase the treasure for himself. This would have been a smart elucidation, but it left several questions unanswered: what was this treasure and where could one find it, topping the list. The more spiritually knowing realized that God indeed planted His treasure, His truth, throughout the land, placing it where He knew people would find it. Only those who understood its value would give up everything to own it.

Today, anyone who so chooses can hold this priceless treasure simply by picking up a Bible. The words of heaven's eternal promise are the jewels in this trove of godly wisdom. Any smart person who discovers it will indeed want to return to it time and again. No worldly treasure can compare. Money, though something we need to survive, can't buy salvation, any more than it can buy health, lasting beauty, committed relationships, love, or happiness. Only faith in Jesus affords us all that and more.

Today's passage is an eloquent reminder, for those of us who have received this incredible gift, that we too happened upon our heavenly reward in someone else's field. We saw the riches another person had, and wanted them for ourselves. Realizing the value of what we had discovered, we gladly traded things we formerly esteemed of value for this unmatched fortune. However, when we went to pay for full access to this wondrous thing, the former owner gave it to us free of charge: a gift.

We can live a heaven-focused life only when we really understand that the knowledge of heaven is the reward worth risking everything for. And it's only when we truly live a heaven-focused life that we can be the Christ-like example He longs for us to be.

In the end, one question remains: "What will you do with your treasure?" Jesus hopes you will encourage others to make the same smart investment.

Stepping In: Read Proverbs 2:1–5; Isaiah 55:1–3; 2 Corinthians 4:7; Philippians 3:7–9; and Hebrews 12:1–2. Considering these scripture passages, reflect on today's passage using the Rewrite It method. (See appendix). Pray for an opportunity to share God's eternal promises with someone whose treasure consists only of earthly, perishable things.

Stepping Out: This week, contemplate the fact that someone else could discover their treasure in *your* field. Be ready with an example to share about how the gospel truth has enriched your life and given you hope.

May 19
Diligent

"Enter through the narrow gate. For wide is the gate and broad is the
road that leads to destruction, and many enter through it. But small is
the gate and narrow is the road that leads to life, and only a few find it."
—Matthew 7:13–14

Many cities in the ancient world were fortified, including some in the region of Galilee where Jesus spent much of His ministry. Protection against foreign invaders came from the strength of their walls and gates. The people listening to Jesus' teaching understood the necessity of secure points of entry. Jesus spoke practical and spiritual truths when He chose the imagery of gates. Access to a place of true security may not lie on the road most traveled, nor can one gain access through just any door.

Those who discerned Jesus' teaching understood that He was equating heaven to a walled city. No one wanted to be outside the locked gate in the city wall after sundown, or outside heaven's gate for eternity. The wise and diligent traveler took care to remember the way back to safety, and planned to avoid being swept off course by the crowds hurrying to the wide gate at dusk. The traveler knew that the foolish and untrustworthy masses congregated at the broad entrance, where unsavory behaviors and ill-intent could go unnoticed. The wise traveler stuck to the lightly worn path leading to the unnoticed gate—Jesus.

Gated communities still exist today. Unlike the fortified cities of old, these exclusive enclaves are always securely locked. Unauthorized guests are not allowed at any time of the day or night. To protect the inhabitants, a keeper at the gate ensures maximum security.

Jesus, who is the Gate to the kingdom of heaven, serves this same purpose. However, His gate is open to all who choose to enter. Exclusivity is not what Jesus had in mind when He made His analogy all those years ago. Like the traveler who ventured beyond the city wall, people today must occupy this planet such as it is: fallen, corrupt, dangerous. Yet Christians, though we live *in* the world, are not *of* the world. Consequently, followers of Jesus must not be like lemmings, mindlessly following the crowd off a cliff. We are not to conform to the patterns of the world, allowing our lives and destinies to be dictated by the dominant culture. Our path is the road less traveled, and our gate the narrow one.

So, in our time remaining on earth, we must choose a safe community in which to dwell, with safe neighbors and a trusted gatekeeper. A large proportion of the world's population will choose the path of least resistance and miss out on the destination Jesus wants for them. The diligent few will enjoy the life He has promised inside the security of His kingdom.

Stepping In: Do you avoid being viewed as narrow-minded to the extent that you do not diligently defend the word of God on *all* matters? Read and meditate on John 10:1–9, 14:6, 15:19, and 17:15; and Romans 12:2. Jesus is the "narrow gate," regardless of popular opinion. Pray that others find the right path … soon.

Stepping Out: This week, ask someone whom you have been shepherding (building a relationship with) what they think about today's passage. Start a spiritual dialogue. Let your example lead them to the right gate.

May 20
Unburdened

"They tie up heavy loads and put them on men's shoulders, but they
themselves are not willing to lift a finger to move them."
—Matthew 23:4 (Mt 22:41–23:4)

During the last year of Jesus' earthly ministry, various Jewish sects coordinated their efforts to bring His ministry and life to an end. During a time of teaching in the temple courts in Jerusalem, Jesus warned His listeners about the hypocrisy of the religious elite, telling them not to these follow "blind guides." Today's verse emphasizes the self-serving practices that the elite thought had gone unnoticed. Their religiosity was worthless, insincere, and strictly for show. These two-faced bullies were ruthless enforcers of rules they themselves did not abide. Instead of unburdening the people of their spiritual loads, the elite taught that these burdens were somehow the plight that people deserved. Jesus let them know otherwise.

Of the many objections nonreligious people today hold against Christianity, the hypocrisy of its members ranks near the top. While we look down our noses at the Pharisees, gloating over their ignorance and lack of true faith, it may be sobering to realize that many unbelievers view us in the same way.

The truth is, often our words and beliefs do not match up with our actions and attitudes. We too often fail to practice what we preach. Today's verse is a stark reminder for all who claim an affiliation with God. As people whose sin-burden has been lifted, we must help others become similarly unburdened. To do this, we must display genuine love for others through our words and actions, showing them that the precepts and commands of the Lord are good and not burdensome. In this way, we begin to deal with the hypocrisy epidemic.

The word "hypocrite" means an actor, deceiver, pretender, *or Pharisee*. Ouch! Who wants to be known by titles such as these? No one. A quick and easy way we can ensure against being lumped into this category is to make sure we pass the double-standard test. Simply put, if we examine our moral, ethical, and religious values and find that we do not personally adhere to all of them, we fail the test. We must remove the planks from our own eyes before unburdening our friends of the speck in theirs.

Stepping In: Read Matthew 7:3-5, 11:28-29; Acts 15:10–11; and Galatians 6:12–15. Are you or someone you know burdened with sin, guilt, shame, worry, anxiety, or confusion? Pray for God to replace this heavy burden with His light and easy yoke of hope and truth.

Stepping Out: This week, take your own double-standard test. If you fail it, fix it. Humbly work to correct hypocrisy in your life and your church. Help to unburden those who suffer under the weight of spiritual uncertainty and falsehood.

Of Service

> "Now that I, your Lord and Teacher, have washed your feet, you also should wash one another's feet."
>
> —John 13:14 (Jn 13:1–17)

In an upstairs room in a Jerusalem guesthouse, Jesus sat down for a final Passover meal with His disciples. After giving thanks to His heavenly Father, Jesus broke the bread and passed the wine, instructing His men to remember Him when they partook of these elements, honoring the sacrifice He was soon to make.

As the disciples dined and bantered about who might be the greatest in the kingdom, Jesus got up from the table, removed His outer clothing, and tied a towel around His waist. Fetching a basin of water, He approached the table and began to wash the disciples' feet. He knew that His disciples could not understand the meaning of this gesture. He informed them that, in time, they would comprehend its significance.

When it was Peter's turn, he flatly refused to allow his Master to perform a task that was normally relegated to the lowest household servant. Speaking of the spiritual implications of this humble act, Jesus told him, "Unless I wash you, you have no part with me" (Jn 13:8). Still not understanding, Peter offered his whole body for cleaning. Jesus explained that He was not offering Peter a bath, but a symbolic cleansing with deep spiritual meaning. Peter acquiesced.

When Jesus had finished, He returned to the table and prompted His men to consider what had just taken place. Adding to the confusion and embarrassment the disciples were already experiencing, Jesus issued the command that they should wash one another's feet. He smashed their notions of status and hierarchy. He made it clear that being of service to one another should be their new priority, even to the point of performing the lowliest tasks.

If you have ever participated in this ritual of foot washing, you can relate to the disciples' discomfort. Especially if you are washing or being washed by someone you don't know very well, this activity is awkward at best. The truth is, it is meant to be humbling, even if it is not quite as demeaning and objectionable now as it would have been to the first-century participants. But even today, getting up close and personal with someone's feet can feel inappropriately intimate. The feet of our modern-day counterparts are far cleaner and less worn than those in Jesus' day, but feet are often not so great to look at (or smell).

Jesus chose this act intentionally. By giving tender care to someone in this way, both parties work through their issues around pride and vulnerability. Jesus wants the barriers between His children to come down, especially between those doing work for His kingdom. As His disciples, we are to honor and serve one another in any and every way, building enduring bonds of trust and unity. This is the example Jesus set, and it is our privilege and duty to follow it.

Stepping In: Read Isaiah 52:7; Luke 22:14–30; Romans 12:9–13; Philippians 2:5–7; and 1 Peter 5:1–5. How are you currently being of service to fellow believers? How willing are you to do menial tasks for your brothers and sisters in Christ? Pray that God will bless you with a humble spirit and eyes to see the needs of others.

Stepping Out: This week, among your small group or some fellow Christians, perform this humble act of foot washing. It does not need to be reciprocated, but it is best if each person can have a shared experience. Afterward, talk about how it made you feel, and discuss Jesus' example.

Accommodating

> "Go to the village ahead of you, and at once you will find a donkey tied there, with her colt by her. Untie them and bring them to me. If anyone says anything to you, tell him that the Lord needs them, and he will send them right away."
>
> —Matthew 21:2–3 (Mt 21:1–11)

With His last long trek from Galilee to Jerusalem nearly over, Jesus paused to give His disciples some final instructions. He was tired from the journey, and certainly looking forward to riding the rest of the way. Jesus also had other reasons for sending two of His men to fetch the donkey and her colt. As was always the case, His requests provided His disciples and others an opportunity to trust Him and to respond in obedience. And, as was often also true, this occasion was yet another fulfillment of prophecy. Though many likely failed to recognize it at the time, the act of Jesus riding triumphantly into Jerusalem on the back of an unbroken colt signified the beginning of His foretold messianic sacrifice—the culmination being His work on the cross.

The disciples, not understanding the significance of their actions, accommodated their Master's wishes. The two who were dispatched found things just as Jesus had said. After laying their cloaks on one of the animals as a makeshift saddle, they placed Jesus on its back. He entered the city, and the people responded to Him as they would a king. They laid palm branches and cloaks on the road, and shouted a joyful welcome. Only later would they realize that Jesus was indeed their eternal King and Savior.

Jesus is still in the business of miracles. His main concern remains the saving of souls. Prophecies are still being fulfilled, and will be right up to the end of the age. Many in our world, like many who witnessed Jesus in person, miss or downplay the significance of these occurrences. As Christians, with the help of the Holy Spirit, we can discern when Jesus is asking us to do something for Him. If we are paying attention and are aware of what the Bible tells us will happen, there is a good chance that we will be a participant in or witness to prophecy's fulfillment in our lifetime.

By the time the disciples were nearing Jerusalem, they had been with Jesus for three years. Jesus had proven His power, authority, and trustworthiness to them. They were willing to act in faith, even if it didn't make much sense. This same test of faith will come in every Christian's life. We are called to be obedient and accommodating when the Lord asks us to serve Him. More times than not, this will involve stepping into the unknown. A lonely and frightening place though this may be, we are never alone. Jesus is there with us and *in* us.

Stepping In: Read 2 Kings 9:13; Psalm 118:25–29; Isaiah 62:11–12; Zechariah 9:9–13; and Matthew 21:1–11. After reading these scripture references, reread the Matthew passage and reflect on it, using the Envision It method. (See appendix). Who did you identify with and why? Pray and ask God what He is teaching you through this passage.

Stepping Out: This week, take a step of faith by being obedient and accommodating to Jesus' requests.

May 23

Reassured

"Go back and tell John what you have seen and heard: The blind
receive sight, the lame walk, those who have leprosy are cured, the deaf
hear, the dead are raised, and the good news is preached to the poor."
—Luke 7:22 (Lk 7:1–35)

Before Jesus officially entered His public ministry, His cousin, John the Baptist, was sent by God to prepare the way for the coming Messiah. Obeying his calling from God, John preached a gospel of repentance and baptism in the wilderness. Jesus, also in obedience to the Father, went out to be baptized by water.

Recognizing Jesus as the "Son of God, who takes away the sin of the world" (Jn 1:29), John was briefly apprehensive about obliging Jesus' request to be baptized. Jesus reassured him that it was proper and good. What a blessing John's obedience would be! All who witnessed the event saw God's sign of peace descend on Jesus like a dove, and heard the Lord's audible voice praising His Son.

After His baptism and time of temptation in the desert, Jesus began teaching about God's kingdom and healing the sick and demon-possessed. Soon Jesus had a large following, and twelve chosen disciples. He also had a growing contingent of opponents. When the Pharisees realized that John's ministry was linked to that of Jesus, they had John arrested. John's disciples, seeking a new master, began following Jesus.

Some of these disciples visited John in prison and brought back a request for reassurance from him to Jesus. Jesus sent it. This eyewitness report would certainly have helped assuage John's doubt and fear.

John's story could have occurred in any time and place in history: someone puts their faith in someone or something until circumstances change. Any one of us can easily recall a time in our own lives when this has happened, maybe even with Jesus. We question, "Does this person really love me, or is it just my imagination?" Or, "Did I do something to deserve this situation, and what possible good can come from it?" Or, "What could I have done differently, so that I didn't have to go through this difficult time?" John had to have been thinking these same thoughts.

When it comes to human relationships, heartache and disappointment are to be expected. With Jesus, however, we should never doubt His power, His authority, or His love. He reminds us time and again that we can take Him at His Word. Better yet, He tells us to trust Him because of the wonders He has done in and through our own lives and the lives of others. It is these reliable accounts that are particularly reassuring.

Stepping In: Read Deuteronomy 3:24–25; 1 Kings 18:37–38; Psalm 77:14-15, 78:1-4; and Isaiah 35:3–6, 61:1-3. Have you ever questioned God? Do you sometimes feel like your prayers are not heard, or that you are being treated unfairly? Do you wonder where God is in your troubles? We all do. Pray and ask Jesus to forgive your human weakness. Ask Him for reassurance that He is who He claims to be. Thank Him for all He is doing and will do for you.

Stepping Out: This week, compile an eyewitness account of the miracles you, your family, and your friends have experienced. Make a copy for each to share with others as the Spirit leads.

Eager

> "But seek first His kingdom and His righteousness, and all these things will be given to you as well. Therefore, do not worry about tomorrow, for tomorrow will worry about itself. Each day has enough trouble of its own."
>
> —Matthew 6:33–34 (Mt 6:25–34)

In the Sermon on the Mount, Jesus repeatedly emphasized the importance of having a right understanding and relationship with God the Father. He assured the crowd that faith was built on love and trust, and went on to teach about the futility of worry for those who belong to God. Jesus explained that, where pagans fret over food, clothing, and material possessions, those who are eager to please God above their own desires can confidently rest in the assurance of God's provision. Speaking practically, it's true that worrying about the future serves no useful purpose. Spiritually speaking, it equates to a lack of faith.

Today, we have a term for the type of worrying Jesus is referring to: "future tripping." Worry is still futile and a very harmful form of unbelief. But, let's face it, in a world full of uncertainty and chaos, it is difficult not to get caught up in worry occasionally. For many, the struggle to provide even basic needs for one's family is a justifiable concern.

However, there is a difference between addressing necessary matters of concern when they arise, and allowing oneself to be consumed with worry over them. Jesus tells us that because God already knows what we need, we should focus on seeking "His kingdom and His righteousness" before settling into panic mode.

Among the people who do this well are foreign missionaries. These are folks who, having been called by God to selflessly serve, rely on God for everything. Though this is far from an easy existence, these people have a front-row seat for the miraculous ways God provides. They experience unexplainable peace in return for their eagerness to obey. If the average Christian committed to trusting God even half this much, worry might cease to be.

Stepping In: Read and meditate on Psalm 23. Pray it back to God, thanking Him for the way He does all that He promises in these verses. Ask Him for a greater awareness of these blessed provisions, and the faith to let Him lead you in His ways.

Stepping Out: This week, as an example to others, live out your trust and faith in God's provision. Let your words and actions reflect your assuredness that God has your best interests in mind and is in control of the situation. Commit to refusing to worry. Instead, be eager to demonstrate to a watching world what true faith (trust, obedience, dependence, and love of God) looks like.

Adopted

> "I tell you the truth, everyone who sins is a slave to sin. Now a slave
> has no permanent place in the family, but a son belongs to it forever.
> So if the Son sets you free, you are free indeed."
>
> —John 8:34–36 (Jn 8:31–47)

For the entirety of His ministry, Jesus gave special attention to His own people: the Jews. As was part of God's prophesied plan, salvation would come from the Jews. Therefore, Jesus trained up His Jewish disciples to offer eternal life—the adoption of souls—first to their fellow Hebrews, and then to the Gentiles in the days to come.

Contrary to what the Jews believed, this inclusion in the family of God was not a human birthright. It was a gift of God given to those who chose Christ as the saving Son. Many did not. Among those most vehemently opposed to this notion were the Pharisees and teachers of the Law. With hatred toward Him most intense in Judea, Jesus nevertheless went to Jerusalem to again teach the Jews about the Father's plan.

Jesus explained redemption through the forgiveness of sins. Most of the pious Jews falsely believed that, because they were descended from Abraham and strictly adhered to the law of Moses, they were not in need of forgiveness. Jesus plainly stated that even these religious men should expect neither a position in God's family nor freedom from sin without the Son's blessing. To be God's heirs, they, like everyone else, had to first be adopted by Jesus.

Jesus is speaking several important truths in today's passage that apply as much to a modern audience as they did to the Jews in the temple. The most foundational truth is that Jesus is God. Unless we accept this, all the other things we put our faith in are going to leave us short. The other key point is that all people are sinners in need of saving grace through the forgiveness of sin, which only Jesus can offer.

All of us must choose between a life of bondage or freedom. Using words He knew would elicit an emotional response, Jesus equated sin's entrapment to slavery. For most of us, the thought of being a slave conjures up the ultimate in human degradation, oppression, humiliation, and powerlessness. Slavery is a place of perpetual misery without hope. Jesus is telling us that to deliberately sin is to choose a life of bondage, controlled by Satan. This is not the life He wants any of His children to experience.

The third concept this teaching highlights is a notion of permanence. For the Jews, the belief that their bloodline afforded them a permanent position with God was their downfall. However, we who have been forgiven by the Son also inherit His royal bloodline; we have been adopted by Jesus Himself, and promised a permanent home with Him.

Stepping In: Read Romans 6:16-18, 8:1-2, with 8:15; 2 Corinthians 3:17; and Galatians 3:28–29, 4:7, and 5:1. How have you responded to the freedom you have in Christ? Ask Him to protect you from Satan's attempts to lead you astray.

Stepping Out: This week, with your small group or some friends, listen and discuss your reaction to the song "No Longer Slaves" by Jonathan and Melissa Helser. Praise God for liberating and adopting you.

May 26

Practical

> "If any of you has a sheep and it falls into a pit on the Sabbath, will you not take hold of it and lift it out? How much more valuable is a man than a sheep! Therefore, it is lawful to do good on the Sabbath."
> —Matthew 12:11–12 (Mt 12:1–12)

After being questioned about the unlawfulness of His disciples' behavior on the Sabbath, Jesus explained to a group of enraged Pharisees that, as the "Lord of the Sabbath," He had the authority to grant His hungry disciples permission to collect grain on their day of rest. Then Jesus and His disciples went to the temple to worship. The indignant Pharisees followed them, intent on gathering further incriminating evidence against Him. They pointed out a man with a shriveled hand and asked Jesus if it was lawful to heal on the Sabbath. Aware that they were trying to force Him to confess that He had broken the Sabbath laws, Jesus posed the question about rescuing a sheep. Clearly, the answer was yes, such rescue was lawful.

Beyond the practical aspect of saving one's flock, Jesus wanted to remind the Pharisees that doing what was right and merciful, regardless of the day of the week, pleases the Lord more than following rules made by men. God desires "mercy, not sacrifice." (Hosea 6:6). To demonstrate, Jesus healed the man's hand. The man praised God for his healing, and the congregation gathered around to celebrate the miracle.

The Pharisees, however, were all the more enraged. Filled with indignation and humiliation, they focused on the source of their discomfort: Jesus, the lawbreaker and blasphemer. Behind their laws, their pride, and their spiritual blindness, the Pharisees were neither godly nor practical.

Every Christian has their own understanding of what keeping the Sabbath means. There are still denominations that adhere to a strict interpretation of what is acceptable and what is not. Most people think of Sabbath restrictions as antiquated and impractical. Unlike other imperative commandments, like "Thou shalt not murder" or "Thou shalt not steal," the notion of observing a day set apart for the Lord tends to fall into a "that's a nice idea" category.

Regardless of where one falls on the spectrum on Sabbath strictness, Jesus reminds us that it has never been about simply following rules. He wants us to keep it simple—and practical. He wants us to enjoy the benefits of spending an uninterrupted day with Him: learning from Him, refreshing ourselves in His presence, realigning ourselves with His plans, and serving Him. He wants us to understand that the Sabbath is not about what God wants *from* us, but what He wants *for* us. When we set aside special and intentional time for Jesus, we find that He provides for us wisdom, renewed strength, and vision for how we can benefit His kingdom. Practically speaking, it is the best use of our time.

Stepping In: Read Exodus 31:12-18, 35:1-3; Mark 2:23-28 and Luke 14:5-6. Take an honest look at your typical Sunday. Pray that God enables you to make appropriate changes to your focus, attitude, and behavior.

Stepping Out: This week, take an actual day of rest. Seek to please God as you find refreshment in Him. Pray for clarity about what practical and "good" things need to take place, and what does not.

147

Courageous

The following night the Lord stood near Paul and said, "Take courage! As you have testified about me in Jerusalem, so you must also testify in Rome."

—Acts 23:11 (Acts 21:27–30; 22:30–23:11)

At the end of his third missionary journey, having been compelled by the Spirit, Paul made haste to Jerusalem for the celebration of Pentecost. Paul did not hesitate to obey his calling, regardless of the persecution he would face there. He was undaunted by the threat of violence and searing ridicule, and courageously entered the city.

While faithfully mentoring believers regarding the inclusivity of their new faith, he was seized by Roman guards, arrested, and led away in chains. Before he was taken to be tried under Roman law, Paul testified before an angry mob of his peers about the miraculous encounter he had had with the Lord Jesus, and his devotion thereafter. The crowd would not hear it. Neither would the Roman commander, who planned to have him flogged—until the commander realized that Paul was, like him, a Roman citizen.

To find out what charges the Jews had against Paul, the Roman commander took him to the Sanhedrin (the Jewish ruling council) the next day. There, Paul proclaimed before God and man his hope in the Resurrected One, and was again met with a violent response. His claim temporarily served as a diversionary tactic to distract the Pharisees (who believed in the afterlife) and the Sadducees (who did not) from the matter of finding fault in him. It worked almost too well—a near-riot broke out, which Paul only narrowly escaped. That night, when Paul was alone in the Roman barracks, Jesus spoke to him the motivational words in today's verse. The encouragement spurred Paul to further courageous acts of faith, in Rome and elsewhere.

One could easily read this passage and miss the miracle in it. Though most red-letter verses in the book of Acts are quotes from those who heard Jesus speak in person, today's verse was spoken directly to Paul by Jesus *after* He ascended to heaven. The author, Luke, tells us that "the Lord stood near Paul" and spoke. It is not clear how the Lord appeared, whether He was in His resurrected body or some other manifestation. The implication is clear, however, that the form He took had legs to stand on. In that moment, Paul's fear of not making it out of Jerusalem alive would have been replaced by fresh courage to meet the next challenge.

This is a wonderful example of how Jesus shows up in our lives and turns our darkness to light. We face nothing alone. His holy presence not only stands *beside* us, but it is *within* us. Confident in this reality, we can persevere in our duty to testify to the faith in which we believe, wherever it takes us.

Stepping In: Read Deuteronomy 31:6–8; 1 Chronicles 28:20; Psalm 27:1; Proverbs 3:5–6; Matthew 1:23, 28:19-20; and Luke 24:13–16. How do these verses encourage you to persevere for the kingdom? Pray for courage to heed your calling.

Stepping Out: This week, share your testimony with three new people. Tell them of all the Lord has done for you.

Forthright

> "Again, you have heard that it was said to the people long ago, 'Do not break an oath, but keep the oaths you have made to the Lord.' But I tell you, do not swear at all: either by heaven, for it is God's throne; or by the earth, for it is His footstool; or by Jerusalem, for it is the city of the Great King. And do not swear by your head, for you cannot make even one hair white or black. Simply let your 'Yes' be 'Yes,' and your 'No,' 'No'; anything beyond this comes from the evil one."
>
> —Matthew 5:33–37

Throughout His Sermon on the Mount, Jesus sought to stretch His audience's understanding of cultural mores and God's laws. Where they had "heard it said," He would add, "But I tell you …" In today's verses, Jesus was teaching about the difference between the old way of honoring one's word—an oath—and the new way, which was at the same time simpler and more difficult.

Jesus concluded that they were making the whole affair too complicated. Oath-takers had no business promising something they could not deliver. Jesus chose His examples with exacting purpose. People swore by heaven, God's throne, the earth, Jerusalem, and their own heads because these were touted as infallibly solid collateral, Jesus reminded them that these things were not theirs to wager. If they could not so much as influence the color of their own hair, how could they possibly offer anything God had made and had control over as payment for a lost bet? Jesus reminded His audience that if anyone could not be trusted with their words, how could they be trusted with anything else? Untrustworthiness and falsehood came from "the evil one."

Somewhere along the line, a person's word seems to have lost its value. "Oath" is an antiquated term no longer used in our day and age. Oaths, like handshake agreements, do not have the same binding implications they once did. Over time, people seem to have lost trust in a person's promise. Jesus tells us where this influence comes from: "the evil one." Now, we hardly hire someone to mow our lawn without a signed legal contract.

Where trust has gone down, the exaggerated response to unfulfilled promises has gone way up. Lawsuits are now the norm rather than the exception. The things we used to stand on as evidence of our trustworthiness, like God as our witness, no longer hold sway. Jesus was and is calling for a revival of unwavering dependability, with forthrightness as the catalyst to bring about a renewal of unquestionable trustworthiness. As Jesus' witnesses, Christians must lead the way in this charge.

Stepping In: Read Leviticus 19:12; Numbers 30:2; and Matthew 23:16. How trusting and trustworthy are you? What influences you? Pray that God will give you a Spirit of reliability and forthrightness in all your dealings.

Stepping Out: Let your yes be yes and your no be no. Mean what you say and vice versa. Period.

Alive

> "I tell you the truth, whoever hears my word and believes him who sent me has eternal life and will not be condemned; he has crossed over from death to life."
>
> —John 5:24 (Jn 5:1–30)

During the second year of His ministry, Jesus went to Jerusalem for one of the Jewish feasts, as was customary. He visited the pool at the Sheep Gate and healed a crippled man on the Sabbath. Armed with the evidence needed to have Jesus arrested and killed, the Pharisees looked for the right moment to use it.

Jesus addressed His persecutors. He implied that all the wondrous things they had seen him do were the work of He and His Heavenly Father. He added that they should not be surprised to see even greater works in the future. Ignoring His antagonists' outrage, Jesus said that He, the "Son," was not only the giver of life, but also the judge. Then Jesus summarized the essence of His gospel message: redemptive grace would be freely administered, not to the pious and ultra-religious, but to those who trusted Him and took Him at His Word. Those who believed would be truly alive.

There have been many people throughout history who, like the Pharisees, have been incensed by the exclusivity of Jesus' message. For Christians, this is fantastic news. By our faith, we have been pardoned our death sentence and given eternal life instead. The unbeliever, however, hears only the converse of this statement: those who deny Jesus as Lord remain condemned.

It seems ludicrous that anyone would choose to remain condemned, but many do. Globally, of those who say they have a religious affiliation, only one third are Christians. (According to a 2010 Pew poll). This means that most people on the planet are currently not saved from eternal damnation. They are not "alive in Christ." Contributing to this stark reality are the many false beliefs about who is in charge and what happens to us when we die.

The truth is, we will all find out in the end—either the end of our lives, or the end of time itself, whichever comes first. The inclusive promise of being alive in Christ comes to *all* who hear and believe that Jesus is Lord. This wonderful news must be shared with those who currently believe otherwise.

Stepping In: Read Genesis 15:6; Romans 8:1-2, 10:9-15; Ephesians 2:1–10; Philippians 3:20–21; and Colossians 1:13–14. Meditate on these scripture passages. Then praise your Father in heaven that He made you alive in Christ.

Stepping Out: Consider the Romans 10 passage. This week, be the one to bring God's saving news to the ears of those who have not yet heard it, as a matter of eternal importance.

Forgiving

> Then Peter came to Jesus and asked, "Lord, how many times shall I forgive my brother when he has sinned against me? Up to seven times?" Jesus answered, "I tell you, not seven times, but seventy-seven times."
>
> —Matthew 18:21–22 (Mt 18:15–22)

Toward the end of His earthly ministry, Jesus began to prepare His disciples for what must soon take place: His arrest, death, and resurrection. This news caused a crisis of belief among the disciples. The hopes they had for Israel's promised redeemer—the one who would rescue God's people from Roman oppression—faded with the thought of their beloved Master's death. Though Jesus had revealed His divine power to them and proven Himself faithful, the disciples allowed their confusion, fear, and pride to diminish their faith. Doubts even rendered them unable to drive out some demons. Pride led them to arguments about who would be the greatest in the kingdom of heaven.

Jesus knew that He had to put an end to this kind of thinking. Calling upon a child to aid His illustration, He instructed the disciples stop behaving like little children, but to have hearts and attitudes like them instead. He told them to rid themselves of their selfish notions of grandeur, and get back to a place of humble submission, dependence, and trust in God alone. He reminded them that, it was not about who they could impress, but who they could serve—beginning with each other. He needed them to understand that divided they were powerless; united, nothing would be impossible. And, since unity is dependent on reconciliation, Jesus explained in the above verses, one could not ever be too forgiving.

It is probably true in any generation, that there are some who are the "forgiving kind," and there are those who aren't. While some people are quick to forgive and forget, others harbor unresolved grudges indefinitely. In today's verse, Jesus makes it clear which attitude we should have. For Christians, this issue of forgiveness is more than just a social matter, but a spiritual one as well. Especially among believers, being able to reconcile and move on is essential to the unity of the "body." Since we model after Jesus, who spoke regularly about the importance of an unselfish attitude toward God and others, we too must strive not to let petty (or even serious) issues hinder our ability to rise above our differences. As is always the case, Jesus leads us back to the condition of our hearts. He prompts us to question our motives, and whose best interest we have in mind. He cautions us not to take the short-sighted approach. As ones who have been forgiven, we are commanded to do unto others as we would like them to do to (and as Jesus has already done for) us: joyfully extending grace and mercy to others. Our spiritual health and ministries depend on it.

Stepping In: Read Genesis 4:24; Matthew 6:14; Luke 23:34. After reflecting on these verses, what is your attitude about forgiveness? Praise God that He has forgiven you, and ask for a heart that is willing to forgive others without reservation.

Stepping Out: This week, let your gratitude for your own forgiveness, spill over to others.

May 31
Pertinacious

"I must preach the good news of the kingdom of God to other towns
also, because that is why I was sent."

—Luke 4:43 (Lk 4:38–44)

After being rejected by the people of His hometown, Nazareth, Jesus returned to the town of Capernaum near the Sea of Galilee. His authoritative teaching and acts of miraculous healing there captured the attention of many. Soon He had throngs of diseased and burdened people seeking His wisdom and touch. All who encountered Jesus could see that He was more than just a wise rabbi; even the demons He expelled recognized Him as the "holy one of God." Jesus was happy to relieve possessed souls, but He often had to rebuke the exiting demons, because it was not time for His identity to be revealed.

One of Jesus' followers, Simon (Peter), invited Him to his home. There, they found Peter's mother-in-law lying in bed with a high fever. Everyone in the house was quite concerned. They asked Jesus if He would help her. Full of compassion, He rebuked the fever, and it left her at once. The completely restored woman immediately got up and began to serve her guests. Accepting His host's hospitality, Jesus stayed the evening there.

Early the next morning, Jesus went off to a quiet place by Himself to pray, as was His custom. However, it was not long before an expectant crowd of locals discovered Him and begged Him to stay with them and continue to heal their community. Clear in His purpose, Jesus said He would continue to travel throughout the region and beyond, doing the will of His Father.

As the disciples did when commissioned during Jesus' lifetime, and again when they went out as apostles after Jesus' ascension, modern-day disciples must continue this kingdom work. New Christians may have a sphere of influence only as broad as their immediate family and friends. Mature believers must branch out to further reaches.

Jesus gave His disciples the command to go out into the world and offer restoration and salvation. That command has been passed down through the generations of believers, and now rests on us. He has chosen each of to be a part of His pertinacious team, eager and willing to carry out His mission even in His absence. Only God knows when the Book of Life will receive its last name. Until then, it is our privileged duty to span out in ever increasing circles, telling other about Jesus.

Stepping In: Read Isaiah 61 with Luke 4:18; Romans 10:14-15 and Revelation 3:5, 20:12-15, 21:22-27. Meditate on these scripture passages with your own discipleship in mind. Is God calling you to be a witness to the gospel somewhere in the world? Pray today's verse back to God and ask Him for a clear vision for your next steps.

Stepping Out: This week, be a pertinacious proponent of the gospel. Tell someone outside your immediate circle about the hope you have in Jesus.

June 1

Industrious

"His master replied, 'Well done, good and faithful servant! You have been faithful with a few things; I will put you in charge of many things. Come and share your master's happiness!'"
—Matthew 25:21 (Mt 24:1–3; 25:14–21)

With the days of His earthly ministry quickly dwindling, Jesus spent concentrated time teaching His disciples, often retreating with His elect to the Mount of Olives outside the city. On one such occasion, He explained many details about the "end of the age." Some of His predictions were soon to be realized, while others would be a long time in coming.

Jesus spoke of judgment and calamity, the likes of which none could begin to imagine. He warned His men to stay strong and full of faith, so they would not be deceived by false prophets and phony Christs. He promised His return was assured, but the day and the hour were not known even to Him. To round out His teaching, He told further parables about the kingdom of heaven.

Using the comparison of a master and his three servants, Jesus illustrated the necessity for kingdom bringers to be industrious with the talents God had given them. In biblical terms, a "talent" was a unit of money. Two of the three servants invested this money and gained a return. The third hid the money out of fear. Upon his return, the master praised the first two servants. The third, who had not put the master's talents to work, was scolded and promised a just punishment. The industrious two, however, were rewarded with praise and greater trust. Wanting to hear these words spoken to themselves, the disciples were motivated to do what was necessary to ensure this would one day transpire.

The parable of the talents may show the master's treatment of the fearful servant in a rather harsh light. The punishment given for merely hiding the talent seems disproportionate to the crime, even unjust. Jesus purposefully chose this illustration to emphasize how important an industrious servant is to God in His kingdom's cause.

For Christians today, this is a serious wake-up call. What Jesus is saying is that the "talents" (by which we now mean gifts, abilities, and knowledge) He entrusts us with, we are to use wisely. Simply put, everything God has given us is rightfully His and is on loan to us. As His servants, He expects us to use our talents to expand His kingdom. The return on His investment is the fruit of our labors: people brought closer to God because of us. When God sees our industrious efforts making a kingdom impact, He blesses us with more opportunities to bring Him even more glory. All of us want to hear the words, "Well done, good and faithful servant!"

This verse gives us a clue about how to please God. We must be industrious investors of what we have been given. To squander our talents is a waste.

Stepping In: Reread today's verse, and insert your name after the words "Well done." Pray and ask God how you can honor Him with the investment He has made in you.

Stepping Out: This week, industriously put one of your talents to use for the kingdom of God. Praise Him for using you in increasingly amazing ways as you prove your faithfulness.

June 2
Conformable

"Put out into deep water, and let down your nets for a catch."
—Luke 5:4 (Lk 5:1–11)

Very early in His ministry, Jesus returned to His childhood village of Nazareth, only to find that the people of His hometown considered Him nothing more than a charismatic public figure. Recognizing the futility of preaching to those who flatly rejected Him, He returned to the region near the Sea of Galilee. There, Jesus sought out more conformable gospel recipients to be His first disciples.

One morning, walking along the lakeshore and teaching a large following of eager listeners, Jesus spied some fishermen cleaning their nets. Jesus left the crowd and climbed into one of the boats, giving its owner the command to launch. The tired and confused fisherman, who was Simon, reluctantly obeyed.

Much to Simon's surprise, his net became so full that it started to tear. After his bewildered friends helped him haul in the biggest catch they had ever seen, Simon fell at Jesus' feet and confessed his unworthiness. To Simon and His other new disciples, Andrew, James, and John, Jesus gave a comforting yet puzzling reply: "Don't be afraid; from now on you will catch men" (Lk 5:9).

The story of the miraculous catch is applicable to today's society on multiple levels. Let's explore each of them from Simon's perspective. How does his conformable attitude and response inspire us when we also receive Jesus' unexpected requests?

- *Faith*: Simon had to override his exhaustion, frustration, and doubt to trust his new Master.
- *Obedience*: Regardless of the futility of the situation, Simon honored Jesus by doing what he was told.
- *Bravery*: Scorning skeptical onlookers and fighting back fear of failure, Simon mustered courage and strength to step out in faith.
- *Humility*: Recognizing the divine nature of his blessing, Simon could scarcely accept such a gift. Jesus had nothing but reassurance for his new pupil. When we are faced with similarly daunting circumstances, He will do the same for us—especially when we are as conformable as Simon Peter.

Stepping In: Read Job 42:4–6; Isaiah 6:1–5; and Romans 8:29-30, 12:2. What is your response when Jesus asks you to do something you do not want to do? What is your response when He blesses you more than you can imagine or deserve? Thank Him now for His grace and generosity. Pray for a conformable heart.

Stepping Out: This week, look for deep water in which to cast your net. As you employ Simon Peter's attributes, also respond to Jesus' commands as he did: "Because Jesus says so, I will."

June 3
Transformed

When He had said this, Jesus called in a loud voice, "Lazarus, come out!"
—John 11:43 (Jn 11:1–44)

While in the region of Perea for a brief reprieve from intense persecution in Judea, Jesus received news that His dear friend Lazarus was gravely ill. Jesus reassured the concerned assembly that "this sickness will not end in death" (Jn 11:4). He stayed where He was two more days. Then Jesus set out for Bethany, despite His disciples' pleading to avoid the heated situation in that region.

Lazarus' sister Martha greeted Jesus with the sad news that her brother had been dead four days. Undeterred, Jesus made His way to the tomb and ordered the stone removed from its entrance. A leery crowd of mourners stood by as Jesus issued the command for Lazarus to come forth. To the shock and, perhaps, horror of the witnesses, the dead man obeyed. Any doubt in Jesus' power to overcome death was removed. The transformed man was living proof.

The moment a person believes in their heart that Jesus is Lord, and decides to live according to His will and His ways, they are transformed. The believer goes from dead to alive, from lost to found, from guilty to forgiven, from imprisoned to free. But that is only the beginning of the journey.

We who are born-again Christians, though we are new creations from the moment we first believe, henceforth begin our journey of sanctification - the ongoing process of settling into our roles in the kingdom. Like Lazarus, we first had to overcome our amazement at being saved. We had to take those first steps out of our darkness into the blinding light of a new reality. For many of us, this was overwhelming, causing us to pause on the threshold. Knowing we are different doesn't mean that the world around us has changed. The people in our lives, our environment, and our former beliefs and behaviors are often slow to evolve and accommodate.

Jesus knows that transformation is difficult and sometimes painful. He also knows that staying dead is not the option He wants for us. Today's passage is an awesome reminder that new life begins when Jesus calls us out of our tombs. At the command of our Savior's voice, we are brought to a right-standing before God. As we walk in faith, we show the world that we are transformed in mind and spirit, if not body too.

Stepping In: Read Job 19:25–26; Psalm 49:15; John 10:17-18, 11:25-26, 12:24 and Romans 10:9-10, 12:2 Has Jesus called you out of a dead-end life? How does your life reveal your transformed mind and spirit? Ask the Holy Spirit to increase your ability to hear His voice. Pray for Him to remove obstacles and fear so that you can obey.

Stepping Out: Identify an area in your life where you are resistant to stepping out in faith. Make a move toward obedience this week. Google the phrase "commands of Jesus" and commit to shining the light of scripture into the shadowy places in your life as you heed His words. For inspiration, listen to "Glorious Day," by Passion.

Relational

> "If you knew the gift of God and who it is that asks you for a drink,
> you would have asked him and he would have given you living water."
> —John 4:10 (Jn 4:1–26)

For more than seven hundred years, the Jews and Samaritans had fostered an unrelenting feud. The Jews considered themselves a pure race—God's chosen people—whereas the Samaritans were thought of as a mixed breed of people who followed a hodge-podge of culture and religion, and were scripturally illiterate—unworthy of God's attention. The two groups despised each other, making every effort to avoid interaction.

After the arrest of John the Baptist and the consequent unrest in Judea, Jesus and His disciples headed north to Galilee, purposefully passing through Samaria. Unbeknown to His disciples, Jesus had a divine appointment with a woman at Jacob's well near the town of Sychar. Everything about this plan must have seemed wrong to the disciples. Puzzled, they went off to find food, leaving their Master sitting by the well in the heat of the day.

Soon a woman arrived, hoping to complete her daily chore undetected. Regardless of the woman's surprised expression, Jesus spoke to her, requesting a drink of water. Jesus was well aware of the cultural and religious rules He was breaking by initiating a conversation with this outcast, emotionally scarred, and spiritually confused Samaritan woman. To her amazement, this Jewish rabbi seemed to value a relational approach rather than one dictated by human protocol. In the above verse, Jesus made a statement that began to open this woman's eyes to who He was and what His divine purpose was for her. Though her interest was piqued, she continued to hide behind the social barrier between them. Undeterred, Jesus welcomed her questions and her skepticism.

The interaction between Jesus and the woman at the well could easily provide the curriculum for Evangelism 101. We see our Lord's relational approach to inviting someone into an understanding of truth. Stepping across cultural barriers and scorning personal criticism, He went into an uncomfortable situation because that was where He was needed. Jesus engaged the woman in a practical way by initiating the conversation and offering her an opportunity to be useful doing something she was already good at. Slowly, Jesus gained this woman's confidence. Patiently, He assured her that He was safe and trustworthy. Purposefully, He built on her existing understanding of God. With sensitivity, He clarified her misinterpretations of scripture, replacing them with glimpses of His divinity and His grace-filled plan for her. As the woman's comfort level grew, she became receptive to the life-changing message Jesus was sharing. Take note, Christians: this is how it's done.

Stepping In: Read Isaiah 44:3; Jeremiah 2:13; Zechariah 14:8; John 7:37; and Revelation 7:17 and 21:6. How do these passages help you better understand God's plan for salvation? Praise Jesus for going out of His way to build a relationship with you. Pray that He will reveal and remove any barriers that inhibit your relationship with Him.

Stepping Out: What risks are you avoiding in your Christian walk? Is Jesus calling you out of your comfort zone? This week, look for someone who is thirsty and begin this process of engagement.

Sure

> Then Jesus said to the centurion, "Go! It will be done just as you
> believed it would."
>
> —Matthew 8:13 (Mt 8:5–13)

In the days after Jesus' Sermon on the Mount, large crowds of people followed Him into the town of Capernaum, where He continued to teach and to heal. He was approached by an unlikely believer—a high-ranking Roman centurion. The faith of this religious and political "enemy" spurred Jesus to respond to his request to heal someone the centurion cared about—a servant.

As miraculous as the servant's physical restoration was, every aspect of this healing was remarkable. Everything about the centurion's faith was sure and true. Though a foreigner and a pagan, he believed in Jesus' power to heal. Though an enemy of the Jews, he risked his reputation to ask the Jewish leaders for their help in finding Jesus. Though a man of worldly means, he realized that only a man of God could do the thing he asked. Though respected and feared, he humbly acknowledged his unworthiness to have the Lord come under His roof. Above all, the centurion was sure that with a mere utterance from the lips of Jesus, a life could be saved. Because of the centurion's bravery, many more than the centurion's servant were saved that day.

The miracles of God are not contingent on anything we humans say or do, but faith often plays a role. Unfortunately, in our day and age, seeing is believing, not the other way around. Many people are proud skeptics and scientists, always analyzing the data and looking for proofs before they put their faith in something. Most people in our modern age feel that living by blind faith is a foolhardy practice. Believing in Jesus (someone we cannot see) and trusting in the will of the Father (the wrathful God of the Bible) seems a ridiculous pursuit to some.

For Christians, as it was for the centurion, tangible proofs come after our hearts and minds have agreed that salvation is possible through one Man's Word. As we know, it takes a step of sure conviction to propel us past our fears and doubts. Today, we call the people who risk everything to save someone else "heroes." The Roman centurion set an example for all Christians to follow.

Stepping In: Read 2 Corinthians 5:6–9. Take some time to consider how often you prefer the comforts of the safe and familiar to the discomfort of stepping out in faith. Pray that God helps you to recall the many ways His Word has proven true in your life. Make a list of the times you have stepped out in faith and been astounded by the results.

Stepping Out: This week, be an example of someone who demonstrates how sure they are in Jesus' power and abilities. Be on the lookout for opportunities to share how Jesus' healing power has been proven in your life.

June 6

Eternal

"I am the Alpha and the Omega," says the Lord God, "who is, and who
was, and who is to come, the Almighty."

—Revelation 1:8 (Rv 1:1–8)

The apostle John, one of Jesus' disciples and closest companions, boldly promoted Christianity throughout the ancient world, establishing many churches along his route. From his prison cell on the Greek island of Patmos, John was taken in the Spirit to the throne room of God, where Jesus Himself dictated portions of the letter he was to write. John quoted Jesus' explanation of His eternal nature, using the Greek letters *alpha* and *omega* (the first and last letters in the Greek alphabet) to express that He was the beginning and the end of all things. At that moment, John fully understood that God's power was unsurpassed. His love for those who were faithful was unfailing. John was given a glimpse of the immeasurable vastness of God as the Creator and Sustainer of all things, the One who had always been and would always exist. God's message to the leaders of the churches was a reminder that Jesus was the fulfillment of God's plan. Therefore, the churches could stand firm in His eternal promises.

Many modern-day Bible readers shy away from the book of Revelation because of its frightening imagery and difficult symbolism. Yet, from the opening verses of this book, the author establishes the foundational truth of God's good nature. Though wrath will be a part of the justice God's sovereign plan ensures, John wants believers to rest in the "grace and peace" our salvation has afforded us.

Very few things in life are completely reliable, but God's Word is. Moreover, God's Word is complete and trustworthy because He Himself is "Faithful and True"; in Him there is nothing false.

In times of grief and loss, humans may utter the hopeless cliché, "Oh well, nothing lasts forever." As far as worldly things go, this is true. However, believers must remember that as children of the living and eternal God, our souls are eternal. God, who is almighty, has saved us from the death we deserve. Because God's eternity stretches forever in both directions—He was, is, and is to come—we can be sure that His perspective includes every detail of our past, present, and future. He knows us and loves us. We are His forever. This is the central message of the book of Revelation.

Stepping In: Read Deuteronomy 33:27; Psalm 48:14; Isaiah 40:28; Romans 8:29–30; Ephesians 1:4–8; and Hebrews 13:8. How does knowing that God is eternal encourage or challenge you? Praise Him for the peace you have in your eternal security.

Stepping Out: This week, write down the ways God has blessed you with grace and peace in the past, how He is blessing and providing for you now, and what promises you are looking forward to in the future. Share this with another person or in your small group.

Savvy

"Again, the kingdom of heaven is like a merchant looking for fine pearls. When he found one of great value, he went away and sold everything he had and bought it."

—Matthew 13:45 (Mt 13:24–45)

In the second half of His earthly ministry, Jesus began to teach by way of parables. These analogies taught His disciples to listen for the deeper spiritual meaning in His words. Parables were also necessary to disguise His meaning from listeners who were looking to use His words against Him. For the masses of not-yet believers, these parables offered little more than a quaint word picture or perhaps a tidbit of advice. For the first Christian converts, however, these teachings contained much spiritual wisdom—wisdom they would need to carry out the mission ahead.

Central to the gospel message was the theme of heaven. Though His men could not fully comprehend that this place was both physical and eternal, Jesus plied them with many comparisons of heaven's splendor and worth. After equating the kingdom to a treasure, Jesus reiterated the preciousness and value of heaven. His listeners may have thought the story was about a foolish man who squandered his wealth for a single pearl, their take-away being, "Beware of impetuousness, for it leads to financial ruin." His discerning and spiritually savvy disciples, however, understood that godly wisdom was the "pearl." This latter group cherished each of Jesus' precious and highly valued words, treasuring them in their hearts and minds.

In our world, money talks. The very measure of success in our modern culture is monetary wealth. Today's merchants are still searching for items of great value, which they can then turn around and sell at a profit. Though Jesus knows that we need money to live, He also knows that we are easily lured into thinking that it is the most important of all pursuits—even above God.

Therefore, Jesus taught about money more than nearly anything else. He used illustrations like the one in today's passage to get our attention and shift it back to what is important. What Jesus is calling "fine pearls" is the knowledge that faith in the one true God will be rewarded with eternal blessings in heaven. There is nothing more valuable, more priceless, or more important for humanity to know. And it is nothing any of us can earn or buy. Like the parable of the treasure hidden in the field, this thing of great value is worth trading everything else to acquire.

As savvy Christians, we must not take this teaching lightly. This priceless gift came at the highest cost to our Savior. Let us not forget nor fail to appreciate this wonderful blessing. Let us not neglect telling others of this limited-time offer, before it is too late.

Stepping In: This week, listen to the song "One Thing Remains" by Jesus Culture. How do the words of this song comfort you? How do they inspire you to share this beautiful pearl of wisdom? Pray for a willingness to step out in faith to tell other of Jesus' unending love.

Stepping Out: This week, fast from something worldly that you value (car, TV, Facebook, cell phone) as a reminder to place a higher value on more important, imperishable things.

Proven

"But wisdom is proved right by all her children."
—Luke 7:35 (Lk 7:1–35)

In the middle of His public ministry, Jesus' hope and healing were transforming countless lives. His popularity and influence also attracted the attention of those who questioned His authority and methods. Already miffed by the influence of Jesus' predecessor and cousin, John the Baptist, these falsely pious men sought to disrupt the spread of the gospel by arresting John. Jesus and His disciples, though saddened by this turn of events, carried on nonetheless.

Jesus went on to teach the ever-present crowd about the contrast between the truly faithful and those who were imposters. Offering John's teaching and baptism as an example, Jesus pointed out that those who accepted John and His message did so because they believed John was a prophet, a messenger of God. Those who rejected John did so because he did not fit their assumptions of someone who could be of such caliber. Their human perception and preconceived religious notions blinded them to the truth. These same hard-hearted souls rejected the One who came after John—the Son of Man—for the same reasons. It would be a long time before they would realize the fact that Jesus had proven John's wisdom all along.

Today's verse should cause each person who calls himself or herself a follower to take a good hard look in the mirror. Do our words, beliefs, and actions reflect the wisdom Jesus has bestowed on us? Is this same wisdom proven by those whom we have influenced, including our children?

The truth is, we all leave a legacy: good or bad, honorable or dishonorable, godly or worldly. It is not enough just to acknowledge Jesus as God. Once we have accepted Him as our personal Lord and Savior, we must start to live according to His standards and not those of our culture.

Concluding the passage in which Jesus reassures His cousin John and us that He is God, the all-wise One, Jesus gives His audience a clue as to where to find lasting proof: in those who come after. What comes out of the heart of a true believer is evidence that Jesus is Lord. Christians must strive to impress truth on those in our sphere of influence. This will be our proven legacy of wisdom.

Stepping In: Reread today's full passage. Take some time to meditate on these verses. Can you relate to Jesus' description of those who reject the gospel message based on preconceived notions and appearances? Do you see this type of rejection elsewhere too? Ask God to reveal any prejudices you may have regarding His ministry or those who offer it. Seek His wisdom in aligning your heart and thoughts to Him instead.

Stepping Out: This week, ask yourself how you would like your Christian wisdom to be proven. Write out what you think your spiritual legacy will be. Use this as a gold standard for your thoughts and actions in the future.

June 9

Sincere

"Everything they do is done for men to see: They make their phylacteries wide and the tassels on their garments long; they love the place of honor at banquets and the most important seats in the synagogues; they love to be greeted in the marketplace and to have men call them 'Rabbi.'"

—Matthew 23:5–7 (Mt 22:41–23:10)

Jesus told the temple crowd and His disciples to obey God's laws, but not to follow the wretched example of the self-righteous Pharisees who imposed them. He pointed out how the Pharisees lived for the adoration, respect, and honor they receive from men, rather than to bring glory to God through their service. This news would have stunned Jesus' listeners. The men they had trusted to be their spiritual leaders, it seemed, were only pretending to care about them and God.

A modern-day example of this behavior is the putting on of one's Sunday best. Six days of the week, Christians all over this planet go about their business, making deals, trying to get ahead, following the patterns of world. On Sunday, they suddenly look quite different. A miraculous transformation? Not in most cases. Often, this is nothing more than a Pharisee-like act, all for show.

Unfortunately, even when our intentions are good, many of us struggle to fully practice what we preach. Today's passage is a reminder for Christians to be sincere. The person we present to the world should be the same one God sees when no one is looking. Our efforts should go toward pleasing and impressing God rather than fickle people. Besides, even if we fool others, we will never fool God. He knows our hearts, so we might as well be real. Redeemed by His blood, we do not need to pretend to be more than we are. There is only One we need to impress: God.

Stepping In: Read Deuteronomy 6:4–9; Micah 6:8; Romans 12:3; 2 Corinthians 5:17; and Galatians 6:14. How do these verses help you understand the ways God wants you to show you belong to Him? How sincere are you in revealing your true self? Pray and ask God to gently guide you toward more sincere and humble practices this week.

Stepping Out: This week, do nothing for show, even at church. Look for an opportunity to give up your seat, so to speak. Allow someone else to have the place of honor on the bus, in line, and so on.

Content

"Look at the birds of the air; they do not sow or reap or store away in barns, and yet your heavenly Father feeds them. Are you not much more valuable than they? Who of you by worrying can add a single hour to his life?"

—Matthew 6:26–27 (Mt 6:25–34)

As he preached the Sermon on the Mount, Jesus looked at His burdened audience with love and compassion. He wanted them to know how valuable they were to God, and that they could be content in the knowledge that their heavenly Father was happy to provide for their spiritual and physical needs. His analogy of the birds was intentional. Knowing that many Jews struggled to afford even the smallest temple sacrifice, which was birds, Jesus explained that the sacrifice of their true devotion was worth far more to God. Jesus' words would have drawn them closer to God—unlike the message the people received from their religious leaders, which pushed them further away.

Possibly one of the New Testament's most famous passages, the Sermon on the Mount is still teaching Jesus' followers the basics of Christian living. In a nutshell, the message is to love God and others well. Throughout this teaching, Jesus challenges His listeners to consider where we place our heavenly Father on the list of things we prioritize in our lives. He implores each of us to examine our hearts for things that inhibit or diminish our ability to trust Him fully, like pride, fear, worry, and discontentment. Satan loves to use these things to distract us from God's truth and love.

While Jesus used some strong language to point out where we may need to recognize our faulty thinking and behavior, He also blessed us with wonderful words of instruction and encouragement. Jesus made it clear that God values us greatly and is aware of our needs. Throughout the generations, these words of Jesus have reminded His followers that, regardless of the struggles we face, we can be content in knowing that He is the great provider, now and forever.

Stepping In: Read Romans 8:14–17 and 1 John 3:1. Pray to your heavenly Father. Cry out, "Abba, Father." Ask Him for the faith to trust Him in all areas of your life. Praise Him for knowing your needs and providing for you. Enjoy being a well-cared-for child of God. Be content in His love and promise.

Stepping Out: This week, meet every anxious thought with a trusting smile toward God. Let this smile of contentment live on your face throughout the week for all to see. When asked, share about the confidence and contentment we find only in Jesus.

Dependent

"By myself I can do nothing; I judge only as I hear, and my judgment
is just, for I seek not to please myself but him who sent me."
—John 5:30 (Jn 5:1–30)

One day, the religious elite set out to accuse Jesus, and were treated to a lengthy teaching on Jesus' unity with God the Father. Even knowing that most of His audience would interpret His speech as further proof of blasphemy, Jesus chose to hold nothing back. In plain language, He claimed His authority as the Son of God, and said that He did not work independently of God's will. He made the distinct claim to be the giver of life. He stated emphatically that those who chose to believe that He was sent by the Father would live eternally, while all others would remain condemned. He also asserted that He was the judge. Anyone who heard these words was amazed; some were amazed at Jesus' audacity, others at His authenticity.

Christians are very Jesus-oriented, and rightfully so. He is, of course the "Author and Perfecter of our faith." (He 12:2). We should also pay attention to Jesus' focus throughout scripture on the Father as the One who reigns on high. Jesus, though He is all-powerful of His own accord, defers to His Father; He makes His dependence known throughout His teaching. While Jesus was in His human body, though also fully God, He continually looked to His Father for guidance and strength. Above all, He sought to please and do the will of His Father.

As Christians, we must acknowledge this holy hierarchy and be similarly dependent on it. If Jesus looked to the Father, we would be wise to do the same. Trusting in the marvelous mystery of the Trinity, we can utilize each of its three aspects to maximize our spiritual growth and missional effectiveness. Beginning each day with the Lord's Prayer, we submit our will to the Father, just as Jesus did. Then we can confidently call out to Jesus by name and be comforted to know that He hears us and is working in our favor. By staying in tune with the Holy Spirit within us, we can discern God's good, pleasing, and perfect will for us each day. If Jesus could do nothing by Himself, why would we think that we can?

Stepping In: Read Matthew 6:9-13, 26:42; John 15:5; Romans 8:28, 8:34, 12:2; 1 Corinthians 8:5–6; Ephesians 4:4–6; and Hebrews 12:1–2. How do these verses inform you about the role of God the Father? Whom do you currently seek to please, and why? Talk to God about this. Praise Him for His understanding. Seek dependence on God.

Stepping Out: This week, in your small group or with some friends, listen to "This I Believe" by Hillsong Worship. Talk about ways you live out this faith by submitting to the Father's will just as Jesus did. Model for one another a dependence on the Father; encourage each other to do the same.

Satisfied

"A wicked and adulterous generation asks for a miraculous sign! But none will be given it except the sign of the prophet Jonah. For as Jonah was three days and three nights in the belly of a huge fish, so the Son of Man will be three days and three nights in the heart if the earth."
—Matthew 12:39–40 (Mt 12:38–45)

Jesus' words and ways looked very different from those of a typical Jewish rabbi in His time. Though the teachers of the Law and the Pharisees acknowledged Him as a teacher, they hardly agreed with His message or His methods—certainly not His claim to deity. At best, they thought Jesus was a misguided nuisance and a thorn in their sides. At worst, He represented a real threat to the ideology and rigid structure from which their power stemmed. Jesus' message of love, rather than fearful obligation, captivated a weary and waiting population, much to the chagrin of those who benefited from keeping the people in a state of perpetual dependence.

Following a scathing rebuttal to accusations that His power was from Satan, Jesus reprimanded the religious leaders for demanding a sign. After telling the religious men exactly what He thought of them, Jesus reminded them that as they had known about many miraculous signs in ancient and recent days, they would be privy to another one soon. The prophetic nature of His words—which pointed to His own entombment and resurrection—were no doubt lost on the spiritually blind Jewish leaders. None hearing this statement could have known what it meant at the time. But they would.

Many Christians grew up hearing the Bible story of Jonah and the whale. We understand the lesson behind it, but we pay little attention to the validity of the event itself. The story may be metaphorical or not. Still, none of us should question God's ability to perform such miracles. Truly, where would we begin to draw the line? We necessarily believe in His power to resurrect the dead. Without that, our faith fails. Nevertheless, sometimes we are tempted to draw the line between fact and fiction with far-fetched examples like Noah and ark, the parting of the Red Sea, and Jonah's giant fish debacle. No one could survive three days inside a fish—that is what makes it a miracle.

God is still in the miracle business. Given a moment to think, each one of us can conjure personal accounts of miraculous events and healings. Yet we continue to ask for signs from God. Jesus warns us not to follow the wicked down that path, but to be satisfied with our faith in God's power instead.

Stepping In: Read the book of Jonah. How does your life resemble his? Do you suffer from doubt and fear? Are you scared of, resistant to, or satisfied with the calling God has placed on your life? Pray for greater faith in who Jesus is, what He has done, and how He will bless and protect you always.

Stepping Out: This week, in your small group or with some Christian friends share your miracle stories.

Fortunate

"Blessed rather are those who hear the word of God and obey it."
—Luke 11:28 (Lk 11:14–28)

During the height of His ministry, with a mixed crowd of supporters and opponents present, Jesus restored speech to a formerly mute man. While most were duly amazed, some claimed that Jesus had used forces of evil to perform the miracle. Apparently emboldened by the suggestion that Jesus' authority was in question, other antagonists began to ply Him for proof that His authority was from heaven.

Matter-of-factly, Jesus explained the absurdity of thinking that evil could drive out evil. He spoke of physical strength metaphorically to illustrate the craftiness and power of evil influences. Jesus cautioned His listeners not to trust their spiritual safety to their own will or abilities. He warned that anyone who took the presence of evil for granted and did not replace evil with good would certainly invite unwelcome hauntings.

Perhaps moved by Jesus' wisdom, or wishing to come to His defense, a woman in the crowd called out a blessing on Jesus' mother for having birthed and nursed Him. In response, Jesus told His audience that the truly fortunate were those obedient to God's Word.

Many Christians today do not fully realize just how blessed we are. The heartfelt blessing that came from the woman in today's story, though it was sincere and kind, still missed the mark. Even in her attempt to honor the young rabbi's mother, her adoration was misplaced. Far closer to recognizing the deity of Jesus than the Pharisees, the woman still failed to understand that the power Jesus used was from God; it was the Father who should have been praised.

Jesus always points us back to the source of all wisdom and power: God. He always reminds us to not only hear God's Word and praise Him for it, but to obey it. In a world where independence is so highly valued, and those who question authority and buck the system are admired, we must remember who is sovereign and in control, whose power in unmatched in all the world. We must also heed Jesus' warning to replace evil with truth—the Word of God. How fortunate we will be if we do these things.

Stepping In: Read Luke 1:37; John 1:5, 5:24; Romans 8:35-37, 12:21; 1 Corinthians 1:18–19; 1 John 5:4; and Revelation 3:19–20. What is Jesus trying to teach you about acknowledging His authority, hearing His voice above all others, and obeying? Ask God to reveal any evil that needs to be replaced with good. Praise Him for your fortunate status in His kingdom.

Stepping Out: This week, turn your words into actions. In addition to verbal praise, show God you love Him with what you do for others. Show Him whose voice you are really listening to—your own, the world's, or His.

Zealous

"It is written," he said to them, "'My house will be called a house of prayer,' but you are making it a 'den of robbers.'"
—Matthew 21:13 (Mt 21:10–15)

Jesus, having entered Jerusalem for the last time in His earthly ministry, followed His custom of going to the temple to worship. As He had expected, droves of devoted Jews were there to offer their sacrifices, since Passover was just getting underway. Once inside the temple courts, however, Jesus found a scene He had not wanted to see: His Father's house had been turned into a marketplace. Instead of keeping this sacred place holy, the religious leaders had decided to capitalize on the opportunity to exploit the obligated masses. Full of righteous zeal, Jesus dispensed with the money changers and merchants by upending their tables and scattering their wares across the floor, quoting the prophets Isaiah and Jeremiah as He did so. Everyone present would have been stunned, none more than the chief priests and teachers of the Law.

With order restored, Jesus resumed the purpose of His visit: praising God and offering acts of mercy to those in need. However, the religious elite were none too pleased by Jesus' supposedly unauthorized command of the temple, not to mention having their lucrative venture so rudely cut short. Indignant and filled with rage, they would soon instigate the beginning of Jesus' end.

Jesus continues to love His church with a protective zeal. Today's passage is an example of the importance of defending the sanctity of God's house. Even today, believers must zealously insist that our places of worship be free from corruption and evil influences.

This is easier said than done. It can be difficult for a church to fit into a melting-pot culture and be relevant in society while remaining faithful to biblical doctrine. Wanting to present a comfortable all-inclusive atmosphere, some churches become more focused on image than on God. In our "bigger must be better" world, some churches resemble malls more than sacred places of worship.

Selling books and coffee in a church is not taboo per se, but these practices can be a symptom of spiritual drift—a leaning more toward the cultural norm than a biblical standard. Jesus has some strong words for churches that sacrifice the purity of the sanctuary to create a place where almost anything goes. He still expects His temples to be houses of prayer, regardless of cultural influences or financially driven decisions. He still has the power and authority to make sure they are.

Stepping In: Read Psalm 69:6-9; Isaiah 56:6-7; Jeremiah 7:9–11; and John 2:13–17. How do these verses help you understand Jesus' zealous protection of His sacred places? How zealously do you protect God's temple—your church and your body? Pray for wisdom to know how to honor God with both.

Stepping Out: This week, make a point to be humble and direct with church officials if you see God's temple being used less like a house of prayer and more like a den of robbers.

Motivated

"Let us go somewhere else—to the nearby villages—so I can preach there also. That is why I have come."

—Mark 1:38 (Mk 1:14–38)

Early in His ministry, with His first disciples at His side, Jesus began teaching a message of repentance and hope throughout Galilee, "as one who had authority." When He also began healing in miraculous ways, the people were amazed, and news about Him quickly spread. However, Jesus was careful not to allow His identity to be known by many. He had only three years to complete the tasks His Father had sent Him to do, so every minute was intentionally utilized.

Thus, Jesus made a habit of rising before dawn to privately consult with God and determine His Father's will for the day. In one such instance, Jesus was in a solitary place, and Simon and a few others went out looking for Him. When they found Him, they explained that everyone was anxious to know where He had gone. Jesus, aware of the far-reaching needs of Israel, suggested they all go somewhere else.

Jesus began traveling throughout the region, teaching in the synagogues, healing the sick, and driving out demons from tormented souls. His new disciples eagerly soaked in all their Master's wisdom. Motivated by the example of Jesus' compassion and servitude, the disciples' love for God and faith in Jesus grew.

Jesus knows what is important. Throughout the gospels, He shows us what it means to be a Christian. He gives us two examples of a proper approach to ministry in today's passage. First, before He did anything, He prayed. This is such a wonderful reminder for us today! In our busy, often frantic lives, we sometimes fail to make time to align ourselves with the will of the Father. Is it any wonder that we struggle? Following Jesus' example, we must not succumb to the pressures of the world that vie for our attention. Instead, we are wise to do as He did: start the day in submission to the Father, offering ourselves to Him before anyone else, and seeking true wisdom before letting worldly influences in. Second, Jesus saw a need and went to meet it—regardless of where it took Him. As we see in this section of scripture, Jesus saw the interruption of His personal quiet time as an opportunity to serve those He cared about. Sacrificial giving was a part of His nature.

As new creations in Christ, sacrificial giving is in our new nature as well. Motivated by love and guided by prayer, we too must be willing to "go somewhere else" to serve others in need.

Stepping In: Read Psalm 119:147; Isaiah 61:1–3; Micah 6:8; and John 5:19 and 6:28–29, 38. How do these verses help you understand what motivated Jesus? Are these the things that also motivate you in your Christian walk? Pray for a willingness to be led by Jesus wherever He might lead you.

Stepping Out: Each day this week, rise early and align yourself with God's will for your day and your life. Spend time in prayer, silence, and His Word. Be filled with the Spirit before filling your day with busyness.

June 16

Unashamed

"Whoever acknowledges me before men, I will also acknowledge him before my Father in heaven. But whoever disowns me before men, I will disown him before my Father in heaven."
—Matthew 10:32–33 (Mt 10:1–42)

Jesus chose His twelve disciples with a clear purpose in mind: they were to be His ambassadors to the world, beginning with their own people, the Jews. After leading, teaching, and training His men for two years, Jesus felt it was time to send them out to minister to the lost sheep of Israel. Before sending them, Jesus sat them down and gave them a lengthy teaching on what to expect on their missionary journeys. They were promised both power and peril. They were instructed and encouraged. Eagerly, the newly appointed apostles accepted their calling.

Yet Jesus knew that human loyalty can be a fickle thing. He understood that most of His devoted apprentices would fail to acknowledge Him as Lord when under pressure. Jesus emphasized the necessity of their verbal conviction in today's verses. Their devotion would be tested. Jesus' words made it clear that anyone who proved faithless would have far more to fear than men. The severity of this message was necessary to impress upon the Twelve the extreme importance of an unashamed faith in Jesus—the proof of which was fearless acknowledgement of His Lordship in every circumstance.

Today, the term "evangelist" tends to be wrought with negative connotations. Some of us automatically envision overdramatic television preachers and their sobbing wives plying the viewing audience for money. Many of us have personally experienced the guy with a bullhorn, shouting, "Repent or die!" This is not the type of acknowledgement Jesus is talking about in today's verses.

Though there is always a relevant application in all of Jesus' teachings, it is also good to consider the context in which they were spoken. Jesus knew each of His men's strengths and weaknesses. He knew who would defend Him and who would eventually deny Him. He knew their hearts, and He knows ours.

Jesus created each of us to bring Him honor and glory, and to serve Him uniquely. Some of us will be called to bold acts of sacrifice and servitude. Others will share God's love in more quiet and subtle ways. However, *all* Christians are called to proclaim Jesus as Lord when prompted by the Spirit. For those of us who have the love of Jesus in our hearts, this unashamed proclamation of His Lordship will come naturally. For those who refuse to accept His saving grace and will not acknowledge that He is Lord of their lives, their denial will go without saying.

Stepping In: Read 1 Peter 3:15. Pray this verse as an affirmation back to God, changing the words to indicate your emphatic loyalty. Pray also for opportunities to share your unashamed witness.

Stepping Out: This week, acknowledge Christ unashamedly whenever the Spirit leads you. Live out the 1 Peter verse to the best of your abilities.

Culpable

"If you were blind, you would not be guilty of sin; but now that you claim you can see, your guilt remains."

—John 9:41 (Jn 9:13–41)

Already irate over Jesus' blasphemous claims and disregard for Sabbath laws, the Pharisees were ready to arrest Him when they learned that He once again had healed on the Sabbath. The Pharisees questioned the man whose sight Jesus had restored, as well as the man's parents. They did not want to hear the man's declaration that only "a man of God" could have done such a miraculous deed. The religious leaders threw the formerly blind man out of the synagogue.

What the Pharisees intended as a humiliating penalty, Jesus used for the benefit of others and for His own glory. He spoke to the healed man and identified Himself as the Son of Man. The formerly blind man put his faith in Him. As for the Pharisees who were listening in, Jesus made today's observation about their guilt. For all the knowledge about God these learned men claimed, they were ultimately culpable for their lack of spiritual wisdom.

We are all responsible for what we know or don't know. Anyone who has tried to plead ignorance as a defense for breaking a law soon finds out that the excuse does not hold water. Though motive does help explain one's intent, it does not excuse one's actions. This is also true when it comes to our spiritual lives. Because we have ample evidence of the existence of God—the wonders of nature, the miracle of life, the Holy Scriptures, the testimony of saints, the conviction of the Spirit—we are without excuse for not agreeing with it.

Moreover, once we profess a belief in God, there is a spiritual progression we are expected to engage in as we walk in faith. This is where the Pharisees' spiritual development became arrested. When Jesus presented Himself as the Messiah, the Jewish leaders ignored the evidence and denied the validity of the facts. Though Christians may not suffer from this kind of spiritual blindness, we are sometimes guilty of stopping at an intellectual belief in God rather than taking the next steps toward a personal relationship with Jesus.

Spiritual maturity takes intentional obedience and cognitive effort. Today's verse is a reminder that if we don't keep our eyes on Jesus and go where He leads us, we too can succumb to sinful attitudes or behaviors. When we are guilty of wearing spiritual blinders, we are responsible for the consequences.

Stepping In: Read Isaiah 59:1–2, 9–10; Matthew 6:23; Romans 1:20, 2:17-21; 2 Corinthians 4:4; and Ephesians 2:1–2. Has Jesus given you spiritual sight? If so, what is the evidence of it in your life? Pray for God to reveal where you may be culpable of blindness or obstinacy. Ask Him for forgiveness.

Stepping Out: This week, pray for the eyes of the blind to be opened in your family, community, church, nation, and world. Pray especially for our leaders to have spiritual vision. If there is culpability that must be acknowledged and answered for, by you or other guides, now is the time to deal with it.

Stoical

> "You have heard that it was said, 'Eye for eye, and tooth for tooth.' But I tell you, do not resist an evil person. If someone strikes you on the right cheek, turn to him the other also."
>
> —Matthew 5:38–39 (Mt 5:38–42)

The reference Jesus made in the first part of today's verses was found in the writings of Moses, and was commonly known as the "law of retaliation." (Ex 21:24; Lev 24:21; Dt 19:21). The Pharisees and teachers of the Law likely knew exactly where this quotation could be found. However, for a young rabbi to add to the letter of God's law, as Jesus did in the second part of His statement, would have been perceived as taking His teaching authority too far.

This was only the beginning of the controversial theology Jesus would impart throughout His life and ministry. Rather than suggesting that anyone behave in a way contrary to God's commands, Jesus challenged His audiences to go beyond a normal course of action—to be motivated by love for God and others rather than by one's emotions alone. Throughout His Sermon on the Mount, Jesus laid the foundation for a new way of thinking and living based on love, not on retaliation, corruption, greed, or other evils. Essentially, He was telling His audience not to do as evil does. This new way of thinking challenged His listeners to be stoical beyond what they would have thought reasonable, to the point of putting instinct and reflex to the test.

The words of today's verses are still a hard teaching. Many of us consider this teaching to be hyperbole, not to be taken literally. Some commentaries suggest that we ought to view it in the context of legal proceedings, where punishment should be commensurate to the crime. Jesus would flip this notion around, saying that one should not fight evil. One should overcome it through non-offensive resistance and stoic fortitude undergirded by the Spirit's power.

In the kingdom Jesus initiated, a godly person will seek reconciliation rather than retaliation, and peaceful process rather than a quick fix. The godly allow God's moral law to dictate their actions, rather than their volatile human emotions. Even in the face of great adversity, the faithful should do better than simply get even with those who bring them harm. Instead, we should lead others toward a better way through Jesus, which starts with love—even for our enemies.

That said, Jesus does not want us to be foolishly vulnerable or spineless pushovers. We must employ spiritual wisdom in all our interactions, especially those of a contentious or potentially dangerous nature. With godly guidance, we will know when to stand up for what is good and right with everything we have, and when to let God take over.

Stepping In: Read Proverbs 11:21; Matthew 5:44-45, 10:12-15; 28; Luke 6:27–36; and Romans 12:17–21. In what ways have you been faced with the choice to retaliate or remain stoic? How did you respond? Pray for the strength to stand up for good when appropriate, when to leave the distribution of justice to God, and the wisdom to know the difference.

Stepping Out: This week, repay evil with acts of generosity and kindness. Allow the rude customer in line behind you to go first. Compliment a critical coworker. Smile at everyone.

June 19
Reconciled

"Therefore, the kingdom of heaven is like a king who wanted to settle accounts with his servants."

-Matthew 18:23 (Matthew 18:21-35)

After the disciples had learned that Jesus was soon to die, grief and confusion overwhelmed them. The onslaught of human emotions threatened their spiritual progress, the effectiveness of their ministry, and their personal relationships. Fear and doubt sapped their healing powers. Selfishness and pride led to disputes among them. Jesus knew that jealousy, bitterness, and unresolved conflict amongst the disciples would destroy their usefulness in the kingdom of God. Thus, He told the above parable to illustrate the necessity of forgiveness, mercy and reconciliation. In the story, a man who had been forgiven a considerable debt by a king had gone on to deal harshly with someone who owed him only a small amount. When the king learned of this, he became angry with the man and ordered that he receive an even harsher punishment than he had doled out to his own debtor. The point Jesus was making was clear: forgiveness, mercy, and reconciliation were not optional for those in His kingdom.

Jesus is the King who wants to 'settle accounts with His servants.' He wants us to be reconciled to Himself; our debts erased, our sins forgiven. Those of us who have received this gift of grace and mercy know how liberating it is to be free from the bondage of a debt we could never pay. Beyond just atoning for our sins with His blood, Jesus redeemed (purchased, bought back) our inheritance in heaven at the highest cost of all. With clean slates, we look forward to eternity with God, full of hope and joy.

Two thousand years later this tale of self-righteous pride and entitlement among "the forgiven" deems this parable more relevant than we would like to admit. Jesus does not want this point to be lost on anyone who is a servant of the Almighty King. He calls us to a higher standard where love, mercy and forgiveness are foundational attributes we must strive for. They are the verbs of the Christian script. If we are to be the united force Jesus gave His life to establish, we must set an example of reconciliation for all to see. Considering what great a debt Jesus paid for us, it is the only appropriate response.

Stepping In: Reread the entire Matthew passage along with Leviticus 25:39-43, Ephesians 4:32, and Colossians 3:13. How do these verses help you understand the mercy and forgiveness of God? How do they inspire you to be merciful and reconciled with others? Pray that God reveal any unforgiveness you may be harboring and for the strength to settle your own accounts.

Stepping Out: This week, let the Spirit guide you to forgive someone a "debt."

Overcoming

"He who overcomes will, like them, be dressed in white. I will never blot out his name from the book of life, but will acknowledge his name before my Father and his angels."

—Revelation 3:5 (Rv 3:1–6)

John, an apostle of Jesus, was chosen by God to record His revelation of the end times for the benefit of the seven churches in Asia Minor, so that they could be encouraged, warned, rebuked, and instructed. Jesus first commended the church leaders for their faithful obedience and perseverance, then brought to their attention any matters needing improvement.

To the church in Sardis, however, Jesus had no compliments to pay. This was a wealthy church whose appearance and deeds were superficially lovely, but it was spiritually dying as a body of believers. Jesus issued Sardis a stern wake-up call to repent and revive the Spirit or suffer the consequences. In today's verse, Jesus explained to the spiritually apathetic church leaders that they would be wise to follow the example of those who had "not soiled their clothes" with the attitudes and behaviors of the dominant culture. In His love—even for those who had let their lives of luxury lull them into a spiritual stupor—Jesus offered them a wonderful promise. To receive it, they would have to change more than their clothes; they would have to undrego a change of heart as well.

The reference to clothing is not an accident. Jesus spoke of gleaming garments because the city of Sardis had earned its fame and fortune as the textile capital of Asia Minor. The people who lived there knew about luxurious fabric. Yet Jesus spoke of robes of white, not the richly hued garb of the wealthy. White to them would have seemed pedestrian, at least until they realized how special the brilliant colorless garments were. White clothes were reserved only for the pure and blameless who had been given the right to wear them.

Today, beauty and fashion are big business. Keeping up appearances is a top priority for most people, in Western cultures anyway. We, like the Sardisians, can easily let our desires to fit in, be admired, and enjoy the finer things in life distract us from the things that are of eternal value. Christians are called to look different, act differently, and be different. It saddens Jesus when His chosen ones become indistinguishable from unbelievers. If we dress, act, and speak like everyone else, we run the risk of forgetting who we are: overcomers, clothed in royal robes of righteousness.

Stepping In: Read Job 29:14; Isaiah 61:10; Zechariah 3:4–5; John 5:24, 16:33; Philippians 3:20–21; 1 John 3:14; and Revelation 6:10-11, 20:11-15. How do these verses encourage you to embrace your role as an overcomer? Thank God that He chose you to exchange your filthy rags for robes of righteousness!

Stepping Out: One day this week, celebrate being an overcomer by dressing all in white.

Commanded

"A new command I give you: Love one another. As I have loved you,
so you must love one another."

—John 13:34 (Jn 13:1–38)

With His ministry nearing its end, Jesus met with His disciples in an upper room in Jerusalem for their last Passover meal together. It was His Last Supper before His death, and Jesus gave His men the command to love one another. This message was of top importance—the effectiveness of the apostles' ministry would ride on their adherence.

The command to love the Lord and your neighbor had already been given before Jesus spoke this "new command." Jesus re-administered the imperative *specifically* to those who would be carrying on His name. As Christians, we are Jesus' disciples. As disciples, we are ambassadors in Christ. We are the hands, feet, and face of Jesus in our world. Whether we like it or not, we represent the Lord in everything we do and say; the eyes of a critical world are watching us closely.

Sadly, we often are poor representatives of Christ. In our humanness, we tend to let our negative attitudes and bad behaviors show through more than our Christian character traits of humility, empathy, compassion, forgiveness, servitude, kindness, generosity, and above all, love. Without these, we do not look any different than anyone else.

Jesus wants us to stand out. He has commanded us to love others, including other believers, even when no one else does. By this, people will know that we belong to Him. It is the least we can do to honor the One who loved us first and best, giving His own life to prove it.

Stepping In: Read John 13:35, 15:13; Romans 12:9–13; 1 Corinthians 13:4–7, 13; Galatians 5:13–14, 22–23; and 1 John 4:7. What do these verses teach about the importance of love to God? How seriously do you take the fact that you have been commanded by Jesus to love everyone? Pray for a heart overflowing with love for others. Pray for those you struggle to love.

Stepping Out: This week, love a fellow believer in the same way Jesus has loved you. Offer help, forgiveness, grace, humble service, or gentle instruction; or simply take them out for coffee.

June 22
Balanced

"I am sending you out as sheep among wolves. Therefore, be as shrewd
as snakes and as innocent as doves."

—Matthew 10:16 (Mt 10: 1–16)

Jesus spoke these words of warning and instruction during the lengthy pre-commissioning pep talk He gave to His twelve newly appointed apostles. Even after two years with Jesus, learning from Him, witnessing His power, and being promised power of their own, these first-ever Christian missionaries were most likely overwhelmed by the enormity of the task ahead. This vision of going out as weak and helpless sheep simply did not match the healing and saving mission they thought they were about to embark upon. These men had probably seen the results of a wolf attack on livestock, and neither snakes nor doves would have seemed a sufficient defense against the beasts Jesus said they would face, literally or figuratively.

It was the spiritual wolves Jesus wanted His men to be cautious of—those who would forcefully reject both the messenger and the message. When faced with such vehement opponents, the disciples would be wise to employ a balanced spiritual approach to fend off their enemy. Learning from the crafty snake, they should avoid predators, be coiled and ready to move, poised to strike with the sword of truth if necessary. Taking a lesson from the dove, they should always strive to be ambassadors of peace. Regardless of the tactics they used, their success would ultimately rest in the hands of the One who was sending them: Jesus.

The modern-day, postindustrial way of saying what today's verse implies might be, "It's a dog-eat-dog world." In so many aspects of our lives, especially in business, we are taught early to always keep our wits about us and watch our backs. The only way to get ahead in this world is to be the smartest, if not craftiest, among our peers. Always working the "angle," we strive to impress those who can help us gain an advantage and to maneuver around those who might inhibit our progress. Competition is fierce. This is the way of the world.

Christians, who promote and live by a different set of standards, can be perceived as a threat to the status quo. Today's passage reminds us that a balance of tactics is necessary for dealing with society's reaction to our faith. Like the savvy businessperson, we must read our audience to know if we are dealing with sheep or wolves, then make the appropriate adjustments to our missional approach. Jesus doesn't want us to be sitting ducks. He wants us to be "salt and light" (with a side of fish) instead.

Stepping In: Read through the book of Proverbs. Meditate on the wisdom therein. Camp out on and pray about the verses that speak to your heart and/or conscience. Make any necessary adjustments as God leads you.

Stepping Out: This week, employ a wise and balanced approach to life and ministry. Pray for a deeper faith to trust Him who sends you out among wolves.

Unapologetic

> "And anyone who does not carry his cross and follow me cannot be my disciple."
>
> —Luke 14:27 (Lk 14:25–35)

Throughout His ministry, as John the Baptist had done before Him, Jesus spoke resolutely about the coming kingdom of God. This was a welcome message for the Jews, who assumed it meant that the Messiah was an earthly king who would end Roman rule and the societal oppression under which the Jews lived.

The years went by, and it became clear that Jesus was not the type of king the people had hoped for. Many lost interest in His so-called kingdom. The division between those who put their hope and faith in the gospel and those who continued to cling to their righteousness through the law became a widening chasm. With the end of His ministry in sight, Jesus spoke unapologetically about the choice each person would have to make: continue to trust in a defunct system, or follow Him into the future.

As we see in today's verse, Jesus made it clear that choosing a life of faith required sacrifices beyond what His listeners could imagine, though no one could fully understand what He meant at the time. To His audience, the cross was nothing more than a barbaric Roman torture device reserved for the execution of criminals. That anyone would choose to subject themselves to it was totally absurd. Those who had sworn loyalty to Jesus, even unto death, were hard-pressed to accept such an assertion. Until they understood that death—even on a cross—was not the end, this was a difficult command to follow.

Modern readers of this passage, without the help of the Holy Spirit, can likewise struggle with its meaning. At face value, it seems to say that devotion to Jesus is a death sentence. At the very least, it requires incredible strength and determination to share His load.

In a sense, both these postulations are true. To be born again of Christ means a death to self. Once saved, we are new creations, no longer bound by the ways of sin and final death. We are heirs to the kingdom of heaven. Yet, while saved from eternal damnation, the lives we live on earth will not be without pain and struggle. The heaviness of the world's hostility toward Christianity and the weight of our own sinful nature make the cross difficult and awkward to carry, if not dangerous.

Jesus minces no words when He tells us that families, communities, and nations will be divided because of Him. People still trust in worldly power for their hope and security, and those who do not subscribe to this line of thinking are seen as narrow-minded and foolish. As they always have, Christians represent a threat to human authority, and will continue to be opposed and oppressed until Jesus returns. This is our cross to bear. May we carry it humbly and unapologetically each day.

Stepping In: Read Mark 8:34–38; John 16:33; Romans 8:3-4, 12:1-2; 1 Corinthians 1:18; and Galatians 2:20, 6:14. Take some time to consider what the cross means to you. Pray that God will reveal to you any area of your life you have not yet surrendered to Him, and that you would have the willingness to do so now.

Stepping Out: This week, help a Christian brother or sister who is struggling to carry their load. Help them to know that they never have to apologize for needing help with their cross—Jesus did.

June 24
Joyous

"How can the guests of the bridegroom mourn while He is still with them? The time will come when the bridegroom will be taken from them; then they will fast."

—Matthew 9:15 (Mt 9:14–17)

Today's verse may have seemed an incongruous reply to a question posed by the disciples of John the Baptist regarding who should fast and when. They might have thought, "What does fasting have to do with guests of a wedding?" and "Who is this bridegroom and why must he be taken?" All John's disciples really wanted to know was why they had to fast if Jesus' disciples did not.

Jesus answered their inquiry with an analogy He would use frequently when referring to His relationship with His church and the kingdom of heaven: that of Jesus as the Bridegroom and His church as the bride. Fasting, in the Jewish culture, was a common practice. People fasted for religious reasons, mostly in combination with sincere repentance, grief, or fervent prayer. No one fasted during a celebration such as a wedding.

John's disciples were most likely fasting while praying for the release of their teacher from prison. Jesus' disciples, on the other hand, were in the midst of a joyous time of having their Teacher with them in the prime of His life, and therefore had no need of fasting. Perhaps to placate John's followers, however, Jesus did add that His disciples' time for fasting would come.

Though most Jews today do not observe the long list of fasting days that their ancestors did, many still observe the fasts associated with Rosh Hashanah and Yom Kippur. In our modern culture, most of us have moved away from old traditions and strict religious practices. There are many reasons for this, time certainly being one of them. Fasting takes time, effort, and energy. Most of us are not willing or able to commit to this discipline even if we wanted to. Busy lives require us to be on top of our game, not preoccupied and fatigued. Moreover, most people in our self-satisfied, comfort-based culture can see no reason to deprive themselves of food or anything else.

Students of the New Testament learn that the occasional practice of self-denial and absolute reliance on God during times of prayer and spiritual seeking are not only appropriate but expected. Jesus states this in Matthew 6:16: "When you fast ..." Notice that "when" is an assumption that you will fast—Jesus does not say "if." As followers of Jesus, we are to abide by *all* His teachings, not just the ones we like.

Thankfully, today's verse reminds us that our Lord wants us also to celebrate the blessed union we have with Him and joyously look forward to the banquet feast yet to come.

Stepping In: Read Isaiah 62:5; Psalm 19:4–6; and Revelation 19:7. Take some time to consider your relationship to the Bridegroom. Read Matthew 9:15 again. Use the Own It method (See appendix) to reflect on this verse. Is now a time for fasting or celebrating for you? Prayerfully seek God's will, being willing to sacrifice your comforts for Him when appropriate.

Stepping Out: This week, share a fellowship meal with other believers. Discuss what being the bride of Christ means to you. What are you most looking forward to when you arrive at the Big Soiree?

June 25
Strengthened

"But I have prayed for you, Simon, that your faith not fail. And when
you have turned back, strengthen your brothers."
—Luke 22:32 (Lk 22:7–38)

On the day of His betrayal and arrest, Jesus had His last Passover supper with His disciples in an upper room in Jerusalem. As the evening progressed, what would have normally been a celebration became heavy and clouded with mystery. Jesus indicated that Satan himself was already at work trying to take the disciples' focus off Him, and that even Peter would briefly be led astray. In His tenderness, Jesus let Peter and the other faithful apostles know that He would spiritually intercede on their behalf so that their time of rebellion and confusion might be short. In prophetic words, Jesus told Peter plainly that although Peter was destined to fail on some accounts, he would again be strengthened by faith. He would become the rock of strength among his brothers in due time. His old name and life were exchanged for new, purpose-driven ones.

Jesus knows our weaknesses. He understands our temptations. He created us and knows our thoughts and desires. He sees into our hearts. Like Peter, even the most devoted and zealous of Christ followers will have moments of confusion and doubt. When pressured, we may even deny Jesus—maybe not verbally, but with our attitudes and actions.

Jesus' encouragement to Peter was meant for all believers in all generations. The promise and the prediction still stand. Jesus is praying for each of us, that our faith may not falter under fire. Yet He knows that it is likely to happen nonetheless. He wants us to use the lessons we learn in our faith struggles to help others. In twelve-step programs, they call this sharing one's experience, strength, and hope. We can do this also when we turn back to God and do as we are prayed for and commanded to do.

Stepping In: Read Job 1:6–12; Matthew 16:18; John 17:6–12; Romans 8:34; Philippians 4:13; and Hebrews 7:25. How does knowing that Jesus Himself is interceding for and strengthening you bring you comfort? How do these verses help to strengthen your faith? Thank Jesus for always looking out for you.

Stepping Out: This week, strengthen your brothers and sisters in Christ by sharing the experience, strength, and hope you developed while working through your own struggles in faith.

June 26

Humble

> "I tell you the truth, unless you change and become like little children, you will never enter the kingdom of heaven. Therefore, whoever humbles himself like this child is the greatest in the kingdom of heaven."
>
> —Matthew 18:3–4 (Mt 18:1–6)

During His last season as an earthly rabbi, Jesus concentrated His efforts on preparing His disciples for His imminent departure. These men, who had lived with and loved their Master, who were devoted to the bitter end, and who had seen His miracles, and some had even seen His glory, were beginning to understand that Jesus was no ordinary man. Yet, because they held out hopes that Jesus would be the promised redeemer king, they often lost sight of the eternal kingdom Jesus was trying to teach them about. Though Jesus' ominous promise about "going to the Father" continued to cause them fear and confusion, their worldly perspective caused them to contemplate their own power and prestige as heirs to the kingdom to come.

To put a quick end to their prideful thinking, Jesus spoke about becoming "like little children." For an adult to be called a child in this ancient culture would have been an extreme insult. Children were, and sometimes still are, considered foolish and insignificant. Jesus, however, wanted His men to consider the childlike qualities that equated to greatness in His kingdom: innocence, unquestioning trust, lack of pretension, utter dependence, and humility. Adopting this perspective would require a change of heart, mind, attitude, and behavior among His disciples.

As we read through the New Testament, it is clear that Jesus cares greatly about the condition of our hearts. This imperative to have a pure heart is second only to the imperative to love God and others. Time and again, Jesus talks about humility, honesty, and good intentions.

Like His disciples, we often need reminders about the futility of pretending with God. He knows our thoughts and motives before we do. From the time of the apostles, followers of Jesus have been in a constant battle between our earthbound realities and our eternal destinies. We are all trying to understand our roles here on earth while at the same time attempting to see ourselves in heaven. Though it may seem that Jesus is implying that believers risk losing their salvation from a lack of childlike qualities, that is not so. Jesus is merely emphasizing that it is unquestioning faith in His saving grace that distinguishes true believers from those who "will never enter the kingdom of heaven."

Christians must remember to keep their focus heavenward and not on dazzling worldly distractions. Jesus spells out the solution: "change and become like little children." By living in the moment, delighting in the promise of gifts from above, and trusting fully in our heavenly Father, we can (re)gain the heavenly perspective Jesus wants all His children to have.

Stepping In: Reflect on today's verse using the Own It method. (See appendix). How does this personalized message change its meaning for you? Does it surprise you to realize how important unreserved trust and humility are to Jesus, and how much they reflect faith? Pray for a humble, childlike faith. Thank God that you are saved by grace through faith in Jesus.

Stepping Out: This week, act like a child! View God, yourself, and others through a childlike lens of trust and faith. Remove all pretentiousness from your words and actions. Be playful, humble, honest.

June 27

Judicious

"You are a king then!" said Pilate. Jesus answered, "You are right in saying I am a king. In fact, for this reason I was born, and for this I came into the world, to testify to the truth. Everyone on the side of truth listens to me."

—John 18:37 (Jn 28–40)

After being bound and taken from the garden of Gethsemane by an armed militia, Jesus was brought to the Jewish high priest for questioning. An illegal evening assembly of the Jewish council of elders tried in vain to agree on a legitimate charge against Him. Soon to lose their cover of darkness, they brought Jesus to the Roman governor, Pilate, in hopes of finding help from the presiding authority.

As the new day dawned, word of Jesus' arrest had spread throughout Jerusalem, and soon a riled mob gathered outside the governor's house, shouting for Jesus to be crucified. The Jews, hoping to avoid being implicated in the shedding of a man's blood and therefore rendering themselves ceremonially unclean, encouraged Pilate to make a quick decision in Jesus' case.

After questioning Him, Pilate too found no valid charge for which Jesus should be executed. However, being concerned with his public image, Pilate was keener on appeasing the crowd than on seeking justice. Pilate then asked Jesus about the charge the Jews had brought against Him—was He indeed the "king of the Jews"? Jesus replied that His kingdom was not of this world. Pilate seized upon only one thing—that Jesus was claiming to be a king. This could be construed as a political crime against Roman rule. Pilate asked the crowd to choose who should receive the traditional Passover pardon, Jesus or Barabbas, a known criminal. Their verdict: freedom for the guilty man, and crucifixion for the innocent One.

Though each of the four gospel writers includes different details about Jesus' arrest and trial, they all agree that it was a farce—a travesty of justice based on an inexcusable debacle of due process. Those who were supposed to uphold the laws of God and man abused those laws in the most egregious of ways—mocking His Son and having Him killed in cold blood. Those who were supposed to employ judicious diligence caved under pressure and became equal partners in the crime of putting an innocent man to death.

In John's version of this story, we are given a clue as to where it all went wrong. Pondering Jesus' kingdom claims, Pilate asked, "What is truth?" This is the crux of the issue for us all. Even those who met Jesus in the flesh, who had visual and tangible proofs of His divinity, who heard from His own lips the very words of God, still had to wrestle with this question. Today, the question remains.

The truth for most people is that "truth" is relative. Even if there is a God, they think they don't need Him. They may know about Him and even like the idea of grand force of good, but they have no interest in having a relationship with Him. Another segment of the population flat-out does not believe. It is a Christian's duty and honor to set the record straight: Jesus' innocent blood bought salvation for believers.

Stepping In: Read Isaiah 53; John 3:32-34, 8:18, 8:47; and 1 John 4:6. What truth about Jesus is revealed in these verses, and what is your heart's response? Praise God for sending His Son for your redemption.

Stepping Out: This week, ask everyone you can Pilate's question. Listen respectfully and share humbly.

Petitionary

"Ask the Lord of the harvest, therefore, to send out workers into his harvest field."

—Matthew 9:38 (Mt 9:35–38)

The command to ask the Lord to send out (mission) field workers was given after Jesus informed His disciples that the harvest of souls was abundant, but the people willing and able to do the work were few. Jesus hoped to both warn and encourage His men that their missionary labor, well spent, would bring a good return.

By reminding the Twelve to "ask the Lord" to direct and assist them, Jesus communicated that they would not be going into the unknown alone. Before, as young Jewish men, the disciples had approached God through strictly observed religious practices and the mediation of the high priest. As Jesus' chosen instruments for spreading the gospel, the disciples' petitionary stance would become a direct line to the Lord Himself. Intellectually, they were beginning to understand that God and Jesus were one and the same. They would in time come to believe it in their hearts as well. In the meantime, they would have to trust that their requests for help would be answered.

Most vocations still require teaching and training before the worker is set to task. Some fields are very specialized and are only suitable for the called and the gifted. Ministry is one of them. In a world where two-thirds of the population claims a religious affiliation other than Christianity (per a 2010 Pew research report), the potential missionary field is dauntingly large and the workers still few. However, according to Jesus, this is not our problem alone. Though all Christians must work for the kingdom, God oversees personnel recruitment, not us.

We do, however, have an important role in the process: praying. In addition to bringing our praise, worship, and repentance to God, our prayer requests are vital. Jesus encourages us to be specific. Throughout scripture, Jesus explains how we should pray. Sometimes He even tell us why. To fulfill the Great Commission, God needs willing and able folks to be His petitionary partners as well as His crusaders. Though it is not explicitly stated, we also know that those who have the skills and the knowledge to do this work already must teach and train others to share the task. Ask, and God will answer His petitionary people.

Stepping In: Read Romans 8:34 and Hebrews 7:25. Turn today's verse into a prayer. Ask Him to reveal to you your role in this work. Thank Him for allowing you to join Him in what He has already begun. Know that you are someone else's answered prayer.

Stepping Out: Where is the Lord of the harvest leading you? Are you answering the call? This week, take some first steps toward becoming an employee of God's kingdom.

Aware

> "When evening comes, you say, 'It will be fair weather, for the sky is red,' and in the morning, 'Today it will be stormy, for the sky is red and overcast.' You know how to interpret the appearance of the sky, but you cannot interpret the signs of the times."
>
> —Matthew 16:2–3 (Mt 16:1–4)

After news that Jesus had fed five thousand in Galilee reached the ears of the Jewish leaders, they were all the more determined to find a way to discredit Him in the eyes of the public. They came to Jesus and demanded He perform a "sign from heaven." In response, Jesus used the same scalding language He had used before when asked for a sign, perhaps by some of the same men. Jesus implied that all the signs they could possibly want were already before their eyes, as obvious as the weather—though the Pharisees were unaware.

Ignorant and incredulous as the Jewish leaders may have been, their demand for proof of Jesus' authority was to be expected. Though they were touted as experts in godly wisdom, these men's hearts were far from God. They were blinded by worldly desires and self-interest. They had lost their ability to discern the workings of God and were unaware when He was standing in their presence.

Today, most people suffer from the same condition. Even Christians, trying to stay aware of God in their midst, struggle against the me-centric dominant culture. Sometimes, in desperation, we call out for signs of His activity in our lives and world. We want proof that He is there, and that He cares.

Regardless of our beliefs, we all want to make sense of the world. We want the "experts" to inform us of our best and safest options in nearly every category of our lives. Yet, because of the busyness and chaos of life, we often neglect the Expert on all things: Jesus. Today's verses remind us to pay attention and be aware of the signs Jesus is giving us. With God's Spirit in us, we can recognize and interpret signs far more impressive than an accurate weather forecast.

Stepping In: Read Matthew 12:38–42. Have you ever asked God for a sign? Have you ever doubted His love or power? Take some time to recall occasions when Jesus gave you clear directions. Thank Him for them now. Pray for an increased awareness of His presence and provision.

Stepping Out: This week, be aware of the clear signs the Holy Spirit is showing you. Make a list of them and thank God for His expert advice and wisdom.

Dauntless

"You of little faith, why are you so afraid?"
—Matthew 8:26 (Mt 8:23–27)

In the middle of His earthly ministry, Jesus and His disciples found themselves again in Galilee. They wanted to cross from one side of the sea to the other, and got into a boat. Not long after they set out, a storm cropped up, threatening to swamp the vessel and toss its passengers into the turbulent waters. Despite the jostling of the boat and the rising panic among His men, Jesus—exhausted from countless days of missional work—slept unperturbed. Frantically, the disciples called out, "Lord, save us! We're going to drown." The disciples' faith was momentarily tested by human fear. They lost sight of their "anchor in the storm" because they thought Jesus was either unaware or uncaring of their plight. They forgot that Jesus was not a mere mortal.

Perhaps Jesus caused the storm. Perhaps He decided to make use of the given circumstances to teach His disciples a faith lesson. Regardless, a lesson was taught that day. Jesus waited for His men, most of them experienced sailors, to call out to Him in utter dependence before He stepped in to help. Before He relieved them, He asked them why they were afraid. Though His disciples were devoted, they had a long way to go before they could tout a dauntless trust in Jesus during life's storms.

Those who read the Bible today, and know the whole story, probably react to this verse with a mixture of amazement and disappointment. Some may smugly consider the disciples ridiculous for not recognizing Jesus' power and authority, especially since they had experienced so much of it firsthand. Most of us believe that if we were in the disciples' place, we would not fear the storm.

However, Christians who take an honest look at their own reactions to life's scary moments come away humbled and embarrassed. Even when we know that Jesus is *with* us and *in* us, we still tend to panic when catastrophes strike. We don't hear Jesus' reassuring words until after He has calmed the storm. Perhaps because we have become accustomed to things going smoothly, we react poorly when things disrupt our routines. We quickly go into fix-it mode, wondering why such circumstances happened.

The question we really ought to be asking instead is "Where is Jesus in all of this?" If we look for Him, we will see that He is right in the boat next to us. Then we can proceed undaunted into anything.

Stepping In: What storms are you in the middle of right now? In a word, how would you describe your reaction or your state of mind? Pray that God replaces any negative reaction with a sense of peace and security. Ask the Holy Spirit for a dauntless faith, regardless of circumstances.

Stepping Out: This week, be a strong and dauntless support to someone dealing with a storm. Let Jesus' calming presence in you be a calming presence for them.

July 1
Measured

> "According to your faith, will it be done to you."
> —Matthew 9:29 (Mt 9:27–34)

As Jesus moved from town to town in Galilee during His second year in ministry, people flocked to Him for wisdom and healing. Near the town of Capernaum, He healed two blind men who had called out to the "Son of David," asking the "Lord" for "mercy." In a world where these men had nothing, hope was enough to inspire a motivating faith.

Jesus gave them what they asked for, and He told them why. He explained that the amount of faith these men had demonstrated would surely be measured back to them. The first of many ways occurred at that moment: their sight was restored. Though not stated, the ways in which their lives were redeemed would have led to many more blessings for them and others. Excited as they were, Jesus instructed them not to tell anyone how they were healed, or by whom. Unable to contain their glee, the two men quickly spread the news.

Most people have heard the phrase, "You get what you deserve." Usually it is used in the context of a punishment. It can also be said that according to what you have done, it will be done to you as well. That means that to the same measure or degree that you do something to others, it will be done to you. This can go in the positive or negative direction.

In our world, we take the negative side of this notion far beyond what is reasonable. In the United States, one look no further than our jammed court systems to see just how sue-happy a nation we are. We often want more than just to be paid back in equal measure to what we have lost—we insist that the offender suffer much greater losses. Jesus wants us to get back on the right side of the scale here. Technically speaking, the two blind men had done nothing to deserve Jesus' favor. But because they pursued Him in faith, He rewarded them with gifts beyond measure: physical sight and an eternal perspective by which they could view the world. In faith, they had asked for mercy. That is what they were given, tenfold.

Stepping In: Read Psalm 51:1–2; Isaiah 35:3–5, 61:1; Ephesians 3:20–21; Hebrews 4:16. Is your faith measured by the world's measure (sight), or according to God's accounting (belief)? When you call out to God, is it for things you think you want, or is it for His mercy—according to what He knows you need? Pray for His mercy and will to be done.

Stepping Out: This week, tweak the golden rule. Instead of doing to others what you would like them to do to you, treat other's as Jesus would (and does). Praise God for such opportunities.

July 2
Protected

"Since you have kept my command to endure patiently, I will also keep you from the hour of trial that is going to come upon the whole world to test those who live on the earth."

—Revelation 3:10 (Rv 3:7–13)

Jesus gave the apostle John the task of recording His revelation of the end times. This apocalyptic letter begins with an address to each of the seven churches of Asia Minor. The sixth church mentioned is the church in Philadelphia.

Typically, Jesus bestowed words of encouragement on each church He mentioned. Philadelphia received that encouragement. Yet, unlike the first five churches, the church leaders in Philadelphia did not then receive scalding words of rebuke. Instead, Jesus commended them. Even in their weakness, they persisted in professing His name. Alluding to the calamity that was to come, Jesus encouraged Philadelphia to remain obedient. He promised protection for their faithful endurance. He went on to tell them that, though they lacked strength, they would become "pillars in the temple of God" when the New Jerusalem came down from heaven.

The hope and promise of this passage has long been an anchor to the souls of believers. As Jesus tells us, this earth is not our home. We are aliens here because our true citizenship is in heaven. However, while we wait for Jesus to return and reclaim His people and His kingdom, we must, like the Philadelphians, patiently endure life in our fallen world.

Christians in ancient Philadelphia, the "city of brotherly love," received the most wonderful of blessings for doing what was honorable and right before God and man. They kept His Word and did not deny His name. Therefore, they would be spared the plight the rest of the world would face upon His return.

This promise is for all, then and now, who faithfully endure trials because of Jesus' name. Patience and perseverance are needed to stay strong in faith and actions as the days get increasingly evil. As Christians, we must shrug off the rejection and ridicule doled out by the egocentric and self-satisfied culture in which we live. We must resist the temptation to engage in spiritually compromising attitudes or behavior in our attempts to fit in. Above all, we must lead others to the only door through which all must enter heaven: Jesus. We must help them to be among those protected inside when it shuts for good.

Stepping In: Read Deuteronomy 31:6; Matthew 24:12–14; John 14:2–3; Acts 14:27; 2 Thessalonians 3:3; Hebrews 6:16–20; 2 Peter 2:4–10; and Revelation 2:10. Praise God that His promises are faithful and true. Pray for the protection and salvation of souls; those who do not yet know the truth, that they will come to a saving faith soon.

Stepping Out: Each day this week, pray for a different person who is need of Jesus' protection.

July 3

Vigilant

"Be careful," Jesus said to them. "Be on your guard against the yeast of the Pharisees and Sadducees."

—Matthew 16:6 (Mt 16:1–12)

After two years of traveling throughout Israel with Jesus, sharing in His ministry and proclaiming the gospel, the disciples prepared to set out once again across the Sea of Galilee with their Master. No doubt tired from the physical nature of their work and constant harassment of the Jewish leaders, they headed for their home base at Capernaum, eager for a rest.

At some point in the journey, the men discovered they had forgotten to bring bread to eat. They mentioned this to Jesus, and He gave them a seemingly random warning against the yeast of the Pharisees and Sadducees. Confused, the disciples whispered among themselves, maybe blaming each other for their negligence and wondering, "Hadn't Jesus recently equated yeast in the dough to the kingdom of heaven?" Yet here Jesus was clearly equating it to something nefarious.

Seeing that His students were feeling remorseful and bewildered, Jesus explained that He was not angry about their absentminded mistake, but about their lack of faith. Didn't they remember that He could supply bread if that was what was needed? Indeed, this lesson was not about bread, or the leavening agent therein, but about the dangerous infiltration of false teachings. Jesus needed His men to trust His words, remember His actions, and be vigilant not to let cultural or religious pressures diminish their faith.

Even more than in the ancient world, today's seekers of truth must beware of unbiblical teaching masked under the cloak of religion. With so many spiritual paths to choose from, the way to God seems to be anyone's guess; one need only choose one's own adventure. Once a person determines that there is a higher power other than themselves, the search for answers begins. Though some seekers prefer not to give God a name or title—because that would imply a recognition of an external authority and require a level of accountability they would rather not be burdened with—some do grasp the monotheistic view. Even so, plenty of religions worship God under names like Buddha, Allah, or some version of Jesus as prophet. These are false teachings.

The only way for a seeker to know if they are on the path toward eternal salvation is if the God they believe in is the Triune God: Father, Jesus, and Holy Spirit. Any teaching that does not point to Jesus as Lord is yeast that must be vigilantly avoided.

Stepping In: Read Matthew 15:7–9; Luke 12:1; and 1 Corinthians 5:6–8. Where have you seen subtle influences of false teaching in your family, community, or church? Pray for boldness to expose hypocrisy and unbiblical doctrine in your sphere of influence. Pray that God give you strength and wisdom to be vigilant.

Stepping Out: This week, make sure that the things that influence you are truthful and honoring to God. View everything, including what you read, listen to, and watch, through a biblical filter. One day this week, fast from leavened foods as a reminder to be on guard against falsehood.

Liberated

> To the Jews who had believed him, Jesus said, "If you hold to my teaching, you are really my disciples. Then you will know the truth, and the truth will set you free."
>
> —John 8:31–32 (Jn 8:31–41)

Preaching in the temple in Jerusalem during the Feast of Tabernacles, Jesus clearly explained the dire consequences that would befall unbelievers. Some wisely opted to put their faith in Him thereafter. Jesus imparted liberating news to His new followers: the truth would set them free. But there was a caveat, an "if," reminding them that their decision would require mental, physical, and spiritual commitment on their part.

It is amazing how such a short word can yield such power. This same two-letter word, "if," continues to hold Christ followers accountable today. It is not enough to casually agree that Jesus is Lord. To be a true disciple, one must hold to His teachings. This means we must know what His teachings are in the first place. He commands His disciples to do more than just memorize lines of scripture; they must embody His teachings in their hearts and lives. Knowledge of God is good, but it is only the beginning. We need to not just know *about* Jesus, but know Him *personally*.

As Jesus extended this invitation to those who stood in His presence two thousand years ago, He extends it to us today. Like the Jews in the temple, we have a choice: remain bound by the Law, held captive by our fear of change, and dead in our sin—or allow our faith in our redeemer, Jesus, to set us free.

Stepping In: Read Psalm 119:45; Isaiah 61:1; John 3:16; Romans 6:22-23, 10:9; Corinthians 3:17; Galatians 5:13–14; and James 1:22. Look again at today's verses. Reflect on this scripture passage using the Own It method. (See appendix). Write it so that it is a personal declaration of your emancipation in Christ. Praise Him, you are liberated!

Stepping Out: This week, with your small group or some friends, review Jesus' teachings from Matthew chapters 5 through 7. Talk about what challenges you, what encourages you, and what is currently inspiring you to act. Make a plan to hold each other accountable to any changes you decide to make.

Charitable

"The King will reply, 'I tell you the truth, whatever you did for one of the least of these brothers of mine, you did for me.'"
—Matthew 25:40 (Mt 24:1–3, 25:31–46)

Having fulfilled His Father's will to offer His message of salvation throughout Israel, Jesus obediently went to Jerusalem to make one last Passover sacrifice: Himself. He spent time in the temple courts, preaching the good news and warning the people about the religious leaders' wicked and hypocritical ways. With just two days remaining before He would be handed over to the authorities, Jesus took His disciples to a remote place. Speaking in parables, He explained how the Son of Man would come like a shepherd to cull the flock: the good sheep to His right side and the wicked goats to His left. Jesus described how His "sheep" had fed, clothed, and cared for Him, even visiting Him in prison. Not recalling having done any of these things for the King, the confused sheep asked for clarification and were enlightened.

Today's verse has become quite well known and highly quoted; a helpful person's creed, if you will. And truly, Jesus would want it that way. Amid this roundabout story of sheep and goats, Jesus is reminding all His followers to treat everyone the way He does—as wonderful and deserving creations. He expects His flock to do for others what we would without question do for our Lord. To Jesus, they are one and the same.

Choosing His words carefully, Jesus touched on the crux of the issue for many by calling the recipients of charity "least." Notice that He also referred to them as "brothers." More than invoking a sense of familial obligation, Jesus nudges us toward sincere compassion for those in need. Bringing the sheep and the goats back into the equation, He tells us in no uncertain terms what will happen to those inside of His fold and those on the outside. Charitable behaviors are not a prerequisite for salvation, but they certainly ought to be a natural response to it.

Stepping In: Read Ezekiel 34:11–17; Malachi 3:17–18; John 10:14; and Hebrews 13:1–3. How is God stirring in your heart after reading these verses? Is there some generosity you are withholding? Pray for eyes to see everyone as worthy of care, and for a charitable heart to serve others as you would Jesus Himself.

Stepping Out: This week, do one or more of the charitable actions Jesus describes in Matthew 25:35–36, not out of mere obligation, but as a form of worship to God for all His generosity toward you.

July 6
Equipped

"When I sent you without purse, bag or sandals, did you lack anything?"
"Nothing," they answered.

—Luke 22:35 (Lk 22:7–38)

In an upper room in a Jerusalem guesthouse, Jesus and his twelve apostles sat down for a longed-for Passover meal. Excitement and anticipation filled the room. So much had transpired in the days leading up to this moment, everyone could hardly wait to break bread and enjoy the celebration. Still elated from the triumphal entry Jesus had received only days before, the apostle's expectations for their holiday meal were quite high.

The mood quickly shifted as Jesus gave thanks in a disturbingly unfamiliar way. Using bread and wine to symbolize His body and blood, broken and spilled for them, He implored them to eat and remember Him. This was to be a lasting covenant. Confused, the disciples argued among themselves until Jesus reminded them to stop thinking about who they would be in His kingdom, and to think instead about *whose* they would be.

Turning to His most vocal and zealously loyal disciple, Jesus rebuked Peter personally by stating that Satan himself would bring testing to his faith. Peter adamantly asserted that he was willing to die for His Master. Jesus reiterated that indeed, before the night was over, Peter would deny knowing Him three times.

Before Peter could say anything more about it, Jesus reminded all His men that He was always aware of their needs and would never fail to adequately equip them. Thus, they could trust and rely on Jesus completely. They should take Him at His Word, even if they could not fully understand it. Jesus asserted that for the journey they were about to embark upon, they should this time go prepared with bag, cloak and sword.

Jesus has been asking His disciples this same question—"Did you lack anything?"—for millennia now. In the simplest terms, He has been telling us that He is all we will ever need to do His kingdom work.

In the way this part of the gospel develops, it might seem that Jesus is telling us something completely different. Peter, confused, equipped himself literally and wound up using a sword to cut an ear off one of the mob members arresting Jesus. But that is not what our Lord had in mind. Violence is never the answer.

What Jesus is saying is that we need to be prepared with the provisions He has equipped each of us with. These look different for each person because the provisions are based on the gifts and talents Jesus gives to us according to our mission. Some will be blessed with money, which they can use for God's purposes. Others will be given the gifts of organization and administration, which they can put to good use in kingdom work. Regardless of our unique equipment, we are all to carry a sword—that is, the Word of God.

Stepping In: Read Matthew 10:9–10; Romans 12:6–8; 1 Corinthians 12:7-11, 12:27-31; and Ephesians 4:11–13 and 6:10–17. How has God equipped you for doing kingdom work? Pray and seek His guidance and a willingness to use it well.

Stepping Out: This week, look up "Spiritual Gifts Assessments" on the web, and take it. Then, choose one of your spiritual gifts to focus on and put it to good work at your church or in your community.

July 7
Compassionate

"Take heart, son; your sins are forgiven."
—Matthew 9:2 (Mt 9:1–8)

Jesus spent a good deal of time in the regions surrounding the Sea of Galilee. After giving a multi-day sermon on a mountainside nearby, Jesus saw the need for and receptivity to His message among the people of that area. Thus, He stayed with them a while, teaching, healing, and sharing His love and truth.

On one occasion, a paralyzed man was carried by his friends to the house where they had heard Jesus was staying. When they got there, though, they could not even reach the door because of the crowd. Bravely, the invalid's committed companions hauled him up onto the roof and lowered him on his mat through the ceiling, placing him right in front of Jesus. Everyone was astonished. Jesus Himself was moved to compassion by this bold act of faith and brotherly love.

The words of forgiveness Jesus spoke, though comforting to the fully restored paralytic, were words of pure blasphemy to the legalistic Jewish leaders present. Only God could forgive sins, or miraculously heal for that matter. The Jewish leaders, hardened by lives dictated by rules, not only lacked the compassion their supposed godliness should have inspired, but were also blind to God's own Son in their presence. The healed man and his friends, however, would have taken to heart Jesus' words and action that day.

Certainly, heroic acts such as the one in today's passage have happened throughout human history. Plenty of examples of courage, bravery, and selflessness can be observed in times of tragedy. But to see a group of friends put forth such a monumental and risky effort, simply out of compassion, is somewhat unheard of. It is not that we don't care; it is just that we are often too busy, distracted, or complacent. We often lack belief that we have the knowledge, ability, or fortitude to bring about life-changing restoration. In other words, it's complicated.

Luckily for the paralytic, his friends did not suffer from this limiting attitude. They weren't confused about where healing power came from. All they had to do was get their friend to Jesus and He would do the rest.

Empowered by the comforting and life-giving words of this verse, all believers can demonstrate compassion to those who still need to hear them, even if means carrying those in need to the feet of Jesus.

Stepping In: Read Mark 2:1–7 and Luke 5:17–26. Use the Envision It method to reflect on this scripture passage. (See appendix). Who in the crowd do you relate to and why? Imagine being the paralytic. How would it feel to be similarly loved and cared for by your friends? What would it be like to be comforted and healed by Jesus? Pray that you are filled with compassion like that of the invalid's friends.

Stepping Out: This week, help a friend find their way to the feet of Jesus. Look for an opportunity to carry another's burden and initiate spiritual and physical restoration.

Liberal

"This is what the kingdom of God is like. A man scatters seed on the ground. Night and day, whether he sleeps or gets up, the seed sprouts and grows, though he does not know how. All by itself the soil produces grain—first the stalk, then the head, then the full kernel in the head."

—Mark 4:26–28 (Mk 4:1–29)

Jesus taught about the progression of faith that those who accepted His new theology would experience, stating that the kingdom of heaven is like the mysterious ways in which seeds take root and grow. Unlike a similar parable about soil, which referred to the condition of the receiver's heart, this parable emphasized the power of the seed, or the Word of God, regardless of the soil or the sower. Seemingly of its own accord, the truth contained in God's Word could take root in a person's heart, simply by its inherent power.

Of the four gospel writers, Mark was the only one to record this parable. And what a great message it has been for Christians in every generation since! Its simple message is that all of us should liberally share the Word of God, knowing that it contains power to change hearts and lives. Often, we get hung up on our own ability (or lack thereof) to successfully cast the seeds of the gospel. Most of us feel woefully inadequate to disseminate scriptural knowledge or effectively evangelize. Moreover, we tend to pre-assess the condition of the soil, judging it unsuitable or infertile.

Today's verses should help us rethink these faulty notions. According to this bit of good news, neither the giver nor the receiver of the truth are fully responsible for the outcome of the sowing. Amazingly enough, once the Word of God reaches the ear of the hearer, the truth has already begun to grow in that person. Like any growing thing, it will start small and get bigger until it has reached maturity—all by God's design and in His timing. That said, Jesus still needs us to liberally plant and attend to His seeds.

Stepping In: Read Luke 8:11; John 1:1–14; 1 Corinthians 3:6–9; 2 Corinthians 9:6–11; and Ephesians 6:17. What do these verses say about the Word of God? How liberal are you in sowing His seeds? Ask God for the courage to share His truth with others. Trust that His power is enough to germinate the seeds you plant in His name.

Stepping Out: This week, cast seeds liberally. Set a goal to share God's truth at least once a day.

Just

"Once again, the kingdom of heaven is like a net that was let down into the lake and caught all kinds of fish. When it was full, the fishermen pulled it up on the shore. Then they sat down and collected the good fish in baskets, but threw the bad away. This is how it will be at the end of the age. The angels will come and separate the wicked from the righteous and throw them into the fiery furnace, where there will be weeping and gnashing of teeth."

—Matthew 13:47–50 (Mt 13:24–51)

Essential to the teaching Jesus' disciples needed to grasp was the concept of spiritual life and death. Using a series of analogies to describe what the kingdom of heaven is like, Jesus taught His men about those who would accept His gospel message and those who would not. Perhaps reminding some disciples of His promise to make them "fishers of men," Jesus stated that God will also cast a net at the end of the age. Believers would be caught up to heaven, and all others would be thrown into the "fiery furnace." Jesus needed His apostles to understand that God was merciful and just, and that soon they would need to bravely cling to this whole truth as they cast their evangelical nets.

For many of us, communicating the truth of these verses is difficult. It is easy enough to talk about the wonderful promises of forgiveness, joy, and blessings that faith in Jesus brings. What we tend to avoid sharing is the part about judgment. Yet justice and mercy are two sides of the same coin. It is important to remember—and to talk about—that the judgment God will bring is His holy response to the crimes against Him and His people. It will be justice finally and forever enacted.

Like a dramatic courtroom battle, when the Judge reappears, each defendant will get what he or she deserves. At the end of each person's life—or at the end of the age, whichever comes first—a verdict will come down from heaven. Offenders, the deniers of God, will go to a place apart from Him "where there is weeping and gnashing of teeth." The innocent, who are washed by Jesus' blood, will be released from the bondage of this life and granted access to paradise. A Christian's duty is to swim among the fishes and lead as many as possible into the safety of Jesus' net.

Stepping In: Read Numbers 16:28–30; Psalm 9:17–18; Ezekiel 18:20; Matthew 4:17–20; Hebrews 4:12–13; and Revelation 14:9–11. How do these passages motivate you to reach out to people you know who are perishing from ignorance about or rebellion against God? Pray for an opportunity to explain the Judge's just nature.

Stepping Out: This week, practice with your small group or with some Christian friends how you would explain the day of judgment to an unbeliever. Who are the wicked and who are the saved? How does one make sure they get caught up in the net of salvation?

In the Know

"I, Jesus, have sent my angel to give you this testimony for the churches. I am the Root and the Offspring of David, and the bright Morning Star."

—Revelation 22:16 (Rv 22:1–21)

After scribing Jesus' encouragements, rebukes, and warnings to each of the seven churches of Asia Minor, John was guided by an angel of the Lord through the scenes of justice and judgment that will come to the earth and its inhabitants. The overwhelming beauty and graphic horror he was shown was difficult to take in and even more challenging to describe. Finally, the scene changed to reveal the fulfillment of prophecy. Heaven and earth were restored; what was left of humanity was saved when the Lamb of God returned to finish the battle with evil. Jesus identified himself and plainly told John that the testimony was complete. Those who received the revelation letter would then be in the know: Jesus was the Creator, Sustainer, Judge, and Redeemer.

Today, we who are in the know are called to be Jesus' messengers. The evangelic torch has been passed down to us. As we mature from new believer to disciple and then to apostle, we take on more responsibility to share truth with others. It is a natural progression. The more we learn about our Savior, the more we grow to love Him. The more we love Jesus, the more we seek to please Him. The more we seek to please Him, the more we are willing to serve Him. And, the more we serve, the more Spirit-guided serving we are given to do.

As Bible readers reach its final chapters, it becomes clear that the time is now for believers to share not only the good news of God's saving grace but also the promised consequence for rejecting Jesus' gift of salvation. Though we are not responsible for saving souls—only God can do that—we are called to be fishers of men and sowers of seeds. We are commissioned to "Go and make disciples of all nations." (Mt 28:19). Being rooted in faith, and guided by the ever-present light of the bright Morning Star, we can walk with "feet fitted with the readiness that comes from the gospel of peace," (Eph 6:15), knowing that the Word of God does not "return empty."

Stepping In: Read Isaiah 55:9–13; Malachi 4:1-5; Matthew 22:42-45, 28:18-20; Romans 10:14–15; Ephesians 6:10–17; and 2 Peter 1:19–21. How do these verses encourage or challenge you? As someone in the know about God's plan, how are you going to share this life-saving information with others? Pray for God's clear direction as you step out in faith to share His whole truth.

Stepping Out: This week, share your testimony with at least one unbeliever or seeker. Remember to include scripture, as it will not return to God's ears empty.

July 11
Heart-Smart

"You diligently study the Scriptures because you think that by them
you possess eternal life. These are the Scriptures that testify about me,
yet you refuse to come to me to have life."

—John 5:39 (Jn 5:16–47)

While in Jerusalem during one of the religious holidays, Jesus healed a lame man on the Sabbath. Later, in the temple, He was confronted by the teachers of the Law and the Pharisees, who accused Him of breaking Sabbath regulations. Instead of defending Himself, Jesus launched into a sermon about His unity with His Father, God. Before these Pharisees could react to this apparent blasphemy, Jesus told them about the many ways He and the Father worked together. Not only had the Father granted Jesus the power to give life, but Jesus had also been given the authority to judge. Jesus validated His claim by citing a number of supportive testimonies. Bringing the focus back to the religious leaders' faulty beliefs, Jesus reminded them that, though they had plenty of head-knowledge, they were certainly not heart-smart about God.

The human mind is the pinnacle of God's creation, His masterpiece. The human intellect is a wonderful gift of God. Yet from the beginning, humanity has used it to try to outsmart God. Deeply ingrained in our ancestral memory is a desire to obtain forbidden knowledge. An instinctual urge to understand the meaning of life has been passed down through the generations. For some, it is their highest goal.

Many of us have been going about this quest in the wrong way. Using the latest technologies and advances in science, we have made a lot of what and how discoveries, but have neglected the why. We can test and prove the first two. The last one tends to stump us. There is an invisible, internal struggle between the things we can prove and the things we just know, the things we think and the things we feel, the things we can figure out and the things we can't. Like the Pharisees, we look to our books, our degrees, our training, and our results to show that we have all the answers we need. Today's verse is a reminder that godly intelligence resides in the heart, not the head. Sadly, we can know everything about God and yet not know Him. We can literally be too smart for our own eternal good.

Stepping In: Read Deuteronomy 18:15–22; Proverbs 3:5, 4:23; Matthew 5:8, 6:21, 19:16-21; Luke 24:44; Acts 13:27; and Romans 2:17–24. What head-knowledge gets in the way of fully trusting in God's Word? Pray that your heart is softened to the truth of scripture.

Stepping Out: This week, with your small group or with some friends, examine Old Testament passages that point to Jesus. Discuss whether they have been, now are, or will be fulfilled. Which ones are you most surprised by or excited for?

Exalted

"For whoever exalts himself will be humbled, and whoever humbles himself will be exalted."

—Matthew 23:12 (Mt. 22:41–23:12)

Only days before heading to the cross, Jesus spoke in Jerusalem's temple courts about the hypocritical ways of the religious ruling class. He pointed out specific ways these falsely pious men went about putting on a show of their religiosity to gain the honor of men. They were more interested in exalting themselves than God. In today's verse, Jesus plainly explained His backward kingdom in a nutshell. Unfortunately for the Jewish leaders, their idea of being exalted did not fit His mold.

Jesus' upside-down theology is still baffling audiences today. Christians puzzle over these nonsensical truths: that those who suffer and serve, those who are humble and meek, and those who seek the approval of God, not man, will be first in His kingdom. Jesus' warning is a stark reminder of pride's dangers. In a world characterized by a "me first" mentality, this whole passage is all too relevant.

Jesus wants us to embrace the truth of this verse. In fourteen words, He tells us the right and the wrong way to seek advancement in His kingdom—which just happens to be the opposite of the way the world does it.

It is difficult to consider others before ourselves. It is even trickier to always honor God rather than seeking the approval of peers. But it is not impossible. Truly, it is only a matter of perspective. By focusing on who we are in the grand scheme of things, and remembering who really is in charge, we go up a level in God's eyes. It is much easier to be humble when we consider not who we are, but *whose* we are: God's! We are His humble servants on earth, His exalted ones in heaven.

Stepping In: Read 1 Samuel 2:6–8; Psalm 18:27; Proverbs 3:33–35; Isaiah 57:15; Luke 1:49–52; Romans 12:10; and 1 Peter 5:6. Meditate on these verses. Pray and ask God for a humble and contrite heart, and the strength to use it to bring glory to His name. Praise Him that He has chosen to lift you up in due time.

Stepping Out: This week, practice humility in everything you do. Look for ways to honor others above yourself. Let your life demonstrate your hope in the promise of a high position in heaven.

July 13
Freed

When Jesus saw her, he called her forward and said to her, "Woman, you are set free from your infirmity."

—Luke 13:12 (Lk 13:10–21)

One day while teaching in a synagogue, Jesus brought forward a woman who had been bent over and crippled for eighteen year and relieved her of her suffering. Standing up tall, the woman immediately sang praises to God. The synagogue leader and Pharisees did not, however, share in her joy. Instead of recognizing the miracle they had just witnessed, they were outraged that Jesus had (once again) healed on the Sabbath. Jesus disregarded their looks of indignation and gave the self-righteous hypocrites a firm scolding. These were the men, after all, who should have offered the woman God's love and compassion, but instead had treated her as an outcast. Jesus, a true man of God and Lord of the Sabbath, saw a need and went to it, freeing the woman and proving His authority.

Today, there are many longing to be freed like the crippled woman. Whether you look at this woman's infirmities as literal or symbolic, many of us can relate to the crippling fear of social humiliation, rejection, or public shame we have experienced simply because we are different. Satan, the master of lies, capitalizes on our weakened state and adds to our burden of shame, doubt, and hopelessness, forcing us to look down. Society doesn't know how to deal with such burdened people. They get pushed to the sides, marginalized, and forgotten. Or worse, such people become feared and villainized.

Those who have faith may turn to God as their only respite. Yet, as we see in today's example, acceptance and compassion are not always found in our places of so-called worship. Like the Pharisees, Christians sometimes offer only pity when they ought to be offering hope.

Jesus made a point of demonstrating what true godliness looks like in action. He called the woman, He sent her demon away, He touched her, and He freed her from her physical and spiritual bondage. Today's verse is a reminder that Jesus is still in the business of liberating souls, and we are His business partners. Because we have been freed, we can bring others to Jesus for restoration. Standing tall, we the freed can look up to Jesus and praise God in heaven.

Stepping In: Read Psalm 82:3–4; Isaiah 61:1–3; Micah 6:8; Matthew 23:2–4; Romans 15:1–2; and James 1:27. What message about God's inclusive mercy do you hear in these verses? Is God prompting you to action?

Stepping Out: This week, as one who has been freed, come alongside someone who is looking down and encourage them to look up to Jesus.

Assured

> "Therefore, I tell you, do not worry about your life, what you will eat or drink; or about your body, what you will wear. Is not life more important than food, and the body more important than clothes?"
> —Matthew 6:25 (Mt 6:25–34)

During His Sermon on the Mount, Jesus spoke of the believer's role in seeking out and maintaining a right-standing with God, and how to improve relationships with others. In today's verse, Jesus began a lesson about the human tendency to worry, and how worry only served to diminish one's faith.

Some hearing these words may have thought this young rabbi idealistic or naive. Others may have thought this foolish advice for a people who struggled to survive; naturally they worried about the necessities of life! Ardent Jews, however, should have been reminded of God's provision of food (manna) and clothing during their exodus from slavery in Egypt. To worry was to forget the greatness and goodness of God. To pine for worldly things rather than focus on God's trustworthiness was a lack of faith. Those who were tracking Jesus' line of thought realized that He was assuring everyone that their Father in heaven was aware of and caring for all their needs. Life was found in God, not in material things.

Food and clothing are still a focal point today, yet for very different reasons than were true for first-century peoples. For us, these things are far beyond basic needs; they are now often objects of vice. It is no longer about survival, but about indulgence, vanity and competition. The attention and money spent on designer shoes, trendy clothes, specialty foods, and diet plans is staggering. To say that the pursuit of these commodities has become an obsession would be putting it mildly.

This is not the life Jesus wants for His people. God knows what we need, of this believers can be assured. Worry is a form of unbelief. Confidence in God's care and provision will result in relief from worry.

Stepping In: Read Exodus 16 and Deuteronomy 8:4 and 29:5. What do you worry about? Are clothes and food things you obsess over? Take some time to think about where these concerns stem from. Are you letting circumstances influence your faith? Confess your worries and unbelief to God. Pray that He replaces your worries with peace and assurance in His faithful provision.

Stepping Out: This week, volunteer with a food and/or clothing ministry. Share God's love in a tangible way, and point to Jesus throughout the experience. Praise God for a fresh perspective on needs.

Positive

> "Do not let your hearts be troubled. Trust in God; trust also in me."
> —John 14:1 (Jn 13:1–14:6)

At the end of their last Passover meal together, Jesus spoke words of comfort to His remaining eleven disciples. He prompted them to remain positive even in the face of troubling events to come. He urged them to continue to trust in Him and in God. There were many things they did not understand: Why must Jesus die? What would become of them without Him? What would become of His ministry? How was the Messiah supposed to reign if He was not alive? What had just happened with Judas Iscariot? Surely, these good Jewish men believed in God. They knew the prophecies and scripture well. However, this was not the way they had envisioned redemption coming to Israel. They could not imagine life without their Lord and Rabbi. They had been with Him, witnessed His power, and experienced His love; they were devoted.

Jesus, knowing that uncertainty and worry could easily erode his apostles' faith, reminded them that they were safe. To further assure them, Jesus let them know that He was going to His Father's house to prepare rooms for them, and that He would return for them in time. Until the following Sunday, however, their hearts would remain troubled. On that day, a positive light of understanding would replace their fear.

In America, our printed currency boldly proclaims, "In God We Trust." For many Americans, this statement is mostly true. Many people the world over say they believe in God. Others say they believe in *a* god, or in a "higher power." Clearly, monotheistic faith is something humanity has long struggled with. Indeed, some may even cite today's verse as an example of God's duplicity.

This is not the case! Time and again, especially in the book of John, Jesus emphatically states that He and the Father are One. The reason for the double imperative was to remind His wavering disciples that the God they had always relied on and the One they had come to know more recently were still there for them. Jesus was and is saying, "Yes, trust in your scriptural knowledge, but also trust in the One who has been with you: Me." Even today, in the turmoil and confusion of our world, Jesus wants us to come to Him for comfort and strength. By trusting in the Holy Trinity—Father, Son, and Holy Spirit—we may live positive, untroubled lives, regardless of our circumstances.

Stepping In: Read Exodus 15:2; 1 Chronicles 16:11–13; Proverbs 3:5; Isaiah 41:10; Jeremiah 29:11–13; Matthew 11:28; John 16:33; and 1 Peter 5:7. What do these verses teach you about God's trustworthiness? How do they encourage you to remain positive even through the hardships of life? Pray for a deeper level of trust, and for "peace that surpasses understanding" (Phil 4:7).

Stepping Out: This week, show God you trust Him with your life. Choose one or more of the following and take a step of trust in that area: finances, job, children, relationships, sexuality, bad habits.

July 16
Steely

"When an evil spirit comes out of a man, it goes through arid places seeking rest and does not find it. Then it says, 'I will return to the house I left.' When it arrives, it finds the house unoccupied, swept clean and put in order. Then it goes and takes with it seven other spirits more wicked than itself, and they go in and live there. And the final condition of that man is worse than the first. That is how it will be with this wicked generation."

—Matthew 12:43–45 (Mt 12:1–45)

Jesus often used figures of speech and parables in response to the persistent and vehement questioning of the Pharisees and Jewish teachers of the Law. Equating the wickedness of His audience to vacant (if not inherently bad) souls, Jesus made it clear that they were just the type in which insidious spirits liked to dwell.

Christian or not, most people agree that there are forces of good and evil in the world. A plethora of books, movies, songs, and video games have been written on the subject, each attempting to adequately depict the battle and its players. It would seem that humans have more than a simple fascination with these opposing powers. Though cheering for the good guys may be more politically correct, demons get the lion's share of the press.

According to the teachings of Jesus, this should not surprise us. Satan is the prince of this world, and he does not work alone. In today's passage, Jesus reminds us that no soul is a vacuum. It will either be occupied by God's Spirit or become a dwelling place for ungodly spirits. Like dust that seems to appear out of nowhere, ungodly spirits must be swept out and replaced by godly ones. To keep the demons we send packing from returning with their friends, we must call on Jesus' power to cast them out for good. Then, we must stand guard with steely determination so as not to let Satan's demons back in.

Stepping In: Read Psalm 1:1-6, 62:5; Proverbs 22:5; Mark 5:1–20; and John 14:30. What is the condition of your soul? Do any demons (things other than God that control your heart and mind) dwell there? Ask Jesus today to cast them out for good, and He will. Replace them with things that are true, noble, right, pure, lovely, admirable, excellent, and praiseworthy (Phil 4:8).

Stepping Out: This week, let your steely resolve not to be controlled by the world be an example to others.

Instrumental

> But the Lord said to Ananias, "Go! This man is my chosen instrument
> to carry my name before the Gentiles and their kings and before the
> people of Israel."
>
> —Acts 9:15 (Acts 9:1–19)

During the time Jesus walked Judea in His resurrected body, revealing to all His victory over death and speaking of the kingdom of God He had successfully established, a new resurgence of faithful followers stirred into action. Christianity (the Way) was born. And while thousands were coming to faith, persecution was also on the rise. In an effort to eradicate the Way and its followers, ardent Jewish purists sought out, arrested, and even killed those professing allegiance to Jesus.

One such man was Saul of Tarsus, an educated tentmaker, respected businessman, and strict Pharisee. Angered by the increase of Christ followers, even after the death of their leader, Saul set out from Jerusalem to round up Christian converts in Damascus. Along the way, Jesus Himself stopped Saul in his tracks. Blinding Saul with the brightness of His presence, and speaking to him with the voice of God, Jesus began the transformation that would change Saul's life in every way. In a vision, Saul saw a man named Ananias restoring his sight. Meanwhile, Jesus was instructing Ananias about his instrumental role in Saul's conversion. Jesus firmly directed a leery Ananias to assist Him in bringing to the nation, and indeed the world, an unlikely instrument of God's evangelical movement. Neither man could have known how their lives would change the course of history forever.

And neither do we. Just as Saul could not have been more surprised by his encounter with Jesus, we too can receive a calling from our Lord at any time. And just as Saul must have thought himself the most unlikely person to represent a faith he had adamantly opposed, many of Jesus' ambassadors have been selected from a pool of similarly improbable candidates.

Reading the verses leading up to today's passage, we hear Ananias reasonably question Jesus about the wisdom and safety of getting involved with one of His known enemies. Any one of us would no doubt have made the same rationalization. But that is the exact point of this passage: we do not know who Jesus plans to use for His kingdom's work. Therefore, we are not to question His choice of who He prompts us to engage with.

The truth is that none of us are worthy of our calling. It is only because of God's grace and through His power that we can advocate for our Savior. It is our honor, privilege, and duty to bless others as we have been blessed. Only God can see all the instruments in His grand orchestra. Until we hear His heavenly symphony, we are not to judge a horn by its rust.

Stepping In: Read Acts 13:2–3; Romans 1:1; 1 Corinthians 1:28–31; and 1 Timothy 1:12–14. Consider the unlikely people God has chosen to use: Moses, Rahab, Jonah, and Paul, just to name a few. Do you question your or another's ability to be instrumental in God's kingdom? Why? Ask God how you can play in His orchestra today.

Stepping Out: This week, go beyond your comfort zone to reach an unlikely person for Christ.

Fruitful

"I tell you the truth, if you have faith and do not doubt, not only can you do what was done to the fig tree, but also you can say to this mountain, 'Go throw yourself into the sea,' and it will be done."
—Matthew 21:21 (Mt 21:1–11, 17–22)

After the excitement of Jesus' triumphal entry into Jerusalem had subsided, He and His disciples went to Bethany to spend the night with some close friends there. The next morning, as they walked back into Jerusalem, Jesus spotted a fig tree and looked among its leaves for some fruit to eat for breakfast. He was dismayed to find not a single fig. In what would appear to be an act of unwarranted anger at the fruitless tree, Jesus cursed it, and it immediately withered. The disciples were stunned and asked Him why this had happened. Jesus did not answer their question directly, but told them that they in faith could do the same and more.

Jesus' disciples understood that when their Master began a teaching with, "I tell you the truth," what followed was of particular importance. At this late stage of their training, there was no longer room for doubt in His disciples' minds about His supreme authority. He needed His men to trust that they would soon inherit great power to live fruitful lives and move many mountains—meaning obstacles that get in the way of one's relationship with God, such as fear, pride, worry, doubt, and ignorance. In time, the disciples pulled the fragmented pieces of their training together and realized that the figurative fruit of the fig tree represented the faith-filled, love-based actions and attitudes of a mature Christian. Then they understood why the fruitless tree withered and died. This was a lesson Jesus needed them to learn.

This story is one for the ages. It is our story. There are two parallel themes that are brought to light in it. First, there is the fruitless tree. The tree represented the Pharisees and religious leaders. These men claimed religious maturity and looked the part, but they had no love in their actions and no true faith. Their outward appearance masked a withered relationship with God, and they would soon perish from spiritual starvation.

The other lesson, the one that undergirds the story as a whole, is that of faith without doubt. Jesus wanted His disciples and us to understand the difference between the appearance of faith and true faith. To be followers of Christ as true believers, we must grow in our faith and mature spiritually. Once we have gone beyond doubt, we are to show our convictions through our actions. We must bear fruit. When we stay attached to the Vine, we can bear much fruit; apart from Jesus, we can do nothing of kingdom value.

Stepping In: Read Isaiah 34:1–4; John 15:5; 1 Corinthians 13:1–3; Galatians 5:22–26; and James 1:6–8. Thank God for your salvation and the ability to be fruitful through the Spirit. Ask for faith to move mountains. Ask Him to remove all doubt.

Stepping Out: This week, demonstrate your love for God and others by exhibiting the fruits of the Spirit (see Gal 5:22–26). Choose one to be particularly diligent about and put it into practice.

Genuine

"Be careful not to practice your 'acts of righteousness' in front of
others to be seen by them. If you do, you will have no reward from
your Father in heaven."

—Matthew 6:1 (Mt 6:1–4)

Jesus chose His words carefully, and many of them He chose to repeat for the benefit of His audiences.
During His Sermon on the Mount, given early in His ministry, Jesus outlined the dos and don'ts of
godly living. Word of His bold teaching, compassionate healings, and miraculous powers drew many
into the Galilean hill country to witness what this young rabbi would say and do. Speaking of humble
acts of righteousness, Jesus reiterated what He had stated previously—that by letting "your light shine
before men … they may see your good deeds and praise your Father in heaven" (Mt 5:16). One's
intention to please God would be revealed. Jesus touched a raw nerve in some listeners, since the Jewish
leaders in the audience were prone to gratuitous displays of generosity done only to gain attention.
Jesus wanted to be certain that His message was clear: God recognizes the difference between genuine
acts of service and ones done only for show.

Though not fully expanded upon in the Old Testament, the concept of heavenly rewards is very
well illuminated throughout the pages of the New Testament. Though equipped with knowledge
about the good things God has in store for those who prove their faith, today's Bible reader is just as
likely to suffer from worldly character traits, such as arrogance, pride, and selfish ambition, as our
first-century counterparts.

From a young age, many of us were taught to "show others what we are made of." Throughout our
lives and careers, we have learned to promote ourselves by proving we have useful abilities. It only
makes sense that this would carry over into our spiritual lives as well. Yet Jesus tells us to be careful
not to allow our self-serving nature to rob us of the reward God has promised those who humbly
and privately serve Him. Even those saved by grace through faith in the resurrected Lord must guard
against the temptation to seek personal recognition from anyone other than God. God desires our
hearts to be genuinely His. Our actions will show if our hearts are or are not.

Stepping In: Read Proverbs 11:2; Luke 11:41; Ephesians 4:2; Philippians 2:3; and Hebrews 13:16.
Consider how important good deeds done with a pure heart are to Jesus. Pray for pure motives and for
insight for when they are not. Pray that He replaces any desire you have for selfish gain with genuine
care for others.

Stepping Out: This week, let the Spirit move you toward genuine acts of kindness and generosity.
Check in with your motives before you act, being careful to guard against showy displays of generosity
for personal gain or attention.

Nonresistant

> We all fell to the ground, and I heard a voice saying to me in Aramaic,
> "Saul, Saul, why do you persecute me? It is hard for you to kick against
> the goads."
>
> —Acts 26:14 (Acts 26:1–32)

Though not officially charged with the crimes of being a traitor and an insurrectionist, Paul was brought before two successive Roman governors by Jews hoping for his conviction. Neither governor could find reason to kill Paul. To appease the Jews, he was put in a Caesarean prison until further evidence emerged.

Two years later, when the Roman emperor, King Agrippa II, came to visit the region, the Jews thought it an opportune time to plead their case against Paul to the highest court. Much to the Jews' dismay, Paul was allowed to tell the king his story: his history as a Pharisee and persecutor of the Way, his conversion – including the words Jesus had spoken to him about the futility of resisting God, and his consequent obedience in following the Lord's commands. He also informed the king about his mistreatment at the hands of the Jews.

At that, the trial was interrupted by the current governor, Festus, who claimed Paul was insane. The king was not persuaded by Festus's or Paul's claims. He was convinced of two things, though: Paul was not guilty of any crime, and because Paul had appealed to Caesar, to Caesar he would go.

Anyone who does not recognize and acquiesce to the Lord's authority is "kicking against the goads." Paul humbly agreed with Jesus' assertion that his aggressive denial of Christ's authority was like a stubborn ox resisting the gentle prodding of the Master's oxgoad. He stated unequivocally that it had been with much difficulty that he had pushed the truth aside, resulting in unnecessary hardship—three days of confusion and blindness, followed by humble acceptance of his grievous mistake.

Some of us know exactly what Paul means. Like willful oxen, humans tend to fight against authority. We think we know better than our parents, teachers, pastors, bosses, law enforcement, and even God, and we attempt to maneuver around their influence. Any one of us can list the consequences we have faced for such futile opposition.

Jesus, our God, Master Teacher, loving Parent, wise Leader, and sovereign Lord, implores us to take a nonresistant approach to relinquishing our will and our lives to Him. He can see the future and is always at work, guiding us rightly. Pushing against the Sword of Truth is both futile and painful.

Stepping In: Read Psalm 73:21–24; Proverbs 16:20, 22:6; Romans 13:1–2; Ephesians 6:1; and Hebrews 13:17. Are you currently resisting God's or another's authority? To what end? Ask God to help you understand and perhaps change your attitude so that you can be used by Him more effectively. Pray for God to reveal your next right move.

Stepping Out: This week, commit to an attitude of nonresistance toward authority, especially God's.

July 21

Reverent

"Do not suppose that I have come to bring peace to the earth. I did not come to bring peace, but a sword. For I have come to turn 'a man against his father, a daughter against her mother, a daughter-in-law against her mother-in-law—a man's enemies will be members of his own household.'"

—Matthew 10:34–36 (Mt 10:1–36)

Before sending His twelve disciples to bring healing and restoration to the Jewish nation, Jesus spoke to them at length regarding the challenges they would face. Some of the greatest opposition they encountered would come from their neighbors and relations. The Jews were a stubborn people, deeply committed to their religious heritage, not easily swayed in their thinking or beliefs—even if the good news was brought by their own brothers. Regardless of how wonderful their message was, the disciples were asking the people to give up everything they had ever known for something they could not see. Many resisted, preferring their world to remain unchanged. Others gladly exchanged death for life. Between the two groups, there was no peace. This was the reality Jesus needed His men to understand.

This is a hard teaching, even two thousand years later. This world is not a peaceful place. One need only turn on the news to see more than enough evidence of this sad truth. From the time the first humans sinned in the garden of Eden until Jesus returns, a spiritual war will rage among the earth's inhabitants. The planet itself is suffering in its fallen state.

Jesus does not tell us about disharmony to discourage our faith. It is a reminder that this earth is not our permanent, perfect home. Our perspective must be heaven-focused; our hearts must be in reverent submission to our sovereign Lord. In the battles we fight to bring God's kingdom to earth, the only sword we need is the Word: Jesus.

Stepping In: Read Micah 7:5–6; Ephesians 6:17; Hebrews 4:12; and Revelation 19:11–15. Take some time to think about how the sword of truth, the Word, has penetrated your conscience lately. Pray for a reverent respect for God and His wisdom, even in the difficulties of living in a sin-stained world.

Stepping Out: This week, strive for peace in your home. Respectfully and humbly share your faith with members of your family who struggle with belief. Trust God with the outcome while praying for their salvation. Let God's sword fight your battles. Speak the name of Jesus and let it sink in.

Unselfish

"Watch out! Be on guard against all kinds of greed; a man's life does
not consist in the abundance of his possessions."
—Luke 12:15 (Lk 12:1–21)

During the third year of His public ministry, Jesus traveled extensively from Jerusalem up to Capernaum, and throughout the regions along the Jordan River. In each town and village, Jesus was greeted with excitement and anticipation. Large crowds gathered around to hear Him speak about the kingdom of God. On one occasion when Jesus was speaking before a large gathering, a man asked Him to tell the man's brother to share his inheritance with him.

Though Jesus truly was the Judge of all humanity, He told this fellow that it was not His business to settle civil matters of this nature. Instead of agreeing with the unfairness of the man's situation, Jesus warned that he would be wise to examine his own motives. To emphasize His point, He went on to tell a parable about a foolish rich man who unwittingly forfeited his life for the sake of his possessions. Jesus wanted the crowd to understand that, though life may not be fair, one should never place one's security in worldly wealth. They should be unselfish, especially toward God.

Jesus is still trying to send this message to the people of the world. Is anybody listening? By appearances alone, it would seem that the answer is no. Since the industrial revolution and the advent of our modern banking system, monetary wealth has become the indicator of both success and security. People believe that the more they have, the happier and safer they will be.

When we are comfortable, healthy, and financially secure, we tend grow complacent in our relationship with God. However, when our perceived safety is threatened, we call out to Jesus for help. Like the man in this story, we approach our Lord as if He were a cosmic vending machine or a public servant, there to make things go in our favor. But Jesus has never been as interested in satisfying our physical needs as He is in attending to the needs of our souls. Verses like today's are meant to shake us out of our selfish, me-centric focus and back into the safety of a right relationship with others, with money, and most of all with God. True life and satisfaction are found in no other source.

Stepping In: Read Job 20:19-20, 31:24-28; Matthew 6:24; John 5:22; and 1 Timothy 6:10. Take some time to reflect on these verses. What is your current relationship to money? Are you selfish or generous with God and others? Ask God to reveal any false securities you have and replace them with His peace.

Stepping Out: This week, make a comparison list of "What I rely on money for" versus "What I rely on God for." Discuss this with your small group or some other Christians you trust. Thank God for this eye-opening perspective, and consider what you need to change. Start by committing to doing one completely unselfish act each day this week. Be rich toward God and others!

Inseparable

"Haven't you read," He replied, "That at the beginning the Creator
'made them male and female,' and said, 'For this reason a man will
leave his father and mother, and be united to his wife, and the two
will become one flesh'? So they are no longer two, but one. Therefore,
what God has joined together, let man not separate."

—Matthew 19:4–6 (Mt 19:1–9)

The Pharisees cornered Jesus one day and asked about the lawfulness of a man seeking to divorce his wife "for any and every reason." Because this was a much-disputed subject between two of the Jewish sects, they hoped to involved Jesus in their rift, thus forcing Him to choose sides. Curtly, Jesus gave the above reply, insinuating that these learned men should already have known the answer to their question. The Pharisees referenced a command of Moses that allowed divorce. Calling their scholarly bluff, Jesus pointed out that their misunderstanding of God's intentions was due to their "hard hearts."

Clearly, much has changed in our world since these words were spoken, and mostly for the worse. Sadly, across our globe, divorce is increasingly common. In most modern societies, the stigma and difficulty attached to the dissolution of marriage have all but been eliminated. Where it was once rare, it has become a norm. Where it was at one time only a male prerogative, it is now a gender-neutral decision. Like the Pharisees, we seem to want to interpret scripture to suit our fickle loyalties and cater to our selfish interests. The dominant culture obviously subscribes to Moses' rendition of the Law, giving anyone the right to divorce for "any and every reason" under the sun.

Under the Son, this logic does not stand. Jesus makes it clear that God intends for marriage to be an inseparable bond, an unbreakable covenant not to be taken lightly. Jesus acknowledges that there are a couple of valid exceptions to the rule, death being one and infidelity another. In either case, the marriage is dead and can be considered null. Christians are to set an example in this area for a watching world, like it or not. Therefore, we should enter into marriage thoughtfully and biblically, with the intention of keeping our vows, period.

Stepping In: Read Genesis 1:27, 2:23-24; Deuteronomy 24:1-4. What are your thoughts on marriage and divorce? Are they mostly biblical or secular? Pray for your heart to align with God's on this matter.

Stepping Out: This week, be aware of and stop any behaviors that contribute to weakening God bonds. Make all your vows inseparable!

Bequeathed

> "Peace be with you! As the Father has sent me, I am sending you." And with that he breathed on them and said, "Receive the Holy Spirit."
> —John 20:21–22 (Jn 20:1–23)

After Jesus had been taken down from the cross and laid behind a large stone in a stranger's tomb, His disciples hid themselves for fear of meeting a similar end. Some of the women who loved Jesus, however, lingered near His grave, awash in their grief and loss, leaving their post only at night and on the Sabbath.

One of them, Mary Magdalene, returned to her vigil very early Sunday morning and discovered the stone removed and the tomb unoccupied. Thinking someone had taken Jesus' body, she ran and told Simon what she had seen. He and John went to see for themselves that the tomb was indeed empty, but in such an orderly state that it could not have been robbed. They went away, scratching their heads, leaving Mary alone again in her grief.

Looking into the tomb, Mary saw two angels, one at the foot and the other at the head of the platform where Jesus' body had been. They asked her why she was crying. "They have taken my Lord away," she answered. Just then, she turned and saw a man who asked her the same question. Not realizing it was Jesus, she gave the same reply. Then Jesus called her by name and her eyes were opened. In a firm but comforting voice, Jesus told Mary not to cling to Him, but to go and tell the disciples that He was alive.

But the men did not believe her until Jesus Himself appeared in their locked room. He greeted them with the traditional salutation, "Peace be with you." The disciples (minus Judas, who had committed suicide, and Peter, who had not yet arrived) thought they were seeing a ghost. Jesus showed them His hands and His side, and they believed and were filled with joy. Jesus reminded them of their mission as apostles. He breathed on them, giving them a foretaste of the Spirit they would receive in-full fifty days later. From then on, bequeathed with the indwelling Holy Spirit, they would no longer doubt.

Thankfully for us, when we accepted Jesus as Lord and Savior, we didn't have to wait to receive the Holy Spirit. Our employment begins the moment we committed to following Jesus. Bequeathed with everything we need—joy, gratitude, truth, the Bible, wisdom, discernment, comfort, and guidance from the Holy Spirit—we may boldly embark on our commissioned kingdom work.

Jesus knows that this is a daunting and sometimes dangerous task. Therefore, He began His statement with a proclamation of peace. Filled with the peace Jesus gives us, we can confidently share His life-saving message with a perishing world. Unless people know about the salvation found in Jesus alone, they remain stuck in their sin, unforgiven and doomed to an eternity apart from God. We cannot forgive sins, but we can and must lead people to the One who is willing and able to do so: Jesus!

Stepping In: Read Genesis 2:7; Exodus 25:17–22; Psalm 29:11; Matthew 28:10; John 14:27; Acts 1:8 and 2:1–4; and Philippians 4:7. How do these verses help you appreciate the cross, the mercy seat, and the Spirit? How have you responded to being bequeathed with the Holy Spirit? Pray for peace and guidance to obey your commission.

Stepping Out: This week, share your testimony with one or more unbelievers. Give your reasons for the hope and peace you have in Christ, while you gently share the truth about salvation (1 Pt 3:15–16).

Guarded

"Be on guard against men; they will hand you over to the local councils
and flog you in their synagogues. On my account you will be brought
before governors and kings as witnesses to them and to the Gentiles."
—Matthew 10:17–18 (Mt 10:1–18)

If anything could have discouraged Jesus' newly appointed apostles and caused them to question their calling, it would have been the long and detailed pre-commissioning speech they received from their Master. This speech was meant to prepare the Twelve for events in their near and distant futures, and to foreshadow Jesus' fate as well. Their faith, endurance, and devotion would surely be put to the test. Their words and deeds would be seen as blasphemous and worthy of severe punishment. Jesus did not want them to be unaware of the treatment they would face—some of which they would be able to guard against, and some they would not.

There have always been two types of people, the trusting and the guarded. Regardless of the type of venture one enters—business or pleasure, secular or religious—the people who employ a more guarded approach tend to fare better in the end. It is good to be open-minded and trusting, but one should also be on guard against those who may have only their own self-interest in mind.

Let's face it: it can be a cruel world out there. As people struggle to get ahead, they look for every advantage to maneuver in front of the competition. An inherent fear of missing out drives some to irrational and mean-spirited acts. In the business world, such people may take credit for another's work, do or say things to discredit another's efforts, or pursue legal action against those they feel even slightly wronged by. Even in a Christian setting, Jesus warns us to watch out.

In our walk with Christ, we will encounter people who go to great lengths to defend their worldly ways. So, while we stand firm in our faith, we heed Jesus' warning to avoid confrontations before they arise, whenever possible.

Stepping In: Take some time to think about the persecution you have faced because of Jesus. Was some of it from within your own family or social group? How did you guard yourself? Pray and ask the Holy Spirit to protect your heart and mind against such negativity.

Stepping Out: This week, listen to the ways other brothers and sisters in Christ evangelize. Observe the reactions they receive. Learn from their successes and failures.

Appreciative

"Therefore, I tell you, her many sins have been forgiven—for she loved much. But he who has been forgiven little loves little."

—Luke 7:47 (Lk 7:36–50)

Perhaps because Jesus had healed him of leprosy, a Pharisee named Simon invited Him to his house for a meal. While Jesus reclined at the table, a "sinful" woman came in and began anointing His feet with her tears and expensive perfume. Simon, clearly annoyed by the intrusion, wondered why Jesus allowed a woman of ill-repute to touch Him.

Perceiving Simon's thoughts, Jesus told him a parable about the forgiveness of a large debt and a small debt. The person who was forgiven the greater debt was more appreciative than the one forgiven less. It was apparent that Simon considered himself to be far less of a sinner than the woman. Jesus pointedly reminded him that Simon had failed to offer Him water to wash His feet, but the woman had offered something far better. She was aware of her lowly position and was grateful to do even the most menial of tasks. She offered all she had as a show of appreciation to her Lord for who He was, what He had done, and what He would soon do.

Many people today simply do not believe they need a savior. The notion of sin seems foolish and antiquated to those who do not understand the nature of God. Views on this topic range widely. Some think sin does not exist. If there is a God, then why would He allow people to possess this negative trait? Others prefer to downplay sin's destructive influences and consequences, believing that everyone is basically good, and those who are really bad will get the punishment they deserve. Yet another group is like the Pharisees of old, believing that because they adhere strictly to their legalistic practices, they are exempt from God's wrath. The unfortunate truth is that even some Christians see themselves this way: saved and therefore above reproach.

Jesus makes it very clear that a right relationship with God and others is centered in love. The natural reaction to receiving His love, mercy, and forgiveness is to be humbly appreciative. Out of the "overflow of the heart" will pour love, mercy, and forgiveness for others. It's that simple.

Stepping In: Read Matthew 12:34, 23:1-7, 23:12; Romans 3:21–27; and Ephesians 1:7–10. How do these verses help you understand the beauty and necessity of forgiveness? Thank Jesus for the undeserved grace He has given you. Ask Him for an appreciative heart, full of love and forgiveness toward others.

Stepping Out: This week, seek the forgiveness of someone who holds something against you, *and* do the same for someone else as well.

Purposeful

"Do not go among the Gentiles or enter any town of the Samaritans. Go rather to the lost sheep of Israel. As you go, preach this message: 'The kingdom of heaven is near.'"

—Matthew 10:5–7 (Mt 10:1–8)

This statement was part of the first commissioning of Jesus' elect Twelve. Thus, the disciples became His apostles, sent out as missionaries of their faith in Jesus as Lord. Jesus specifically instructed them who should receive His message and who should not. This request would not have seemed odd or discriminatory, as Jews and Gentiles, especially Samaritans, did not mix, culturally or otherwise.

Yet that was not the reason Jesus instructed His missionaries to seek out their own. According to the plan that had been in place from the beginning, salvation through the Christ would come from the Jews. After His own people had been offered life through the Messiah, all other groups would receive it. The Jews were God's chosen people, the ones He had made His original covenant with. He had given them His laws and commandments. Now they would be given the first opportunity to take part in the new covenant—to choose to live under the new laws and accept the Messiah. They were first in line for the kingdom of heaven, if they chose to accept it. Obediently, the apostles enacted this plan.

God does not play favorites. Contrary to how it may look in this passage, God does not discriminate or endorse nepotism. He is a covenant-keeping, loyal, faithful, wholly trustworthy God who honors His commitments. When He established a lasting contract with the Jewish nation, He intended to fulfill His promises to them—and He has. This is what Jesus did when He sent His apostles out among the Israelites. Those who read on in the gospels know that Jesus later commissioned His followers to go out and make disciples of *all* nations.

The lesson we learn from today's scripture passage is that evangelism starts at home. Beginning in our own families and spreading in an ever-widening sphere of influence, Christians are to share the joy of salvation our Savior offers to all who choose Him. We must model ourselves after our Good Shepherd and attend to our flock purposefully and well. The better we do this, the more attractive and effective our broader missionary ventures will be.

Stepping In: Read Isaiah 53 and Romans 1:16. Meditate on these scripture passages. Thank God that salvation through Jesus was always His plan. Thank Jesus for willingly shedding His own blood to fulfill it.

Stepping Out: This week, be purposeful in your interactions with family members, making the most of every opportunity to share God's truth and love. Share with them the hope you have in Jesus with gentleness.

Quenched

"Everyone who drinks of this water will thirst again, but whoever drinks the water I give him will never thirst. Indeed, the water I give him will become in him a spring of water welling up to eternal life."
—John 4:13–14 (Jn 14:1–26)

As Jesus rested by a Samaritan well, His disciples went in search of food in a nearby village. Shortly thereafter, a woman came to draw water. She was alone, and it was an improbable hour for her task. Clearly, she had her reasons for wanting to avoid the other woman of her village.

Jesus, of course, knew all about her troubles—that was why He was there. Breaking numerous social and religious customs, Jesus asked the woman for a drink. Stunned but curious, the woman cautiously questioned Him. Jesus engaged her in conversation, slowly revealing His divine nature and plan for her. Building on her limited knowledge of God, Jesus opened her eyes to the undiscriminating and boundlessly generous nature of God that was available to her. Though Jesus cared about this woman's difficulties, His greater desire was to quench her soul with His "living water."

Jesus knows what is troubling each of us, even more than we know it ourselves. Like the woman at the well, many of us also practice avoidance so that we do not have to face the pain and humiliation of dealing with our issues. Jesus goes out of His way to meet us. Unlike the rest of society, Jesus accepts us exactly as we are: broken, hurting, marginalized, rejected, misunderstood, religiously damaged, and spiritually bankrupt. He wants us to know that while we are focused on just getting through the day, He is behind the scenes, orchestrating an encounter with Himself. While we are merely addressing our paltry physical needs, He seeks to meet our deepest spiritual need—the salvation of our souls. Because He knows us fully and He loves us completely, we can come to Him to be quenched. With the Holy Spirit flowing through us, we can be deeply satisfied in a way that the worries of this life can't diminish. There is no shame or condemnation, only abundant grace and eternal satisfaction.

Stepping In: Read Psalm 139; Isaiah 12:1-3, 44:3, 58:11; John 7:38-39; Romans 8:1-2; and Revelation 21:6. How do these verses give you confidence and joy in this gift of living water? How has God quenched your spiritual thirst? Thank God and Jesus for the gift of His Spirit, and for the eternal life you have been promised.

Stepping Out: This week, hand out bottled water to those who thirst. Pray for opportunities to share about the eternal spring Jesus offers to those who seek it.

Welcoming

> "And whoever welcomes a little child like this in my name welcomes
> me. But if anyone causes one of these little ones who believe in me to
> sin, it would be better for him to have a large millstone hung around
> his neck and to drowned in the depths of the sea."
>
> —Matthew 18:5–6 (Mt 18:1–6)

During His ministry, Jesus taught many tough lessons to those who were willing to listen and learn. He presented new definitions of the scripture, proclaiming a fresh theology to supersede the old. He filled synagogues with astonished listeners. When inside venues became too restrictive, He taught and healed the masses on hillsides, even using a small boat for a pulpit when necessary. When the Pharisees and teachers of the Law questioned Jesus' authority, He switched to speaking in parables, befuddling the undiscerning. In His miracles and His quiet moments, Jesus always consulted His Father.

This example was essential for the disciples' training. Bit by bit, their faith in God and in Jesus grew. They were starting to make the connection between God the Father, Jesus the Son, and the kingdom of heaven. Two hurdles still stymied their progress, however: the cross, and the philosophical switch from an earthly perspective to a heavenly one. Indeed, the disciples' confusion over their roles in the kingdom sometimes turned to arguments.

Seeing how childishly His men were acting, Jesus explained how they should be more childlike instead: humble, trusting, innocent, gentle. For those who did not possess these traits, heaven would be unattainable. Jesus emphasized His point by painting a dire illustration of the extreme consequences for failing to trust Him without reservation. A similar fate would befall anyone who led the innocent away from God's saving grace. Jesus needed His apostles to demonstrate how to love God by loving and welcoming even the least members of society. To do otherwise was folly.

Children in Jesus' day held a position near the bottom of the social strata. Along with women, the mentally ill, and the disabled, these little ones had no authority of their own. They were to be seen and not heard. Certainly, they were expected to stay out of the way of the men. Yet Jesus encouraged the children to come to him.

The same is true today. Jesus not only appreciates their innocence, He uses their unquestioning trust as an example of pure faith—the kind of faith needed to gain access to heaven. In today's passage, Jesus demanded that His followers protect the absolute dependence and vulnerability of the child. This is the responsibility of all who represent Christ, both emulating and protecting childlike assurance in God. We are to make every effort to invite the simpler-of-mind into our midst and encourage their journey of faith. It is our obligation to avoid placing any stumbling blocks in their path of faith. Christians today, as the hands and feet of Christ on earth, should see each next generation as potential disciples. In the name of Jesus, we are to nurture and not discourage their closeness to the Lord. To not do so would be disastrous.

Stepping In: Read Deuteronomy 4:9–10; Psalm 4:9-10, 78:5-7; Proverbs 22:6; and 1 John 3:1–3. Think about your childhood. Can you think of someone who encouraged you in your life and faith? Thank God now for that gift of provision.

Stepping Out: This week, be welcoming to little ones, employing sound doctrine and love.

July 30
Giddy

"Blessed are you who hunger now, for you will be satisfied. Blessed are you who weep now, for you will laugh."

—Luke 6:21 (Lk 6:17–26)

One day, after an evening of prayer, Jesus came down from a hillside and began to teach His disciples, speaking of the blessings they would receive for maintaining a heart for God regardless of circumstances. A great crowd gathered to listen, but He spoke directly to His newly appointed apostles, preparing them for the work they would soon begin. By example and through His teachings, Jesus taught them that God was the Sustainer and Lover of souls. Those who received the apostles' evangelical message and put their faith in God and His Son would hunger not for food that perishes, but for spiritual food that truly satisfies. They would gain a new perspective: able to see past the hardships of their current situations to fix their eyes on eternal hope. They would become increasingly joyful at the prospect of what was to come.

Throughout the generations, readers of the Sermon on the Mount have found comfort in Jesus' words. Even today, it is a relief to know that whatever we faithfully endure, our Savior has blessings in store for us. Though Jesus cares about our physical condition, His primary concern is for our spiritual well-being. It is important for us to remember that each of the Beatitudes are meant to encourage us to seek God more fully and consider our current situations in light of an eternal perspective, not a temporal one.

In our consumption-focused world, the need for spiritual revival is great. For most, it is personal pleasure that make us joyful, not God. Jesus knows our human weakness and our inclination to seek comfort and safety above most everything else. He understands our need for reassurance in trying times. That is why He offers us these beautiful blessings. He does not promise a trouble-free life, but for those who believe, He offers peace.

Stepping In: Read Isaiah 55:1-3, 61:1-3, and Revelation 7:16–17. What do you hunger and weep for? Do you worry about not having what you need? Does uncertainty steal your joy? Pray that God turns your sorrows to giddy excitement in the knowledge of His love, promise, and provision.

Stepping Out: This week, be a blessing to someone who is hungry, spiritually or otherwise. Comfort someone who is sad. Let your joyful faith uplift everyone you encounter.

Virtuous

"For I tell you that unless your righteousness surpasses that of the Pharisees and the teachers of the law, you will certainly not enter the kingdom of heaven."

—Matthew 5:20 (Mt 5:17–20)

In His Sermon on the Mount, Jesus crafted each of His statements to address the spiritual needs of the general audience as well as the hard-heartedness of the religious leaders. Many times, over the course of His multiday teaching, Jesus mentioned the kingdom of heaven. In today's verse, He again boldly stated that a right-standing with God was needed to enter the kingdom—a relationship greater than the superficial self-serving kind demonstrated by the Pharisees. The righteousness Jesus talked about was not the unattainable legalistic version the religious leaders dictated. The kingdom Jesus would usher in required a righteousness of the heart. It was more about humility and love than about power and control. It was contingent on virtuous love for God, rather than the mere appearance of it.

Today, those who study the life of Jesus understand that He is offering an invitation rather than a condemnation in today's verse. Biblical scholars can easily point to the folly of the Pharisees: their pride, arrogance, spiritual blindness, and self-serving attitudes. We are happy to surmise that if we avoid these same pitfalls, our righteousness will surpass that of the Pharisees.

But we should not be so quick to move past this issue. We would be wise not to discount our own self-righteous tendencies. How often do we judge others by imposing our standards on them, compare our positive traits to another's negative ones, and justify our own bad behavior?

Everyone sins, even the most virtuous. We all fall short of God's criteria for righteousness. Thankfully, there is grace. Realizing that we are reliant on God for His forgiveness and acceptance, we understand that God is God, and we are not. We look to Him, His laws and commands, and not our own knowledge, status, or abilities to gauge our performance. Virtue is good, but God and His grace are best.

Stepping In: Righteousness is an attitude of humility and contrition, as well as an outward expression of morality, virtue, and lawfulness. Prayerfully seek God's help in becoming a more virtuous person.

Stepping Out: This week, look up synonyms for the word "righteous" and practice one or more each day. Enlist an accountability partner to provide honest feedback about your efforts.

August 1
Compliant

"But when they arrest you, do not worry about what to say or how to say it. At that time, you will be given what to say, for it will not be you speaking, but the Spirit of your Father speaking through you."
—Matthew 10:19–20 (Mt 10:1–20)

From the time Jesus called His twelve disciples, He trained them to carry on His ministry. Before sending them out, He gave them specific instructions, commands, and warnings to heed while ministering to the lost sheep of Israel. He promised them power and authority to evangelize and heal, but He also cautioned them about the difficulties and dangers they would face. Believing that their Master was trustworthy and good, Jesus' first missionaries were compliant to their calling.

In most places in the world today, Christians needn't fear such harsh consequences for practicing their faith as the first evangelists did. We have the advantage of being able to read the full story of the Bible; we know who the players are and how the story ends. We also know that the Spirit of the Father, to whom Jesus referred, is the Holy Spirit of God—the very Spirit that lives in all believers. (Imagine what those twelve overwhelmed men must have thought He meant.)

Nonetheless, persecution and resistance are still a reality. The words of today's passage, spoken thousands of years ago, remind us that though there may be dangers involved in sharing the gospel truth, we still need not fear the outcome. We only need willing and compliant spirits. When we open our mouths in Jesus' name, the Holy Trinity will fill in the blanks.

Stepping In: Read Exodus 4:11–12 and Acts 4:8–10. Does the fear of persecution, resistance, or rejection deter you from speaking truth about Jesus? Talk to God about this today.

Stepping Out: This week, pray before you speak. Ask the Spirit to give you the words. When He does, speak them confidently with love. Then thank Him that He has the outcome under His control.

August 2
Unfeigned

> "Yet a time is coming and has now come when the true worshipers
> will worship the Father in spirit and truth, for they are the kind of
> worshiper the Father seeks."
>
> —John 4:23 (Jn 4:1–26)

Speaking to the Samaritan woman at the well of Jacob near the town of Sychar, Jesus offered her "living water." She gave Him a feeble response based on her limited knowledge of the Prophets and Jewish worship. Jesus explained that, though her beliefs about worship were unfeigned, they were based on limited information. That day, a new way would be revealed.

Only God is omniscient. As much as we know (or would like others to think we know), our minds are finite. The most studied theologian or historian can only know so many facts, and these are subject to perspective, opinion, and bias. Through the story of Jesus and the Samaritan woman, we see that God wants everyone, even the unlikely, to have accurate knowledge about salvation. It is a perfect illustration of how God goes out of His way to bring restoration where it otherwise would not have gone. Jesus has tender care for those who are hurting and in deep need of physical and spiritual life-change.

Using the themes of this passage, we can recognize that where there is thirst, the offer of quenching drink does not go unnoticed. Where there is skepticism, humble confidence is readily welcomed. Where there is confusion, direct clarification is eagerly accepted. Where there are false assumptions at play, unfeigned truth brings comfort. Though there is no absolute formula for speaking truth into people's lives, Jesus gives us some clear parameters. Trust precedes knowledge. Knowledge precedes truth. Truth precedes faith. Faith precedes worship.

Stepping In: Read Deuteronomy 29:18; 1 Chronicles 16:23–31; Isaiah 29:13; and Romans 12:1. How do these verses help you to understand what true, unfeigned worship looks like and your role in it? Ask the Spirit to enliven your thirst for truth. Worship Him with all that you have.

Stepping Out: This week, invite someone who needs refreshment to worship with you at church.

August 3
Expressive

"But what about you?" He asked. "Who do you say I am?"
—Matthew 16:15 (Mt 16:13–20)

In His final year of ministry, Jesus and His disciples traveled north from their home base on the Sea of Galilee to the pagan town of Caesarea Philippi. They taught and healed, drawing their typical crowds. Even in this secular environment, the people were abuzz about the charismatic and authoritative young rabbi. Could He be the Christ, as some claimed? Could He be the Messiah or Son of Man, as He would later testify?

Perhaps during a rare quiet moment, Jesus asked His disciples who the people of this region said He was. Peter, in his bold fashion, spoke up. He reported that people believed Jesus to be John the Baptist, Elijah, Jeremiah, or some other prophet reincarnate. Jesus asked Peter what Peter thought. Without hesitation, Peter expressed his heartfelt belief: "You are the Christ, the Son of the Living God!" Jesus praised Peter's faith and promised him that because the Father had revealed this truth to him, he would become His church's foundation—His "rock."

Jesus very intentionally waited to ask Peter this question until He and His disciples were surrounded by unbelievers. After getting confirmation of the general misconception, Jesus turned to His followers and asked them about their belief. Jesus imparted to Peter the blessing he would need to endure the torment of his upcoming denial of Jesus.

This poignant lesson about faith and loyalty still applies to all believers today. Jesus knows us fully. He perceives our questions from afar and tests our anxious thoughts. He is aware of our fickle tendencies, that many of us prefer to blend in with the dominant culture rather than stand out. However, in an increasingly non-Christian world, this can lead to a harmfully stifled faith. Peter overcame his fear of affiliation with his countercultural Leader, going on to become Jesus' strongest proponent. So must we. In a world where most people do not know who Jesus is, believers must be the ones to boldly express truth.

Stepping In: Read Psalm 139 and John 18:12–27. How does knowing that Jesus knows you completely help you to trust Him? Is there any fear of rejection or confrontation that you need to confess? Thank Him now for empowering you to stand up in faith, enabling you to express your belief in the one true God.

Stepping Out: This week, respectfully ask several people who they say Jesus is. When it is your turn to share, let the Word of God support your humble testimony.

August 4
Happy

"Rejoice in that day and leap for joy, because great is your reward in heaven."

—Luke 6:23 (Lk 6:12–26)

When Jesus started His Sermon on the Mount by listing the ways suffering people would be blessed, He was expressing more than compassion for the physical neediness of the majority. He was also tenderly assuring the faithful minority—including His disciples—that in His kingdom, all wrongs would be made right. The poor would inherit the kingdom, the hungry would be satisfied, mourners would laugh, and joy would come to those persecuted because of His name.

Jesus added the above promise—that ill-treatment was to be expected, but the reward would make it worthwhile. He reminded His listeners that those who persevere will be in good company: all the prophets before them had also been treated poorly and had received the reward of eternal happiness.

For most of us, the idea of being unfairly persecuted or even abused for our faith does not conjure up happy thoughts. Yet Jesus tells us that "in *that* day," meaning the day we experience suffering for our affiliation with the Lord, we should "rejoice and leap for joy"! Even with the hope of heaven as our reward, many of us wonder, "Is this even possible?"

Especially in America, where most of us are well fed, comfortable, and free to practice our religion without fear of persecution, we tend to downplay the significance of this promise. Most of us have a hard time contemplating the ability to rejoice during times of abuse. So focused are we on our personal needs and desires, we forget that the spiritual battle Jesus is talking about rages on all around us. Scripture tells us time and again that the forces of darkness will continue to oppose truth until Jesus returns. Jesus continually emphasizes that His followers can expect resistance. However, because worldly suffering is only temporary, and our Savior has already crowned us victorious, we can be happy.

Stepping In: Read Psalm 20:1–5; Romans 5:1–5, 8:17-18; and 2 Corinthians 4:16–18. What is your normal reaction to insults or aggression? Do you react differently when they are faith-based assaults? Pray for strength and courage to view such incidences in light of future glory. Thank Jesus for being your suffering Savior.

Stepping Out: This week, do not shy away in fear from shining your Christian light. Instead, welcome any negative repercussions and be happy that people recognize Christ in you.

August 5
Munificent

"When she poured this perfume on my body, she did it to prepare me for burial. I tell you the truth, whenever this gospel is preached throughout the world, what she has done will also be told, in memory of her."

—Matthew 26:12–13 (Mt 24:1–3, 25:14–46, 26:1–13)

Shortly after teaching His disciples about the coming judgment, Jesus descended the Mount of Olives and went down into Bethany. There, He and the Twelve were invited to dine in the home of a man known as Simon the Leper—a Pharisee whom Jesus had likely healed. As Jesus enjoyed the meal given in His honor, Mary, the sister of Lazarus, whom Jesus raised from the dead, came in with a jar of very expensive perfume and began anointing Jesus with it.

Seeing this, the men at the table became indignant and voiced their displeasure at such a wasteful act. Jesus rebuked the men and explained that what Mary had done was "beautiful"; her awareness of who Jesus was, and what He was about to do, motivated her to do what was necessary, regardless of the cost. Apparently, this woman understood more fully than the disciples and the religious leaders what Jesus would go through in a matter of days. Out of love and devotion for her Lord, this woman gave to Him the best she could offer: a munificent gesture and a sacred act.

Most Bible readers today are familiar with the stories about Jesus' good friends Lazarus, Martha, and Mary. Of the three, we know that Mary loved Jesus more than anything else—even more than her domestic duties, much to her sister's chagrin. Because Mary prioritized sitting at Jesus' feet and listening to Him, she learned that Jesus was more than a good teacher. He was God incarnate. She understood that He was Lord of all, and she trusted Him.

What a fabulous lesson for believers in every generation! It would serve all Christians well to be more like Mary: valuing Jesus more than worldly riches, paying attention to His words, willingly sacrificing ego and agenda to bring glory to the Lord, and offering Him our best. Today's passage is a reminder not to lose focus of what truly matters: honoring Jesus. No gift is too munificent for Him.

Stepping In: Read Deuteronomy 15:7–11; Mark 14:3–9; Luke 7:37–38; and John 12:1–8. Compare the different accounts of Jesus' anointing. What do you learn about beautiful and extravagant acts of love? How munificent are you in loving Jesus by serving the poor? What is God impressing on you about His command for genuine generosity? Seek a willingness to serve the needy.

Stepping Out: This week, make a generous offering of something of value, like your time, to help someone in need. Give a hand up, not a handout.

August 6
Sagacious

"Therefore every teacher of the law who has been instructed about the kingdom of heaven is like the owner of a house who brings out of the storeroom new treasures as well as old."
—Matthew 13:52 (Mt 13:24–52)

During one of His teachings to the disciples, Jesus spoke extensively about the kingdom of heaven. He asked if they had understood His teaching thus far. Without hesitation, they answered yes. After using seven different parables to teach the eternal value of taking to heart the Word of God, Jesus made this last comparison to the owner of a house. Ironically perhaps, Jesus chose to draw a parallel between kingdom work and the work of Jewish disseminators of knowledge—the scribes and the teachers of the Law, who were Jesus' greatest opponents.

The Twelve might have been taken aback by the mention of heaven and their Master's enemies in the same sentence. What they didn't understand was that *they* were to be the new teachers of the Law. They were to be the owners of the house, who would wisely treasure both the old and the new teachings of God. They were to be the sagacious new leaders of the faith.

In modern vernacular, Jesus is saying that accepting the Old and New Testaments as a complete and congruous teaching is truly having the best of both worlds. However, helping people to see it that way can be a challenge. Many view the Old Testament as a collection of stories about the ancient Jewish race, and therefore irrelevant to us. Some think of the God of the Old Testament as a God of wrath, while the God of the New Testament is a God of mercy.

Jesus would disagree. God is the same yesterday, today, and forever! From the opening pages of Genesis to the closing statements in Revelation, the story of Jesus and the coming kingdom can be traced. Though the new covenant put an end to the old sacrificial system and God's wrathful punishment of His rebellious people, the foreshadowing of the final judgment should not be ignored.

Thanks to the work of the apostles and the New Testament scribes, today's Christians can see the two halves of the Bible as God's complete story of redemption. As sagacious owners of the old and new treasures combined, today's Christians can confidently carry on the work of teaching Jesus' law to the next generation of believers.

Stepping In: Skim Deuteronomy 5 and 6; Nehemiah 8:1–18; Ezekiel 37:15–28; Matthew 5:17–20; Acts 5:29-42; and Hebrews 13:8. Consider how these verses emphasize the role of the chosen to proclaim the Word of God, both in the past and now. Is the Holy Spirit prompting you be a teacher of God's law? Pray for a sagacious and responsive spirit.

Stepping Out: This week, spend some time with the Old Testament, reviewing prophecies of Jesus. Share with someone at least one fascinating fact you discovered there.

Giving

"Heal the sick, raise the dead, cleanse those who have leprosy, drive
out demons. Freely you have received, freely give."
—Matthew 10:8 (Mt 10:1–8)

On sending out His twelve apostles, the first Christian missionaries, Jesus gave them simple instructions about their assigned tasks. For two years, these men had been devoted students of their Master and Teacher, Jesus. They had witnessed and participated in many wondrous acts and miraculous deeds. The time had come for them to put their training to good use. Jesus reminded His apprentices, "Freely you have received, freely give." Jesus had always provided everything they needed: knowledge, power, and authority to carry on His ministry. In addition, they received abilities for the mission they had been assigned. The assignment was clear: by the power Jesus gave them, they were to give others health, peace, hope, and joy—just as Jesus had given these things to them.

To this day, God is still in control of all things. He alone has the power to give and take life. He decides who gets sick and who is healed. In a world where modern technology is king, we often forget this important fact. We trust in doctors and surgeons. We put our faith in computers and science. We rely on the wise and learned to guide us through our difficult days. All the while, God is quietly orchestrating every detail according to His plan, not ours.

That said, training and education are still very important for leading a successful and productive life. The apostles trained under Jesus' tutelage for years before He felt they were up to task. Likewise, most of us need plenty of practice and instruction before we feel competent to perform well on our own. But when we are called to do kingdom-bringing work, none of that really matters. It is not, and never was, by human strength, knowledge, or talent, that miracles happen. It is by Jesus and for Jesus, according to His will and in His timing. We are merely instruments—His hands and feet—giving away the gifts we have been freely given.

Stepping In: Read Proverbs 18:16; Luke 6:38; and Romans 12:4-8. What has God feely given you? Pray about what gifts and talents He would like you to share for His kingdom's sake.

Stepping Out: This week, put one of your God-given abilities to work in the name of Jesus. This could be a physical or intellectual talent, or a spiritual gift Jesus gives you for a specific purpose. Pray that God reveals the details of your mission. If you are unsure about your spiritual gift(s), take a spiritual gifts assessment on the internet, to discover where God has gifted you.

Thrifty

"Gather the pieces that are left over. Let nothing be wasted."
—John 6:12 (Jn 6:1–15)

As He was entering His third and final year of ministry, Jesus left Capernaum for a quieter place on the opposite side of the lake. A large crowd, amazed by the miraculous signs and healings they had witnessed, followed the boat by land, hoping to experience more. Near the town of Bethsaida, the two groups converged. Despite His thwarted plans, Jesus had compassion on them and sat down to teach.

Jesus suggested that Phillip go and buy some bread for the hungry crowd. Phillip balked at the impossibility of this task. Andrew offered Jesus the only food he could find: a boy's small lunch. Jesus had the assembly, more than five thousand in number, sit down. He thanked His Father for the food and had the disciples distribute the five barley loaves and two fishes. Being thrifty not to waste anything—not least of which were the lessons of this miracle—Jesus had His disciples gather the leftovers. There were twelve baskets' worth, one for each of them.

Aside from the empty tomb, the feeding of the five thousand is the only miracle recorded in all four gospels. It is the quintessential example of Jesus' power and God's provision. It is the ultimate illustration of blessings being poured out beyond anyone's wildest imagination. It is a perfect reminder of why we are to trust Jesus without reservation.

Yet how often are we like Phillip, only seeing the impossibility of the situation and forgetting who our Lord is? On a good day, we might be more like Andrew, bringing what we have to Jesus regardless of how inadequate it may be. Jesus "had in mind what He was going to do" even before the boy's lunch was brought to Him. He knows what He is going to do in our lives each day as well. Tests, in the form of preposterous scenarios, become opportunities for God to do what only He can do. That's the very definition of a miracle—if only we remember to let Him!

Today's verse brings our focus back to our role in helping to preserve and utilize the gifts Jesus bestows, being thrifty with miracle leftovers. By sharing the nuggets of truth we have collected in our spiritual feasts with Jesus, we feed many souls.

Stepping In: Read Isaiah 55:1–3; John 4:32–34; 1 Corinthians 4:1–2; 2 Timothy 1:14; and 1 Peter 4:10. After rereading John 6:1–15, reflect on the passage using the Envision It method (See appendix). Who did you identify with and why? What is God teaching through this scripture passage about being thrifty with the gifts He has given you? Pray for wisdom.

Stepping Out: This week, plan a service project with your small group, utilizing the various gifts you each possess.

Appointed

"Now get up and stand on your feet. I have appeared to you to appoint you as a servant and as a witness of what you have seen of me and what I will show you."

—Acts 26:16 (Acts 26:1–32)

Twenty-two years after Paul's miraculous conversion from murderous Pharisee to ardent believer in Jesus' Lordship, he stood trial before Rome's appointed ruler. Instead of extraditing him back to Jerusalem, where they had a better chance of manipulating the system in their favor, the Jewish leaders were forced to stand up against Paul in front of King Agrippa. To their added dismay, the king gave Paul permission to speak first. Paul retold the story of his former ways as a Pharisee and his life-changing encounter with the resurrected Jesus. When Jesus finally opened Paul's eyes, He also opened his mind, heart, and soul to the truth.

For every Christian, alive or dead, there was a moment in time when they realized who Jesus was. More than that, at some point they came to understand who He was to them *personally*: Lord, Savior, heavenly Father, Wonderful Counselor, Teacher, Friend, God. Then, after humbly admitting their sinful nature and consequent need for a Savior, they accepted His forgiveness and committed to following Him.

That is the moment of transformation, rebirth, redemption, salvation. Jesus planned and orchestrated each of these encounters. For some, it was a natural transition. For others, like Paul, it came as an utter surprise. All whom God has chosen, He draws to Himself. Once called, He appoints and equips His children to serve His kingdom and to testify to the truth of the gospel. Each person who calls themselves a Christian has been appointed to be Christ's hands, feet, heart, and voice to those who have not yet had their moment of truth. Like Paul, we must stand up and follow Jesus' instructions, regardless of where they take us. We must never forget that we owe the Lord our very lives and eternities.

Stepping In: Read Isaiah 61:1–2; Ezekiel 2:1–8; Daniel 10:11–12; Acts 22:14–16; Romans 8:28–39; and Ephesians 4:11–12. How do these verses encourage or challenge you? If you don't know what your appointment is, pray about it.

Stepping Out: Each morning this week, before you stand up, get on your knees in prayer, praising God and seeking His will in everything.

Productive

"A farmer went out to sow his seed. As he scattered the seed, some fell along the path, and the birds came and ate it up. Some fell on rocky places, where it did not have much soil. It sprang up quickly, because the soil was shallow. But when the sun came up, the plants were scorched, and they withered because they had no root. Other seed fell among thorns, which grew up and choked the plants. Still other seed fell on good soil, where it produced a crop—a hundred, sixty, or thirty times what was sown. He who has ears let him hear."

—Matthew 13:3–9 (Mt 12:1–13:9)

On a day when the crowd was too large even for Jesus' own mother and brothers to reach Him inside a house, He opted to move out-of-doors. He made His way through the pressing throng to the edge of Lake Gennesaret, the Sea of Galilee, and employed a small fishing vessel to take Him just offshore. From the safety and acoustic advantage of His floating venue, He began teaching the crowd.

Compassion, and perhaps a sense of urgency, filled Jesus' heart as He looked out at the expectant audience. He saw their need. He also saw their potential. The parable He spoke in today's passage, though an accurate illustration of managing crops in difficult terrain, was also a depiction of the spiritual landscape that sowers of the seeds of truth would encounter in the mission fields to come. Only a few of His listeners comprehended the mystery of the soil and the seed. Those who understood knew that this was a call to take up their seed bags and begin casting liberally, aiming for the most productive soil they could find.

Jesus is still recruiting fishermen and farmers alike to do their bit for the harvest of souls. Though most of us no longer live in agrarian societies, it is easy enough to decipher Jesus' meaning in these verses. One need only read on in the chapter for Jesus' own full explanation. These verses, though cleverly disguised as tips one might find in the *Farmer's Almanac*, have much to teach us about the spreading of God's truth.

As Jesus' representatives, today's Christians must be the ones to share His life-saving message far and wide. We must persevere through the droughts and failed attempts at coaxing new spiritual growth in places where we can. We must come alongside those who are blossoming in their faith, helping them to put down secure roots based in eternal promises, while at the same time knocking back choking vines of falsehoods and deception that shade the facts of the gospel. Most importantly, we must trust the Gardener to do the work only He can do: changing hearts, minds, lives, and souls. Adhering to His growing schedule is the most productive use of our time.

Stepping In: Read through the above verses again. Make a mental list of people you know in each of these soil groups. Pray for wisdom to improve their receptivity. Ask God to help you to be a productive sower.

Stepping Out: This week, sow gospel seeds liberally. Pray and trust God to do the rest.

Fiery

> "To the angel of the church in Laodicea write: These are the words of
> the Amen, the faithful and true witness, the ruler of God's creation.
> I know your deeds, that you are neither cold nor hot. I wish you were
> either one or the other!"
>
> —Revelation 3:14–15 (Rv 3:14–22)

Almost seventy years after Jesus' ascension into heaven, the apostle John received his calling to record God's end-times revelation. In His message to the angel of Laodicea, the seventh church, Jesus imparted the harshest criticisms He made of any of the Asia Minor churches. Some of the other churches were warned about succumbing to the adulterous ways of the dominant culture, or told to guard themselves against false teachings. The church in Laodicea was accused of the grievous offense of having lukewarm faith.

Like the church in Sardis, the church in Laodicea was guilty of the rich man's plight: greed, pride, gluttony, and selfish ambition, resulting in blatant spiritual blindness and apathy. Jesus reminded those who claimed to uphold His name that, as the sovereign God of the universe, He would not tolerate their tepid devotion. He clearly disapproved of their self-aggrandizing attitudes and false piety.

But Jesus went on to encourage them to use the generous gifts He had given them, so they could come back into a right relationship with Him before it was too late. Out of love for His church, Jesus offered to clothe the shamefully naked, open the door to heaven wide, and seat them alongside Himself on His throne—all in exchange for a reignition of fiery faith.

Some who read these verses today may think that Jesus is being unduly harsh with the people in Laodicea. From a worldly perspective, who could blame them for simply enjoying the abundant life they had made for themselves? After all, they were decent, churchgoing people who believed in Jesus and gave to worthy causes. They did what was expected of them, and they weren't doing anything the rest of their community wasn't doing. Maybe they didn't go above and beyond their call of duty, but at least they weren't hurting anyone.

Sound familiar? It is an unfortunate human flaw to want to choose the path of least resistance, the easy way. When things are going well, we accept it and settle into a life of ease without thinking much about it. When there is money in the bank, good food in the cupboards, nice clothes on our backs, and oodles of options for our entertainment, we quickly lose sight of anything else. And why not? We have everything we need.

Jesus gives us some clear warnings about being deceived by the ways of this world, a way that leads to destruction. He doesn't want any of us to forget who created us, who gives us all good gifts, who bought our salvation with His own blood, and who has numbered our hairs and our days. He wants us to remember why we are here: to honor and glorify Him with our words, lives, and actions as people on fire for the Lord.

Stepping In: Read Genesis 3:8–13; 1 Chronicles 16:23–31; Psalm 90:12; Isaiah 29:13–14; and Romans 12:1–2. Are you on fire for Jesus, or are your actions lukewarm? Praise your Creator for loving you, and exalt Him above all else.

Stepping Out: This week, let your deeds reflect the blazing affection you have for the Lord.

August 12
Sighted

"Woe to you, teachers of the law and Pharisees, you hypocrites! You shut the kingdom of heaven in men's faces. You yourselves do not enter, nor will you let those enter who are trying to."
—Matthew 23:13 (Mt 22:41–23:14)

With His life and earthly ministry soon to come to a grand conclusion, Jesus held nothing back from His most ardent opponents. He spent countless hours teaching and promoting the gospel in the temple courts. On one such occasion, after warning the crowd not to behave as the hypocritical Pharisees did, Jesus launched into a sermon proclaiming seven woes on the religious elite. He explained that even their righteousness was invalid. He called them "blind guides," "fools," "snakes," "brood(s) of vipers," "murders," and "sons of hell." He exposed their deceit, greed, and corruption. He accused them of their crimes against God and humanity. He predicted their fate and their role in His own. In the hearing of many, Jesus unreservedly exposed the religious leadership's sin and ignorance. Jesus let His audience, including the Pharisees, know that only those with eyes to see who He was would gain access to heaven. The anger these words induced in His enemies would lead them to unwittingly aid in the fulfilment of God's redemptive plan: calling for Jesus' death.

In our day and age, we have a church entity known as the "holy huddle." This is a group of believers who prefer to keep only the company of other believers. They do not like to mingle with the unsaved due to the risk of being contaminated by sinful influences. They discourage the unchurched from participating in the saving grace they themselves enjoy.

Sadly, this very closely resembles the religious elite of old. Jesus had some very strong words for the Pharisees and the teachers of the Law because of their hypocritical and deceitful practices, and He is shouting out a warning to us today for the same offenses. These "woes" can easily apply to us as we blindly continue in our self-serving and hypocritical ways. We too may feel superior to others based on our biblical knowledge or conservative behavior. We too may hold ourselves to a different standard than others, or even withhold love and truth from those we deem unworthy. We too are at risk of being blind guides. Yet for those who are willing to look, they will see a simple solution: lose pride and gain humility. The humbly sighted see things and people the way Jesus does.

Stepping In: Read Isaiah 5:8, 5:20-21, 10:1-2; Habakkuk 2:4–6; and Malachi 2:7–9. Pray that God reveals any falseness or pride in you. Pray that He replaces any spiritual blindness with godly vision.

Stepping Out: Make a commitment to regularly step outside your own holy huddle. This week, find ways to be inclusive rather than exclusive.

August 13
Saved

"Your faith has saved you; go in peace."
—Luke 7:50 (Lk 7:36–50)

Late in Jesus' ministry, a woman of ill-repute came in to where He was sharing a meal and anointed His feet with her tears and expensive perfume. Simon the leper (a Pharisee) was miffed by Jesus' acceptance of the woman's affection. Simon muttered to himself, "Surely if this man was a prophet, He would not allow this sinful woman to touch Him." Jesus did know about this woman's life, and He knew the hardness of Simon's heart as well. After telling a parable about love and forgiveness of sins, Jesus told the woman that hers were forgiven. To further emphasize His authority to do this divine act of mercy, He added the above statement.

Each of the characters in today's story took calculated risks. This is something humans have been doing since the dawn of time. Some risks we take pan out, while others do not. Inherent in these ventures is the possibility of losing more than we gain. We have all played this game; we know how it works. Sometimes the stakes are very high.

In this passage of scripture, we see that the Pharisee risked scorn from his religious brethren for associating with Jesus, a known adversary. Simon figured that he might do well to get on Jesus' good side. He took his chances and was treated to a lesson in humility.

Jesus too took a risk in accepting the invitation. He knew that his host offered only a cursory interest in Him. The Pharisee's display of hospitality was nothing more than a strategic maneuver to win His graces. Simon's heart was so far from God that he did not realize that God's Son was sitting at his table. Nonetheless, Jesus accepted, knowing the good that would come of the event, even if it also served to aggravate His opponents further.

Of the three, though, the woman risked the most. Already an outcast, rejected and humiliated by society, she took the one thing she had of value and poured it out on the Lord's feet. She humbled herself completely and honored Jesus in a very special way. She risked much but gained everything. Her bold faith had saved her, as it will all who seek Him.

Stepping In: Read Numbers 6:24–25; 1 Samuel 1:16–18; Mark 5:34; and Luke 8:1–2. Has your faith in Jesus healed and saved you? Think of the times you have risked something for Jesus. Was it worth it? Thank Him now.

Stepping Out: This week, because of your love and faith, take a risk. Go in peace into your sphere of influence.

August 14
Uncontainable

"No one sews a patch of unshrunk cloth on an old garment, for the patch will pull away from the garment making the tear worse. Neither do men pour new wine into old wineskins. If they do, the skins will burst, the wine will run out and the wineskin will be ruined. No, they pour new wine into new wineskins, and both are preserved."
—Matthew 9:16–17 (Mt 9:14–17)

When John the Baptist was convicted and sent to prison for offending Herod Antipas, the tetrarch of Galilee, John's disciples realized that Jesus' disciples were not praying and fasting as they were in response to this sad news. They asked Jesus about this. He told them that it was not yet the time for his disciples to mourn and fast, because He was still with them.

Jesus then used the illustrations of the cloth and the wineskin to help them understand that they needed to stretch and adapt to the new order of things He was ushering in. His truth and His message could not be contained nor understood by those who could not conform to a new ideology. John's disciples had to choose between joining Jesus' uncontainable movement or getting out of the way.

Most of us can recall a time when we went to our parents, complaining about the unfairness of life—perhaps wanting to know why an older sibling got to stay up later. We hoped for some sympathy, or for the authorities to see the error of their ways. We typically received neither.

Like a patient parent, Jesus tries to help us see beyond how things are, or even how we think they should be, to the way they must be in His kingdom. He encourages us to stop trying to squeeze God into our own understanding just so He makes sense to us or fits our preconceived notions of who He should be. God is not containable, and neither should our faith be.

Stepping In: Take some time to think about the belief system in which you were raised. How has it influenced your faith today? Pray that the Holy Spirit reveals any old ways or beliefs that no longer serve a purpose, and for the willingness to let them go.

Stepping Out: This week, invest some time and/or resources in a faith-based youth development program. Pray that God fill those new wineskins with new wine.

Thriving

> "The thief comes only to steal and kill and destroy; I have come that they may have life, and have it to the full."
> —John 10:10 (Jn 9:13–10:10)

With only a few months left in His earthly ministry, Jesus made the most of every teaching opportunity. Teaching in the temple courts in Jerusalem during the Feast of Dedications, Jesus boldly stated His purpose as the One sent to do the redeeming work of the Father. Most of the religious leaders' hearts were far from God, and the truth Jesus spoke fell on deaf ears. Because of their spiritual blindness, they could not see the Messiah even as He stood in their midst proclaiming His identity.

Jesus spoke of Himself as the Shepherd, His sheep hearing and responding only to His voice. Those who were not His sheep did not recognize His voice at all. He was also the Gate. Only His sheep entered through the Gate—all others were imposters, thieves, and murderers. Jesus summarized His position in today's verse, letting the implied choice hang in the air while His opponents scoffed and fumed.

Satan, the master of lies, is still very much at work in our world today. His only goal is to steal us away from God, so he can have us on his side. He is a crafty opportunist who preys on the weak. He capitalizes on our moments of doubt, pain, fear, confusion, anger, jealousy, worry, and temptation, magnifying them so that we feel that our loving God has abandoned us. Conversely, when life is good, Satan tries to convince us that we are self-sufficient and don't need God. He attempts to lead us through the wrong gate, which only leads to destruction and death. He is a clever demon, but he is easily outsmarted.

Though Satan would love to distract us from this fact, Christians have the power to vanquish him with a single word: Jesus! Once we have claimed Jesus as our Lord and Savior, our ears become tuned to hear only His voice and obey only His commands. Jesus leads us through the Gate to safety and a thriving life within the fold of God.

Stepping In: Read Psalm 16:11, 23:1; Isaiah 40:10-11, 56:9-12; Ezekiel 43:1–2; Matthew 6:31–33; John 14:6; and Romans 5:17. What do these verses teach you about the abundant and secure life Jesus offers? How is it different from the ways of the world and Satan? Are you thriving in the fold of God, or languishing in want and worry? Pray for an ability to hear Jesus' voice above all others, and allow Him to lead you through His Gate.

Stepping Out: This week, write out the ways "the thief" has attempted to steal your faith and joy. Perhaps there was a time when he succeeded. Contrast this list with a list of ways Jesus has enriched your life and blessed you beyond your dreams. Share these two lists with your small group or some friends.

August 16
Imploring

"If you believe, you will receive whatever you ask for in prayer."
—Matthew 21:22 (Mt 21:1–11, 17–22)

Having slept in the nearby town of Bethany, Jesus and His entourage went into Jerusalem early one day. On the way, Jesus was hungry and went to a fig tree for some fruit to eat. Finding none, He cursed the tree, causing it to wither and die. The disciples were amazed and asked Jesus why this had happened. He explained to them that if they had faith, without doubt, they could do far greater things than this. He told them to express this faith by asking in prayer.

After three years as Jesus' apprentices, the disciples had heard this teaching before. Jesus had been supplying them with all they needed to do miraculous works. But soon He would be leaving them, and they would have to depend on a supernatural connection to the Father through the Spirit to accomplish their evangelical goals. In a matter of days, they would no longer be able to ask Jesus to aid them. Henceforth, they would be imploring the unseen God of the universe through prayer.

Jesus chose His words carefully. He meant what He said, even when speaking figuratively or in hyperbole. When He told His disciples to pray, they had not yet received the Holy Spirit, nor had they been fully trained. Still, they had witnessed Jesus praying to His Father on a regular basis and knew how vital it was for Him.

As Christians today, we often take the wonderful privilege of prayer for granted. When most of us read today's verse, we tend to emphasize the word "whatever." Jesus wants us to focus on the word "believe." Moreover, some of us completely miss the word "if." Like so many passages in the Bible, if taken out of context or misunderstood, this verse can lead to false doctrine and faulty belief.

Jesus is speaking literally here—with a caveat. He is saying that if we truly believe in the unity and power of the Holy Trinity, we will have a heart for what pleases God. With a heart for what pleases God, we will seek to do His will above our own. When we truly seek to do what God wants, we will pray for His will to be done. When we implore of Him to enact His will, it will be done. The only limiting factor in getting what we ask for in prayer is our capacity to believe that God can and will answer—according to His plan, timing, and will.

Stepping In: Read Matthew 7:7; John 11:41–42; Philippians 4:4–7; and James 1:5–8. After reading these verses, take some time to reflect on today's passage, using the Emphasize It method (See appendix). Thank God for giving you an imploring and trusting heart, and for faithfully answering your prayers.

Stepping Out: This week, make a list of prayers God has answered. Note how many were answered the way you expected. Share this list with a friend and compare notes.

Shrewd

"But God said to him, 'You fool! This very night your life will be demanded from you. Then who will get what you have prepared for yourself?' This is how it will be with anyone who stores up things for himself but is not rich toward God."

—Luke 12:20–21 (Lk 12:1–21)

As the intensity of His final year of ministry pulsated around Him, Jesus kept focused on God's plan, highlighting truth in every situation. He used each teachable moment as an opportunity to develop His disciples' understanding of spiritual matters, as well as to educate the general populace about right living before God. Full of compassion, and possessing the utmost patience, Jesus continually met the demanding mental, physical, and spiritual needs of the people. Above all, being the Good Shepherd that He was, Jesus cared most deeply for the lost souls of those who regularly gathered around Him.

And so, as He traveled between Judea and Galilee, Jesus preached the good news to the crowds and healed the people of many ills. On one such occasion, a young man asked Jesus to arbitrate a financial matter between himself and his brother. Jesus declined to do so and warned the young man against greed. Jesus then told a parable about a rich man who, in preferring the finer things in life, failed to see that soon he would have no life at all. Jesus explained bluntly how that story would end—a greedy, short-sighted approach to life was sure folly.

Jesus always cuts right to the heart of the matter, especially when it concerns one's attitude toward God. Time and again throughout scripture, Jesus issues these types of warnings to stir people toward awareness and repentance. His direct approach leaves us with no excuse but to respond.

Those who have the Spirit of God dwelling within them respond with an attitude of humble conviction and are spurred toward corrective actions. Those whose hearts are hardened toward God tend to react with contempt. Some will be offended by the accusatory tone and the suggestion that enjoying one's financial success is somehow ungodly. Surely there is nothing wrong with acquiring wealth and reaping the rewards of one's labor. That is not the issue here. God has nothing against rich people—far from it. It does not matter how much one has or does not have. What God cares about is how tightly one holds on to what one has.

The shrewd Christian knows that all one has is a gift from God, and is happy to give back to Him generously. As for those who believe that they deserve to keep their riches and do as they please? They will always be wanting, always striving, always worrying, and never finding true satisfaction.

Stepping In: Read Deuteronomy 15:7–8; Leviticus 25:35–38; Psalm 39:4–8; Matthew 6:19–21; and 2 Corinthians 8:12–15 and 9:6–9. God has plenty to say about the shrewd management of resources, generosity, and unselfish giving. What is He saying to you about these things? Ask Him to free you from any love of money that may be holding your heart captive.

Stepping Out: This week, be rich toward God. Follow the Spirit's prompting and give Him something of true value, be it your money or your time. Do this as an example to a watching world.

Obedient

"Not everyone who says to me, 'Lord, Lord,' will enter the kingdom of
heaven, but only he who does the will of my Father in heaven."
—Matthew 7:21 (Mt 7:15–23)

One can only imagine the expressions of shock on the faces of those who heard Jesus' words in His
Sermon on the Mount. This statement would have been considered outright blasphemy by many in
attendance. Could this young Jewish teacher, the son of a carpenter from Nazareth, truly be claiming
to be the Son of God?

Certainly, there were some in the crowd who did believe Jesus to be the Messiah. Some believed
that He was sent by God to be Israel's new earthly king. Many others agreed that He was a talented
healer and a wise man, but remained skeptical about His divine authority. Though most of the
audience knew very little about the kingdom of which Jesus spoke, they most certainly understood
that it was a place they wanted to go. Some believed they had an automatic right to be included there.

Jesus, in His bold and unapologetically truthful manner, let His audience know that only those
who were obedient to God's will would see heaven. In other words, it would take more than just words,
religiosity, or ancestry to ensure one's position in that lofty place.

Like the Jews of Jesus' day, many people today believe that their place in heaven is secure simply
by association. But saying you believe in God is not enough. Jews, God's chosen people of old, believed
that they would inherit the kingdom solely because of their lineage. Many now falsely assume that
since they were created by God and are mostly "good," they are necessarily heaven-bound. There
are even some who know about Jesus but refuse to accept Him as Lord and Savior, and nevertheless
believe that their association is enough to secure their eternity. These are the ones Jesus is referring
to in today's verse, the ones paying Him only lip service.

Jesus calls such people's bluff. As is true for all His teachings, it always comes down to a matter of
the heart—the heart and obedience. Jesus knows our hearts. He doesn't need our words to tell Him
what He wants to hear. Our actions will speak louder than anything that comes from our mouths.

Stepping In: Read Psalm 40:8–10; Matthew 26:39; Romans 12:2; and Ephesians 5:17–20. What do these
verses tell you about God's will? What specific behaviors mentioned do you think God is calling you
to change? Pray for an obedient heart to do God's will and not your own this week.

Stepping Out: This week, set an example of obedience to God's Word. From the above scripture
passages or one of your own choosing, obey the commands He is leading you to follow. Whisper,
"Lead me Lord," and then show Him you mean it with your actions.

August 19
Rejuvenated

"Come with me by yourselves to a quiet place and get some rest."
—Mark 6:31 (Mk 30–44)

After spending many months training His twelve disciples, Jesus commissioned them as apostles and sent them out to minister on their own. Using the power and authority He had given them, the Twelve were able to preach with boldness, heal many illnesses, and drive out demons among the people of Israel. After their successful missions, they reunited with Jesus near the shores of the Sea of Galilee. As they gave their reports, a large crowd gathered, creating a chaotic scene.

Recognizing His disciples' need for rest before the pressures of their work began anew, Jesus issued a command for them to come with Him. Leading them to a solitary place, Jesus provided for His disciples' physical and spiritual needs. However, their time of rest was soon cut short. The people discovered their location and began arriving in droves. Jesus, having compassion on the masses, sat down to teach and feed them by His miraculous power. Many that day went away satisfied in their bodies and souls—rejuvenated.

Jesus knows what we need and when we need it. It saddens Him to see His people running themselves into exhaustion, even in the cause of His kingdom. He knows we need times of rest, refreshment, and spiritual rejuvenation. Time with the Father was of the utmost importance to Him, as it should be for us as well.

Jesus opted to start each day in quiet prayer and devotion to God, aligning His life to the will of the Father and committing His first and His best. We often give God only our leftovers. Jesus recognized a need to take God breaks in the midst of the chaos. We are often too caught up in it to realize how spiritually depleted we are becoming. Today's verse is a reminder and an encouragement to prioritize soul care. Notice that Jesus didn't ask the men if they wanted to take a break. He *told* them to join Him in a time of rest. It was and is not a suggestion, but a command.

Stepping In: Read Exodus 33:14 and Psalm 23:1–3 and 62:1–2, 5–6. The Bible has plenty to say about rest. How do these verses or others encourage you to take this command seriously? Pray that the Spirit guides you to times of needed rejuvenation, and that you have the wisdom to take them as directed.

Stepping Out: This week, as the Spirit prompts you, join Jesus in times of rest and rejuvenation, so that you can be your best self for Him.

August 20
Unhindered

"Let the little children come to me, and do not hinder them, for the
kingdom of heaven belongs to such as these."
—Matthew 19:14 (Mt 19:13–15)

Having left Galilee for the last time, Jesus and His disciples began the journey toward Jerusalem. While they were in the region of Judea, they crossed over to the other side of the Jordan River to minister to the people there. At that time, some children were brought to Jesus so that He could lay hands on them and pray for them. When the disciples saw this, they tried to dissuade the people from troubling their Master in this way. Jesus rebuked His men and told them to bring the children to Him, and to never discourage the little ones from seeking His presence.

His disciples should have known that Jesus would react this way. They had only recently been instructed to protect and provide for the spiritual growth of the innocent, vulnerable, pure of heart, and utterly dependent. In fact, Jesus had told them plainly that they would have to adopt these qualities if they were to inherit the kingdom of heaven. Jesus reiterated this notion in today's verse. The disciples apparently needed the reminder.

To their credit, they were probably only doing their best to ensure an atmosphere conducive to healing and teaching. Culturally speaking, children were not allowed free access to important adult matters, especially of a religious nature. However, as was typical with Jesus, He bent the norms of His day because they no longer fit in His theological model. Jesus wanted His followers to see children as the next generation of believers, and never to hinder their pursuit of Him.

The encouragement in today's verse is for all generations of Christians, from Jesus' day until His return. We too must view children as the ones who will continue the work of spreading the gospel once our day is done. The kingdom of heaven belongs to them.

Jesus is still the Master Rabbi. He still speaks to those who have ears to hear. As parents and adults, it is our responsibility to provide our children every opportunity of church, home, and community to be brought up in the Word. This means that our children must learn about the Bible, the Trinity, and the promise of heaven from an early age.

It also means that the adults in these children's lives must set the best possible example of walking daily with Jesus. Sadly, many of us were hindered spiritually by growing up in "religious" homes, where spiritual neglect and hypocrisy were the example set. Many of us stumbled or even left our faith as a result. Some have not yet found their way back. Jesus is telling us not to let this happen to the next generation, but to usher in an unhindered faith.

Stepping In: Read Matthew 18:3–6 and 25:34. What was your own "religious" experience as a child? Were you led to Jesus, or was your spiritual growth hindered? Pray and thank God for those who helped you find your way.

Stepping Out: This week, look for and remove any hindrances you may be putting in the way of the little ones—those with immature faith—coming to Jesus. Instead, let your Christ-likeness guide them closer.

August 21

Led

"I am the way and the truth and the life. No one comes to the Father except through me."

—John 14:6 (Jn 13:1–14:6)

In an upper room in a Jerusalem guesthouse, where Jesus and His disciples ate their last Passover meal together, Jesus spoke comforting words about going to prepare a place for them in His Father's house, and that He would be back for them. When Jesus stated that they already knew the way to this place, Thomas voiced the group's doubt, asking how they could know the way to this mysterious destination. Jesus explained that He was the way: they knew the way because they knew the Savior. They would be welcome in the Father's house because they had believed in the Son. To follow Jesus was to be led into paradise.

Today's verse is probably one of Jesus' most famous and most divisive statements. It is the gospel message in a nutshell, the plain and simple truth of the way to salvation. For Christians, this statement is the proclamation of our faith. Jesus is the way to gain access to God—the only source of spiritual truth and the only path to eternal life. For non-Christians, this emphatic declaration is proof of our religion's exclusivity.

Without really thinking it through, many people view the notion of there being only one way to heaven as narrow-minded and discriminatory. However, from an objective standpoint, that is a nonsensical argument. Heaven, the place where God lives, is a Christian construct. Therefore, one should not expect to gain access there unless one subscribes to Christian belief. What's more, it is unclear why anyone who does not believe in Jesus would want to go to where He is.

That said, Jesus does want all to know about Him and to choose freely to be led by Him. As His disciples, we must explain to a skeptical world that, though salvation is exclusive to those who acknowledge Jesus as Lord, it is an all-inclusive offer.

Stepping In: Read Matthew 7:13–14, 21; Luke 13:24–25; John 5:24, 6:44; Romans 10:12–15; Ephesians 2:8–10; and 2 Peter 3:9. How does your faith in these verses encourage you to lead others to Jesus? Praise God for drawing you.

Stepping Out: This week, pray for God to draw those who don't yet know Jesus as the way, the truth, and the life. Lead others to be led into a relationship with Christ. Invite some to church.

August 22
Devoted

"No one can serve two masters. Either you will hate the one and love the other, or you will be devoted to the one and despise the other. You cannot serve both God and money."

—Matthew 6:24 (Mt 6:19–24)

Everyone in attendance during Jesus' Sermon on the Mount would have been familiar with the master-slave relationship. They lived under oppressive Roman rule, many in servitude to the greedy and corrupt foreign officers placed over them. For the Jews, who shared a sad history marked by long periods of captivity and slavery, the thought of serving yet another master surely added insult to injury. Some slave masters, however, were cut from a more humane cloth, and would therefore have been worthy of a slave's respect and devotion—perhaps even love in some rare instances.

From a strictly financial standpoint, the slave trade was extremely important in the ancient world. Dynasties were literally built on the backs of this free labor source. Masters needed their slaves and were protective of their investments. A loyal slave was highly valued and often treated accordingly. A smart slave worked to please the master, demonstrating a strong work ethic, trustworthiness, and devotion.

The slaves Jesus was talking about were not just those owned by another person. He implied that greater powers had the potential to own a person: financial lust or godly pursuits. To those who loved money and the power it wielded, this message of misplaced devotion would have stung.

The bosses of today are our closest equivalent to the masters of old. They too fall into the loved and the despised categories. We often feel like we are working for slave drivers: underpaid, overworked, and way underappreciated. Yet, as Jesus reminds us, allegiance can be a fickle thing, especially when it concerns money. Most of us think we can manage our pursuit of wealth and keep our godly perspective in check. But, really, can we?

Jesus thinks not. When we cast our morals and ethics aside in the pursuit of the almighty dollar, we alienate our true Master in the process. Jesus talks a lot about our relationship with God and with money because He knows our hearts and our tendencies. As He wrapped up the "treasures in heaven" portion of His sermon, Jesus let us know that He was aware of the enduring struggle between love of stuff and love of God.

In a world of easy access and abundance, we are desensitized to the enslaving effect worldly pursuits have on us. According to the blog site *Nerdwallet* (2016), the average American family's debt sits at more than $132,000, with interest costing upward of $1,300 per month. Clearly, the master/slave relationship Jesus spoke of two thousand years ago still very much applies to us today—and then some.

Stepping In: Read Malachi 3:10; Luke 21:1-3; 2 Corinthians 8:2-5, 9:7. Where does your devotion lie—with the pursuit of wealth or of God? Just for fun, acknowledge God each time you think of or use money. Keep track and pay yourself (maybe a quarter) for each time you spend money this week. Give the accumulated payments as an extra tithe this weekend. Test this and notice the blessings you receive.

Stepping Out: Commit to a Malachi 3:10 lifestyle. Practice 10/10/80 financing (see appendix).

August 23
Sought

"In the same way, I tell you, there is rejoicing in the presence of the angels of God over one sinner who repents."

—Luke 15:10 (Lk 15:1–10)

With a crowd of social outcasts gathered around Him, and a group of Pharisees looking on, Jesus told a series of parables about the joys of finding a lost treasure. One was about a woman who lost a valuable coin. After a thorough search, she recovered the coin. In her joy, she went out and shared the good news far and wide. The moral of these stories revealed how God rewarded those with pursuant faith—and how well-aware He was of those who clearly lacked it.

As easy as it is to look down on the Pharisees, it is important to remember that Jesus died for them too. God sought them out just as He seeks us out. This is a beautiful and underrated truth. Before any one of us came to know Jesus as Savior, God was drawing us to Himself. Even in our sinful, fallen state, He sought us out and adopted us as His own. All of heaven rejoices when one of the lost is found. God is glorified when the stubborn drifter turns back toward Him and accepts His saving grace. Yet, to a dying world, these notions are of little interest or use.

For the Pharisees, whose academic knowledge and religious rigidity became their god, the words of the cherished repentant sinner were lost on them. Pride and spiritual ignorance cause their hearts to drift further and further away from the God they loved, until they didn't recognize Him when He was standing right in front of them.

This is the unfortunate way of the world. Each person creates their own truth based on what they see and know. With so many choices, distractions, and temptations, it is easy to see how the head rules the heart. Yet God does not give up. He leaves the flock to track down the one lost sheep. He searches high and low until each lost one is found. He is relentless. Hidden in each person's heart is a transponder, a beacon of hope signaling to God, if not too buried.

Stepping In: Read Genesis 3:8–10; Psalm 139; Matthew 18:12–14; John 6:44, 10:14–16; and 1 Corinthians 1:26–31. In what ways do you let pride, shame, or fear keep you from allowing God to pursue you, or keep you from seeking God above worldly desires? Pray that He softens your heart so that it yields to Him in every way. Thank Him for seeking and finding you.

Stepping Out: This week, be an example of one who turns from sin and does what is right is God's eyes. Be an encourager, not a stumbling block, for others to do the same. For inspiration, listen to "Relentless," by Hillsong United.

United

> "Every kingdom divided against itself will be ruined, and every city or household divided against itself will not stand. If Satan drives out Satan, he is divided against himself. How can his kingdom stand? And if I drive out demons by Beelzebub, by whom do your people drive them out? So then, they will be your judges."
> —Matthew 12:25–27 (Mt 12:1–27)

When Jesus spoke these words to a confrontational group of Pharisees, He had just healed a demon-possessed, blind, and mute man. The Pharisees saw this as another example of Jesus' unauthorized use of power. Blind to His divine nature, the Pharisees were convinced that Jesus' miraculous abilities had to derive from the master of evil, Beelzebub or Satan.

Instead of engaging His opponents in an angry dispute, Jesus answered their accusation with pure logic. He highlighted the importance of operating within a unified organization. The Pharisees could not have understood just how divided their nation would become over such issues as distribution of power and religious authenticity. Jesus wanted them to know that much more than mere human influences would eventually determine whose side each person was on: God's or Satan's. In time, representatives from each side would claim their own.

"Unity" is a nice word—a churchy word, even. But do we actually take the time to think about what it means and what it entails? Do we make an effort to live in unity with others? When we examine our fickle history, a sad reality emerges. We have a collective tendency to bail out of uncomfortable situations rather than persevere for the good of the institution. Simply put, when tensions run high, we put our own interests and needs ahead of the collective unit. If we don't like people, we unfriend them. If we don't like our jobs, we quit. If we don't like our spouses, we get divorced. When we don't like the way things are going in our church, we leave it—sometimes leaving our faith at the door as well.

As humans, we possess a basic need for cohesiveness and structure. We are designed to live in community with God at the center. When we cut God out of the equation, we are left at loose ends until we find something or someone to replace Him. Satan takes advantage of floundering souls, leading them further away. All through scripture, believers are called to be united in word, thought, faith, and action. Together we stand; divided we fall.

Stepping In: Read Psalm 133:1; Romans 15:5-7; Ephesians 4:3–6; Philippians 2:1–4; and Colossians 2:2-3 and 3:14. Pray for unity in your home and church. Pray that Jesus wins back those who are lost in this struggle.

Stepping Out: This week, prioritize group harmony over self-interest at home, school, community, and church.

August 25
Sanguine

> Then he said to Thomas, "Put your finger here; see my hands. Reach
> out your hand and put it into my side. Stop doubting and believe."
> —John 20:27 (Jn 20:1–31)

Jesus' disciples were crushed by the death of their Lord and Master. Fearing for their own lives, they huddled together behind locked doors, unsure of their next move. For three days, the disciples attempted to reconcile what they thought they knew about Jesus and what they had seen happen to Him, trying to figure out what went wrong.

Three days after Jesus had been placed in the tomb, ten of the disciples were treated to quite a surprise when the resurrected Jesus appeared to them in the flesh, proving His power over death. Thomas, who had suffered the loss more than most, was not present for that glorious moment. When he returned, the other disciples told him the wonderful news. Instead of being thrilled and relieved, Thomas doubted; he required tangible proof of the miraculous claim. One week later, that is exactly what Jesus provided. Thereafter, the disciples' view of their future turned from pessimistic to sanguine.

In a "seeing is believing" culture, most of us can easily relate to Thomas' skepticism. It would be like someone in your family telling you that they had won the lottery. You would want to see the winning ticket—or, better yet, the money—before you were convinced. News like that is usually too good to be true, and even the most honest of people are not infallible.

But Jesus is! Everything He says is true. Everything He has said would happen has happened. Everything He has told us will happen, will happen. He is trustworthy. However, because He knows that most of us have been conditioned to be mistrusting, He offers proof to back up His claims. Sometimes the proof comes in the form of physical evidence. At other times, it may arrive in our mind by way of an unquestionable peace or assurance given to us by His Spirit.

One day we will all get to put our fingers in Jesus' wounds and see with our own eyes that He is who He claims to be. Until then, we must live by faith and not by sight, confident of His power and His promises, and similarly sanguine in our view of what is to come.

Stepping In: Read 2 Samuel 7:28; Psalm 22:4–5; Isaiah 25:9; and 2 Corinthians 5:7. How do these verses encourage your faith? Do you view difficulties as unfair tests or as opportunities? Is your attitude pessimistic or sanguine? Take some time to reflect on today's passage using the Envision It method (See appendix). Could you relate to Thomas' doubt, or were you drawn to the optimism of the others? Ask God to help you to trust Him more.

Stepping Out: This week, make a list of the convincing evidence Jesus has given you that allows you to be sanguine about Him and His abilities and promises. Share this list with those needing convincing.

August 26
Perseverant

"Away from me, Satan! For it is written: 'Worship the Lord your God, and serve him only.'"

—Matthew 4:10 (Mt 4:1–11)

Two significant events initiated Jesus' earthly ministry. First, when He was thirty years old, He was baptized in the Jordan River by His cousin John. Second, He was led by the Spirit into the desert to be tempted by Satan. On the day Jesus was baptized, the voice of God was heard acknowledging and praising His Son. The people saw the Holy Spirit descend on Him like a dove. Immediately following this glorious event, the Holy Spirit led Jesus into the desert for a time of intense isolation, fasting, and temptation.

All of this was very intentional. The ministry Jesus was about to embark on would take strength and fortitude, the kind only achieved by the testing of endurance and faith. Satan tried to break Jesus' resolve by tempting Him with the thought of food during His fast, and by enticing Him to use His power to rescue Himself. Satan went so far as to offer Jesus the whole world in exchange for His worship. Jesus did not take the bait. Instead of arguing with His tempter or trying to reason with him, Jesus repeatedly used the power of scripture to put Satan in his place. Being a coward and sore loser, Satan fled the scene without further ado. In the battle of perseverance, Jesus won.

In many parts of the world, life has become very easy. Convenience is expected; instant gratification is the norm. The line between wants and needs has become blurry. Especially in America, the pressure to appear like we have it all (beauty, riches, intelligence, health, a perfect family) fuels our greed and leads to self-aggrandizement. In our modern world, the individual is king. Our money and our stuff have become objects of worship. We have forgotten our place in the world God created. We have forgotten that we are nothing and we have nothing without the grace of God. He gives, and He takes away.

The devil wants to convince us otherwise. Satan, the prince of this world, wants us to believe that we are in control, and that we deserve to have whatever we want. Satan tempts us with the things that are within his dominion—the things of this perishable world. But all he can provide is a fleeting and fruitless fantasy.

Only God can offer lasting treasure. Only God is worthy of our praise, worship, faith, and service. Today's verse reminds us to tell Satan that you are not interested in him or his empty promises. Our devotion belongs to God. Following Jesus' example, we too must combat evil with God's Word and perseverant faith.

Stepping In: Read Job 1:21; John 8:42–44; and 2 Corinthians 11:3. Pray to God for wisdom to recognize Satan's schemes and for the strength to stand up in faith against them. Start by using your voice and the name of Jesus to send him away. Devote your day of rest to worshipping God and serving Him.

Stepping out: This week, verbally ask God to adorn you with His protective armor (see Eph 6:11–17). Call on the name of Jesus to help you persevere through Satan's attacks.

August 27
Safe

"Woe to the world because the things that cause people to sin. Such things must come, but woe to the man through whom they come!"
—Matthew 18:7 (Mt 18:1–9)

At the time in Jesus' ministry when He felt His disciples were ready to take their faith to the next level, He began to teach them about their role in the coming kingdom. Along with inspirational lessons of encouragement, Jesus also spoke plainly about the hardships and dangers of following Him. Yet, their human minds could not yet perceive of the deep spiritual meaning behind His teaching; they certainly could not grasp how the sin of the world would lead to His impending martyrdom. Though these faithful Jewish men knew that sin was offensive to God and deserving of His wrath, they did not yet understand how insidious a threat undealt-with sin was. Moreover, as the warning in today's verse implies, the disciples had to learn to realize that each person, including themselves, would be held responsible for their sin-inducing influence. Jesus taught His disciples that, though evil "must come" to fulfill prophecy, they would be safe with Him.

By reading through the Old and New Testaments, Christians today can trace sin back to its origin with the fall of man, as well as project its course forward to its demise when Jesus returns and brings it to a final end. We understand why sin exists and why it must be atoned-for.

To an unbelieving world, sin is not real. Most think that circumstances are dictated by chance or luck. Some attribute our manifest destinies to karma. Christians understand about the good and evil spiritual powers at play in our lives and world. While God will win, Satan will not go down without a fight. Jesus needs all His followers to know how to stay safe in this perishing world by staying close to Him.

The teaching in today's scripture passage is a warning and a reminder: sin doesn't just come from without. It also can come from within. We must claim our safety in Christ alone, arming ourselves with the gospel and fending off Satan's attacks at every turn. It is for our protection and for that of others as well. Jesus makes it clear that the person who is blindly unaware and ignorantly contributes to sin heaps calamity on him - or herself. We can expect it.

Stepping In: Read Ephesians 6:10–17 and Revelation 13:7–10. Do you feel prepared to defend yourself against Satan's attacks? Pray for awareness of things that can cause you to sin. Wear God's armor each day.

Stepping Out: This week, be hypervigilant to avoid temptations and not tempt others to sin. Pray each morning that God will keep you safe and protect you from Satan's deceptions.

August 28
Somber

"Daughters of Jerusalem, do not weep for me; weep for yourselves and for your children. For the time will come when you will say, 'Blessed are the barren women, the wombs that never bore and the breasts that never nursed.'"

—Luke 23:28–29 (Lk 23:26–43)

Just five days after He had been given a king's welcome into the city of Jerusalem, Jesus staggered out of the city gates carrying the device that would end His life: the cross. He strained toward Golgotha, the place of the skull, with two heavy, rough-hewn planks pressed to His raw shoulders. Each step was extremely painful and slow. Wanting to get their gruesome task over with, the guards leading Jesus forcibly recruited a man named Simon from Cyrene to carry the cross the rest of the way.

A large crowd of mourners followed. Some were true believers, and some possibly professional mourners hired by the Jewish leaders. Jesus' concern was for those around Him. Speaking in utter sincerity to the women in the crowd, He expressed a somber truth about the mourning to come. How it saddened Jesus to know that so many of His own people had been blind to the Messiah in their midst. And how sad it would be on the day when they were held accountable for their unbelief.

Truly, there is very little on this earth that is sadder than watching people make irrevocably bad choices, especially having to do with their eternity. Scripture makes it all too clear that when Jesus returns to earth, He will justify the righteous and judge the unrighteous. These are the somber facts. Until that moment, people will still have a choice to believe in Jesus and be saved, or continue to reject Him and be condemned.

Jesus, like any good parent, does not want His children to head down a path of destruction. Yet He gives us free will to choose. Christians know this truth and must share it with those who are blindly careening toward an endlessly hopeless future. These verses remind us of how incredibly heartbreaking it is for someone to miss out on salvation. For them, death will be final and terrifying. For the saved, it is only the beginning of eternal joy.

Stepping In: Read Daniel 12:1–4; Joel 2:28–32; Matthew 24:14–21; Acts 17:29–31; and Romans 1:20. How do you feel about Jesus' return? Are you excited? Nervous? Ready? Fearful? Somber? Worried about friends and family who do not yet know the truth? Pray for opportunities to share this life-saving news. Thank Him that He prayed for you while you were one of the lost, and is praying for you still.

Stepping Out: This week, wear the clothes of a mourner as a reminder to pray for and share the gospel with those who are "dead in their transgressions" (Eph 2:1–5).

241

August 29
Grace-Filled

Three times I pleaded with the Lord to take it away from me. But he said to me, "My grace is sufficient for you, for my power is made perfect in weakness."
—2 Corinthians 12:8–9 (2 Cor 12:1–10)

After Jesus' ascension to heaven, His apostles brought the gospel out of Israel in ever-broadening waves of influence. Among them was Paul, who traveled widely throughout the Mediterranean region and Asia Minor, professing the truth of Jesus as the resurrected Lord, planting churches of new believers, and encouraging the faithful to stay strong.

In the middle of his third missionary journey, Paul spent several years ministering to a young church in Ephesus (Turkey). From there, in the spring of AD 55, he wrote his first letter to a struggling church in Corinth (Greece). Later that same year, Paul penned a second letter from somewhere in Macedonia, again addressing the church leaders in Corinth.

In his first letter, Paul's goal was to encourage spiritual maturity and unity in the body of believers. In his second, he hoped to warn against false teachings that had been springing up, causing confusion and division among believers. Paul refuted rumors that he too was lacking integrity, rendering him untrustworthy to be their advisor.

In defense of his ministry and himself, Paul always pointed to Jesus, giving credit to the only One worthy of boasting. Toward the end of his second letter, Paul affirmed his love for the believers in Corinth by listing the sufferings he had endured in his efforts to be their best spiritual guide. Adding credibility to his witness, Paul told them about how, in a vision, Jesus had allowed him to see Paradise. In this vision, Jesus acknowledged that Paul was suffering from "a thorn in my flesh, a messenger of Satan," but did not offer to remove it (2 Cor 12:7 NIV). Jesus simply reminded Paul that His grace was all Paul needed. Paul touted how God was revealing His power through him, and that by the grace of Jesus, the Corinthians' lives could also be used for the kingdom.

Scripture does not tell us what Paul's "thorn" was. It was bad enough that it caused him to repeatedly beg God to remove it. Each of us will, at some point in our lives, likewise call out to God to remove our ailments. God does sometimes grant us relief. Even if He doesn't, Jesus can redeem the situation for good.

In God's kingdom, pain has a purpose. It leads us away from its cause and into the loving arms of Jesus. It develops in us perseverance and a right-size perspective that can be an impressive example to others in similar circumstances. The only limitation is whether we allow God into our troubles, letting His grace and peace shine through us to the watching world.

So, what is this grace? It is the gift of free and unmerited favor, the blessing of forgiveness from God. It is a contractual bond that binds us to our Savior in a love embrace so safe that nothing can touch us. To experience it, we must be willing to change our perspective on life's circumstances. Where we see our troubles as obstacles, Jesus sees them as opportunities, for us and for Him. Living in the hope of our eternal security and choosing to trust in God's plan and provision, we allow Jesus' grace to transform us spiritually, if not mentally and physically. This allows His power to be displayed through us in amazing ways. His grace *is* enough.

Stepping In: Read Job 6:8–10; Psalm 34:18; Acts 6:8–10; Romans 8:17–18, 26–30; 1 Corinthians 2:3–5; 2 Corinthians 4:16–18; and Hebrews 2:18. Ask God to make you more aware of how grace-filled you are. Pray that this grace in you overflows, revealing God's power in you.

Stepping Out: This week, be a support to someone else who suffers from your same issues.

Dedicated

> "Anyone who loves his father or mother more than me is not worthy of me; anyone who loves his son or daughter more than me is not worthy of me; and anyone who does not take up his cross and follow me is not worthy of me."
>
> —Matthew 10:37–38 (Mt 10:1–38)

Jesus told the Twelve that devotion to him must come before all other allegiances—including blood relations. Even so, the newly appointed apostles were committed to Jesus and ready to obey His commands. All of them no doubt sought to be worthy of Jesus and were willing to do anything for their Lord. Without knowing what it meant, they agreed to carry their crosses and endure any other hardship to succeed in their calling. By faith, they willingly dedicated their lives in service to the cause of the gospel, loving Jesus more than anything or anyone else.

Today, many Christians blaze past today's verses, paying them little credence. Perhaps we, like the disciples, do not know what they mean. These are true statements, regardless of if we understand them, or how we feel about them. The concept of worthiness is a touchy subject. It falls in line with acceptance and competence. It becomes an indicator of identity, causing many to work extra hard to be regarded as meritorious in the view of others. We believe worthiness is something we can earn. Even in families, we often feel that our actions deem us worthy or not of our parents' approval and love.

Thankfully, none of God's children need ever worry about being worthy of our heavenly Father's love and acceptance. By our commitment and dedication to Jesus, we prove that our love for Him surpasses all others. It is not that Jesus wants us to stop loving our families. No; it is by our love for others that we will be known as true disciples. It is just that we are to love, obey, and be dedicated to Jesus most. In His eyes, we are worthy. By our dedication and obedience, we claim our worth.

Stepping In: Read Luke 14:26–27. Meditate on these verses. Do you feel worthy of Christ? Why or why not? Ask Him for a heart of unreserved dedication to His causes, and a willingness to act on them.

Stepping Out: This week, follow Jesus where He leads you in acts of obedience, changed behaviors, and loving others, putting Him first. Trust in your worthiness as a child of God.

August 31
Enduring

"Blessed are those who are persecuted because of righteousness, for theirs is the kingdom of heaven."

—Matthew 5:10 (Mt 5:1–12)

In today's verse from the Sermon on the Mount, Jesus spoke of a hardship His audience was familiar with. They knew about persecution—most lived under strict religious and cultural regulations, and all lived under oppressive Roman rule. On hearing this promise, given that their understanding of heaven was limited, the Jews might have thought it no more than a platitude.

However, the righteousness Jesus spoke of was not the Jews' position as God's chosen people, but a right relationship with God and Himself. The heaven to which He referred was not just an ideological construct, but a real place where the saved would live forever with God.

Today, the whole story of God's redemptive plan is available to anyone with access to the Holy Bible. People now can learn the truth about the only two eternal destinations available: a forever home with God, or a place of everlasting torment. Bible readers can also learn about the cost to many—especially our Savior—for promoting the better of these choices.

Religious persecution is still very much a harsh reality in many parts of the world. For those living in most developed nations, however, it is somewhat of an abstract concept. Though many of us have experienced some degree of harassment or ridicule for our faith, we have not endured physical persecution. It is hard to imagine any persecution being associated with a positive outcome. But what some would use for evil, God can use for good.

Jesus knows that in our pursuit of justice and promotion of truth, we will experience opposition. In living and standing up for a life of steadfast devotion to Christ, believers should expect societal pushback. Righteousness means upholding biblical truth regardless of the cost. For those who faithfully endure, the blessing of a secure eternity is promised.

Stepping In: Read Deuteronomy 26:15; Daniel 4:3, 7:13, 12:3; Matthew 5:10–12; 2 Timothy 3:12; and 1 Peter 3:17 and 4:12–14. What have you had to endure to live out your faith? Thank God for these opportunities to glorify Him.

Stepping Out: This week, do not shy away from spiritual opposition. Confidently stand your ground as you prayerfully follow Jesus' will for your life.

Honorable

"Only in his hometown and in his own house is a prophet without honor."

—Matthew 13:57 (Mt 13:24–58)

Jesus intended to offer His own neighbors, friends, and family in Nazareth His spiritual wisdom about the coming kingdom. Yet they would not accept it. Instead of embracing their own prophet and recognizing His deity, they were miffed by His confidence and authoritative manner. They simply could not acknowledge this young man, whom they knew as the son of a common carpenter, as a person worthy of their respect. Instead of welcoming Him and His message, they rejected both. What should have been a joyful reunion turned into an occasion for jealous skepticism and personal affronts. They even attempted to kill Him. Saddened but not surprised, Jesus and His disciples left that town in search of more receptive audiences.

Throughout history, this scene has no doubt been played out time and again. The upwardly bound often find their harshest critics under their own roofs. Sadly, many of us still firmly believe that it is impossible for an apple to fall far from the tree. Those who have alternative ambitions or differing views commonly must seek acceptance elsewhere to prove their worthiness at home.

Christians seeking a religious platform are often received by family and friends with a mixture of ignorance, jealousy, doubt, and indignation. People fear what they do not understand. Part of our task is to extinguish this fear with genuine love, compassion, and patience. We must remember that it is more honorable to stand on truth and be misunderstood than it is to compromise our convictions to be liked, even if that means moving on to the next town.

Stepping In: Read Luke 4:24–27. Have you ever experienced a similar reaction to your association with Jesus? How did you handle it? Pray for the strength to honor God even when faced with opposition from your own family and friends. Pray for your loved ones to have a change of heart, in God's timing.

Stepping Out: This week, adhere to the 1 Peter 3:15–16 passage, being ready to speak truth gently to anyone who asks about the hope you have in Jesus. Honor God with your hope-filled testimony. Live a life worthy of your calling, wherever you are.

September 2
Affluent

"But woe to you who are rich, for you have already received your comfort."

—Luke 6:24 (Lk 6:17–26)

When Jesus finished comforting the have-nots with his Beatitudes, He began issuing warnings to the haves. He informed the opulent members of the crowd that their riches were perhaps more a curse than a blessing. Those who were generous with the little they had would be given much by God; those who kept their abundance to themselves, however, should not expect any more. In so many words, Jesus explained that affluence consisted of what was in one's heart, not one's pocket.

In our world today, as in ancient times, the discrepancy between rich and poor is vast. No one would deny that our population consists haves and have-nots. Though Jesus stated plainly that those who have large amounts of disposable income have all the comfort they could ever want, He is not paying them a compliment.

This is not to say that wealth is necessarily bad. It is merely a reminder that affluence is not about money—at least not in God's kingdom. The underlying spiritual matter is that those who put their hope in things that money can buy risk missing out on the things only God can provide. Worldly citizens in all generations must know that true safety, comfort, and security come only from one source: Jesus Christ. Sadly, too many succumb to the allure of financial abundance, allowing greed and stinginess to win their hearts away from God. Eternally speaking, richness toward God and others is worth far more than all that glitters in this world. True generosity blesses both the giver and the receiver.

Stepping In: Read Deuteronomy 15:7–8; Psalm 37:16–17; Proverbs 17:16; Ecclesiastes 5:10; Matthew 6:24, 19:21; Mark 8:36; and 1 Timothy 6:10. The Bible has plenty to say about money. Feel free to look up other verses if you want to know more. After reflection, honestly ask yourself how you define affluence. Do these verses help you understand how God feels about the acquiring and allocation of resources? Pray for financial wisdom.

Stepping Out: This week, choose a verse that talks about godly generosity and do the things it dictates. Be a joyful giver as you free yourself from the burden of worldly wealth. Thank God for the spiritual affluence you have both now and eternally.

September 3
Cognizant

> While they were eating, Jesus took bread, gave thanks and broke it,
> and gave it to his disciples, saying, "Take and eat; this is my body."
> Then he took the cup, gave thanks and offered it to them, saying,
> "Drink from it all of you. This is the blood of the covenant, which is
> poured out for many for the forgiveness of sins."
> —Matthew 26:26–28 (Mt 26:17–30)

On the evening of the Passover, the very night He would be betrayed by one of His own, Jesus offered His disciples a new covenant. The disciples understood that blood was an essential part of the covenant process and the forgiveness of sins. But they were no doubt dumbfounded by Jesus' suggestion that they should eat His flesh and drink His blood. Jesus wanted His men to know that this contract was so strong and so binding that He would spare no expense, not even His own life, to see it established.

In today's verses, Jesus used the elements at hand to represent the requirements for the contract He was making between Himself and God, and Himself and His followers. As the disciples would soon find out, the breaking of their Master's body and the spilling of His blood really were the cost of this agreement. And so, in a borrowed upper room in Jerusalem, the Twelve partook of the elements with Jesus, agreeing that they would live up to their side of the covenant agreement. They were only somewhat cognizant of the greater meaning of this first Communion. They nonetheless solemnly consumed the bread and wine.

This tradition, started on that fateful night more than two thousand years ago, has been an integral and enduring part of Christian ceremony ever since. The taking of communion signifies our understanding of the price Jesus paid for our salvation. As Jesus commanded, it is something we do not forget.

Not only are we to remember what Jesus has done for us, we are also to remember that we have a part in the covenant agreement. As adopted heirs to His kingdom, we are offered both privilege and responsibility. Our freedom, though it cost us nothing, is a precious gift not to be taken for granted. The more cognizant we are of our Savior's awesome sacrifice, the more our love for Him should be evident in our obedience to God's will. Jesus gave His very life so that we may live abundantly and fruitfully now and forever. Each time we take the Eucharist, we ought to refresh our commitment to honor Jesus with our lives.

Stepping In: Read Luke 22:15–22. Take some time to look up other verses referring to God's covenant. How do these verses help you understand how seriously God takes His binding contracts? Thank God for sending His Son to fulfill the requirements for the final covenant, and that you are included in it.

Stepping Out: This week, either privately or corporately, take communion. Take time to review your agreement and to remember Jesus.

Entrusted

Then Jesus declared, "I who speak to you am he."
—John 4:26 (Jn 4:1–30)

Alone at Jacob's well, Jesus waited. Soon, an outcast Samaritan woman came to collect water. This shame-filled, emotionally overwrought, and spiritually depleted woman was the one Jesus had come to see. Jesus revealed to her everything about herself, including her prejudice, her cynicism, her religious ignorance, and her troubled past. He then entrusted her, a stranger and an enemy, with His divine identity. With it came the offer of salvation. Immediately, she accepted. Leaving everything behind, she ran to her village and told everyone that she had met the Christ. She invited them to come and see, thus bringing eternal hope to that formerly God-forsaken place.

Christians should never take for granted the blessing of knowing Jesus. In the days when He walked the earth, His divine identity was extremely privileged information. Jesus only entrusted this knowledge to those He knew would use it to promote His kingdom. He chose His words and their recipients carefully. The truth of who Jesus was, whispered in the wrong ear at the wrong time would have jeopardized His ministry. Yet because of the eternal impact His confession would make, He told a dejected woman that He was indeed the Messiah.

Today, Jesus is still meeting people at the well. He is still reassigning the rejects in society to positions of great importance in His kingdom. He is still mending broken vessels so they can carry the message of salvation to others, who will in turn bear witness to their miraculous transformation. Jesus made a point of entrusting His identity to a lonely Samaritan, who then brought her whole village to faith.

The ripple effect is still being felt. Christians must remember that we too have been entrusted with knowledge of who Jesus is and what He has done. We too must run and tell others about Him.

Stepping In: Read Exodus 9:16; Joel 2:32; John 2:23–25; Philippians 2:5–8; and 2 Timothy 2:1–2. How do these verses encourage you to honor the duty you have been entrusted with? Pray for strength and guidance. Ask Jesus to show you who you should run and tell about Him.

Stepping Out: This week, look up and work into conversations the many names of Jesus. Make sure to clarify any confusion that people may have about His identity.

September 5

Restorative

"I am willing," He said, "Be clean!" Immediately he was cured of his
leprosy. Then Jesus said to him, "See that you don't tell anyone. But
go, show yourself to the priest and offer the gift Moses commanded,
as a testimony to them."

—Matthew 8:3–4 (Mt 8:1–4)

Not long after Jesus concluded His Sermon on the Mount, He encountered a man suffering from leprosy. The stricken man called Him "Lord" and asked Jesus to make him clean. The hushed onlookers gathered in close to see what the young rabbi would do, expecting perhaps a prayer or a blessing. But Jesus did the unthinkable, He touched and healed an "untouchable." In so doing, He not only broke a societal norm but rendered Himself ceremonially unclean in the process. Knowing full well that word of this event would quickly spread, Jesus nevertheless instructed the man to keep quiet. Then Jesus sent the happy man to show the priests his drastically changed state. Restored in body and spirit, the man could finally rightly stand before God.

Modern Christians have the advantage of the same instantaneous cleansing. The moment a person claims Jesus as Lord, he or she receives the message that Jesus is willing and able to restore us to spiritual health, to cleanse us of our sin. What is harder for us, unless we too are miraculously physically healed, is showing this change to the world around us as proof of our internal transformation.

However, with the help of the Holy Spirit, we can prove that true restoration has occurred through our Christ-like behaviors and compassionate interactions. This requires us to do more listening than talking, more asking than telling, and more caring than criticizing. In so doing, we build a new foundation for relationships that may otherwise be strained. When our friends and family see how genuinely changed we are because of Jesus, they too may want the same restorative power to be at work in their own lives.

Stepping In: Read 2 Corinthians 5:17–21; Galatians 6:1; Ephesians 4:2–3; and 1 Peter 3:15. How restorative are your relationships? How do today's verses help you understand the importance of your Christian influence? Pray for the Holy Spirit to enable you to reach people gently yet intentionally for His kingdom.

Stepping Out: This week, let your changed-ness be your testimony. Let your actions, not just your words, reveal Christ in you. Let your Christian witness be a living example of Jesus' restorative power. Strive to let your words and actions bring restoration in all your relationships.

September 6
Heralding

> On the Lord's Day, I was in the Spirit, and I heard behind me a loud
> voice like a trumpet, which said, "Write on a scroll what you see
> and send it to the seven churches: to Ephesus, Smyrna, Pergamum,
> Thyatira, Sardis, Philadelphia, and Laodicea."
> —Revelation 1:11 (Rv 1:9–20)

In the sixty-seven years from the time John was first called as a disciple of Jesus to when he wrote the book of Revelation, He remained faithful to his calling. He was a leader in the church in Jerusalem for forty years, until threats to his life forced him to flee to Ephesus. There John stayed for another twenty-five years and wrote his gospel account, as well as his first, second, and third epistles. During his year on the island of Patmos, John received a revelation from God. As instructed by Jesus, John wrote down everything that he witnessed for the benefit of the seven churches in Asia Minor. This was an unexpected ministry opportunity to aid the churches he had helped to plant, a way he could encourage and warn those he and God cared very much about.

God has many ways of communicating with his people. Throughout scripture, He often used dreams or visions to impart wisdom, warnings, instructions, and encouragement. Today, these methods are less common. We have access to the Bible and other resources, so God does not need to use such dramatic methods to get his messengers' attention. Christians now enjoy unlimited access to God through His Holy Spirit.

The unfortunate downfall to having Jesus available anytime, anywhere, is that we are prone to take Him for granted. In a world of self-satisfaction, Jesus often gets placed on the back burner until we need Him.

In the book of Revelation, John was given a privileged glimpse into heaven. He was entrusted to disclose the end of the Bible story—and of world history. The gravity of this job was not lost on John. It should not be lost on us either. As is clearly emphasized in Revelation, there are only two eternities: life with Jesus or death without. Christians are the heralds of the life-saving message.

Stepping In: Read Exodus 20:18–20; Isaiah 52:7–9; Ezekiel 20:19–20; Luke 9:26; Acts 4:29, 9:28; and Romans 10:13–15. Are you keeping the Sabbath holy so that you can hear from God? Pray for forgiveness and repent.

Stepping Out: This week, write a letter to someone who needs encouragement. Express how the gospel has positively impacted your life. Write to a friend, family member, pastor, coworker, teacher, missionary, or inmate in prison. Be the herald God has called you to be. (Heb 2:2-3).

September 7
Knowledgeable

"The knowledge of the secrets of the kingdom has been given to you, but not to them. Whoever has will be given more, and he will have an abundance. Whoever does not have, even what he does have will be taken from him."

—Matthew 13:11–12 (Mt 13:1–15)

Jesus gave this reply to His disciples when asked why He spoke to the people in parables. Because His opponents were looking and listening for evidence that would warrant His arrest, Jesus chose to protectively cloak His messages within the context of a story. With little time to lose, He carefully revealed the secrets of the kingdom only to those He could trust with the information.

Today's verses informed Jesus' chosen men of their privileged position. Having been gifted with spiritual wisdom, the disciples continued to gain understanding about the kingdom soon to be initiated. Those who refused to recognize the myriad evidences of Jesus' deity only became increasingly blind to God's plan as it unfolded before them.

This stark reality still rings true today. Those who have the ability to discern spiritual matters will only gain more godly wisdom; those who are ignorant of truth will become steadily less aware of the terrible fate that will befall them. The former will be blessed with spiritual abundance, now and forever. The latter may enjoy many earthly pleasures in the short term, but will lose everything in the end.

As students of the only Teacher of truth, Christians are to take their studies seriously. The more we seek to know Jesus and to follow His lead, the more He bestows on us and the more spiritually knowledgeable we become. The converse is also true. Those who ignore biblical wisdom, choosing instead to live by their worldly vision, will remain blind to God's secret knowledge. Those who prefer the shadowy places, where the light of the gospel cannot expose their sin, will wind up completely in the dark when the day of judgment comes.

As Christ's faithful followers, we should read this passage as a prompting to assist Him in bringing lost ones into the light, striving to make *all* knowledgeable.

Stepping In: Read 1 Corinthians 2:6–10; Colossians 1:27; and 1 John 2:20. Do you consider yourself a knowledgeable Christian? Are there spiritual things that still seem mysterious to you? Pray that God open His Word to you more, and that the Spirit whispers tangible truths in your ear, drawing you closer in your relationship with Him.

Stepping Out: This week, share of your abundance, both spiritual and physical. Bless others as God has blessed you. Share a bit of spiritual wisdom and a cup of coffee with someone new to faith.

z

251

Privy

> "The knowledge of the secrets of the kingdom of God has been given to you, but to others I speak in parables, so that, 'though seeing, they may not see; though hearing, they may not understand.'"
>
> —Luke 8:10 (Lk 8:1–15)

As Jesus traveled throughout Galilee, sharing the good news and healing the infirm, many people joined His entourage. Among them were several women who had received Jesus' healing touch. These women helped to finance His ministry using their own money. This was very uncommon in that day and age. But then again, many things about Jesus were out of the ordinary, including His teaching. Sometimes He spoke in parables: stories that could be taken at face value or plumbed for spiritual depth. Jesus had control over who perceived which interpretation.

Many Christians today may not realize that the gift of spiritual discernment was not always available. Until Jesus appeared on the first Easter Sunday and breathed on His bewildered disciples, the Holy Spirit had previously only been doled out on an "as needed" basis. After Pentecost, the Holy Spirit became available to all who had been saved by grace through faith in Jesus, immediately and permanently.

Jesus knows that Christians will still sometimes struggle to understand His words and His ways. That is why He is always encouraging His followers to draw from the source of all wisdom: God. He set the example of seeking the Father's will through daily scripture reading and fervent prayer. Jesus showed us how to best utilize the awesome power we have been given. Because of Christ's great love for us, we are privy to many of God's secret thoughts. This is a privilege we should not squander.

Stepping In: Read Deuteronomy 29:29; Isaiah 6:8–10; John 20:19–23; Romans 11:33–34; 1 Corinthians 2:9–10; and Hebrews 4:12–13. Take some time to thank God for being privy to His thoughts and able to understand them. Pray for even greater discernment as you prove your trustworthiness.

Stepping Out: Reread Luke 8:1–15. Then, conduct an honest soil test on your spiritual life. What type of soil is the Word of God germinating in? Is it time for an upgrade? This week, enrich your spirit with the wisdom of God by reading chapters 2 and 3 in Proverbs.

Good

> "Do people pick grapes from thornbushes, or figs from thistles? Likewise, every good tree bears good fruit, but a bad tree bears bad fruit. A good tree cannot bear bad fruit, and a bad tree cannot bear good fruit. Every tree that does not bear good fruit is cut down and thrown into the fire. Thus, by their fruit you will recognize them."
> —Matthew 7:16–20 (Mt 7:15–23)

To the people of Israel, a largely agrarian society, the words Jesus spoke in today's passage would have sounded like familiar farmyard banter. His rhetorical question may have been taken as comic relief after the harsher topics that preceded it. Indeed, as the audience digested meatier teachings about adultery, revenge, worry, and judgment, it may have seemed incongruous to be hearing about fruit.

Jesus was not speaking some random thought here. He was connecting the dots of His message about how one's internal life, one's heart, manifests externally as fruit. In a parable-like format, with which his audience would not yet be familiar, Jesus was spelling out the hard facts of the gospel message. Some will be saved and others will perish.

This passage directly follows one about false prophets and wolves in sheep's clothing, so those who were tracking Jesus' message might have figured out that the focus had shifted from the enemy without to the enemy within. Those whose hearts were good and pure would produce evidence of their right-standing with God in the form of love, obedience, and loyalty: good fruit. Those whose hearts were callused and far from God would have lives marked with relational dis-ease, futile pursuits, and bitterness: bad fruit.

Barring the farmers among us and those possessing particularly green thumbs, this agricultural reference might not resonate with most modern citizens. In fact, most city slickers these days probably can't tell the difference between figs and thistles. But the hard truth of today's passage remains. Some people are children of God and others are not. This is a matter of choice. Once we know who Jesus is, we can choose to accept Him as Lord and start to bear good fruit, or we can deny Him and continue to produce nothing of lasting value. Not only is this a stern warning for those heading for destruction, it is also a strong reminder for Christ followers to yield a lasting crop.

Stepping In: Read Galatians 5:22–26 and Philippians 1:9-11, 2:3-4. What good fruit are you producing in your life? What areas of character development is God currently working on? Pray for a yielding spirit to take Jesus' commands and warnings to heart, changing attitudes and behaviors as needed.

Stepping Out: This week, in all your interactions with others, practice one or two of the fruits of the Spirit (see Gal 5:22–23). Maybe even choose the ones that you struggle with most as a good character-building exercise, as well as a good example of Christ-likeness.

September 10
Filled

"I am the bread of life. He who comes to me will never go hungry, and he who believes in me will never be thirsty."

—John 6:35 (Jn 6:16–59)

By His third year in active ministry, Jesus was well known for performing wondrous signs and miracles. Wherever He went throughout Israel, people came to Him out of great need and out of curiosity as well. When word of His feeding five thousand near Bethsaida got out, many more people flocked to Jesus, hoping for a free meal. The weary and burdened masses likely missed what He was truly dishing out – an offer of imperishable spiritual sustenance. The hope of an effortless food source was an even greater enticement. Their physical need to be filled outweighing any spiritual need they might be aware of.

Knowing this, Jesus patiently explained that the bread He offered was better than that given to them by Moses in the wilderness. Jesus Himself was the bread. The Jews in the crowd might have wondered if Jesus was claiming to be greater than their forefather Moses. They had to be asking how they could get this everlasting bread. They had not made the connection that Jesus was God and could indeed honor His outrageous claim. Those who accepted this teaching came to Jesus to be filled. Most, though, refused His offer and became disillusioned about His kingly purpose.

Those of us who are familiar with the gospels in the New Testament understand this notion of Jesus as the Bread of Life. For those hearing these words two millennia ago, however, this would have been a very foreign concept. Even so, the idea of eating the Master's flesh and drinking His blood is a strange, powerful analogy. When we eat and drink of this truth, our temporal bodies take in eternal wisdom. Though we remain in our flesh until He takes us to be with Him in heaven, we are no longer merely human. We are also spirit and in the Spirit. We are wholly new creations. We hunger and thirst for truly satisfying spiritual food. We do the will of the Father, engage in the work He has given us to do, experience His blessings, endure pain and suffering with joy that can only come from the Lord, and live with assurance of salvation. This is the life Jesus offers, and He wants us to enjoy it to the full.

Stepping In: Read Exodus 16:4, 15; Psalm 63:1; Matthew 5:6, 26:26-29; John 4:32–34, 10:10; and 1 Corinthians 10:16–17. What do you see the world hungering and thirsting for? How has a life with Jesus filled you up? Pray for those who are yet unsatisfied.

Stepping Out: This week, along with your small group or some friends, volunteer with a food ministry or hand out bread to people on the street while you engage them in a conversation about Jesus as the Bread of Life.

Humanistic

"Woe to you, teachers of the law and Pharisees, you hypocrites! You give a tenth of your spices—mint, dill, and cumin. But you have neglected the more important matters of the law—justice, mercy and faithfulness. You should have practiced the latter, without neglecting the former. You blind guides! You strain out a gnat but swallow a camel."

—Matthew 23:23–24 (Mt 22:41–23:24)

During the final days of His earthly ministry, Jesus spent much of His time preaching in Jerusalem's temple courts. During a scathing sermon regarding the phony religious leaders' many woes, Jesus pointed out the folly of their legalistic practices. Where they had been careful to obey the precise letter of the Law for the sake of public recognition, they had utterly failed in the humanistic aspects of their faith. In today's passage, Jesus used a comical illustration to make His point, but the religious leaders' loveless offerings and thoughtless disregard for the people was no laughing matter.

In our hectic world and busy lives, finding time to meet all our obligations can be very challenging. Even our service to the Lord can become an item to tick off the list. This is when deeds become duties, when love becomes legalism. In today's verses, Jesus gives a two-part directive. Yes, one should joyfully give the full tithe and whatever offerings one has in one's heart. *And*, one should joyfully also give to others one's love and attention.

Jesus says that anytime we put rules before people we are swallowing the camel despite the gnat. Anytime we nitpick the details of another's faith-walk, we run the risk of straining the love from our good intentions, leaving everyone with a bad taste in their mouths. Thus, Jesus wants us to take a humanistic viewpoint of loving and serving God instead, obeying both the law of the Lord *and* the law of human decency.

Stepping In: Read Exodus 23:2, 6; Leviticus 27:30–33; Micah 6:6–8; Malachi 3:10; Matthew 22:37–40; 1 Corinthians 13:1–3; and 2 Corinthians 9:6–9. Reflect on these verses and feel free to look up more regarding justice, mercy, and faithfulness if you wish. What is God impressing upon you now? Is there anything you are holding back from Him that you need to confess? Talk to God and ask Him for a compassionate and generous heart.

Stepping Out: This week, be humanistic. Seek to uphold the rights of others through acts of justice, mercy and faithfulness done in love. Out of the riches God has given you, give generously back to Him and others.

September 12
Ripe

"As soon as the grain is ripe, he puts the sickle to it, because the harvest has come."

—Mark 4:29 (Mk 4:1–29)

In today's passage, Jesus told a parable about a man who cast seeds onto the ground, but had no idea how they came to grow and mature. Seemingly all by themselves, the seeds took root and flourished. Once the plants matured, the time was ripe for collecting the harvest. To the layperson, this was an unsurprising tale of basic farming. For the spiritually wise, however, this parable explained that there was an awesome power hidden in the seed, the Word of God, itself. Once the Word of God had been spread to all the places it could go and had produced a ripe harvest, it would be time to gather *all* the fruit. This reference to the end times most likely went over even the disciples' heads.

Christians, for the most part, do not like to talk about end times. Though we love to share the good news of grace and forgiveness—and rightly so—we rarely bring up the necessary judgment that will take place when Jesus returns. We boast about mercy but shy away from justice.

Mark, the only one of the four gospel writers to include this parable, felt it important to add this last statement about the harvest. If he had opted to stop after explaining how the seed had the power to mature on its own, and that the soil and the sower have little to do with the matter, we would be left thinking that we are off the hook.

Today's verse is a reminder for Christians to prepare themselves and others for the day of harvest. When the time is ripe, there will be no more chances for those who have not accepted Jesus as their Lord and Savior. When the sickle hits the stalk, all the fruitless souls will be left behind. The time to sow and nurture seeds is now!

Stepping In: Read Joel 3:13 and Revelation 14:14–19. How do these images of the coming judgment motivate you to share God's truth before it is too late? How much ripe fruit do you see around you? Pray for courage and guidance to plant and water as many seeds as you can.

Stepping Out: This week, do not shy away from telling people the whole truth. Talk about both grace and judgment. Ask the Holy Spirit to help you explain why both are necessary.

September 13
Careful

"He who is not with me is against me, and he who does not gather with me scatters. And so I tell you, every sin and blasphemy will be forgiven men, but the blasphemy against the Spirit will not be forgiven."
—Matthew 12:30–31 (Mt 12:1–31)

After He healed a demon-possessed, blind, and mute man, Jesus was engaged in debate by the Pharisees and teachers of the Law. They said that He was driving out demons by the power of Satan, and accused Him of breaking Sabbath laws. Jesus turned the line of questioning back to the Pharisees. If they could not be trusted to recognize the power and presence of God, how then could their godly authority be trusted? Taking His argument one step further, Jesus made the two poignant statements in today's verses. All who did not accept His authority would be found guilty; they would be wise to carefully reconsider their alliances. In short, He was saying that sins of ignorance could be forgiven, but intentionally denying the existence and sovereignty of the Spirit of God was unforgivable.

These verses are difficult to understand even today. Simply put, there are two spiritual forces vying for people's devotion: the force of evil, which pulls people away from truth, and the force of good, which draws people into the light of God's love and forgiveness. Those who doubt Jesus do not like to be alone in their uncomfortable confusion. They cast a net of contention, skepticism, and fear all around themselves. Without the Spirit of God, the mysteries of Jesus' life, death, and resurrection remain hidden from them. Consequently, they continue to blindly sin and blaspheme God.

Yet proof of God is everywhere for those who seek it. As the apostle Paul wrote in the epistle to the Romans, because "God's invisible qualities have been made clear … people are without excuse" for knowing and believing in Him (1:20). With eternity at stake, Christians must encourage the doubtful to make a careful examination of the facts about God, Jesus, and salvation. Even in a world that scatters, we must use the Spirit's power to gather evidence in our case for Christ.

Stepping In: Consider what it means to be for Jesus. In what ways are you helping Him to gather rather than scatter? Pray for guidance for next steps.

Stepping Out: This week, be careful to speak God's whole truth. Omissions may be considered an endorsement of what's unsaid. Be for Jesus in your words as much as your actions. Speak of your personal experience with the Spirit.

257

September 14
Waiting

"The master of the servant will come on a day when he does not expect him and at an hour he is not aware of. He will cut him to pieces and assign him a place with the unbelievers."

—Luke 12:46 (Lk 12:1, 35–48)

On an occasion when Jesus was teaching a sizable audience about the virtues of attentiveness to the coming kingdom, Peter asked Jesus if He was speaking in a parable or to the crowd. Without answering Peter directly, Jesus told a parabolic story about an impatient servant whose unfaithfulness led to his ruin. In today's verse, Jesus spelled out the dire consequences for false devotion. To the undiscerning, His illustration might have seemed like an unjustly harsh reaction to negligence and bad behavior. For Jesus' disciples, it would have been a reminder that, because their Master was trustworthy and faithful, they could expect His return. Those who would be found patiently waiting would not be severed from the eternal promises the Master would bring upon His return.

Readers of the New Testament could easily mistake this passage as a claim that one could lose salvation due to impetuousness and sinful acts. This is not what Jesus is implying here. To the contrary, Jesus is stating that those who pledge only superficial allegiance to the Master are the ones who will become impatient and complacent while waiting for His return.

As Jesus emphasizes time and again, head knowledge of God is not enough for salvation. One is only saved when the idea of Jesus as Savior moves from the head to the heart. When one accepts Jesus as *personal* Lord and Savior, a life-changing, life-saving shift happens. The old, self-serving, desire-driven person dies; a new Christ-focused self is born. Thereafter, the truth of today's verse is no longer threatening.

Christians who truly believe receive the Holy Spirit, who helps them to hear and heed the Master's call. Those who look to any other master will perish. While we are waiting for Christ's return, it is our privileged duty to share the truth of Jesus with those who don't know Him.

Stepping In: Read Matthew 25:21; John 3:16–18; Romans 10:9–10; and 1 Thessalonians 5:1–6. Who is your master? Is it the Lord Jesus, yourself, or the things of this world? If you have not accepted Jesus as Master of your heart and life, will you do so now? Pray to Him, confess your sin, ask for forgiveness, and invite Him to be your Lord. What or who are you waiting for?

Stepping Out: This week, behave as if Jesus is coming tomorrow. As you await your beloved Master's imminent return, clearly and with gentleness and humility, share your excitement and hope for that glorious day.

Selective

"The eye is the lamp of the body. If your eyes are good, your whole body will be full of light. But if your eyes are bad, your whole body will be full of darkness. If then the light within you is darkness, how great is that darkness!"

—Matthew 6:22–23 (Mt 6:19–24)

Today's passage was purposefully sandwiched between a message regarding the value of eternal longings rather than worldly desires, and a choice about whom one serves, God or money. Jesus' audience might have puzzled over the seeming incongruity of this statement. Indeed, this statement was not meant to be easily understood. Much like the parables Jesus used throughout His ministry, today's passage required a discerning mind to be understood. Even His disciples may have been somewhat confused.

Having already talked about how to be light to the world, Jesus may have been hoping that many would put the pieces of the puzzle together to see the bigger picture. Eyes are a feature of the body that receive, and perceive, light (truth). Eyes that do these tasks well bring benefit to the whole body. Eyes that fail in these regards bring calamity.

This was Jesus' first reference to believers as the body (of Christ). With the help of the Spirit, these verses would eventually come into focus. Until then, first-century listeners might have only come away with a warning to be selective in what they chose to gaze upon.

Jesus spoke about humanity's relationship with money and other lustful things almost more than any other topic. In today's verse, He used the analogy of the human eye to illustrate how easy it is to be seduced by worldly treasures. Truly, we need only to set eyes on something desirable and already our faith is put to the test.

More than our other senses, our sight allows us to see what the world has to offer. We can easily turn away from things that are ugly, but we equally easily find ourselves captivated by things of beauty. If we like what we see, we admire it. After admiring something, we start to want it. Soon, we convince ourselves that we need it. Once we have it, we want more of it. What starts off with an innocent glance becomes an obsession—if we allow it to.

Jesus reminds us that the eye is but a tool—a filter, if you will—that serves our hearts and minds, directing our thoughts, attention, and eventually devotion. It can lead to honest and pure pursuits, resulting in light streaming in, or it can take us down dark paths of corruption and debauchery. When it comes to how we choose to spend our time and money, our eye more than our wallet needs to be kept in check. To reflect God's light, the lamp of the body must be selective.

Stepping In: Read Psalm 19:8 and 119:105; Matthew 6:22–24; Ephesians 1:18; 1Timothy 6:10; Hebrews 13:5; 2 Peter 2:14; and Revelation 3:17. How do these verses help you understand the correlation between the eye and the dangerous love of money? Pray for the Holy Spirit to direct your attention and help you be selective in what you view.

Stepping Out: Be selective about what you choose to focus your eyes on. If it is not God-honoring, skip it. One day this week, do a visual fast from ungodly viewing (i.e., social media, television, magazines, people-watching). Remember: good in, good out, and vice versa.

September 16
Amenable

"I will also ask you one question. If you answer me, I will tell you by what authority I am doing these things. John's baptism—where did it come from? Was it from heaven, or from men?"
—Matthew 21:24–25 (Mt 21:23–27)

During the last week of His ministry, Jesus spent most of His remaining time teaching and healing in Jerusalem's holy temple. After receiving a king's welcome into the city, and following His righteous tantrum in the public courts of the temple, the religious leaders were anxious to have Jesus arrested. They again questioned Him about His authority. In today's passage, as He often did, Jesus returned their questions with a question of His own.

The religious leaders knew that if they said John's baptism came from heaven, they would look foolish for not believing John. If they said that it came from men, the people would be indignant because they believed John to have been a prophet. Either way, their reputations were at stake.

In the end, they told Jesus that they didn't have an answer for Him. Consequently, He did not have one for them either. His divine authority would soon be revealed, but Jesus kept it concealed for the time being. Explaining that He was God to this unamenable audience would not only have been futile, but it would likely have resulted in a premature end to His final hours of teaching.

Clearly, it is within our human nature to question authority. Beginning in the garden of Eden, we have always tested the limits imposed upon us. It is a way of establishing a sense of control over our circumstances. This is true in our families, communities, schools, workplaces, social groups, and churches. Like the chief priests in Jesus' day, we question God's authority in our world and over our lives.

Though devout Christians emphatically believe in the all-powerful creator God, we often fail to trust His sovereign authority over every aspect of our lives all the time. The Spirit reminds us of who is ultimately in control by sending messages of discomfort and conviction to our consciences. Then we are faced with a choice. Do we acknowledge Jesus' authority, or do we pretend we didn't hear the question? Are we amenable, or do we tell Him, "Thanks, God, but I can handle this on my own?"

Stepping In: Read 2 Chronicles 20:5–6; Job 9:1–12; Psalm 135:6–7; and Romans 1:21-25, 9:19-21. Think of the times when you have questioned authority. How many of those occasions turned out the way you wanted them to? How many times have you questioned God's authority over your life? How did those occasions play out? Pray and ask for forgiveness. Pray for an amenable spirit.

Stepping Out: This week, set an example for your family, friends, and acquaintances of one who is joyfully under the authority of the Lord. Humbly submit to His statutes and commands. Speak of the benefits of being amenable to God's will. Explain that obedience is liberating and not burdensome.

September 17
Shepherded

"I am the good shepherd. The good shepherd lays down his life for the sheep."

—John 10:11 (Jn 9:13–10:21)

For the entirety of His earthly ministry, Jesus outwardly expressed His love, power, authority, and spiritual wisdom so that the people could recognize His deity and see Him as the Messiah, the One sent by God to redeem His people. Though His kindness, compassion, charismatic manner, and miraculous abilities attracted large crowds, the pervasiveness of spiritual blindness continued to be a faith barrier for many. His contrary religious message and unorthodox methods earned Him fierce opposition from Jewish leaders. By the third year of His ministry, the religious elite wanted Jesus dead.

Incensed that Jesus had healed on the Sabbath, the Pharisees again questioned His standing as a man of God. Using the image of a shepherd protecting his flock, Jesus explained that He alone would lay down His life for the sheep. Jesus as the Shepherd knows and protects His sheep, and His sheep know the Shepherd and follow only Him. Though His audience would not have understood that He was once again forecasting His atoning death on the cross, Jesus made this analogy to inform them of His intentions. More puzzling, astonishing, and perhaps maddening to His listeners was His claim to possess the authority to both lay down and take up His life.

Throughout the gospel of John, the reader is offered a clear picture of Jesus' relationship with God the Father. Their union was and is more than just a human father/son bond or an inherited connection with one's forefathers. Jesus continually emphasized the unity, the oneness, of He and His Father. He met with difficulty and resistance when communicating this key fact to His first-century audience, but it was a point He insisted that they hear.

Jesus' claim to deity is the very basis of our faith. From beginning to end, scripture provides more than enough proof that our triune God (Father, Son, and Holy Spirit) is the sovereign Lord of all. God is Creator, Sustainer, Protector, Provider, Friend, Counselor, Judge, Physician, and most of all, Savior. Not only did our Good Shepherd lay down His life for us, His sheep, He continues to shepherd His otherwise helpless followers. When we listen to His voice, He leads us away from harm and into a safe and joyful life.

Stepping In: Read Ezekiel 34:11–16; Luke 12:32; John 6:25-29, 14:6; Hebrews 13:20–21; 1 Peter 2:25, 5:2-4; and Revelation 7:17. Do you allow yourself to be shepherded by Jesus alone? What other enticing voices do you follow? Pray for strength to follow close behind Jesus each day. Praise God that you have a sacrificial Savior.

Stepping Out: This week, model for other Christians what it looks like to be shepherded by the Good Shepherd. Look for opportunities to show unbelievers the way into the fold of God.

September 18
Enlightened

"All things have been committed to me by my Father. No one knows the Son except the Father, and no one knows the Father except the Son and those to whom the Son has chosen to reveal him."
—Matthew 11:27 (Mt 11:1–27)

By His second year as a public figure, the impact of Jesus' kingdom message and miraculous ways was stretching far and wide. Yet people were unsure. The Jews were hearing one thing from the religious leaders, but learning quite a different theology from this young rabbi. Moreover, many wondered if it was safe to associate with promoters of His new faith.

At that time, the religious climate was abuzz with change. John the Baptist had been thrown in prison for preaching the coming Christ and calling all to repent of their sins. Jesus' apostles were exhibiting His power through their healing and preaching. Jesus Himself was performing miracles and ministering to the towns and villages of Galilee. Clearly, there was a movement afoot.

Though most people believed in God, and many believed Jesus was a man *of* God, few truly understood that Jesus *was* God. Even his cousin John's disciples were confused about who to follow and to whose authority should they submit. They wanted to know if Jesus was the man of whom John had spoken. John himself sent his disciples to ask Jesus that very question.

Jesus told them to report to John the miraculous things they had witnessed firsthand. He wanted them to discover the connection between those works and the supernatural powers at play, powers that could only have come from God in heaven. In the humblest of ways, Jesus pointed to His source of power and authority in today's verse. Jesus praised His Father in heaven for His sovereign choice of who would be divinely enlightened.

The full authority of the Father is something many of us struggle to grasp today. We know of the Trinity. We love Jesus and call Him Savior. We also experience the guidance of the Holy Spirit. But by and large, the Father may seem abstract and distant.

Most of us consider all parts of the Holy Trio to be equal. But does Jesus see it that way? If we take a closer look at scripture, we find that Jesus always defers to the supreme authority of His Father. Time and again, He tells us that no one, not even Himself, can do anything apart from the will of the Father. So for us to know Jesus and thereby get a glimpse of the Father is an extreme privilege. He is the source of all wisdom and power, and certainly not to be underestimated. It is an undeniable honor that God, through the wondrous acts and ministry of Jesus, enables us to be enlightened about His eminence.

Stepping In: Read John 3:31-36, 5:19-21; and Philippians 2:5–11. Pray and ask God to reveal more of Himself as you read through scripture and contemplate the work of the Trinity.

Stepping Out: This week, acknowledge the Father in your inward and outward prayers. Thank Him for the gift of His Son and the gift of salvation you have received because of Him.

Cultivator

> "'Sir,' the man replied, 'leave it alone for one more year, and I'll dig around it and fertilize it. If it bears fruit next year, fine! If not, then cut it down.'"
>
> —Luke 13:8–9 (Lk 13:1–9)

Jesus came to earth to fulfill a specific mission for His Father in heaven. He made a way for sinners to receive salvation through their faith in the Savior, not by their efforts to follow the letter of the Law. This was the new covenant which Jesus came to establish first with His own people, the Jews, and then with the Gentiles.

Among His most staunch opponents were the men who held the highest positions in the Jewish religious order. These pious men wielded the power to decide who was acceptable before God and who, because of their sin, deserved to be shunned. Jesus, naturally, had much to say about these men's attitudes and approach.

So when someone in a crowd Jesus was speaking to asked about a supposedly sin-related tragedy, Jesus saw an opportunity to correct everyone's misconceptions and expose the hard-heartedness of the perpetuators of this erroneous notion: the Pharisees and teachers of the Law. Using an agricultural allegory, Jesus explained that, unlike those who were quick to chop a tree down, the gardener was a patient cultivator. In other words, though the Pharisees were quick to condemn sinners, God offered mercy.

There are a few ways to interpret this parable, both in the context in which it was spoken and for today's audience. When Jesus told this story, it was a response to the barbaric enforcement of broken ceremonial laws. People were killed in the temple for noncompliance. The religious leaders had blood on their hands. These phonies were the tree, God was the vineyard owner who ordered the tree cut down, and Jesus was the gardener who asked for one more year.

In our context today, the same scenario is still being played out with a different cast of characters. Today, the tree represents those who persist in their unbelief. God is still the vineyard owner. True believers, filled with the Spirit, assist the gardener Jesus in advocating for mercy. With Jesus as the Master Gardener, we help bring new life to barren wood. Let us be cultivators of a heavenly harvest!

Stepping In: Read 1 Kings 4:25; Proverbs 27:17–18; Micah 6:8; Matthew 3:7–10; and John 15:5–8. How do these passages help you to understand how important it is for Christians' actions to line up with their words and beliefs? Ask God to reveal areas where you can be more fruitful in your Christian walk.

Stepping Out: This week, look for opportunities to cultivate new spiritual life into fruitless friends and neighbors. Humbly use words and actions to enrich the soil of their Christian faith. Remember to plead for mercy on behalf of those who will perish in their stubborn resistance and ignorance.

September 20
Dutiful

"Why do you ask me about what is good?" Jesus replied. "There is only
One who is good. If you want to enter life, obey the commandments."
—Matthew 19:17 (Mt 19:16–26)

A rich young man approached Jesus and asked him, "What good thing must I do to get eternal life?" Jesus responded with today's verse. Seeming to have heard only the last part, the young man asked, "Which ones?" Jesus listed the laws most commonly revered, adding His own summation. The young man claimed to have dutifully obeyed all these. Jesus then gave a command the man did not expect: "Sell your possessions … give to the poor … follow me" (Mt 19:21). At this the man went away sad, unwilling to do what Jesus required. The disciples would have been greatly encouraged to know that they had made the better choice.

One of the most common misconceptions about heaven is that anyone who is "good" gets to go there. This erroneous belief apparently has not changed in the millennia since Jesus walked the earth. Yet, as Jesus reminds us, only God is truly good---"all (else) have sinned and fall short of the glory of God" (Ro 3:23). Human nature strives for the path of least resistance. We would much prefer to take the shortest and easiest route to get from point A to point B.

Like the rich young man, most of us also want to know exactly what our faith requires, so we can do just those things. Even some Christians still falsely believe that salvation is something earned through good prayers and deeds. But it is not about what we do. It is about what Jesus has already done.

Jesus knew that the young man had been an obedient Jew. He also knew that the young man's heart was with his earthly treasure; money, status, and stuff. In our affluent society, most of us are sadly like the man in this story. We reject today's difficult teaching. We must all honestly admit where our treasure lies. Then we must choose to be dutiful to the righteous cause or to succumb to worldly ways.

Stepping In: Read Deuteronomy 5:6–21; Matthew 22:36–40; Luke 12:34; and Romans 3:21–24. Take some time to consider where your treasure is. Are you willing to give up what you have to follow Jesus? Why or why not? Pray and ask Jesus to soften your heart to make you a joyfully dutiful and sacrificial servant.

Stepping Out: This week, follow the Spirit's leading to obey the commandment He is putting on your heart. Go above and beyond what is required in your journey toward your heavenly home. Seek to please God more than your own desires.

September 21
Longed For

"So he got up and went to his father. But while he was still a long way
off, his father saw him and was filled with compassion for him; he ran
to his son, threw his arms around him and kissed him."

—Luke 15:20 (Lk 15:1–32)

For three years, Jesus preached scripture with authority, proclaimed the coming kingdom of heaven, and displayed His power through miracles of many kinds. Because of His bold and different take on God's Word and ways, people's reactions to Him varied greatly. Some agreed with His teachings and were amazed by His wondrous abilities. Others were blind to His identity, threatened by His authority, and therefore rejected Him fully. There were also those who considered themselves unworthy of God's compassion because of what the culture and religious leaders had told them.

One day, while speaking to a group of acknowledged sinners, Jesus told a series of parables about the joy of finding something that was lost: a sheep, a coin, a son. In a third parable, He spoke of a man whose youngest son demanded and then squandered his inheritance. Alone and destitute, the son realized his mistake and resolved to return to his father and beg his pardon.

Before the son could reach his former home, his father, who had been anxiously awaiting his son's return, rushed out to meet him on the road, offering unasked for and undeserved forgiveness. Jesus explained how great the father's love and compassion were, even for a wayward child. The message is that even the most undeserving are longed for by God.

The tenderness and depth found in the teaching of the Prodigal Son has blessed the hearts of Christians for generations. However, someone not acquainted with Jesus may read this parable and quickly come to the defense of the prodigal's dutiful older brother. It is certainly hard to sympathize with the self-centered, reckless, and destructive behavior of the younger brother. It is equally difficult to understand the father's compassion.

Those of us who do know Christ, however, are humbled to recognize that this is the story of God's grace and mercy toward *us*, for all of us were once wayward children. The good news is that God is the same yesterday, today, and forever. God expects the faithful and obedient to serve Him joyfully and be glad when the lost are found, regardless of the seeming unfairness of it. As the father in the story longed for the reappearance of his hopelessly lost son, God the Father holds out hope for each of his rebellious children to come to their senses and run back to His loving arms.

Stepping In: Read Deuteronomy 21:18–23; Psalm 103; Ephesians 2:4–7; 1 Timothy 2:1–4; and Hebrews 8:8-13, 13:8. Take a minute to consider how gracious and merciful God has been to you. Thank Him that, before you knew Him, you were longed for by Him.

Stepping Out: This week, demonstrate mercy and patience by putting James 1:19–22 into practice. If the opportunity arises, freely offer forgiveness to anyone who offends you.

Gracious

"See that you do not look down on one of these little ones. For I tell you
that their angels in heaven always see the face of my Father in heaven."
—Matthew 18:10 (Mt 18:1–14)

Though the Twelve loved Jesus and hung on His every word, they struggled to perceive the grander plan; their perspective remained focused on the temporal and not the eternal. Their narrow view limited their power to heal in Jesus' name, as was seen in their failed attempt to expel a demon from a young boy near Capernaum.

Jesus brought His disciples in for some private teaching. He explained that if they had unwavering faith, innocent dependence, and absolute trust in God—like that of a child—nothing would be impossible for them. Jesus told His men to take on the humble and accepting qualities of a child, so they could be great in heaven. Moreover, they were to help and protect children in their spiritual journeys. Jesus implored them to do all these things for children graciously, without condescension or reservation. He challenged societal norms by suggesting that His men respect rather than demean children, and see them as valuable members of God's family. To drive the point home, Jesus informed them that angels would be watching to make sure that they did.

Christians in each generation are called to carry on the ministry of our Lord Jesus. Because we are not privy to the timeline in which He will return, there should always be a sense of urgency in spreading the gospel truth. Also, since we cannot know who is in the Book of Life, we must be careful never to exclude anyone from sharing in our joy, be they children or those with lesser faith. These include the people we consider below or beyond us—people we have deemed hopeless because of how they look or act, or what they believe.

Today's verse makes it clear that it is not our job to determine who comes to Jesus. Our attitude should be that of Christ Jesus, seeing all as worthy of God's love. God's angels are always watching over His chosen ones. The thought of this heavenly surveillance is both comforting and somewhat unnerving—certainly a perspective changer and an impetus for action.

Stepping In: Read Psalm 34:7, 91:11; Luke 1:19; Acts 23:8; and Hebrews 1:14. Look up other scripture passages referring to angels if you wish. Meditate on the thought of angels watching over us. Have you had any personal experiences with your guardian angel? Praise God for this heavenly blessing.

Stepping Out: This week, be extra gracious to children and other "little ones." Give a wink toward heaven each time you think of or experience an angel encounter.

Pleading

> "I tell you the truth, anyone who has faith in me will do what I have been doing. He will do even greater things than these, because I am going to the Father. And I will do whatever you ask in my name, so that the Son may bring glory to the Father. You may ask for anything in my name, and I will do it."
>
> -John 14:12-14 (John 14:5-14)

In preparation for His imminent departure, Jesus spoke both comforting and challenging words to His disciples during their last Passover meal together. In an upper room in a Jerusalem guesthouse, Jesus listened as the Twelve recalled their recent triumphal entry into the city and as they wondered aloud who would be great in this new kingdom Jesus promised. However, their elation quickly turned to confusion as Jesus began to speak again of His death. To add to their puzzlement Jesus then washed their feet and predicted that among them was one who would betray Him and another who would deny knowing Him. At hears this, all were astonished and perhaps indignant and doubtful. To refocus His men, Jesus spoke the promises in the above verses. Though they could not fathom how, the disciples would soon discover that humble and honest pleading with God in their master's powerful name would be essential for the success of their apostolic missions.

The above passage contains some of the most inspiring and misunderstood words Jesus ever spoke. To say that there is power in the name of Jesus is a foundational proclamation of the Christian faith. Those who believe, know that when we call on His mighty name all things are possible. Those who know Jesus as their personal Lord and Savior can attest to His healing, protection, guidance, comfort, and assurance. No other person is as faithful, trustworthy and capable. No other person encourages us to bring them all our needs, pleading our case for help and mercy. It is our Christian lifeline, now and eternally. Yet, many misconstrue the latter part of this passage, making it seem as if Jesus grants anything asked of Him. Unfortunately, this faulty notion leaves many disappointed in their unanswered prayers. Over time these seemingly unfulfilled promises cause faith to falter in some. Their error: pleading with God with the wrong motives.

Jesus chose His words intentionally. When we pay attention to only part of His teaching we often miss its true meaning. In the promise Jesus spoke in today's verse, we should not over look the detail about faith leading to doing what Jesus does. Those who know Jesus know that He does only what brings glory to the Father. If that is our same goal then our prayers and supplications will be focused on His will, not our own. This is very different than regarding God as our personal cosmic vending machine. Ask rightly and indeed great things are possible.

Stepping In: Read Matthew 7:21-23; John 15:7-8; Philippians 2:9-11; James 4:3; 1 John 5:13-15. Do you believe that you can do great things for God's kingdom by the power of Jesus' name? Plead with Him to purify your motives and empower your actions.

Stepping Out: This week, look for God at work and join Him. Check your motives and pray for His will to be done.

Objective

"Whoever finds his life will lose it, and whoever loses his life for my sake will find it."

—Matthew 10:39 (Mt 10:1–39)

Like so many of Jesus' teachings, today's verse is an example of His backward and upside-down theology. Readers of the New Testament have wrestled with many of these seemingly absurd notions for centuries. Those who strive to be first will finish last. Those who desire worldly riches will be poor. Those who seek a life of satisfaction will die, and vice versa. With the spiritual wisdom given to us by the Holy Spirit, we can unveil the mystery of such statements. When we look through the lens of love, Jesus' contrary teachings begin to make sense.

As we come to know and love God more, we understand that there is no better or safer place to be than inside of His will. Our earthly searching and worldly desires begin to lose their appeal. When we start to comprehend just how fruitless our personal exploits and earthly treasures are, we realize that we have been looking in the wrong places for a meaningful life. As soon as we trust in the life Jesus has for us, we know we are truly living.

Objectively speaking, those who have considered both side of this equation emphatically conclude that to gain a life everlasting for losing a perishable one for Jesus is a worthy trade.

Stepping In: Read John 12:25–26. Look up and read or listen to the lyrics for "Amazing Grace." Take some time to humbly thank Jesus for saving your life.

Stepping Out: This week, pray fervently for someone you know who has not yet gained an objective view on Jesus' backward theology. Pray for an opportunity to share with them the ways God has made your life meaningful and given you eternal hope.

September 25
Resolute

"Brother will betray brother to death, and a father his child; children
will rebel against their parents and have them put to death."
—Matthew 10:21 (Mt 10:1–21)

In the middle of Jesus' lengthy discussion with His newly appointed apostles about what they could expect in the mission field, He included this statement about familial homicide. The words probably seemed a bit out of place and difficult to comprehend. The apostles could not have known that these things could and would happen in the name of religion. They also may not have believed that anything of this nature could happen in their own families. Sadly, for some, it would. However, considering the many stories passed down through the generations of similar atrocities befalling the Hebrew nation, these men should not have been surprised to hear that they could expect these events to strike close to home. Though war and bloodshed in the name of God were to be expected, in their hearts they may have hoped it could be avoided. Jesus' words served as a stark reminder that, even among their own people, vehement opposition was plausible. It would serve these young missionaries well to be prepared for whatever might come their way. They would have to make a resolute commitment to carry out their orders, regardless of the cost.

The twelve apostles could not have known how today's prophetic statement would play out throughout history. Over the course of millennia, families have been torn apart by clashes in belief. Religious strife has cost the lives of many brothers, sisters, mothers, fathers, friends, and loved ones, with no end in sight. In some parts of the world, practicing Christianity is still punishable by death.

Jesus didn't tell His apostles this shocking news to discourage them. He was simply telling the truth, as He always does. Like His first disciples, whom He lovingly trained and taught, Jesus wants us to be informed about the joys and the trials of a resolute commitment to Him.

Stepping In: Do you quarrel about religious beliefs in your family? Is there disharmony in your church family? This week, pray for resolution and harmony in these arenas. Pray also that Jesus protects all concerned from the killing of relationships, family unity, reputations, and trust.

Stepping Out: This week, strive for family unity in your home and in your church. Resolve to be strong in faith, not in arms.

Disciplined

"Those whom I love I rebuke and discipline. So be earnest, and repent."
—Revelation 3:19 (Revelation 3:14–22)

John, the recorder of these words of Jesus, would have understood them well, including the response commanded. As the disciple whom Jesus loved, John had experienced Jesus' loving discipline on many occasions. Because of this relationship built on trust and respect, John rightly perceived everything he received from Jesus as beneficial.

Addressing the church in Laodicea, Jesus imparted some of His harshest criticism for their lukewarm faith. He wanted them to turn from their self-indulgent and spiritually neglectful practices. Jesus reminded them that everything they enjoyed had come from Him, and that it could just as easily be taken away. Jesus was eager to win back the hearts of those who were slipping into a life of self-satisfied complacency.

Christians over the course of time seem to experience an ebb and flow of closeness with the Lord. Those who are new in faith usually respond with zeal to the blessing of having been saved from a meaningless life and eternal damnation. Their words, attitudes, and actions reflect the fire they have for their Savior. However, over time, it is common for believers to settle into their saved positions as one would into a comfortable chair. From this safe location, it is easy to become content and apathetic. The passion and heat we once felt for Jesus, which inspired us to actively pursue His will and act upon His commands, fades to low embers and we begin to lose our spiritual effectiveness. Many things contribute to this phenomenon, busyness, wealth, and cultural distractions being the biggest culprits. When our personal interests outweigh our need for Jesus, we become lukewarm in our faith.

Jesus wants us to realize that unless we turn the heat back on and repent, what is left of our faith flame may flicker out. Jesus loves us too much to let this happen. Like a loving parent, He gives us what we need to thrive in all ways. He commends our good efforts, administers discipline, and calls us back to Him with the promise of hope that has always been there. Let us embrace this balanced approach to life with Jesus, so we rekindle the love we have for Him.

Stepping In: Read Deuteronomy 8:5; Proverbs 3:11–12; Romans 12:9–13; 1 Corinthians 11:27–32; and Hebrews 12:4–9. How has the Lord rebuked or disciplined you lately? What have you learned from it? What is your response? Praise God that He loves you enough to save you from your folly time and again. Earnestly repent and return to God.

Stepping Out: This week, in humble submission to God's will, revisit the thoughts and actions you had as a new Christian. Show God and others your passion for Jesus through your words and deeds.

September 27
Solid

"Blessed are you, Simon son of Jonah, for this was not revealed to you by man, but by my Father in heaven. And I tell you that you are Peter, and on this rock I will build my church, and the gates of Hades will not overcome it."

—Matthew 16:17–18 (Mt 16:13–20)

To prepare his apostles for the difficulty of maintaining a solid faith amid spiritually confused polytheists, Jesus took them into the region north of Galilee. His men's faith, loyalty, and divine understanding of who He was were tested. Jesus asked them who the people said He was. Simon described the misconception that Jesus was a reincarnate prophet. When Simon expressed his God-inspired faith in Jesus as the Christ, Jesus changed Simon's name to Peter. On Peter's solid confession of faith, the Christian church would be built.

Today, names do not have the same significance they once did. In ancient times, they often communicated the very nature of a person. Whereas the disciples may have called Simon "Peter" in a joking manner, to tease him for his rocky personality, Jesus turned that name into a title of virtue. Jesus saw that His emotional, reactive, and impulsive student also possessed the fiery desire to fully embrace his calling. Because of these characteristics, Peter became the first to be allowed by God to comprehend the spiritual reality of Jesus' Lordship.

Jesus, who is our true Rock and firm foundation, acknowledged His rocky protégée as possessing the qualities necessary to do the biggest job in history—ushering in Christianity. This work continues today, and will until Jesus returns. When Jesus said He was going to establish His church, and that not even death or Hades could overcome it, He was talking about His assembly of people—His movement, not a place. He was not predicting a religion, but a people motivated to love by belief in a risen Savior. Jesus is still looking for those with rock-solid faith, employing unlikely characters to carry on the apostles' mission. Jesus is still the changing the hearts, minds, and names of those He commissions.

Stepping In: Read Genesis 17:5, 17:15-17, 32:24-28; Isaiah 49:15–16; Malachi 3:16; John 1:40–42; Hebrews 12:22–23; and Revelation 3:5. How do these verses help you to understand the importance of names and titles to God? What name or title do you go by? Is God whispering a new name in your ear? Pray for courage to take on the solid new name Jesus wants to give you.

Stepping Out: This week, be the church outside the walls of the church. Live up to your new name.

Steadfast

"Simon son of John, do you truly love me more than these?" "Yes,
Lord," he said, "you know that I love you." Jesus said, "Feed my lambs."
—John 21:15 (Jn 21:1–19)

After seeing the resurrected Jesus, His disciples were filled with new hope for the future. So, while Jesus was away, appearing to others, the disciples resumed normal daily activities. Seven of them returned to their former livelihood of evening fishing.

One morning, after they had caught no fish, Jesus reappeared to them, standing on the shore. They did not recognize Him. As their boat approached the beach, Jesus inquired as to their catch. They replied that they had caught nothing. Jesus then told them to cast their net from the other side of the boat. When they did, their net was immediately filled. It was then that they realized who had provided them with the bounty they now struggled to manage. Peter, in his excitement, jumped off the boat and swam to shore, leaving the others to haul in the load.

Once they had eaten breakfast, Jesus asked Peter if Peter loved Him—not once, but three times. By the third time, Peter was despondent, not understanding why the Lord did not trust his answer. Jesus, however, was not testing Peter's love for Him, but slowly coaxing His rock out of a state of guilt and shame over having denied Him. Jesus reminded Peter to focus on Him and not on anyone else. He called Peter by his old name to remind him of who Jesus had called him to be, He replaced each of Peter's denials with a new confidence and steadfast purpose in Him, resulting in a restored relationship and a complete reinstatement.

Though Jesus knows each of our hearts and minds intimately, He wants us to consider where our true devotion lies. Knowing the self-doubt and unworthiness many of us feel, Jesus teaches us through passages like today's just how patient, kind, and forgiving He is. He reminds us that we too have been given new identity and purpose, which our fickle emotions do not change. Like Peter, each time we fail, Jesus is there to gently reinstate and recommission us.

In the process, He wants us to consider how much we love Him. Is it more than we love the things of this world? Is it more than we love our own plans? Is it more than we love to wallow in our own self-pity and stuck-ness?

Jesus knows we will walk through valleys in life, but He doesn't want us to set up camp there. As His followers, we must march through everything life throws our way, keeping in step with our Leader. Our temporal lives are short; there is no time to waste fretting over the past or comparing ourselves to others. Jesus has work for us to do today. We are to feed His lambs—the young, weak, vulnerable, and spiritually immature. Sometimes the feeding we do is physical, providing literal food or other necessities as an expression of love. At other times, the food we offer will be spiritual and emotional. Either way, this is how we prove our steadfast love for Jesus with more than mere words.

Stepping In: Read Jeremiah 3:15; Ezekiel 34:2; Matthew 16:16–18; Luke 22:32; Romans 8:30; 2 Timothy 4:1–2; and 1 Peter 5:1–7. Is Jesus coaxing you to focus on Him rather than guilt, shame, pride, or envy? Pray for focused and steadfast faith.

Stepping Out: This week, encourage those coming up in faith by volunteering with a youth ministry.

September 29
Supportive

"Blessed are those who mourn, for they will be comforted."
—Matthew 5:4 (Mt 5:1–12)

In Jesus' day, death and mourning were accepted facts of life. Devout Jews understood that suffering and death were the results of sin, which came into the world through Adam and Eve, compromising the perfect union of God with His people. Each death was a harsh reminder of humanity's fallen state.

The sadness of losing a loved one caused an outpouring of contrition among mourners. Grief was commonly expressed by loud wailing and the wearing of sackcloth and ashes, symbolizing a state of discomfort and ruin. It was also the custom that mourners never mourned alone. For seven days, family and friends gathered around the bereaved to just be with them. These supporters didn't try to alleviate the mourners' sorrow or expedite the grief process. They were simply there, experiencing grief alongside their stricken loved one. They did what they could to be supportive: making meals, cleaning, and speaking only when necessary. Mostly they just stayed near and provided a loving presence in time of need. Today, some Jewish sects still observe distinct mourning rituals, including the seven-day community support custom of sitting shiva.

Sadly, in our fast-paced, me-centric, modern society, most people do not embrace or respect the grieving process as we once did. Most of us don't want to linger in our or someone else's misery. Sin almost never comes into consideration, nor our role in it. And, though they say "misery loves company," most people do not like others to see them at their worst. Mourners either buck up or hide. A house full of spectators is unthinkable.

Yet, though it may not be what *we* want, God knows grieving is what we need. Jesus tells us that blessings will come out of acknowledged and dealt-with sorrows. He created us with a wide range of emotions for a reason. He will supply comfort to those who grieve in the form of a loving community and through the eternal hope He bestows on believers—if only we let Him.

Stepping In: Think of a death or loss you have experienced. How did you deal with it? Do you have any unresolved feelings surrounding it? Take some time to revisit your feelings. Allow yourself to cry, be angry, be confused, or even be okay without guilt. Allow yourself to experience the discomfort of that moment. Don't rush it—*just be.* Then whisper a prayer thanking God for never leaving nor forsaking you. Thank Him for caring for you and for taking the sting out of death.

Stepping Out: This week, allow others into your grief. Realize that both parties benefit from coming together in times of need. Fight the tendency to retreat from your feelings and your friends. You need them as much as they need to be needed, whether you like it or not. On the flip side of the coin, also be supportive of others in their grief. If possible this week, make that support happen. Regardless, be willing to be on the giving and receiving end of this blessing.

September 30
Absolved

"Father, forgive them, for they do not know what they are doing."
—Luke 23:34 (Lk 23:26–43)

Among those who dared to linger near the scene of the Master's murder was a sizable crowd of false mourners and mockers. Crucifixion was a spectacle that drew Jews and Romans alike. To most, this event marked only another display of Roman authority, through which all could be warned about the consequence for criminal misconduct. Because they truly did not know what they were doing, people hurled insults at the men on the crosses. Soldiers cast lots for Jesus' clothing. Many sneered, others jeered, and some even spit on Him.

Though He hung in excruciating pain, gasping for breath, Jesus strained to utter His plea for forgiveness. Instead of calling down curses on His abusers, Jesus declared the ones who acted out of ignorance absolved. Instead of calling on angels to rescue Him, He resolved to sacrifice His perfect life for the redemption of souls. Jesus knew that among the gawkers were a paltry few who clung to the hope that had been planted in them—a hope that would awaken in just a short while. Soon, the truth about Jesus Christ would become clear. His words from the cross would be understood. Joy and gladness would replace grief and remorse. For the absolved, new life would come from His death.

The words of today's verse continue to invoke deep emotion in people from all walks of life. Just the fact that any man could forgive such a seemingly hate-filled, murderous crowd is astonishing. It is humbling and awe-inspiring. For Christians, these words are painful reminders that Jesus paid the ultimate penalty for the sins of this world, even the sins of the ones who pinned Him to the cross. Furthermore, even in the anguish of dying one of the most undeniably excruciating deaths, Jesus cared more about the comfort and absolution of others than He did about His own condition.

This is true love. This is true grace. These words were for those standing there on that fateful day at Golgotha. These words are for us today. The ignorance of His executioners and of the crowd did not excuse their guilt, any more than ignorance can excuse our guilt today. Praise God that Jesus declared all who put their faith in Him innocent!

Stepping In: Read Psalm 22:16–21; Isaiah 42:1–4, 53; Acts 7:59–60, 13:27–28; and 1 Corinthians 2:8–10. Take some time to be quiet before God as you contemplate Jesus' great love. Praise Him and thank Him for absolving you.

Stepping Out: This week, pray the above words for the people in your life who continue to live in ignorance and sin. Pray that God illuminate the truth of their need for a Savior, and that one day they too will be absolved of guilt.

Grounded

"All men will hate you because of me, but he who stands firm to the end will be saved."

—Matthew 10:22 (Mt 10:1–22)

Jesus told His apostles plainly that those who had hated Him would hate them as well. However, He encouraged them to remain grounded in their faith, so they could endure until the end. Though they were to minister among their own people, the Jews, familiarity would not make their tasks any easier. These new "men of God" were known in their communities as common folk, fishermen and the like. Not many would take them seriously. But when they started to teach God's Word with authority and heal with miraculous power, some believed. Taking the good with the bad, the apostles stood their ground among the Israelites, bringing salvation to those they could.

The truth of today's passage is still very much a sad reality for Christians today. At the mention of the name of Jesus, people's reactions vary widely. Fellow believers express a happy acknowledgment. Non-Christians usually let their discomfort or disdain show, in body language if not words. Familiarity with those who administer the truth tends to amplify the recipient's response.

The fact is, nothing about Jesus is neutral. From the time He began His ministry, He has stirred people's imaginations and emotions. This will continue until He returns. Those who love Him, love Him completely. Those who hate Him, hate Him with the same vehemence Jesus spoke of when He warned His disciples about the cost of following Him.

As modern-day apostles, we too will face resistance, rejection, anger, and sometimes even violence in our attempts to bring the good news to our family, friends, community, and world. Jesus does not want us to be worried or discouraged. But He does want us to be informed. Holding firm to His promises, we must continue our missionary journeys, grounded in the eternal security He offers.

Stepping In: Read Matthew 5:11, 10:28-36 Luke 6:22–23; and John 15:18–25. Pray that God gives you strength to withstand opposition in your ministries. Praise Him for the ways He has set your feet on solid ground.

Stepping Out: This week, be grounded by scripture relating to Jesus' promises. Talk about Jesus among your family and friends. Stand firm and reflect God's love and truth.

October 2
Nourished

"My food," said Jesus, "is to do the will of him who sent me and to finish his work."

—John 4:34 (Jn 4:1–38)

Having spoken with the Samaritan woman at Jacob's well near Sychar, Jesus was rejoined by His disciples who had gone in search of lunch. Puzzled over what had happened, they encouraged their Master to eat something to regain His strength, if not His senses. Yet Jesus was not hungry for what they offered. Filled with the joy of living in complete submission to the will of His Father, and nourished by the fulfillment of participating in His life-saving work, Jesus was satisfied. His response let His disciples know that the sustenance His soul had just partaken of was more than enough. Satiated in "living water," Jesus' Spirit overflowed with a peace that His men could not yet understand.

When we accepted Jesus as our Lord and Savior, He gave us living water too: eternal nourishment for our souls. This gift is the indwelling Holy Spirit, which connects us to the heavenly realms even while we are still in our physical bodies. We cannot literally live on spiritual food alone, but we can experience the satisfaction of working inside of the Father's will.

Every Christian is employed by the kingdom of God to be the hands and feet of Christ to a needy world. Once we have reached a level of spiritual maturity, as we are expected to do, we are to bring others up in the faith as well.

Further on in today's passage, Jesus discusses the harvest with His disciples. These are the people who are ready and waiting to receive the gospel. Jesus urges all His followers to sow seeds, water crops, reap a harvest, and collect wages. He shows us how this is done throughout the story of the Samaritan woman at the well. He engaged her, gained her trust, introduced her to the gospel, spoke scriptural truth, proclaimed Himself, and offered the gift. The joy in seeing this work done is better than all the money and food in the world. It is what truly nourishes the Christian soul.

Stepping In: Read 1 Corinthians 3:6–9; 2 Corinthians 9:6; Galatians 6:7–10; James 3:17–18; and Revelation 14:15–16. What new inspiration about kingdom work do you gain from these passages? How have you been nourished by the spiritual food Jesus talked about? Pray for a willingness to tend the field God gives you.

Stepping Out: This week, fast and pray for opportunities to participate in the Father's work. Then obey His call.

October 3

Responsible

> "I will give you the keys of the kingdom of heaven; whatever you bind on earth will be bound in heaven, and whatever you loose on earth will be loosed in heaven."
>
> —Matthew 16:19 (Mt 16:13–20)

When Jesus called Simon by the name He had given him, Peter, He also made a grand claim: "On this rock, I will build my church, and the gates of Hades will not overcome it" (Mt 16:18). Peter had to have been stunned. But Jesus was not finished. He concluded His prophetic proclamation by promising Peter the keys to the kingdom, thus bestowing on Peter the authority of an usher at the doors of heaven itself. Though the keys were metaphorical, they signified Peter's duty to lock and unlock the mysteries of the kingdom during His lifetime as a Christian missionary. Peter's astute proclamation, that Jesus was the "Christ, the Son of the living God" (Mt 16:16), earned him a position in the kingdom that would come at great cost, being both a privilege and an enormous responsibility. If only he could have known the treasures he was amassing!

Like Peter, all Christians have been blessed with insight into the mysteries of God through the Holy Spirit. Everything we know about spiritual matters comes from God Himself, and not from our own learning or intellect. With this endowment of privileged information comes a responsibility to use it wisely; for our own good and the good of others. As we walk through our earthly lives, we have numerous opportunities to hold the door open for unbelievers or slam it shut. By our words, attitudes, and behaviors, we can invite skeptics, even haters of God, into the previously hidden world of hope and salvation.

Daunted by the seriousness of this task, many will choose to keep their keys safely in their pockets. However, according to this passage in Matthew, clearly Jesus would like His representatives to actively strive to remove barriers between this world and the kingdom of heaven. Equipped with the tools appropriate for the challenge, and with the unlimited power of the Holy Trinity at work in us, today's disciples must continue the kingdom work Peter started millennia ago. We are the new keepers of the keys. It is still a tough and risky job, but one worth doing responsibly and well.

Stepping In: Read Isaiah 22:20–24; John 20:19–23; Acts 1:7–8; and Revelation 3:6–7 and 20:1–4. How do you feel about having the responsibility to carry on the work of the apostles? Do these verses help you understand what your role is and what it is not? Pray for peace and strength to share God's truth unreservedly.

Stepping Out: This week, let your life be an example of right living before God, showing others that you take your Christian responsibility seriously. Hold the door open for all.

Fulfilled

"Woe to you who are well fed now, for you will go hungry. Woe to you
who laugh now, for you will mourn and weep."

—Luke 6:25 (Lk 6:17–26)

Jesus began His Sermon on the Mount with encouraging words about blessings. However, to those
who questioned His authority or downplayed God's sovereign justice, Jesus issued warnings. To the
self-satisfied and spiritually complacent, Jesus predicted a turning of the tables in today's verse. He
knew that His words would strike a chord with His audience. Some would feel a sense of vindication,
while others would be somewhat perturbed by His message. However, this teaching was mainly for
His disciples. They needed to understand that the nature of God's kingdom was in direct contrast to
the ways of the world, and they would likely encounter resistance because of it. They needed to learn
a new definition of fulfillment.

Life in ancient times was tough. All but the very rich had to work exhaustively just to eat. The
realities of mourning and weeping were sadly common. In our modern world, convenience and excess
have largely replaced struggle and scarcity. At least in industrialized nations, today's verse may have
lost some of its original impact.

We need to remember that Jesus is speaking more about our spiritual condition than about our
physical or emotional state. Over the centuries, human nature has not changed very much. Those
who look for fulfillment and peace in the world have always been left wanting. The fleshly desires to
satisfy one's needs and, if possible, avoid discomfort were passed down from the first people, Adam
and Eve. Lust for forbidden fruit and power still plagues us. Jesus wants us to examine our appetites.
Hungering for anything other than God's will leads not to fulfillment, but to dissatisfaction and
spiritual starvation.

Stepping In: Read Deuteronomy 8:3; Proverbs 14:11–14; Isaiah 65:11–16; and John 4:13–14 and 6:35.
What do you hunger for? What comforts do you feel you could not live without? Are pleasure
and entertainment priorities? Pray for a right perspective. Ask God to reveal areas of greed and
overindulgence that need to be confessed.

Stepping Out: This week, fast from the thing that God revealed to you (food, media, work, recreation),
Devote that time to blessing someone who is hungry or sad, physically, emotionally, and/or spiritually.
Focus on being spiritually rather than physically fulfilled.

October 5

Unfaltering

Going a little farther, he fell with his face to the ground and prayed,
"My Father, if it is possible, may this cup be taken from me. Yet not as
I will, but as you will."

—Matthew 26:39 (Mt 26:17–45)

Overwhelmed with confusion and grief, the disciples followed their Lord into the garden of Gethsemane, just outside Jerusalem. Jesus implored His men to stay nearby while He went a short distance away to pray. Taking Peter, James, and John with Him, He asked His close companions to keep watch and to pray as well. Jesus turned to His Father for comfort and strength. The human side of Him struggled to find a way out of the agonizing fate He faced and asked for mercy. However, the holy side of Him chose what was right over what was safe. He chose pain over comfort. He chose the eternal over the immediate. As His disciples slept nearby, Jesus was truly alone and full of sorrow. Sweat, in the form of blood, rose on His brow. Yet He remained unfaltering in His resolve; He would fulfill the will of His Father at all cost.

How lightly we read these words today. At the slightest discomfort or inconvenience, we plead with God for relief. When we pray, we often toss in as an afterthought, "Oh, and by the way, may your will, not mine, be done." All the while, we hope that they are one and the same.

Imagine if Jesus had taken such a light-hearted approach in the garden of Gethsemane. Imagine if He had let His human frailty rule over His divine nature. On second thought, let's not.

The truth is, asking for the Father's will to be done before our own is no small deal, and it should not be taken lightly. When we honestly mean them, these words profess our faith and trust in the sovereignty of our Lord. By them we give up our rights and our plans, and rightfully so. Jesus chose the holy and just path, and so should we. Not only do we owe this devotion to the One who saved us from eternal damnation, but we stand to gain so much more than we could possibly manage on our own. Simply put, the Father's will may not be the easiest choice, but it is always best. Following Jesus' example, our faith and obedience should never falter.

Stepping In: Read Psalm 40; Isaiah 53; and Matthew 20:21–23. Take some time to meditate on these scripture passages. Picture yourself in Jesus' place on that fateful day when He took on the sin of the world—your sin. Thank Him now and apologize for downplaying the role of the Father's will in your life.

Stepping Out: This week, earnestly pray for the Father's will to be done in and through your life. Then do His will at every opportunity. Practice unfaltering faith and obedience.

Convinced

"Why do you entertain evil thoughts in your hearts? Which is easier to say, 'Your sins are forgiven,' or to say, 'Get up and walk?' But that you may know that the Son of Man has authority on earth to forgive sins …" He said to the paralytic, "Get up, take your mat and go home."
—Matthew 9:4–6 (Mt 9:1–8)

One day, while Jesus was teaching and healing amid a large crowd in Capernaum, a paralyzed man was brought before Him by his friends. Moved to compassion by the faith and loyalty of the man's companions, Jesus comforted the paralytic and forgave his sins. The crowd was astonished. The Pharisees and religious leaders were outraged. When they confronted Jesus about His supposed blasphemy, He gave them the reply in today's verse. If Jesus' forgiveness that day did not convince His audience of His divine authority, His healing ability certainly should have.

Everything Jesus did and said was intentional. Every one of His teachings was specifically crafted to address the issues of those who heard Him. Each of His healings was designed to have the greatest impact on those who experienced them. For the benefit of His disciples, past and present, Jesus employs a variety of tactics to convince people of His Lordship and to teach the lesson needing to be learned.

Since the fall of man, the battle between good and evil, between God and Satan, has raged on. Each of these powerful forces is vying for our hearts and minds. This issue was of first importance to Jesus. People may like to think that there is a distinction between one's thoughts and what is truly in one's heart; Jesus reminds us that the line between the two is thin at best. In fact, He would say that the heart rules the body and the mind.

Notice that Jesus did not ask, "Why do you entertain evil thoughts in your *mind*?" Today's verse is a stark reminder that what is in our hearts will convince our minds of what to think, not the other way around. Good and pure hearts think noble, godly thoughts. Evil and corrupt hearts think blasphemy. Thankfully, Jesus can change hearts that need a "transplant."

Stepping In: Read Psalm 51:10; Proverbs 3:5, 4:23; Matthew 6:21, 12:33-35; Romans 3:38-39, 12:2; and Philippians 4:7. What do these verses teach you about the importance of having and maintaining a pure heart? Do your actions convince others that you belong to God? Pray that Jesus protects your heart from evil influences.

Stepping Out: Read 2 Corinthians 10:3-8. This week, live out these verses. Hold captive every evil thought and replace it with what is "true, noble, right, pure, lovely, admirable, excellent, and praiseworthy" (Phil 4:8).

October 7
Doubtless

"Everything is possible for him who believes."
—Mark 9:23 (Mt 9:14–32)

As Jesus was returning, along with Peter, James, and John, from His transfiguration experience on a high mountain near Galilee, they came upon the other disciples in the middle of an argument about an ineffective exorcism. The crowd around the disciples was upset that Jesus' men could not drive out a demon from a suffering child. Frustrated by the people's lack of faith, Jesus nevertheless stepped forward to help. After the boy's father had explained his son's condition, he asked Jesus if He *could* heal him.

It is in this context that Jesus made today's statement. Immediately, the father professed that he did believe, but then added that he could use some help with his unbelief. Jesus had the boy brought to Him. When the demon saw Jesus, it threw the boy into a violent convulsion on the ground. At Jesus' command, the evil spirit shrieked and left the child. In a final act of tenderness Jesus helped the boy to his feet. Then He left, leaving the crowd standing in awe. As for the boy and his father, they were left doubtless of Jesus' healing power and divine authority.

Today's disciple has the advantage of reading scripture in its greater context. Yet some verses, like today's, are profoundly meaningful in and of themselves. Of the many things Jesus spoke of, doubt in Him and His abilities was something He addressed with emphatic clarity. Today's verse leaves no room for uncertainty about Jesus' power. Moreover, it is a promise that His power in us is also unlimited. He tells us plainly that not just some things, but *all* things are possible for the one who truly believes. What a claim!

Human tendency is to succumb to fear, doubt, and helplessness--- all ploys that Satan still uses today. These negative influences are forms of unbelief. As we mature in our Christian faith and come to know Jesus personally, we should learn to trust Him more. Yet, in our humanness, we slip back into letting our circumstances dictate our faith.

The test comes when hard times prevail. Do we utilize Jesus' power by calling on His name, or do we exhaust every other option first? Do we fall on our knees and pray, or do we complain to and blame others instead?

Jesus had a reason to be frustrated with the unbelief of the people who walked with Him and witnessed His miracles. He has even more reason to call our current unbelieving generation to task; we do, after all, have the complete God-breathed Holy Bible, as well as our own miraculous stories as proof. That said, most Christians can easily identify with the afflicted boy's father, who professed his belief in Jesus yet struggled with uncertainty anyway.

And so we are left with a choice. We can trust completely and see Jesus work wonders in and through us, or we can believe only half-heartedly and never know the fullness of His power. True faith in Jesus should be doubtless.

Stepping In: Read Numbers 11:23; Isaiah 59:1; Jeremiah 32:17, 27; Matthew 19:26; and Philippians 4:13. How do these verses give you confidence in the power of the Lord to work in and through you? Meditate on today's verse using the Emphasize It method (See appendix). Pray for doubtless faith, daily if necessary.

Stepping Out: This week, make a list of impossible things God has made possible for you in your life. Put it somewhere where you will see it every day. Each time you read it, praise God.

October 8
Willing

> "O Jerusalem, Jerusalem, you who kill the prophets and stone those
> sent to you, how often I have longed to gather your children together,
> as a hen gathers her chicks under her wings, but you were not willing."
> —Matthew 23:37 (Mt 22:41–23:39)

Speaking in the temple courts of Jerusalem, Jesus issued "seven woes" upon the Jewish leaders. He ended His scathing sermon with a sentimental lament for the city. Though His anger burned at His earthly contemporaries' hypocrisy and sacrilegious behaviors, His heart clearly ached for their lost souls. There was not much time left to fulfill the Father's will to first call His chosen ones to salvation. Jesus professed His sadness at the hard-heartedness of these men who claimed devout allegiance to God. He concluded by quoting from familiar scripture passages, declaring that their house would be desolate until they willingly acknowledged Jesus as Lord and welcomed Him back with praise and blessing.

This lament continues today for Jerusalem and every nation of the world. Jesus came to call His own people first, but it was always His Father's plan to invite all peoples to His kingdom. After Pentecost, Jesus' apostles went out into the wider world. They spread the good news of the gospel and won many converts to the family of God. Thanks to their brave and tireless efforts, Christianity has successfully reached nearly every part of the globe.

Yet there are still many who are unwilling to join the ranks of the victorious. Some, having missed Him the first time, are still awaiting the Messiah. Truly, anyone reading scripture can pick up a sense of anticipation; the grand finale is still to be seen. As in the days before Jesus was crucified, we feel the urgency to get the Word out to all who have ears to hear. And, as in the days following His ascension, we are once again in a state of suspense over when He will return. There is much work to be done, and no idea of how long we will have to do it.

Until He comes back to collect His children, we are commissioned to gather His chicks under our wings. We must seek out the willing, no matter how hard they are to find, so that together we may say, "Blessed is the one who comes in the name of the Lord."

Stepping In: Read 1 Kings 9:6–7; 2 Chronicles 24:20–22; Psalm 57:1, 118:26–29; Isaiah 31:5–6; and Jeremiah 22:4–5. How do you feel knowing that Jesus grieves over those who refuse His grace, even those who persecuted and killed Him and His followers? How do they encourage you to pray more fervently for unyielding hearts to become willing? Take some time to do so now.

Stepping Out: This week, spread your wings of love and truth over the lost souls in your life. Offer hugs.

Awestruck

"Do not be afraid. I am the First and the Last. I am the Living One; I was dead, and behold I am alive for ever and ever! And I hold the keys of death and Hades."

—Revelation 1:17–18 (Rv 1:9–20)

During His earthly ministry, Jesus instructed the twelve disciples whom He selected, not only to be His companions and apprentices, but also to be His apostles. Of the Twelve, Jesus had three with whom He was closest—His inner circle. Of the three, John was known as "the disciple whom Jesus loved." Unsurprising, when God was looking for someone to do the special work of recording His revelation of the culmination of human history—the final fulfillment of prophesied judgment and salvation—John was chosen.

John gave his full attention to God, and was rewarded by being transported in the Spirit into the very presence of God. He was instructed by Jesus Himself to write down everything he saw and heard, for the benefit of the seven churches in Asia Minor. Turning to see whose voice was coming from behind him, John caught the first of many symbolic visions regarding what was to come. He also saw Jesus in all His glory, a sight almost beyond description. Jesus comforted His awestruck messenger with the most reassuring words of all for those who believe.

Christianity is based on the belief that Jesus, the Son of God, lived, died, was buried, was brought back to life, and now reigns in heaven. Without this, our faith is dead, and so are we. Because we believe that scripture is God-breathed and has been proven valid and reliable, we trust in the many recorded accounts of Jesus dying and then appearing alive. Everything that scripture said about the Messiah, as well as everything Jesus said about Himself, has or will come true. Jesus told His disciples that He would return to the Father, and many eyewitnesses verified that this is what He did. He promised them the Holy Spirit, and when It came, that was an event none present could deny. He has promised to return, and since His Word has never once failed, Christians throughout history have put their faith in Him.

In the meantime, it is easy to forget that we have a living Savior interceding for us, orchestrating His will in our lives, and preparing a place for us in heaven. The book of Revelation reminds us of these facts. We do not need to be afraid—Jesus is alive and in control of our eternal destinies. It is a reminder to share our awestruck amazement at the promise and fulfillment we have come to know and trust.

Stepping In: Read Daniel 7:13–14; Mark 8:31–33; John 5:24; Romans 6:9, 8:6; and 1 John 3:14–15. Are you awestruck or frightened when you hear God's commands? Pray for courage to move from shocked to stoked.

Stepping Out: This week, with a friend or in your small group, listen to or watch the music video of the Newsboys' "God's Not Dead." Discuss how the Spirit of God is roaring like a lion in your life. If it is not, pray that God ignites His fire in your heart, spurring you to proclaim, "Jesus is alive!"

October 10
Proper

"Let it be so now; it is proper for us to do this to fulfill all righteousness."
—Matthew 3:15 (Mt 3:1–17)

Before Jesus began His ministry, His cousin, John the Baptist, preached the coming of the Messiah. John had received a calling from God to go into the wilderness, proclaiming the nearness of heaven's kingdom and calling all to repent of their sin. Regardless of his strange habits and appearance, he gained quite a following because of the impassioned message he proclaimed. Many people, including some of the Jewish leaders and Pharisees, came to the Jordan River to be baptized by him. Filled by God's Spirit, John professed a coming judgment, one that would not stand up against a mere water baptism. He told the people of a baptism by fire and a "winnowing fork" that would separate the faithful from the faithless. He spoke of the Holy Spirit, though he did not fully grasp the significance of this mysterious force.

Jesus, who had also begun to gain recognition for preaching a salvation message, came to John and asked to be baptized. Puzzled and reluctant, John did finally acquiesce. All who were present that day were blessed beyond measure to witness, not only the Holy Spirit's arrival in the form of a dove, but also the audible voice of God praising His beloved Son.

Jesus did not need to be baptized. Yet because of His commitment to always lead by example, He sought baptism nonetheless. Imagine being John when he came to the realization that day that Jesus was the Messiah he had prophesied. And Jesus wanted John to baptize *Him*!

In today's verse, Jesus encourages John to honor His request and reminds John of the purpose for this divine act. Skeptical as he might have been, John was no doubt very glad that he eventually complied. Today, the act of being washed in the water—of being submerged—still symbolizes the death of the old self and the birth of the new. Though one can claim to be born again without undergoing baptism, it remains the proper way to show the world where one's devotion lies. It is a tangible way to follow our Leader.

Stepping In: Read Matthew chapter 3 along with John 1:29–34. Do these verses change the way you look at baptism and its significance for Christian obedience? Is the Spirit prompting you to take any next steps in this regard? Pray for guidance from the Holy Spirit as to where you can increase your compliance with Jesus' requests this week.

Stepping Out: If you have not already been baptized of your own volition, consider taking some first steps toward setting that goal. If you have already made that public profession of faith, then commit to supporting others as they take the plunge of obedience.

Timely

> "The right time for me has not yet come; for you any time is right."
> —John 7:6 (Jn 7:1–13)

With the Feast of Tabernacles approaching, faithful Jews of Galilee prepared to head to Jerusalem to partake of the festivities, as was their custom. Due to the increased opposition He faced there, Jesus decided to postpone His journey. His half-brothers—sons of Mary and Joseph—strongly encouraged Him to go. They wanted their famous brother to show off His awe-inspiring abilities. Seeing Him only as a charismatic and influential public figure, they implored Jesus not to disappoint His expectant Judean fans. They did not understand that Jesus' message and His miraculous signs and wonders were not for show, but were the actual work of God, meant to prove Jesus' divinity. They did not take Him at His Word—that a time was coming, but had not yet come, when He would go to Jerusalem for the last time to officially usher in a new kingdom. Today's verse was yet another reminder of the importance of doing God's will in His timing.

Not that we would be proud to admit it, but Christians throughout history have often behaved as Jesus' brothers did: pushy, demanding, expectant, and prone to promote our own agendas based on a limited spiritual scope. Even with the best of intentions, we ask of Jesus many miracles that are not the will of the Father. We think that our every cause is of first importance, and tend to disregard the myriad reasons why He may not cater to our wishes in a way we deem appropriate. Unable to see across time and space, and unduly influenced by a culture of instant gratification, we become impatient and even disgruntled when Jesus does not give us an immediate response. In honest reflection, we later see that many of the things we thought we wanted, we were glad never transpired.

If only we could remember that God's timing is always perfect! Everything Jesus did and said was according to the detailed plan God laid out for sin's atonement and for salvation to be made available. Jesus fulfilled this plan. We, as His heirs, must use our limited time wisely to tell others of all our Savior has done and will do. By staying in step with Jesus through the Holy Spirit, we can accomplish God's will—which is always to promote and expand His kingdom. Today's verse is as true for us today as it was for the first apostles. The time for us to proclaim Jesus is always right—now.

Stepping In: Read Ecclesiastes 3:1–11; Habakkuk 2:3; Romans 5:6, 13:11; Galatians 4:4–5; 1 Thessalonians 5:1–6; and 2 Timothy 4:1–2. What do these verses tell you about God's perfectly timed plan and what your role in it should be? Is there anything He is revealing to you that requires your urgent attention? Pray for guidance, courage, motivation, and wisdom to step out in faith in a timely manner.

Stepping Out: This week, based on what the Holy Spirit reveals to you, take an action step in your faith walk. Let a sense of urgency drive you to promote God's kingdom in a new and powerful way.

October 12
Composed

"Where is your faith?"
—Luke 8:25 (Lk 8:22–25)

For the first two years of His public ministry, Jesus and His disciples, though they traveled throughout Israel preaching and healing, always returned to their home base in Galilee. On one occasion, Jesus wanted to visit a village on the opposite side of a lake (Sea of Galilee). Underway in a small boat with His disciples, Jesus lay down to rest and was soon fast asleep.

Shortly thereafter, a violent storm cropped up and tossed the boat about mercilessly. The disciples, fearing for their lives, woke Jesus with their panicked cries. They had seen Jesus cure people's mental and physical illnesses, they had witnessed Him teaching with bold authority, and they had even seen Him bring a dead boy back to life. Yet when their own lives were in peril, they lost their composure and their faith.

In today's verse, Jesus questioned His pupils about their emotion-driven response. Though He didn't have to, Jesus then rebuked the weather, calmed the seas, and restored peace to the hearts of the men in the boat.

Most people can relate to the disciples' reaction. How often do we allow fear and uncertainty to take our focus off Jesus and diminish our faith, even if briefly? Truly, when the fight-or-flight response is triggered in one's brain, the ability to think clearly and rationally gets switched off. Even someone of great faith, who has gone through trials with Jesus and normally trusts Him fully, can easily succumb to the deceptive influence of fear.

Satan knows this about people and capitalizes on it at every opportunity. Believers must dig deep and rise above, striving to maintain spiritual composure. To overcome fear's grip, we must look inward to where Jesus lives, and whisper the words, "I trust you, Jesus." Once He has calmed our fears, we will be able to see beyond the situation in front of us.

This takes practice. We can start by trusting Jesus with our small disasters and everyday struggles, so that we build up our faith muscles for the big storms. With time, practice, and the help of the Holy Spirit, we can deal with any situation with a calm reassurance that surpasses understanding.

Stepping In: Read Joshua 1:9; Psalm 23:4, 27:1, 107:23-32; Romans 8:38–39; and 1 Peter 5:6–7. What current or future circumstances cause you to worry and take your eyes off God? Ask Him to remove those fears and replace them with peace. Thank Him for the times He has helped you be composed in difficult times.

Stepping Out: This week, preferably with your small group, listen to "It Is Well" by Audrey Assad and "No Longer Slaves" by Jonathan David and Melissa Helser. Discuss how these songs encourage faith, strength, and courage through Jesus. Cling to the promises of God for help in overcoming fear.

Benevolent

"They do not need to go away. You give them something to eat."
—Matthew 14:16 (Mt 14:1–21)

When the people of Israel learned that Jesus was a benevolent man of God and a compassionate healer, they sought Him out in droves. Jesus tirelessly ministered to the physical and spiritual needs of the masses. On one such occasion, after spending the day healing the sick and sharing words of encouragement, His disciples thought it time to send the people home. They suggested that everyone ought to go find food for themselves. Jesus disagreed. Skeptical, the disciples wondered how they could possibly feed more than five thousand people with only a few loaves of bread and a couple of fishes?

Jesus was undaunted. To show His men that nothing was impossible with Him, He miraculously displayed His powers by demonstrating His unwavering trust in God's mercy and provision. Together, Father and Son provided physical and spiritual food for the masses that day.

How often do we look at a situation and deem it hopeless? How often do we gauge the potential for rectifying a bad scenario by how much strength or smarts we possess? Where does God fit into all of this?

These were the same questions the disciples had to be wondering two thousand years ago. We can read about the many miracles Jesus performed during His ministry, and have probably experiencing a few of our own, but we still tend to prefer to rely on our own abilities rather than trusting in the proven power of God to see us through. The lesson the disciples needed to learn that day on the beach is the same lesson we still need to learn today: stop doubting, start trusting, and follow Jesus' example of benevolent giving.

This is tough for sensate beings, ruled by tangible senses. Faith requires that we believe in God's sovereign power, even in the absence physical proof. We must believe that He is both benevolent and able to meet our needs. The lesson from today's verse, for all disciples throughout history, remains: never let your sight influence your perception of possibilities.

Stepping In: Read Matthew 19:26; Mark 5:36; Luke 1:36–37; Romans 4:18; 2 Corinthians 5:6–7; and Ephesians 3:20–21. What is your typical response to impossible situations? How do these verses help you have faith in the benevolence and power of God? Pray for your faith in Jesus to grow as He reveals miracles in your life.

Stepping Out: In the spirit of benevolence and faith, serve in a food ministry this week.

Attestable

"Do not believe me unless I do what my Father does. But if I do it, even though you do not believe me, believe the miracles, that you may know and understand that the Father is in me, and I in the Father."
—John 10:37–38 (Jn 10:22–42)

Just months before He would go to the cross, Jesus went to Jerusalem for the Feast of Dedication. In the temple, at Solomon's Colonnade, He was approached by a group of Jews anxious to know if He was the Christ. Recognizing many of them as witnesses to His miracles and teachings, He told them plainly that He had already given them ample proof of His deity. Because the Jews had not believed what they had seen, Jesus boldly restated His claim of Oneness with the Father. Instead of greeting their Messiah, the Jews picked up stones to hurl at Him. They could not understand or accept that Jesus was the living God. Jesus reminded them of prophecies and scripture, and added today's verses as a testament to His power and authority. Though His claim was attestable, many remained unconvinced.

When we study the Bible as a whole, as one complete story from Genesis to Revelation, we see the full picture of God's plan for redemption through His Son. It is a joy for Christians and messianic Jews to read through the prophecies in the Old Testament and know that our Savior has and will fulfill them for us. Though the nature of our Triune God is cloaked in mystery, believers do not doubt. We all have our own experiential proofs that each of these three Spirit-Beings exists. Our testimonies are attestable verifications of truth. We understand in the core of our souls that Jesus/God/Spirit lives in us from the moment we profess our faith.

Consequently, today's verses make perfect sense. As God is in the Son, the Son is in us. Our oneness with God allows us to see and do what the Father is doing, just as Jesus did and does. Because our spiritual blindness has been removed, through the Spirit we are able to discern truth, detect miracles, and enjoy the benefits of being in the Shepherd's flock. Not only that, we know the best is yet to come.

Stepping In: Read Genesis 1:26–27 and John 1:1–4, 5:19, 8:17–18, 14:10–11, and 17:20-23. What do these and other scripture passages say about who Jesus is? How does your life bear witness to the validity of Jesus' claim to deity? Pray for the Spirit to open your eyes to everyday miracles.

Stepping Out: This week, look for where the Father/Son/Spirit is working around you. Join in the work. Be prepared to share your attestable testimony with someone seeking proof of Jesus' Lordship.

October 15
Repentant

> "I tell you the truth, the tax collectors and the prostitutes are entering
> the kingdom of heaven ahead of you."
> —Matthew 21:31 (Mt 21:23–32)

Teaching in the temple during the last week of His earthly ministry, Jesus told a parable about a father who asked his two sons to work for him in his vineyard. The first son rather curtly said he would not go, but later changed his mind and went. The second son respectfully said he would go, but didn't. Jesus asked the crowd which of the two sons the father would want to have. They answered, "The first," to which Jesus made the observation in today's verse. He was reminding some hard-hearted listeners that their ability to recognize God's prophets was an issue to be scrutinized. To add insult to injury, Jesus concluded that the lowliest, most ungodly members of society were more spiritually perceptive. These would have been shocking and anger-invoking words for pious men to hear. From a heavenly perspective, however, it was not what one does or says that matters; it is a spiritually aware and repentant heart that pleases God.

In too many cases, Christians today still struggle with this issue of acceptance. Many simply cannot look beyond the outer trappings of a person to see the precious creation hidden just below the surface. To use Jesus' illustration, people like prostitutes, corrupt business owners, and compromised government officials are still considered unwelcome in many religious organizations. Pious members believe that "those people" are best left to their own devices—they can lie in the beds they have made. Some of us believe that these folks are likely to receive God's just wrath, while those of us who look and act the Christian part deserve God's favor.

Naturally, Jesus turns this notion upside-down. What today's passage is driving at it is simply this: anyone who has a truly repentant heart, regardless of what they look like or have done, is a worthy child of God. This is a lesson for the hard-hearted hypocrites in every generation.

Stepping In: Read Jeremiah 31:19; Ezekiel 11:17–19; Zechariah 1:3; Acts 3:19; Romans 2:5; and 2 Corinthians 7:9–10. How do these verses help you understand more about the kind of heart posture God desires? How do they help you understand the importance of repentance, turning from sin to God? Pray for a repentant heart.

Stepping Out: This week, examine your heart for false pride and judgement. Repent of those sins and look for opportunities to show love to those you have formerly deemed unworthy to receive it.

October 16
Sensible

"Do not store up for yourselves treasures on earth, where moth and rust destroy, and where thieves break in and steal. But store up for yourselves treasures in heaven, where moth and rust do not destroy, and where thieves do not break in and steal. For where your treasure is, there your heart will be also."

—Matthew 6:19–21 (Mt 6:19–24)

Jesus alluded to heaven many times in His multi-day Sermon on the Mount. With each illustration, He gave His listeners a bit more detail of what that place was like and who would be there. He slowly but surely painted an ever more complete picture of this mysterious destination.

For the Jews in the crowd, the mention of heaven may have conjured up a variety of images: a resting place with God, a life everlasting, the Promised Land of their ancestors. But none could fathom the splendor and eternal nature of the heaven with which Jesus spoke.

Treasure too was an imaginary concept for the majority of His audience. The temple had many gold and bejeweled articles in it, but these were clearly unattainable. Most people in this society made a subsistence living. Times were hard. The Roman government's corrupt taxation, desperate swindlers, and barbaric thieves were unfortunate realities of life. Treasure and security were believed to be things only money could buy.

But Jesus was not talking about earthly treasures. As He often did throughout His ministry, He was asking His audience to consider their heart condition more than their physical status. Those who heard this teaching should have realized that eternal savings were the most sensible investment.

People today might say "nothing lasts forever" without really giving the impact of this statement much thought. If pressed, many would not know exactly where they stood about that. A popular rock band of the 1970s and 1980s, Kansas, postulated that the earth and the sky were exceptions to the rule, but everything else was "dust in the wind."

These lyrics inch closer to the truth but are still not fully accurate. There is a place that will never perish: the new heaven and earth. Until Jesus returns and replaces both, heaven is in every believer's heart.

Those who live only for today, treasuring what this world offers, will indeed wind up as dust in the wind, destined to swirl discontentedly forever. Even Christians are tempted by worldly treasures and often trust their security to it. We think, "Surely, the more money and possession I have, the happier and safer I will feel." Sensible as this sounds, the truth is that it doesn't work that way. Instead of granting us security, worldly treasures often induce worry, stress, obsession, and greed. Money is not a bad thing. But when we value it above God and His kingdom, we become enslaved by it. Our hearts follow what we value, not the other way around.

Jesus warns us not to invest in things that won't last. He offers a more sensible approach: invest in the kingdom and the King, and await His glorious return. The people of this dying planet need this age-old wisdom more than ever.

Stepping In: Read Matthew 6:19–24 and Luke 12:16–21. Pray that God reveals and removes any greed or stinginess in you. Ask Him to show you ways you can be rich toward God and others this week.

Stepping Out: Make a sensible choice. Replace your thoughts of worldly acquisitions with the things God would love to occupy your heart instead. Look for and treasure the things listed in Philippians 4:8–9.

October 17

Managerial

"I tell you, use worldly wealth to gain friends for yourselves, so that when it is gone, you will be welcomed into eternal dwellings."

—Luke 16:9 (Lk 16:1–15)

During the final year of Jesus' earthly ministry, the loyalty of His followers was put to the test. With each sermon, Jesus made it clear that every person must choose between a life of selfish ambitions ending in death, or a God-centered life resulting in eternal blessings. Many people could not accept this teaching, especially those who believed they were already justified by birthright and the law. Those who had little chance of earning salvation through the Jewish system, however, were eager to hear about the salvation by grace through faith in Jesus. More and more sinners became followers of the Way.

Since the Pharisees watched Jesus' every move, they were naturally present during a talk he gave to a group of His unsavory new friends. Jesus told them a story about an unjust manager of a wicked man's estate. After being fired for wasting his master's money, the crafty man concocted a deceitful plan to win the favor of his former master's debtors. Duped, the corrupt master congratulated the man on his cleverness. Knowing the Pharisees' love of money, Jesus spoke today's verse to remind them of their neglectful use of God's property. They would not "be welcomed into eternal dwellings" until they started employing more generous managerial practices,

Though it may sound like Jesus is endorsing the practice of buying friends, that is not exactly what He meant. Jesus was implying that He was aware of the Pharisees' insincere generosity. Further on in the teaching, He made it clear that one's true character determines how much one will be entrusted with by God. Furthermore, Jesus stated that one "cannot serve both God and money."

That said, as stewards of the gifts God has given each of us, we are expected to make wise, prudent, and honest choices with our wealth. In a world where money is revered as the answer to all problems, it is easy to see the influence it has over people's decisions. Fear of scarcity drives some to take desperate measure to secure their future holdings.

God's economy does not work the way the world's does. Instead of saving and hoarding, we gain our true security from wise planning and giving—good managerial skills. Jesus expects us to share generously and joyfully rather than stockpiling wealth for ourselves. This is how we can gain friends for now and for eternity.

Stepping In: Read Psalm 49:16–20; Matthew 6:19, 25:21; Luke 12:33–34; 2 Corinthians 9:7–9; and 1 Timothy 6:9–10, 17–19. Because a proper perspective on money is very important to God, pray that He give you financial wisdom.

Stepping Out: This week, let a kind and generous act pave the way toward a potential friendship, now and in heaven. Let your good managerial skills prove to God that you are trustworthy with much.

October 18

Percipient

"This is why I speak in parables: 'Though seeing, they do not see; though hearing, they do not hear or understand.' In them is fulfilled the prophecy of Isaiah: 'You will be ever hearing but never understanding; you will be ever seeing but never perceiving. For this people's heart has become calloused; they hardly hear with their ears and they have closed their eyes. Otherwise they might see with their eyes, hear with their ears, and understand with their hearts and turn, and I would heal them.'"

—Matthew 13:13–15 (Mt 13:1–15)

In the region of Galilee, Jesus attracted such large crowds that it was difficult for Him to find adequate venues for His gatherings. One day, Jesus opted to address His onlookers from a boat out on the lake. Using a parable about sowing seeds, Jesus spoke of the various ways people receive God's Word. His disciples asked Jesus why He spoke to the people using figures of speech. Quoting ancient prophecies, Jesus explained that the rejection of His message was to be expected; it had been foretold by several of God's prophets. Because He had much to teach those with percipient ears to hear His spiritual wisdom, Jesus used parables to disguise His meaning from those who would choose to distort the truth and use His words against Him.

For many, scriptural writings are still difficult to understand. Even Christians struggle to fully comprehend many passages. Yet, by faith, we believe in the authenticity and accuracy of the Bible. To the world, the Bible is nothing more than an ancient storybook, full of fictitious adventures and hardline moral edicts. Indeed, without the help of the Holy Spirit, no one would be able to believe in the Bible's challenging precepts.

The words of today's passage, spoken to rejecters of God's Son in all generations, teach us that acceptance and healing go hand in hand. Too few choose it. Even with all the evidence of fulfilled prophecy, miracles of science and nature, the complexity of human life and love, and the availability of hope and renewal, many people choose to keep their eyes closed and ears stopped to the gospel's saving message. The good news is that anyone can turn and be healed by Jesus.

Stepping In: Read Deuteronomy 29:4; Isaiah 6:9-10; Jeremiah 5:21; and Ezekiel 12:2. Are there things in the Bible that are not clear to you or that you struggle to believe? Pray to the Holy Spirit to guide you in truth. Pray for open eyes and ears, and a willing heart to take God at His Word. Being a percipient recipient is an intentional choice.

Stepping Out: This week, experience God with all your senses: eyes seeing God's creation; ears listening to what God is teaching you through the Spirit's whispers, sermons and songs; heart feeling deeply with the mental perceptions and emotions God gave you. Thank God for these precious gifts. Praise the Spirit for being your guide.

October 19
Rightful

"To him who overcomes, I will give the right to sit with me on my throne, just as I overcame and sat down with my Father on his throne."
—Revelation 3:21 (Rv 3:14–22)

The good Jewish men who would become Jesus' disciples, and later His apostles, had a reverent fear of the almighty God. As His chosen people, they believed that their God was not only the Creator and Controller of the universe, but also their Lord and Redeemer. As compassionate and mighty as God was in their minds, however, He was not particularly approachable.

It wasn't until they went under the tutelage of their Master, Jesus, that these men came to know God as a loving, heavenly Father. Through Jesus' life, death, and resurrection, the apostles learned that God was not only a personal God, but He was a *person*!

After Jesus returned to the Father and sent His Holy Spirit on the apostles, the gospel truth was perpetuated under the new name of Christianity. Though many would be martyred in its promotion, the apostle John was thankfully spared that end. As Jesus' scribe, the letter John wrote while on the island of Patmos was addressed to the seven churches in Asia Minor as an encouragement and warning of what was to come. In His address to the seventh church, in Laodicea, Jesus reiterated the theme that recurred in each message. Those who "overcome" will be blessed beyond measure. The faithful and perseverant would be rightful heirs to Jesus' royal throne, seated beside Him in glory.

In this life, there are very few guarantees. But still we think that if we do *this* and don't do *that*, we can somehow influence a positive outcome. It has been said that the youth of today are living in an "entitlement age," meaning they falsely believe that it is their right to enjoy a life of privilege and be rewarded for every effort.

Nowhere in the Bible does it say anything of the sort. Jesus Himself tells us that the first will be last and the last shall be first. Not only should we not expect a life of ease, we should expect trouble. Christians are certainly not exempt from the hardships of life. We should not be surprised when hard times come. Furthermore, because of our affiliation with Jesus, we should expect opposition, rejection, persecution, threats, and even violent anger at times.

However, Jesus implores us to take heart. He has overcome the world. So too have all who rightfully put their faith in Him. No matter what life dishes out, we who stand firm to the end are *guaranteed* a seat next to our Lord and Savior forever. Of this and little else can we be certain.

Stepping In: Read John 1:9–13; Romans 6:5–10; Ephesians 1:4–10; Colossians 3:1–4; 1 Peter 2:9; and 2 Peter 1:3–11. How do these verses help you to have a right perspective on worldly versus heavenly "rights"? Praise Jesus for blessing you with the gift of your royal inheritance.

Stepping Out: This week, with an accountability partner, live as an overcomer by acknowledging your deficits in, and working to improve upon, the Christian characteristics mentioned in 2 Peter 1:5–7.

October 20
Dependent

"With man this is impossible, but with God all things are possible."
—Matthew 19:26 (Mt 19:16–26)

Heading south from Galilee to Jerusalem, on His way to fulfill the last duties of His earthly ministry, Jesus encountered a rich young man seeking the formula by which he could get eternal life. Jesus told him the true cost of inheriting the kingdom of heaven: giving up everything of this world for a life devoted to following Him. This was not the simple answer the rich man wanted. In the end, he chose worldly wealth over eternal treasure.

Turning to His disciples, Jesus compared the difficulty the rich have in inheriting eternal life to the absurdity of a camel passing through the eye of a needle. The disciples understood that either endeavor was nearly impossible. They asked Him, "Who then can be saved?" Jesus reminded His men that "with God all things are possible." It was a matter of being dependent on God's grace, not on oneself or worldly securities.

In our world today, at least in many developed nations, a sense of fierce independence and drive for financial success dominates adult life. By most standards, the amount of money, status, and stuff we have *is* our measure of success. Dependence is a sign of weakness. We value strength, power, confidence, and beauty. We look up to those who possess superior intelligence and business savvy—especially if these qualities are dressed in a designer suit.

These are not the things God values. As Jesus explains, these positive qualities can become hindrances to a Christian's walk. In the end, it will always come down to a matter of the heart. What we treasure there is where our devotion will lie. In other words, what we learn to depend on is where we put our hope. Our heavenly Father wants us to value Him more than our money, our family, or even our own lives. And though Jesus said it is hard for a rich man to enter heaven, He assures us that nothing is impossible for those who depend on and put their hope in God. At the end of the day, we must all ask ourselves what we trust in more: God or money?

Stepping In: Read Genesis 18:13–15; Job 42:1–2; Jeremiah 32:17; and Luke 1:37, 18:27. How do these verses help you to trust God's sovereign power more? Do you depend more on God or on your own efforts for security? In what ways has He proven His miraculous abilities in your life? Take some time now to thank Him for what He has done for you, and will do in the future.

Stepping Out: This week, assess your worldly possessions. Is there anything God is prompting you to let go of? If so, donate that item to a worthy cause. Look to God for a right perspective on worldly wealth and generosity. Then, follow the Spirit's leading to give joyfully.

October 21
Personal

> "But when you pray, go into your room, close the door and pray to your Father, who is unseen. Then your Father, who has seen what is done in secret, will reward you."
>
> —Matthew 6:6 (Mt 6:1–15)

In His Sermon on the Mount, Jesus challenged the conventional wisdom about religious practices, as well as the role of personal accountability to God. In today's verse, He offered a different approach to prayer than the people would have been familiar with. Instead of trusting the priests to intercede on their behalf, or simply performing the rituals to which they were accustomed, Jesus suggested that prayer should be a private and personal matter between an individual and God Himself.

The notion that God could be accessible to the common man anytime and anywhere would have been an entirely new concept to Jesus' listeners. In Jewish belief, God's holy presence was hidden deep in the inner recesses of the temple, inside the ark of the covenant, where it was kept from the sinful masses. Only the high priest could approach it once a year to atone for the people's iniquities. The people would come as close as they were allowed, offer their sacrifices to appease God, and then pray. Prayer outside the temple, though it certainly took place, was probably considered a less effective method. Not only was Jesus reminding His listeners not to pray for the benefit of others who might hear it, He was also introducing a way of praying that the common person would have never considered.

For us today, the issue of needing to be in a specific place to pray no longer exists. Modern Christians are free to pray whenever and wherever we choose. We have the luxury of finding our own special environment in which we connect most closely with God. Because our bodies are God's temples, worship happens wherever we are. Our biggest barrier for drawing near to God is our schedules. Though the message not to pray solely for the sake of being heard is still a valid command, the more relevant pronouncement for this fast-paced society is to commit to actually praying at all.

Jesus, being the practical Savior that He is, tells us what we must do and what we stand to gain if we comply. God deserves our undivided attention. We would be foolish to miss any opportunity to meet privately and personally with our loving Father.

Stepping In: This week, commit to a time of personal and private prayer. Carve time out of your busy schedule to shut out distractions and meet with God. Pray for a willingness to make this practice a routine, regardless of the sacrifice required to make it happen.

Stepping Out: Use a portion of this time to pray for others, especially for salvation for the lost. Pray for our leaders. Pray for revival in our country and world.

October 22

Transparent

"Make a tree good and its fruit will be good, or make a tree bad and its fruit will be bad, for a tree is recognized by its fruit. You brood of vipers, how can you who are evil say anything good? For out of the overflow of the heart the mouth speaks."

—Matthew 12:33–34 (Mt 12:1–34)

Jewish religious leaders regularly cornered and questioned Jesus about the source of His power and authority, as well as His rebellious disregard for Sabbath laws. In today's verse, Jesus responded by revisiting an agricultural illustration from His Sermon on the Mount, regarding the inherent nature of a tree. He was clearly alluding to the innate qualities of the human condition. Jesus reminded His audience that, regardless of outward appearances, the Pharisees' true nature was evil; one needed only to listen to them speak to know.

Today's Bible readers are not as likely to miss the forest for the trees (so to speak). As Christians, we understand that first-century seekers struggled to comprehend spiritual matters because they had not yet received the Holy Spirit. We also know that, the Law God had given to the people for their good, under the management of the Pharisees, became a barrier between its teachers and the common folk. Their words, instead of giving life, brought spiritual death. Jesus called these snakes to task on many occasions. He also warned that an apple usually does not fall far from its tree.

Before the Holy Spirit came and allowed people to see the world from an eternal perspective, they had to rely on their physical senses to inform them of what was real and true. Knowing this, Jesus purposefully used tree fruit to illustrate how easy it is to distinguish the good (appealing, tasty, healthy) from the bad (marred, rotten, diseased). The fruit's quality was obvious to the naked eye. Today's verses remind us that our spiritual fruit, or lack thereof, is equally easy to detect. What is not evidenced by the eye will become clearly known by what we say. The purer the heart, the more transparent it will be.

Stepping In: Read Matthew 7:15–23; Romans 2:1–16; and Galatians 5:22–23. What is the condition of your heart? How transparent are you? Do your words and actions reflect the godly character you would like? Pray for more transparency in your words and actions.

Stepping Out: This week, let the goodness in your heart be what flows out in speech, prayer, and actions. Let your good fruit be appealing to everyone.

October 23
Filial

"If you love me, you will obey what I command. And I will ask the Father, and he will give you another counselor to be with you forever— the Spirit of truth."

—John 14:15–17 (Jn 14:15–31)

In a borrowed upper room in Jerusalem, Jesus and His men ate their final Passover meal together, musing over the splendor of His triumphal entry into the city and the greatness of the kingdom to come. However, the jubilant mood soon changed. Jesus prepared His men for what loomed just ahead, speaking difficult truths about His impending betrayal, denial, and death. He reassured them that His leaving was necessary, and that after He had prepared a place for them in His Father's house, He would return for them. He also promised that He would not leave them alone; He would send "the Spirit of truth" to guide them in their missionary duties. In the days to come, they would cherish the loving supernatural connection Jesus was soon to establish with them.

Today, the moment a person confesses that Jesus is Lord, the Holy Spirit takes up residence within them. Talk about instant gratification! Nothing else in life will ever come as effortlessly and instantaneously as receiving His Spirit. It is the most powerful tool you will ever be given for free.

But there is a fee for its use: obeying the will of the Father. As Jesus explained to His apostles, this spiritual endowment is for holy use only, not to be taken lightly or misused. As wonderful as the Holy Spirit is, it is unfortunately misunderstood by Christians and non-Christians alike. Some view it as a genie in a bottle or a cosmic vending machine—put in your request and out pops the answer.

Jesus never intended the Spirit to be used that way. Time and again, Jesus explains that every good thing that God has promised those who love Him will come when we obey and ask. In this way, we strengthen the filial connection between us and our heavenly Father, enabling the Spirit within us to thrive.

Stepping In: Read Psalm 103:17-19, 139:7-17; John 15:10; Romans 8:14, 26–27; and 1 John 2:3–6 and 3:21–24. What do these verses teach you about the working of the Holy Spirit in your life? Pray for your love and obedience to increase, so that His Spirit may be increasingly awakened in you.

Stepping Out: This week, demonstrate your filial devotion by approaching the Father properly. Love and obey Him first, then ask for the Spirit's blessings. Also, if possible, be a blessing to your earthly parents this week.

October 24
Innocent

"I praise you, Father, Lord of heaven and earth, because you have hidden these things from the wise and learned, and revealed them to little children. Yes, Father, for this was your good pleasure."
—Matthew 11:25–26 (Mt 11:1–26)

Jesus instructed John the Baptist's disciples to report back to their master all that they had witnessed. But, before they left to obey this command, Jesus imparted to them more words of wisdom about the fulfillment of prophecies and imminence of the judgment to come. During this profound speech, Jesus offered the salutation to the Father in today's verses. Jesus informed the skeptical audience that things were not as they seemed: the little children, not the wise and learned, were the ones who understood the ways of God. The innocent and pure were the ones worthy and able to receive God's truth as it was—not the way the majority thought it should be.

All Christians start out young in faith. Wisdom, discernment, and spiritual maturity come with time and practice. Truly, if one wants to become knowledgeable and proficient in anything, one must devote time and energy to it. Christianity is no different from any other study in this regard. All of us start out ignorant and innocent.

Jesus regularly emphasizes the importance of maintaining childlike faith during one's spiritual journey. This means being open to the Spirit's leadings, regardless of how contrary they may be to our preconceived notions of what Christian life should be like. We must be dependent on God and not on the world. Those who consider themselves righteous, holy, intelligent, and above reproach will miss out on the benefits of their knowledge. Because of their arrogance and rigidity, the kingdom of heaven will pass them by.

Experiences in trust building and faith stretching are necessary parts of the spiritual maturation – sanctification - process. Patience and endurance also come into play in every Christian walk. Though we never reach mastery in faith this side of heaven, Jesus praises His Father every time one of His beloveds reaches the next rung on the spiritual ladder, taking one innocent faith-step at a time.

Stepping In: Read 1 Corinthians 1:18–19 and 3:1–9. At what stage in your spiritual journey are you? Pray that God reveals next steps for you in your walk with Jesus.

Stepping Out: This week, build up someone who is newer in faith than you are. Pray for God to assist you in nurturing the "little children" in your life. If possible, volunteer in your church's children's ministry this weekend.

October 25
Acquitted

"I tell you the truth, today you will be with me in paradise."
—Luke 23:43 (Lk 23:26–43)

Having been convicted of crimes He did not commit, Jesus was sentenced to death on a cross. Alongside Him were two rightly accused criminals, facing the sentence they deserved. One of the crucified men joined the crowd in hurling insults at Jesus, saying, "Aren't you the Christ? Save yourself and us." The other criminal, however, rebuked him and recognized Jesus' innocence, even venturing to ask if he would be remembered in heaven.

Filled with compassion and acknowledging this man's faith, Jesus spoke the amazing words of acquittal in today's verse. With most of His devoted followers hiding somewhere in Jerusalem, waiting for the news of His death, Jesus found companionship with the most unlikely of characters just moments before they both would die. No doubt they smiled at the promise of seeing one another in a much better place soon.

What beautiful words to hear from our Savior! Most of us would like to live long and productive lives before we hear them, but some will not have that opportunity. For those whose lives will be cut short by illness or injury, the dream of fulfilling long-term goals will not be realized. Those who are in Christ nevertheless rest in the assurance that they will enjoy much better things in the life to come.

There are those like the criminal on the cross who will wait until they are on death's doorstep to receive forgiveness from Jesus. Though late is better than never, each day without His blessing equals wasted potential. Jesus died so that we could have life to the full, both now and eternally. This is why the gospel is such good news. It is a Christian's duty to let others know that they can look forward to hearing from Jesus one day, either "I never knew you" or "Welcome to paradise." Once a person breaths their last, a verdict is brought down: guilty or acquitted.

Stepping In: Read Isaiah 25:6–9; Luke 13:29–30; John 14:2–4; and Revelation 2:7 and 21:6–8, 18–27. How do these verses help you to better understand your future home in paradise? What is your response to Jesus' sacrifice and promise? Praise Him now for the gift of acquittal you receive upon belief.

Stepping Out: This week, go with a friend or your small group to share the love of Jesus with people in a hospital or nursing home. Pray for an opportunity to share this verse or other promises.

October 26
Yielded

"Repent, for the kingdom of heaven is near."
—Matthew 4:17 (Mt 3:13–4:17)

The warning in today's verse was first spoken by Jesus' cousin, John the Baptist, while he was in the desert, proclaiming the coming Christ and encouraging all to return to God. Through John's efforts, the groundwork for Jesus' ministry was set. For a time, Jesus and John carried out parallel ministries in Israel. After John was arrested, Jesus went to His home region of Galilee to reestablish the ministry His cousin had proclaimed in the wilderness: the ministry of repentance.

The command to repent in response to the kingdom's imminence was both a warning and an invitation. Things were about to change; Jesus wanted His family, friends, and neighbors to be the first to know about the spiritual revival He was about to usher in. With an urgency in His tone, He implored His listeners to stop wandering down paths that lead away from God, and begin walking in the light, life, and freedom of the new kingdom He would bring.

How often in this life do we miss something that is right in front of us? How often do we take for granted the things we care about? Sometimes we are so busy pushing through our own agendas that we forfeit good opportunities. Too often we carry regrets for not giving more of our time and energy to a loved one before it is too late. We let the momentum of habitual life propel us along too quickly, blurring the scenery as we go.

In eight words, Jesus gives a simple perspective alert. Yet most people do not give much thought to sin and repentance. Many people are satisfied with life and don't believe they need to seek God or His forgiveness. For most, God is an abstract notion, a mystical and distant deity.

Jesus shatters that notion in today's verse. God is nearer than you think! He is calling us to stop, turn around, recognize His sovereignty, and move toward Him. He longs for us to realize just how close He is. Maybe He even wants us to contemplate how short life is, and not to waste another moment chasing empty pursuits. His Word reveals to us that our eternity is a choice *we* make. Yielding to Jesus' commands is the proper response, and the only way that leads to the best results.

Stepping In: Read John 1:19–34. What does the "kingdom of heaven" mean to you? Let the things you don't know or understand about that time and place be reconciled by what the Word of God does tell you. Use a concordance or computer word search to look up what Jesus says about His kingdom. Pray for insight, and ask Him how you can be a kingdom bringer.

Stepping Out: The command in today's verse is to repent. That means to do an about-face. Is there something God is putting on your heart to turn from? Start turning your attention toward God today. Take a first step, keeping your eyes on your Savior, trusting His forgiveness, and yielding to His will.

Validated

> "If I testify about myself, my testimony is not valid. There is another who testifies in my favor, and I know that his testimony about me is valid."
>
> —John 5:31–32 (Jn 5:31–47)

On one occasion, the Jewish religious leaders confronted Jesus regarding the validity of His testimony about Himself as the Son of the Father, God. Jesus explained that He did not stand alone in His testimony, which would have rendered it unacceptable according to the Law. He had several highly credible witnesses in His defense, such as John the Baptist and Moses. More than these, Jesus called the Father, God, as His key witness. Without evidence to prove otherwise, Jesus had successfully validated His profession of divine authority.

The Christian faith is built on the unfaltering belief that Jesus' testimony about Himself is true. Indeed, if Jesus is not who He claims to be—the Son of God and the Savior of the world—then our religion is false and pointless. Through the conviction of the Spirit and the God-breathed, inerrant Word of God – His Holy Bible – believers today are convinced of Jesus' truth claim.

Throughout history, many have staked their very lives on the validity of Jesus' testimony. Some have gone on to glory to prove their faith. The men and women who have paid the ultimate price throughout the centuries for proclaiming Jesus as Lord are too numerous to mention. Since people don't generally give their lives for a hunch or an ideal, their testimony gets added to the others in the defense of our Lord.

Today, Jesus continues to be validated by each Christian's testimony. To a critical world, these may be the most credible of all the sources of evidence we can compile in the case of Jesus as Lord.

Stepping In: Spend some time looking up Old Testament prophecies of Jesus and New Testament prophecies fulfilled. How do these verses validate Jesus' claim to deity? Praise God that His Word is faultless and true.

Stepping Out: This week, write up and share your testimony of how you came to faith.

Valued

"What do you think? If a man owns a hundred sheep, and one of them wanders away, will he not leave the ninety-nine on the hills and go to look for the one that wandered off? And if he finds it, I tell you the truth, he is happier about that one sheep than about the ninety-nine that did not wander off. In the same way your Father in heaven is not willing that any of these little ones should be lost."

—Matthew 18:12–14 (Mt 18:10–14)

In a time of private instruction with His disciples, Jesus explained that they must have the innocence and humility of children if they were to reach their heavenly potential. Among the profound truths Jesus was instilling in His men, this notion must have seemed oddly out of place. As Jesus continued to explain, to achieve the necessary link to the unlimited power of God, they needed to take on hearts of absolute trust and reliance. They needed to protect and promote the spiritual path of those who required help, treating even those with lesser faith with respect and dignity. Jesus used an analogy of a shepherd's love for one his lost sheep to illustrate how greatly valued the most vulnerable are by God.

Jesus is the Good Shepherd, and He still pursues the lost in this way. This is a lesson Jesus wants His current disciples to understand and apply today. It is a call to leave our holy huddles and go after the lost, misled, and rebellious.

In the verses leading up to today's passage, Jesus made clear to His soon-to-be evangelists the importance of seeking and doing only the will of God. He reiterated that a childlike dependence on the Father, with a pure heart and a heaven-focused gaze, was what they would need to successfully complete their missions. This is true for all Christians, then and now. We were all once lost sheep. Because someone sought us out and brought us back, we are now safe in the fold—redeemed. Out of gratitude and love for God, we are to follow this example and do the same for others, valuing each soul as God does!

Stepping In: Read Psalm 23; Isaiah 53; Mark 2:17; John 10:11; Hebrews 13:20–21; and 1 Peter 5:1–4. Praise God that Jesus, the slain Lamb, is our Shepherd. Meditate on these verses. How is the Spirit prompting you to emulate the example of the sheep and the shepherd in the flock? Pray for guidance for how to fill both of these roles in your church and beyond. Thank Him for valuing you and teaching you to value others.

Stepping Out: This week, let your loving actions show others how much they are valued by you and God.

October 29
Unprejudiced

"Do not call anything impure that God has called clean."
—Acts 10:15 (Acts 10:1–48)

After Jesus had been taken up to heaven, the apostle Peter set out to preach the gospel, heal the sick, and encourage groups of believers throughout Israel. He brought a dead woman back to life in the town of Joppa, and the townspeople encouraged him to stay a while.

Afternoon prayer time arrived. Peter prayed on a roof and became very hungry. In a trance-like state he saw a vision of a sheet lowered from heaven. The sheet listed a variety of animals, and a voice told him to "kill and eat" (Acts 10:13). Because of his strict adherence to Jewish purity laws, Peter refused. Then Peter heard the voice again, saying the words in today's verse.

Meanwhile, in the nearby town of Caesarea, Cornelius, a God-fearing centurion, was also having a vision. He was instructed to send for Peter, whom he did not know. Once the two were brought together, Peter understood the meaning of his vision. Under Jesus' authority, all people were equal. The rules that encouraged discrimination had been replaced by an unprejudiced, humanitarian, moral law.

In our day and age, Christianity comes in many variations. All Christian groups believe that Jesus is Lord. But there are dozens of separate denominations, and as many doctrinal interpretations therein, to choose from. Churchgoers now have choices. One can choose a small and traditional congregation, with pews and hymns. Or one can choose to attend a megachurch with dazzling entertainment, dynamic pastoral performances, and cutting-edge music.

Regardless of your worship preference, the unprejudiced acceptance of believers established thousands of years ago should hold sway. The lesson we learn from today's passage is that all people should be allowed access to Jesus. As Jesus taught in His earthly lifetime and firmly established through His death on the cross, the worship of God is and has always been a matter of the heart, not a man-made formula or list of rules to follow. The last thing Jesus wants is for modern-day Pharisees to limit a seeker's approach to His saving grace, simply because the seeker looks, acts, or worships differently. He shed His blood so that all could come directly to Him. Our job is to make sure that happens unhindered.

Stepping In: Read Exodus 23:9; Leviticus 19:14–15; and Romans 14. How do these verses encourage you to help and not hinder those seeking to meet with Jesus? Pray and confess any prejudices you currently struggle with. Ask Jesus to soften your heart toward all people.

Stepping Out: This week, identify any religious biases you may have toward other Christians' worship practices. Confess them to God. Then expand your thinking by attending a service at a different church.

Accessible

"He who receives you receives me, and he who receives me receives the one who sent me."

—Matthew 10:40 (Mt 10:1–40)

Before Jesus sent His disciples on a mission to bring the lost sheep of Israel back to God, He imparted to them instructions and warnings for the journey on which they were about to embark. Opposition was to be expected. As people had rejected Jesus, so too would they reject His messengers. However, as implied in today's verse, some would choose to accept both messenger and Master. Those new receivers of the gospel would make the mission worth its risks.

The promise in today's verse continues to encourage believers who choose to embrace their evangelic callings. Those in the modern-day mission fields regularly praise God for this truth. As in ancient times, the best way to evangelize is through relationships. Sometimes people are reached through a powerful sermon, sometimes by religious tracts. In most cases, people learn about Jesus' saving grace through face-to-face encounters with a caring Christian relative, friend, neighbor, coworker, or acquaintance. Each of us has someone to thank for introducing us to our Savior.

We will never know who is ready to receive God's love and truth until we offer it. As Jesus' modern-day apostles, we too must make ourselves and the gospel accessible. Jesus knows that it is not easy—that is why He used so many words to prepare His apostles for the task. Rejection and all manner of angry resistance are often the reward we get for our efforts. But, as Christ encouraged His disciples not to give up, we too must press on for the cause, employing wisdom and discernment in every circumstance. In God's timing, those who will come to Christ, will come; those who do receive Jesus' messengers will receive a reward in triplicate.

Stepping In: Read Luke 10:16 and John 12:44–46. Do you let fear of rejection keep you from sharing the gospel? Pray that Christ's light shines through you so that people receive you well.

Stepping Out: This week, live out Romans 12:9–13. Reach out to others. Build relationships. Make the gospel accessible by making yourself available.

Relaxed

"Do not be afraid, little flock, for your Father has been pleased to give you the kingdom."

—Luke 12:32 (Lk 12:22–34)

After correcting a foolish young man whose ambitions in life revolved around getting his fair share of an inheritance from his father, Jesus turned to His disciples and began to teach about worldly worries. In each of His examples, Jesus contrasted a temporal concern with the lavish generosity of God. There was no human want or need that God was not aware of. To those who put their faith in Him, He would give more than they could possibly imagine. Jesus wanted His men to relax in the knowledge they were safe within His fold, and He urged them not to be afraid. As adopted children of the Most-High God, they literally had nothing to worry about.

Today's verse has been a sweet reassurance for all Christians throughout history. Jesus is the Good Shepherd, and true believers are His sheep. More than ever before, it seems, this fast-paced world is a place of mayhem and confusion. There is certainly plenty to worry about if one so chooses. In a fallen world, this has always been the case.

Jesus wants us to know that we have a choice. We can be fearful, or we can trust. We can be uncertain, or we can be secure. We can be tense, or we can be relaxed. More specifically, we can rely on our own strength and abilities—and be left in a constant state of worry—or we can trust in the almighty God and rest assured that our future is secure.

Jesus is not saying that this is by any means easy. He knows that it is not. He knows that it is our tendency to strive for comforts and pleasures, which left unchecked leads to greed and gluttony. He also knows that every worldly acquisition is temporary and can never fully satisfy. Though we foolishly and repeatedly choose wrongly, Jesus gathers His flock back to Himself and reminds us that *our* Father loves us. Assured, we can step out and offer the hope of Jesus' beautiful promises to those still wandering in the wilderness.

Stepping In: Read Numbers 27:15–17; Psalm 23; Isaiah 53:6; Matthew 9:36; John 10:11; and 1 Peter 2:24–25. How confident are you in the truth found in these verses? Are you worried or relaxed about the future? Confess this to Jesus now and ask for His reassurance. Praise Him for the promise in today's verse.

Stepping Out: This week, if you are inclined to dress up for the pagan holiday, go as a sheep. Use your costume as a way to invite a conversation about your relationship with the Good Shepherd. Better yet, get together with other sheep and flock the town.

November 1
Contagious

"Get up, take your mat and go home."
—Matthew 9:6 (Mt 9:1–13)

When Jesus attempted to conduct private business in people's homes, the crowds were so eager to see Him that soon the house was filled to overflowing. On one such occasion, some friends of a paralyzed man tried to bring their friend to Jesus for healing. Unable to enter the house through the crowded doorway, the daring and determined friends carried the man onto the roof and lowered him through the ceiling in front of Jesus. Everyone was stunned. Jesus was impressed and moved to compassion. He told the man that his sins were forgiven. The Jewish religious leaders in attendance bristled at these seemingly blasphemous words. Knowing the evil in their hearts, Jesus proved His power to heal as well as His authority to forgive sins. As Jesus commanded, the man got up, took his mat, and went home.

Today, we would like to say that the fear of and stigma against sick people, the mentally ill, the disabled, and the developmentally challenged does not exist—certainly not like it did in ancient times. Right? Though prejudice may be now less overt, our society still often fails to treat such individuals with the fairness, decency, and respect they deserve. The practice of avoidance, if not outright ostracism, is still sadly common.

Christians fall into the sin of complacency regarding their role in helping a friend or fellow citizen find healing. Though prayer, and maybe a handout, are a good start, these approaches lack the kind spiritual fervor the paralytic's friends had. They didn't wait for Jesus to come to their friend's aid, they brought their need to Jesus in person. The result speaks for itself. Christians today can learn a lesson from the paralyzed man's friends about turning a fear of contagion into a contagious spiritual and cultural movement of compassion.

Stepping In: Take some time to think about your attitude toward the mentally or physically disabled. Do you tend to go toward them or away from them? Do you have any friends who are disabled? Ask God to soften your heart and give you a willingness to personally bridge the gap.

Stepping Out: Read Romans 12:9–13 and live out these commands this week. Be a contagious Christian!

Relinquished

Jesus called out in a loud voice, "Father, into your hands I commit my spirit." When He had said this, He breathed His last.

—Luke 23:46 (Lk 23:26–49)

After living a perfect, sinless life, Jesus accomplished what He had been sent by the Father to do: create a way for all people to be reconciled to God through one final, atoning sacrifice. By shedding His own innocent blood on the cross, Jesus took away the sin of the world and offered eternal salvation to all who believe in Him.

For the three years leading up to that day, Jesus made every effort to share the good news of the coming kingdom, and the new covenant of love, to those with ears to hear Him. He explained to those who would listen that He was the promised Messiah, the fulfillment of the ancient prophecies. Yet most people either could not recognize Him or refused to relinquish their hearts and lives to His authority. On His last day, even His own disciples abandoned Him, leaving Him to die a criminal's death nearly alone.

Jesus still, as He always had, submitted to the will of the Father. Mustering His last bit of strength, He performed the final miracle of His life. He pulled Himself up by the nail through His wrists, took in a breath, and shouted, "It is finished" (Jn 19:30).

At face value, this section of scripture seems very bleak. For Christians, however, it is a passage of triumph. For people who do not know the full story from Genesis to Revelation, Jesus' death may seem like an unnecessary tragedy. For those who know about God's planned redemption for His beloved creation, we see it as a beautiful act of love and faith.

Crimes cannot go unpunished. Sin, being the most grievous of crimes against God, is punishable only by death. Even now, God and sin cannot cohabitate. Those who are lost in sin because they have not accepted Jesus as Savior may never enter God's presence.

After death, there is only an eternity with God (heaven) or an eternity without Him (hell). God created us to be in a relationship with Himself and to do His will. Jesus set the perfect example of this, even going to the cross to pay the penalty for our sins. To relinquish control to Him is to live in true safety and security.

Stepping In: Read Numbers 21:4–9; Psalm 22; Matthew 26:38–39; John 3:14-15, 12:30-34; and Hebrews 13:20–21. What do these verses teach you about God's plan for redemption? Have you relinquished your will to Him, or are you still insisting on having your own way? Pray for a fully yielded heart and for clarity to know God's specific will for you.

Stepping Out: Based on what the Spirit revealed to you, take a step of obedience this week. Commit to relinquishing your will to the Father each day.

Familial

"For whoever does the will of my Father in heaven is my brother and sister and mother."

—Matthew 12:50 (Mt 12:46–50)

Because of the personal impact Jesus was having on the people of Israel, many were leaving their old faith and religious practices to follow Him. Finding adequately large venues for His teaching was a constant challenge. Once, when a pressing crowd tried to follow Jesus into a house, Jesus' mother and brothers were among those who could not make it in. A concerned member of the household informed Jesus of the situation. He responded with the hypothetical question, "Who is my mother and who are my brothers?" (Mt 12:48).

In a culture that valued strong family ties and respect for its elders, many eyebrows likely went up in response to this statement. Jesus then explained who His true, heavenly family was: those who do the will of the Father. Jesus was not disowning His earthly family; He was expanding the definition of family instead.

Many of us are familiar with the cliché "Blood is thicker than water." Though the modern family seems to have lost much of its cohesiveness, some families still claim this statement as their unofficial credo. For Christians, it takes on a whole new meaning. This "blood" relationship means everything to Christ followers. Jesus freely gave us new life through the shedding of His own blood at Calvary. We are no longer limited by our earthly bonds. For those of us who came from less-than-perfect backgrounds, this is incredibly good news. When we claim Jesus as our Lord and Savior, we are adopted into His Father's family. All He asks is that we do our best to do the will of our Lord in heaven. Considering what this world has to offer, that is a fantastic bargain.

Stepping In: Read Luke 8:19–21; John 15:14–17; Romans 8:16–17; and Ephesians 1:3–10 and 3:6. Take time to thank God for your position in His family and for the rich inheritance that still awaits you.

Stepping Out: This week, embrace your Christian brothers and sisters. Make your best effort to work together in harmony as you do the will of the Father. In familial fashion, share a fellowship meal with some Christian friends or your small group.

Alert

"Watch and pray so that you will not fall into temptation. The Spirit
is willing, but the body is weak."

—Matthew 26:41 (Mt 26:17–45)

At last the time had come for Jesus to begin His final march toward the cross. After sharing the Passover meal with His disciples in an upper room in a Jerusalem guest house, the disciples followed Jesus through the city gates and into the garden of Gethsemane at the foot of the Mount of Olives. Drawing His three closest friends near, Jesus asked Peter, James, and John, to stand guard while He communed with His Father. Soon the three men succumbed to exhaustion and drifted off to sleep, leaving their Lord without human companionship. In today's verse, Jesus pleaded with His men to stay alert and not let their human weakness override their desire to please God. Yet, try as they might, they failed in this—not just once, but three times that night.

Mere humans can never know the anguish Jesus experienced in the garden. Even in the worst of our trials, it is only our temporal bodies and minds that suffer. For Jesus, the upcoming separation from His Father was far more agonizing than any physical wound He could ever endure. This is more than mortal minds can fathom. Our gratitude for this alone should be immense.

But Jesus did not stop there. He allowed His holy and sinless self to be put to death in the most humiliating and excruciating of ways. And what does He ask of us? That we stay awake and alert, and that we not allow our human tendency to "drift off" take our attention away from Him. He tells us to stay with Him and to pray for God's willing Spirit to help us to overcome temptation.

Jesus knows that it is hard to live in a fallen world. He simply asks us to look beyond this world to the destination He paid the highest price for us to obtain, and that we will someday enjoy free of charge. In the meantime, we are to keep our vigil and tune our hearts to the whisper of the Spirit.

Stepping In: Read 2 Chronicles 7:14; 1 Corinthians 10:13; Ephesians 6:18; James 1:13–15; and 1 John 5:13–15. Considering these scripture passages, what are your thoughts about utilizing the Spirit to deal with temptation? Pray for God to guard your heart and mind against the Devil's schemes.

Stepping Out: One evening this week, stay up an hour past your bedtime in fervent prayer to your heavenly Father. Stay alert and keep watch for what God has for you in that sacred time.

Beneficent

"I sent you to reap what you have not worked for. Others have done the hard work, and you have reaped the benefit of their labor."
—John 4:38 (Jn 4:1–38)

After Jesus' encounter with the Samaritan woman at the well, His disciples returned and puzzled over what had transpired. Jesus explained that He was doing the beneficent work of His Father, and that there was work for them to do as well. In fact, an opportunity was coming their way as they spoke. The woman and the people of her village were coming to see the Christ. Jesus informed His men that others (the woman, Himself, and John the Baptist) had readied the people to receive salvation, and the disciples' job was to seal the deal and reap the benefits.

Jesus used the analogy of a harvest field to illustrate the bounty of new believers that are ready and waiting to be gathered into the kingdom. In many ways, our world today is like Samaria of old. In most developed nations, the population is made up a mix of races, cultures, and religions. America, in particular, is considered a melting pot of people and beliefs.

Yet at the core is a foundation of Christianity. Like the Samaritans, who had a basic understanding of Judaism and other religious ideologies, many modern people believe in God. All people are made in God's image and are born with a desire to know Him. It is just a matter of weeding through the half-truths, deceptions, and lies to find Him. Most people have seeds of hope and truth planted in their hearts just waiting for a beneficent gardener to encourage them to grow. Each Christian – who themselves benefited from another's labor - is called to help in the harvest of souls in some way: planting, watering, fertilizing, and cultivating. Jesus tells us that the fields are ripe and ready for picking. Let's pick up our baskets and get to work.

Stepping In: Read Matthew 9:37, 28:18-20; Acts 1:8; 1 Corinthians 3:5–9; and 2 Corinthians 9:10–11. Think back on how you came to faith. Who planted, watered, and cultivated the seeds of hope in you? Take some time to thank God for these individuals. If you can, thank them personally. Ask Him to show you the beneficent work He wants you to do in His name.

Stepping Out: This week, take every opportunity to sow, water, tend, and reap a harvest for God. If you have no idea where to begin, take a Sharing the Gospel seminar at your local church or online.

November 6
Generous

> "So when you give to the needy, do not announce it with trumpets, as the hypocrites do in the synagogues and on the streets, to be honored by men. I tell you the truth, they have received their reward in full. But when you give, do not let the left hand know what your right hand is doing, so that your giving may be in secret. Then your Father, who sees what is done in secret, will reward you."
>
> —Matthew 6:2–4 (Mt 6:1–4)

Jesus made this pronouncement during His Sermon on the Mount, early in His ministry. He spoke directly to the Jews in attendance. Apparently, grand acts of generosity done for the sole purpose of gaining notoriety were commonplace, especially among the Jewish religious leaders.

In Jesus' day, socioeconomic lines were drawn very clearly. The chasm between those with financial means and those without, was vast. Those without a means of supporting themselves were forced to beg. These marginalized members of society relied on the generosity of strangers for their livelihoods. Jesus made a point to expose the hypocrisy of those who gave to such charity for show. It angered Jesus greatly that anyone would capitalize on the neediness of already humiliated persons simply to draw accolades for themselves—especially in the name of God! Jesus emphasized the importance of His words when He said, "I tell you the truth." God knows the difference between genuine generosity and self-serving acts.

Notice that Jesus did not say "if" you give to the needy, but "when." It is easy for us to become desensitized to the plight of the less fortunate. Like the men Jesus was rebuking, we may suddenly feel the urge to be generous when others are watching. In a way, this is just human nature.

This is why Jesus brings up our Father in heaven. He wants us to shift our thinking from a limited, me-centered perspective to an eternal, heaven-focused one. It will always be far more rewarding to please God than to impress people. Though the saved will receive the ultimate reward at the end of this life's journey, Jesus reminds us all that if we seek only the recognition of our peers, that will be the totality of what we receive. God has something far better for those who give generously for no other reason than because it is in their hearts to do so.

Stepping In: Reflect on today's passage using the Own It method (See appendix). Every place that Jesus says "you," it is to *you* He is referring. Ask God for a generous heart and a humble approach to your giving. Ask Him to help you overcome any biases or barriers that keep you from helping others unconditionally.

Stepping Out: This week, choose a charity to give to anonymously. Give generously and joyfully.

Guileless

"Woe to you when all men speak well of you, for that is how their fathers treated the false prophets."

—Luke 6:26 (Lk 6:17–26)

Jesus began His Sermon on the Mount by issuing a series of blessings and woes. For His discerning disciples, this speech highlighted the contrasting heart-positions of those they would soon be ministering to. Jesus needed His followers to understand that there were two very distinct groups of people: the faithful and the false, the godly and the worldly. Jesus reminded the Jews in the audience that they had a history of mistreating true prophets and wrongfully accepting false ones. He spoke of the false flattery religious leaders often used to try to sway prophecy in their own favor. He stated how miserable it was to hear such phony sweet talk, for it could hardly be trusted. The true prophet was better off being jeered and mocked, if by that he remained guileless.

The saying "history repeats itself" is sadly true. Lessons we thought we had learned cycle back around time and again. But why? The simple answer: it is the way of the world. The more complex reason is that fallen humanity cannot help but choose the quicker, easier, wrong solution rather than the one that is more difficult, costly, and right. We tend to choose temporary worldly fixes instead of adhering to God's patient plan.

Today's verse is a reminder for current leaders to beware of two-faced opponents trying to butter up the competition. Sadly, we see too many blatant examples of this in our world politics. There is hardly an honest person to be found on either side of any argument. Politicians and others in power seem to understand the importance of posturing to be viewed in the most favorable light. Though the hurling of slander and insults is common, we also see a fair amount of sugarcoating going on. Jesus tells us that Christians, knowing that the world will hate us as they hated Him, should be more encouraged by the former than the latter. By not returning fire, we remain guileless.

Stepping In: Read Ezekiel 13:8–12; Philippians 4:8–9; and 1 Timothy 3:1–7. How do these verses help you to recognize false pretenses in the world around you or in your own behavior? Pray that you will crave the acceptance of Christ more than the approval of people. Pray for strength to endure both ridicule and false praise.

Stepping Out: This week, in response to this warning about recognizing spiritual falsehood, let every word you say about Christ be guileless. Speak only truth about Jesus—no omissions or sugarcoating. Be prepared to share your reasons for hope (1 Pt 3:15–16).

Accountable

"The good man brings good things out of the good stored up in him,
and the evil man brings evil things out of the evil stored up in him. But
I tell you that men will have to give account on the day of judgment
for every careless word they have spoken."
—Matthew 12:35–36 (Mt 12:1–36)

During an encounter with the Pharisees, after they had accused Him of driving out demons by the power of Beelzebub, Jesus explained that, like fruit from a tree, only good could come from good and only bad could come from bad. Referring to the calloused-hearted Jewish leaders, Jesus warned that all would be held accountable for their beliefs, attitudes, efforts, and words.

All of us have said things we wish we could take back. As one cannot un-ring a bell, words that have left one's mouth cannot be unsaid. Words brought on by intense emotions seem to have minds of their own, making a beeline for their target audience before our logical thoughts can harness them.

Yes, we are responsible for the harm our careless words cause. Yet more important than our thoughts and words are our core values and beliefs. As Jesus mentions in Matthew 12:34, "Out of the overflow of the heart, the mouth speaks." One's heart is at the heart of the matter. Hearts that are far from God cannot help but spill out negative, uncaring, and untrue words.

When we Christians are careless with our words, we send a confusing, if not contradictory message to a skeptical world. Today's passage reminds us that we are held to a higher standard—and rightfully so. We must hold our hearts accountable for our thoughts and words, especially those that are spoken.

Stepping In: Read Matthew 12:37; Romans 14:10–11; 1 Corinthians 4:5; and Revelation 20:1–15. What sin of words or ways is the Holy Spirit prompting you to repent of? Pray for forgiveness and guidance. Be accountable for what you do and say.

Stepping Out: This week, quickly make amends for any thoughtless or damaging words you say. Enlist an accountability partner to help you succeed in making the changes God wishes for you.

Right-Minded

"Stop judging by mere appearances, and make a right judgment."
—John 7:24 (Jn 4:1–24)

In His third and final year as an earthly teacher, Jesus went down to Jerusalem to participate in the Feast of Tabernacles. He made His way to the temple courts before He let His presence be known. Then, holding nothing back, He began to preach.

Quickly His accusers, the Jewish religious leaders, surrounded Jesus and began to question Him. After scolding these men for their hypocrisy, Jesus then in today's verse, reminded them that they were no longer aware of the truth behind the original Law they had been given, rendering them spiritually blind and unable to rightly judge.

If Jesus were walking among us today, He might explain this story of the misguided Jews as a case of not being able to see the forest for the trees. He would tell us not to judge a book by its cover. Before we discredit the Pharisees for their nearsightedness, it would be good for us to remember that most of us suffer from a perspective deficit ourselves. As much as we don't like to admit it, we regularly judge others based on how they look, what they say, or what we think they believe. In a split-second, before we can hold captive our thoughts and sometimes our tongues, we assign people a title: rich, poor, godly, worldly, intelligent, uninformed, uncouth, rigid. This happens even in our churches!

Jesus cautions us not to place our opinions, rules, or denominational doctrine above our love for all of God's people. When we fail in this, we see division among believers. People avoid or leave the faith because of rigidity, hypocrisy, and judgment in the church. Today more than ever, Jesus is imploring His followers to be right-minded, judging rightly based on the doctrine of truth and love, not on mere appearances. We need to take a lesson from the Pharisees on how *not* to represent God. Christians should uphold biblical truth in a palatable, nonjudgmental way, thus attracting more people than we repel.

Stepping In: Read Deuteronomy 1:16–17; 1 Samuel 16:7; Isaiah 11:2–4; Matthew 7:1–2; John 8:15–16; Romans 14:1–4; and 2 Corinthians 10:7. How well do you see yourself and your church doing in this area of unconditional love and acceptance? Pray for yourself and your church to be right-minded in respect to judgment. Replace rigid, critical, or judgmental attitudes with genuine acceptance of all seekers and believers.

Stepping Out: This week, start a positive dialogue with a fellow believer who looks and acts differently than you do. Using the "iron sharpens iron" philosophy found in Proverbs 27:17, humbly engage in an exchange of biblical truth. Who knows? You may just learn a fun new way to meet with God!

Watchful

Jesus answered: "Watch out that no one deceives you. For many will
come in my name, claiming, 'I am the Christ,' and will deceive many."
—Matthew 24:4–5 (Mt 24:1–31)

Just days before Jesus would be betrayed, arrested, tried and convicted, and then crucified, He dedicated much of His time to preaching His gospel in the temple courts in Jerusalem. After several heated exchanges with Jewish religious leaders that left these falsely pious men enraged, Jesus left the temple and made his way up the Mount of Olives with his disciples. Jesus pointed to the temple and said it would be destroyed. Confused and worried, the disciples wanted to know when this would happen and what signs they should expect. In today's verse, Jesus warned them against deceivers. He encouraged them to be ever-watchful, holding fast to their faith. He assured them that, though He would soon be going away, He would return. There would be no mistaking this event—of that they could be certain.

Modern-day Bible readers know this passage as the introduction to the Olivet Discourse. In that sermon, Jesus mapped out the events we know as the signs of the end of the age. Before He answered the disciples' questions, He issued a warning for all Christians throughout the ages. We too must go into the future prepared for the bad things that will come, but not blindly so.

Jesus tells us to watch out. He commands us to be on our guard against false Christs and all kinds of deceivers. They will come, He tells us. We should not be surprised, nor should we be fooled. When He comes back, the whole world will know it. The event will be unmistakable. No one will have to ask, "Is this the Christ?"

Stepping In: Read Numbers 24:15–19; Matthew 7:15–20; John 2:18–22; and Revelation 3:10 and 16:14–15. Take some time to consider how easily people have been led astray by charismatic leaders in the past. How watchful are you for Satan's deceptions? Pray for the Spirit to equip you with strength and knowledge. And it wouldn't hurt to wear the armor of God as well (see Eph 6:10–17).

Stepping Out: This week, help others to understand more about what to expect when Jesus comes back. Share the good with enthusiasm and the bad with genuine concern—but not fear.

November 11
Effective

When Jesus saw that a crowd was running to the scene, he rebuked the evil spirit. "You deaf and mute spirit," he said, "I command you, come out of him and never enter him again."

—Mark 9:25 (Mk 9:14–32)

Jesus was informed that some of His disciples had been unable to cast out an evil spirit from a woefully stricken youth. Frustrated by their collective lack of faith, Jesus voiced His displeasure and asked that the boy be brought to Him. When the evil spirit saw Jesus, it threw the boy to the ground in violent convulsions. The boy's father, beside himself with concern, asked if He could help. Jesus returned the question rhetorically and affirmed that nothing was impossible for those who truly believe. At His command, the evil spirit shrieked and left the boy. Thus, Jesus proved that He had the power to restore a person's body, mind, and spirit. He offered the child a hand up, dusted him off, and sent him back to his father, completely well.

Sometimes Jesus chooses to work His miracles behind the scenes, where only those closely involved in the situation bear witness to them. At other times, as in today's passage, He prefers to make a public display of it. Jesus saw that there were several lessons the audience needed to learn, and opted to capitalize on the opportunity this unsettling event provided.

Frustrated as Jesus was, He still showed patience and compassion for the people who so desperately needed reassurance—as He continues to do with us today. Each of the teaching points of this lesson can easily be applied to our lives. Jesus has a lesson in mind for each person, as He did for those present in today's passage, who experience His power and presence:

- *The disciples*: Jesus wanted to turn their lack of faith-filled confidence into unwavering trust and effective efforts.
- *The crowd*: Jesus wanted to turn them from critical bystanders into compassionate actors.
- *The boy's father*: Jesus wanted to turn this parent from a burden-weary skeptic into an unshakeable believer.
- *Satan*: Jesus wanted to reveal the limited power of this conniving opportunist.
- *The boy*: Jesus wanted to turn this victim into a fully functioning proponent of God.

Jesus didn't give us His Spirit so that we could live easy, trouble-free lives. He expects us to effectively use this gift to our full advantage, confident in the power that is in Him and in us.

Stepping In: Read Phillipians 4:13. Consider each of the above teaching points. Which one seems to apply to you the most, and why? Pray for God's power to help you turn from limited to effective in your ministry.

Stepping Out: This week, exercise confident faith by utilizing the Spirit's help in your ministry efforts. Ask in the name of Jesus, and you shall receive—according to His will.

November 12
Prominent

"You are the light of the world. A city on a hill cannot be hidden.
Neither do people light a lamp and put it under a bowl. Instead they
put it on a stand, and it gives light to everyone in the house."
—Matthew 5:14–15 (Mt 5:13–16)

Jesus knew that among His audience for the Sermon on the Mount were those who came seeking wisdom and truth, as well as those who came only to serve their own interests. After calling the people to be "salt" (to live appealing, God-centered lives), Jesus said that all who worship the one true God are also to be "the light of the world." Likening God's love and truth to the radiance of a lamp, Jesus implored His listeners to boldly reflect their faith to all around. As obvious as it might have sounded, Jesus felt it necessary to state that this light should not be hidden. It should take a place of prominence in the house. Some in attendance preferred to keep this light for themselves. Thus, keeping themselves and others in spiritual darkness. Jesus' words were meant to shine a spot-light on these people's error.

Jesus chose light because it is an enduring metaphor for both physical and spiritual illumination. When we are bathed in light, we can see the world around us, identify what we are looking at, and proceed safely along our path. In the absence of light, we are blind. Without visual input, we cannot determine where we are, what is around us, or whether we are safe.

The same is true for the light of truth that is in Jesus and His followers. Today's passage tells us plainly that, as Christ's ambassadors representing God in this dark world, we must boldly shine our witness everywhere we go. We must bring our light into the gray areas where our culture waters down truth, revealing misconceptions and falsehoods about Jesus and Christianity. We must throw off the covering of fear, doubt, and ignorance that have kept the faithless in the dark. Jesus wants His people in the center of the action, shamelessly pouring out God's truth and love to all around us. By this, others will know that we are Christians. For this, our Father in heaven will be praised.

Stepping In: Read John 8:12. Take time to pray and thank Jesus for His wonderful gift of light. Recognizing that He is the ultimate source of all spiritual illumination, ask Him how you can reflect that light to others.

Stepping Out: Make a conscious effort this week to reflect God's light and love to others. Be a source of warmth and comfort. Like a prominent lampstand, stand tall in your witness for Christ. Humbly and gently speak truth to people living in the dark. Move in closer to magnify the radiance Jesus has given you to share.

Exuberant

"Return home and tell how much God has done for you."
—Luke 8:39 (Lk 8:26–39)

Wanting to expose His disciples to a culturally different environment, Jesus and His men set sail across the Sea of Galilee to a Gentile area known as the Gerasenes. After calming a storm en route, Jesus and His shaken men arrived at their destination. At once they were greeted by a demon-possessed man. This naked and deranged fellow, tortured by many evil spirits, approached Jesus and called Him by name. He also addressed Him as "Son of the Most-High God." The disciples must have wondered how this insane Gentile could have known who Jesus was. After all, many of His own people had failed to recognize His true identity.

Jesus understood that it was the evil spirits within the man who had recognized Him. He also knew that it was not time for His divinity to be made public. So Jesus made a move to silence the demons. They begged Him not to destroy them, but to send them into a nearby herd of pigs. He did so, and the pigs ran into the lake and were drowned. The man was fully restored. The herdsmen, fearful and angry, quickly spread the news about Jesus' miraculous performance. Meanwhile, the exuberant, newly cured man begged to join Jesus and His disciples. Jesus refused and told the man what he was to do instead: go home and spread the word. The man, realizing that Jesus was God, did exactly as he was told, to the benefit of many.

The parallels between this story and similar ones that have played out over the course of the centuries are innumerable. Throughout history, God has selected, called, healed, advised, and saved many from wickedness brought on by external and internal demons. Truly, each of us has our own tale to tell of evil that has caused us physical, social, and spiritual harm. Like the man in this story, many of us have experienced the misery and bondage of life apart from God's presence. Once restored, we too were exuberant and eager to remain only with Jesus. Like the demon-possessed man, we were given the command to return home and tell others about what Jesus has done for us.

For some of us, this command is difficult to obey. Fear of negative reactions, skepticism, and rejection from those who "knew us when" keeps us from bringing God's salvation message home. Today's passage should encourage us to remember all that God has done for us. This inspiration should drive us to be an exuberant witness for Jesus to all.

Stepping In: Reread Luke 8:26–39. Reflect on this passage using the Envision It method (See appendix). With whom did you identify, and why? What is God teaching you about bondage? Is there sin in your life that needs to be confessed and repented of? Is fear, pride, or selfish ambition holding you captive? Talk to God about it. Seek His advice and follow His commands.

Stepping Out: This week, be an exuberant witness. Share with your family, neighbors, relations, and friends all that Jesus has done for you—with enthusiasm! Remember, it is *your* testimony, and no one can take that from you!

November 14
Convicted

"Blessed is the man who does not fall away on account of me."
—Matthew 11:6 (Mt 11:1–19)

At the request of the imprisoned John the Baptist, some of his disciples came to Jesus with questions. John wanted to know if Jesus was the Messiah, the one he himself had prophesied would come. Jesus, instead of being irritated by the lack of faith this inquiry implied, understood the root of John's faltering faith. John, fearing for his life, was concerned about his and his disciples' future. Could he have been wrong about Jesus being the Lamb of God, as many fellow Jews believed? To compound his fear and confusion, John was also likely miffed by rumors about Jesus' disciples' increasing influence and power to perform miracles. Many, including John, wondered how Jesus' disciples—men of humble beginnings and lack of formal training—could so audaciously claim wisdom and wield authority. Seeds of jealousy and discontent were beginning to take root.

Jesus sent John's disciples back to him, telling them to report all the miraculous things they had witnessed and how lives were being changed before their eyes. Jesus let their firsthand accounts speak the affirmation His cousin was seeking—convicting John of what he already knew in his heart.

Many people in this world take issue with God and His unconventional methods. With all the evil we see and all the chaos we face, many believe that Jesus must not be the loving, forgiving, and all-powerful entity He claims to be. If He were, He would put an end to hate, violence, suffering, war, disease, corruption, and poverty. Wouldn't He? If He were God, wouldn't He make His presence known for all to see?

These were and are the kinds of questions people have been asking for centuries. Like John the Baptist, people today are influenced by what they hear and see. We are quick to doubt when tests of faith challenge our convictions. We are prone to fall away when everything around us seems to confirm the rumors that Jesus is not interested or able to intervene on our behalf. Even John, who knew, loved, and trusted Jesus, succumbed to the fearful and doubt-inducing gossip that reached his ears. After all, if Jesus loved him and was capable of anything, wouldn't Jesus get him out of prison?

If maintaining conviction in one's faith was difficult for those who witnessed Jesus' miracles firsthand, how much more is it for us today? That is where the power of the Christian witness comes in. Our absolute faith and conviction, along with the power of the Spirit, helps others not to fall away on account of the things the world wishes Jesus would do and be. Blessings abound for those who take this message to heart.

Stepping In: Read 2 Corinthians 12:20 and Ephesians 4:3, 11–13. How do these verses convict you of the ways you fall short in the areas of unity and unnecessary gossip? Pray for awareness of the ways your witness may send a confusing, negative, or doubt-inducing message. Repent, and let your testimony of personal miracles inspire others instead.

Stepping Out: This week, stand firm in faith and avoid participating in gossip. Instead, look for an opportunity to demonstrate your conviction by sharing your testimony.

Luminous

"Are there not twelve hours of daylight? A man who walks by day will not stumble, for he sees by this world's light. It is when he walks by night that he stumbles, for he has no light."

—John 11:9–10 (Jn 11:1–16)

While Jesus and His disciples were ministering to the people in the region of Perea, word reached Jesus that His dear friend Lazarus was dying. Though this was troubling news, Jesus was not worried, for He knew that the death of His friend would be an opportunity to reveal His power over death. Two days later, Jesus informed His disciples that they should return to attend to Lazarus. The disciples were fearful because of the threat to Jesus' safety and freedom in that region. Responding to their concern in a puzzling way, Jesus spoke today's parabolic verses. His statement offered a double meaning. In addition to the obvious—work is done more safely and efficiently by day than by night—Jesus was also referring to the work of the Father being illuminated by His efforts. When darkness came over the world at the time of Jesus' death, the disciples would then have a clearer understanding of what He had meant by "night."

Even today, this notion of light as good and dark as evil is anything but mysterious. In the light, all is revealed: nothing can sneak up on you, and your path is plainly visible. In the dark, nothing is clear: your eyes play tricks on you, and there is the potential for danger at every turn. Without light, we literally and figuratively stumble around, full of fear and uncertainty.

As scripture repeatedly states, without the penetrating luminosity of Jesus, we are hopelessly lost in a world of shifting shadows, our spirits cloaked in blindness. Today's verse foreshadowed the three hours of darkness preceding Jesus' death, and the hopeless three days when the light of His physical and spiritual presence was not available. It also represents the enduring darkness of unbelief. Until Jesus returns and puts an end to the night our world is experiencing, Christians must use their luminous witness to help others find their way.

Stepping In: Read Deuteronomy 28:1, 15, 29; Proverbs 4:19; Isaiah 9:2, 42:16; Luke 1:76-79, 23:44-46; and John 9:4–5 and 12:35–36. Is Jesus currently revealing an area of darkness in you or in those around you? Pray for the light of His truth to penetrate your heart so that you can combat any fear and allow for deception to be exposed.

Stepping Out: This week, perhaps as a small-group service project, hand out flashlights to the homeless while sharing the love light of God's words of hope. Be like Jesus, shining luminous love.

Contrite

"Therefore I tell you that the kingdom of God will be taken away from
you and given to a people who will produce fruit."
—Matthew 21:43 (Mt 21:33–46)

Just days before going to the cross, Jesus preached and healed in the temple courts in Jerusalem. The Pharisees approached Him, demanding to know by what or whose authority Jesus preached. He avoided giving them a direct answer. Instead, He spoke in parables.

One of the stories Jesus told was about a vineyard owner and his evil tenants. After the tenants refused to give the landowner his share of the crop, they killed his messengers and even his son. The Pharisees did not realize that the evil tenants represented the pious religious elite - themselves. They quickly articulated their condemnation of the murderous rebels. Testing their knowledge of scripture, Jesus then quoted a prophetic psalm denoting their rejection of God's "Capstone." He concluded His thoughts with today's verse, letting His audience know what their ignorance and arrogance would cost them. Only the honest, contrite, and fruitful would see the kingdom of which Jesus spoke.

Christians in all generations have been confused by today's verse. Taken out of context, it seems to mean that a person might lose their salvation if they fail to do good works. That has never been nor will ever be the case. Once a person admits their need for a Savior and accepts Jesus as Lord of their life, they are saved; their eternity in heaven is secure.

What this verse is saying is that those who claim to love God but do not accept His Son will not receive the kingdom, having never been saved in the first place. Jesus is also telling us that we will be known by our fruit. That is, our actions will reflect our love for God or lack thereof.

It saddened Jesus to see the Pharisees' pride, stubbornness, and lack of contrition. It kept them from loving God, accepting His Son, and producing lasting fruit. It saddens Him still when He sees the children He created refuse His gift of salvation. Jesus does not want "anyone to perish, but [for] everyone to come to repentance" (2 Pe 3:9). He expects contrite obedience and fruitfulness from those who have accepted Him. By this we show the world that we belong to Jesus now and forever.

Stepping In: Read John 3:16–18; and Galatians 5:22–26. Take some time to pray and thank God for the gift of salvation. If you are not sure you are saved, don't wait. Admit your need for a Savior, ask for forgiveness of your sins, and invite Jesus to be the Lord of your life. Then share the good news with as many people as possible, so they can celebrate with you!

Stepping Out: This week, really live out the fruits of the Spirit. Choose one or two and give God your best efforts. When you fail, return to Him with a contrite heart, and He will meet you with open arms.

Angelic

"The mystery of the seven stars that you saw in my right hand and of
the seven golden lampstands is this: The seven stars are the angels of
the seven churches, and the seven lampstands are the seven churches."
—Revelation 1:20 (Rv 1:9–20)

From the moment the two "Sons of Thunder" (James and John—Galilean fishermen like their father Zebedee) were called to be disciples, they dedicated their lives to the service of the Lord Jesus. Sadly, James became the first of the apostles to be martyred for the cause. John, however, went on to do much kingdom work throughout Asia Minor, including being one of the founders of most of the seven Christian churches referred to in today's verse.

The book of Revelation is known as apocalyptic literature, meaning to "unveil" or "disclose" what was previously hidden. John, the human author, by means we cannot yet understand, was transported into the presence of Jesus Himself. The experience was so overwhelming that words could not begin to describe it. Yet that was exactly what John was asked to do. Periodically throughout the text, Jesus explains what its overwhelming imagery means.

God made a promise to redeem His children by way of a Savior, which He did through the life, death, and resurrection of His Son, Jesus. He also promised to reestablish His kingdom, at which time justice and judgment will be delivered. The book of Revelation details how this will play out. Christians today are the angels of the church—the messengers of God's prophecy. Seven is the number of perfection and completion. Today, churches provide the guiding light of truth and hope across the seven continents of the world, the lamps of which will never be extinguished. As numerous as the stars, believers reflect God's light to a dark world, generously sprinkling love like stardust wherever we go. Safe in our Lord's powerful right hand, we spread the Word taken from the mouth of Jesus.

Stepping In: Read Psalm 91:9-12, 103:19-21; Habakkuk 2:2–3; Matthew 5:14–16; Luke 15:10; and Hebrews 12:22–24 and 13:2. Is Jesus the center—the only source of light and truth—in your heart, home, and church? If not, take steps to make it so. Pray for God's heavenly guidance.

Stepping Out: This week, be an angel to seven people through evangelism and acts of kindness.

November 18

Kind

"And if anyone gives even a cup of cold water to these little ones because he is my disciple, I tell you the truth, he will certainly not lose his reward."

—Matthew 10:42 (Mt 10:1–42)

Jesus spoke these reassuring words to his disciples before sending them out on their first evangelical mission. His use of the endearment "little ones" was a sweet reminder that their Master and rabbi cared for them. Not only were the Twelve His prophets and righteous men, they were also His little ones—devoted and utterly dependent children. Jesus had instructed His disciples about how they should navigate the path of their missionary journeys. He had warned them about the hardships they should face. Now Jesus brought the focus back to the point of their mission: to seek out those who would graciously receive both the messenger and the message. The apostles, then, would know who was a true disciple by their genuine acts of kindness.

Most of us have heard the saying, "A little kindness goes a long way." For all we know, it could have been coined by one of the little ones all those years ago. And how true it is. In our day and age, kindness seems to be in short supply—the result of an overburdened society. Many of us are too busy juggling jobs, families, hobbies, and other responsibilities to notice others in need. Even Christians succumb to this cultural trap. We rush our kids through breakfast, quickly dust off their Sunday clothes, strap them into car seats, and bolt to church, trying not to be late. Then we hustle them out afterward so everyone can get to their sports practices and piano lessons. Rarely do we stop to visit. Almost never do we stop to thank our pastor or the dedicated church staff. Too often, we are so busy filling our own cups that we forget other people need living water too. We forget that kindness is a two-way street.

Stepping In: Read Proverbs 14:31, 19:17; Matthew 25:40; and Hebrews 6:10. When was the last time you stopped to help someone in need? How do these verses encourage you to prioritize acts of mercy? Pray that God shows you where you could extend kindness to others, inside and outside of the church.

Stepping Out: This week, make a point to thank your pastors and church staff for the hard work and devotion they have for feeding Jesus' flock, yourself included.

Grafted

"I am the vine; you are the branches. If a man remains in me and I
in him, he will bear much fruit; apart from me you can do nothing."
—John 15:5 (Jn 15:1–17)

After the inspiring and confusing events of their last Passover meal with Jesus, the disciples could see that their Teacher was anxious to enact the plan He had long been preparing for. Jesus knew that His disciples would soon be at a loss without their Master, so He took the time to inform and encourage them. Of first importance was for them to know that as He was One with the Father, and that they must stay spiritually connected to Him.

Jesus began His teaching by telling His apostles, "I am the true vine, and my Father is the gardener" (Jn 15:1). For them to succeed in their upcoming missions, they must "remain in" Jesus, as He remains in the Father. The disciples were familiar with the grafting practices of farmers in the region and would have understood the analogy. Once a graft is complete, the two plants are inseparable, the lesser living off the greater. With Jesus as the source of all sustenance, the apostles could thrive and produce a bountiful crop. Without Him, not only could they do nothing of eternal value, they would soon spiritually wither and die. Only the branches grafted to the true vine and tended by the supreme Gardener would bear good fruit.

One does not need to be a horticulturalist to see this passage as a beautiful testament to Jesus' love for us. Of Jesus' seven "I am" statements retold in the gospel of John (6:35; 8:12; 10:7; 10:11; 11:25; 14:6; 15:1, 5), today's verse places an onus on the reader to meet Jesus halfway in the work of the Father.

Considering the opposing forces the world places on us, it will take considerable action on our part to remain in Jesus. The ways of the world promote independence and material success. Christians are called to be different—not conforming to the world, but working for food that lasts. We do this by staying close to Jesus; taking Him in like bread; standing in the light of His truth and reflecting it back; always approaching Him through the proper Gate; showing that Gate to others; following only the voice of our Shepherd; proudly proclaiming His resurrection and life and how it has changed our own lives; maintaining our unwavering belief in His way, truth, and life; gratefully accepting the pain of the Pruner's shears as a necessary part of the spiritual maturation process; and all the while, trusting that the Master Gardener has grafted us in for a reason.

Stepping In: Read Matthew 7:16–20; Romans 11:16-31, 12:2; Galatians 3:26-29, 5:22-23; and Ephesians 2:10–12. Praise God that He grafted you to His vine! Ask Him to reveal and repair areas in your life where you have become detached.

Stepping Out: This week, check your fruit basket to see if you are producing a crop for Jesus. If not, check for any loose connections and apply the glue of love and obedience to them.

Appealing

"You are the salt of the earth. But if the salt loses its saltiness, how can it be made salty again? It is no longer good for anything, except to be thrown out and trampled underfoot."

—Matthew 5:13 (Mt 5:1–16)

Highly valued for its preservative and flavor-enhancing properties, and essential for health, salt was a precious and costly mineral in ancient times. It was literally worth its weight in gold. The audience listening to Jesus' Sermon on the Mount understood the value and importance of salt. The flavor was salt's valued characteristic—without it, the mineral was worthless.

Jesus used salt as a metaphor for the appealing quality of people who radiate God's love and truth. He directed the words in today's verse mainly at the religious leaders and Pharisees as a harsh warning. Aware of their prideful ways and lack of love for those God had given them to shepherd, Jesus made clear that their heartless attitudes and unappealing behaviors would eventually render them useless for God's purposes.

Jesus' statement in today's verse was and is for every believer. Though He originally singled out the Pharisees, He certainly wanted all who heard this message to take it to heart. As Christians, we are the face of Christ to a watching world. We are representatives of our faith. Our attitudes and behaviors are under the constant scrutiny of a skeptical society. When we agree to follow Jesus, we are commissioned to be salt and light to a dark and dying world. Jesus expects us to show that we are worth our salt.

That said, most of us know that finding the right balance between sprinkling our witness too lightly, and pouring it on too thick is tricky business. With God's help, we can genuinely love and serve others without becoming mechanical or overbearing. With guidance from the Spirit, our attitudes, appearance, and behavior can be appealing and not detracting. To remain effective instruments for God's use, we must remember we are the salt of the earth.

Stepping In: How palatable is your Christian witness? Is it a tasty example of joy and hope in action, or could it use a little enhancement? Pray this week for Jesus to reveal areas of your life and ministry where you need to adjust your recipe.

Stepping Out: This week, ask a trusted Christian friend to give you their honest assessment of your Christian appeal. Based on what you learn from them and what the Spirit is telling you, take a first step toward improving your image and/or approach.

November 21
Neighborly

"Which of these three do you think was a neighbor to the man who fell into the hands of robbers?" The experts in the law replied, "The one who had mercy on him." "Go and do likewise."
—Luke 10:36–37 (Lk 10:25–37)

While Jesus was teaching in a synagogue, an expert in the Law asked Him how he might inherit eternal life. Jesus, knowing that the man was hoping to trick Him into a confession of deity, chose to return the question instead and asked the scholar what was written in the Law. The man replied with a summary of the Law's requirements, which he had no doubt heard Jesus quote as the first and second greatest commandments. Jesus agreed.

Puffed up with self-righteousness, the man then inquired as to who one's neighbor might be. Jesus told a parable about a man who was robbed along a treacherous mountain road and left for dead. A priest and a Levite each saw the man and chose to pass by on the other side of the road. However, when a Samaritan came upon the wounded man, he took pity on him and cared for him at his own expense, and at considerable personal risk as well. In today's verses, Jesus not only deflected the implied accusations of the scholar, He successfully exposed the unneighborly attitudes and behaviors of His opponents.

The notions of neighborliness and access to heaven have always been inseparably linked. That is not to say that one inherits eternal life simply by being kind to people. No, one can only receive salvation through faith in Jesus as Lord and Savior. However, once saved, an outpouring of love for others should be our natural reaction to the saving grace we have been freely given—not only out of gratitude for our redeemed state, but also because of the power of the indwelling Holy Spirit. Neighborliness or kindness is one of the fruits of the Spirit, and as such is proof that we belong to Christ.

To refresh our focus on what kindness and mercy mean to Jesus, every Christian should regularly read the parable of the Good Samaritan. Many convicting truths emerge with each reading. Some of us will relate to the "I am smarter than you, and I can prove it" attitude we see in the legal expert's slanted questions and snappy reply. Haven't each of us ridden this same high horse at some point? Some of us, have been that person who walked on the other side of the street to avoid dealing with a situation we did not want to be bothered with. Some of us, sadly, were the ones damaged or abandoned by religion. Jesus makes it very clear, that caring for people in need is not optional for His followers. Neighborliness is a Christian virtue. Period.

Stepping In: Read Leviticus 19:18; Deuteronomy 6:5; Matthew 22:37–40; and Galatians 3:10–11, 22–24 and 5:22–25. How did God speak to you through these verses about love in action? Pray for a genuine desire to be neighborly.

Stepping Out: This week, walk toward someone in need instead of away from them. Be a Good Samaritan and a good representative of Christ.

Righteous

"Blessed are those who hunger and thirst for righteousness, for they will be filled."

—Matthew 5:6 (Mt 5:1–12)

Jesus carefully worded the Beatitudes to address both practical and spiritual matters. In today's verse, Jesus mentioned two very real issues for the common folk: thirst and hunger. Times were hard for the underprivileged majority. Jesus told the eager crowd that satisfaction was within reach for those whose heart-desire was to please God. This same verse, spoken to the pride-filled, self-righteous religious leaders, was a harsh reprimand. For them, there would be no blessing.

Jesus is still addressing the issues of hunger and thirst in our insatiable world. Physical thirst and hunger are sadly an enduring problem in many parts of the world, and the bigger issue of spiritual deprivation seems only to be increasing. This latter concern is what we would call a classic "first world problem." While modern society seeks endlessly to satisfy its lust for more of everything, many of its members are slowly starving spiritually. Like the Pharisees, these folks look and act like they are living close to God, while in reality they hunger only for power and personal gain.

Most people on the planet strive only to feed their own needs, with little or no regard for God. Because they don't know Him, they don't believe they need Him—or they simple don't care. Jesus wants His people (Christians) to be different. He wants us to actively seek to please God, to do His will, and to pursue right living in His eyes. More than anything, Jesus wants us to be blessed.

Stepping In: What do you hunger and thirst for? Do your personal desires hold first place in your life? Is there an emptiness you are trying to fill with food, money, activities, accolades, or worldly possessions? What does God want for you? Ask the Spirit to guide you to verses about living in a right standing before God. Begin to apply them to your life this week.

Stepping Out: Right living begins with a right attitude, followed by right actions. This week, in addition to nourishing your own physical and spiritual needs, look for opportunities to help feed someone else. Consider volunteering at a food bank, homeless shelter, or soup kitchen. Sharing God's love with others is the best way to serve and honor God. Live righteously and be blessed for it.

November 23
Enthroned

"And everyone who has left houses or brothers or sisters or father or mother or children or fields for my sake will receive a hundred times as much and will inherit eternal life."

—Matthew 19:29 (Mt 19:16–30)

Somewhere between Galilee and Jerusalem, Jesus was approached by a rich young man wanting to know what was required of him to "get" eternal life. When Jesus explained that he needed to give away all his money and possessions and follow Him, the man went away sad; he had chosen worldly wealth over eternal treasures. Jesus used the opportunity to educate the disciples on God's plan and their purpose. This lesson was as much for them as it was for the rich young man.

True to his impetuous manner, Peter asked how he and the other disciples would be rewarded for their sacrificial devotion. Jesus explained that, besides inheriting eternal life, they would preside on heavenly thrones and be made judges over Israel. Those who willingly gave up everything they had to bring the gospel to the world could expect more than they could imagine in return. However, while still in the world, they should not expect to be given the status, honor, or respect they deserved.

Like the first disciples, all Christians must understand that the cost of a life devoted to God is often high. However, Jesus tells us that everyone who chooses eternal treasure over worldly wealth will be more than adequately compensated. The reward far outweighs the sacrifice. At the time when all things are renewed—when the old heaven and earth are replaced with the new—all true believers will be enthroned in heaven. As children of God and heirs to His estate, this ancient promise is ours. Until that day comes, we have work to do.

Out of love and gratitude for our Savior's sacrifice, we gladly do what is necessary to promote His kingdom, even if it is costly, uncomfortable, or seemingly impossible. Not everyone is asked to give up everything to follow Jesus, but we all are asked to relinquish our old sin-stained lives for the redeemed life He offers. In the end, the only riches that matter are the ones we store in heaven. Looking forward to our future enthronement, we give our all.

Stepping In: Read Luke 22:28–30 and Revelation 3:21. What cost have you paid in your walk with Jesus? How do you feel about this? Pray for a grateful and submissive heart. Praise Him for the rewards you have already received, as well as for those yet to come—being enthroned with Jesus!

Stepping Out: This week, identify one thing that Jesus is asking you to leave behind for His sake, and then commit to doing so. Wear something purple each day this week to remind yourself of your royal inheritance.

Drawn

"Stop grumbling among yourselves," he said. "No one can come to me unless the Father who sent me draws him, and I will raise him up at the last day."

—John 6:43–44 (Jn 6:25–59)

Jesus' main objective throughout His ministry was to do the will of His Father. Aside from coming to earth to usher in the new covenant, one dictated by love rather than rules, Jesus came to provide the propitiation necessary for all to receive salvation by grace through faith in His name. He was the Messiah sent by God to redeem all whom the Father would draw. Jesus' message and miracles were well received by the spiritually starved masses, but the Jewish leaders and Pharisees refused to believe. More than that, they refused to relinquish their religious authority over the people, especially to a carpenter's son from Nazareth. Jesus was not dissuaded by their denial. Instead, motivated by love to capture the drawn ones to Himself, He pressed on in His ministry – performing ever-increasing wonders.

One such event was the feeding of more than five thousand near Bethsaida in Galilee. Afterwards, when the participants discovered that Jesus had left for Capernaum, they followed Him there. The crowd soon began to argue about where this rabbi and His bread had come from. Many wondered if this man could be greater than Moses, who provided the Israelites with manna in the desert? Jesus told them to stop grumbling. He reminded them that God and the prophets had all spoken of this Bread of Life, which was not only *from* Him but *was* Him. However, when Jesus told them that the bread they must consume to inherit eternal life was His "flesh" (Jn 6:51), it was a difficult message for His audience to swallow.

The words of Jesus have forever been both encouraging and challenging. Consequently, His teachings have been the subject of much debate throughout history. The necessity of consuming His very flesh and blood has certain caused some theological arguments. Regardless of the disagreements about what kind of bread Jesus is offering or where it comes from, Jesus points out in today's passage that arguing such points to those who are not "drawn" by God is futile.

For those of us who are already in a relationship with Jesus, this fact can be sad and frustrating. Nonetheless, Jesus told His disciples and us that, though we should spread the gospel far and wide, it is God Himself who brings people to faith. All Jesus followers must work in cooperation with the Father/ Spirit/Son. We must humbly remember the time in our lives when we were the ones grumbling. Our loving words and actions now, together with God's gentle pull, will lead many to salvation—in time.

Stepping In: Read Jeremiah 31:3, 31–34; John 12:32; 1 Corinthians 2:12–16; 1 Thessalonians 4:9; and 1 Peter 2:9–10. Take some time to thank God for choosing you and drawing you to Himself. Pray for an increasingly yielded heart to serve God by leading others toward Jesus.

Stepping Out: This week, make every effort not to grumble with anyone, especially other Christians.

Self-Controlled

"For it is written: 'Man does not live on bread alone, but on every word that comes from the mouth of God.'"

—Matthew 4:4 (Mt 4:1–11)

Before His public ministry officially began, and even with the eyes of the world watching His every move, Jesus' life was always a perfect example of relying on the power of scripture to overcome temptation. Immediately after being baptized in the Jordan River by His cousin John the Baptist, Jesus was led by the Holy Spirit into the desert to be tempted by Satan. Sometime in the middle of Jesus' forty-day fast, Satan taunted Him by reminding Him that He need only say a word and the stones would become bread. Surely, at that point, even the driest loaf would have sounded very appealing to Him. Imagine the self-control it must have taken not to succumb to that temptation. Even for Jesus, the basic human need for nourishment, combined with survival instinct, would have been difficult to ignore. Yet, instead of getting angry or acting rashly, Jesus quoted a scripture passage Satan would have known from the book of Deuteronomy. Satan counterattacked with the same tactic, quoting Psalm 91. But his attempt at coaxing Jesus to "command His angels" to come to His aid was met only with another scriptural rebuttal. Finally, Jesus commanded Satan to leave Him. Dutifully, he obeyed.

What tempts you? How often do you resist it? How often to you give in? These questions are not meant to induce guilt or shame, but to highlight just how common this plight is. All of us are susceptible to temptation, from Satan and our own sin-nature. It is not a sin to be tempted. If it were, Jesus Himself would have been blemished by it. Temptation only becomes sin when we fail to employ self-control, allowing temptation to become an attitude or behavior that goes against God's laws.

Because Jesus was fully man and fully God at the same time, He understands our weakness and feels compassion for our struggles. He always provides a way to cope with temptation. But we need to learn where to look for solutions to our physical and spiritual battles. Jesus demonstrates how to fortify ourselves against the Devil's schemes: look to God. This means we must know the Word of God; both Jesus as Word and the Word of Holy Scripture.

When we have the life-giving Word of God in our heart, trusting that what He promises is true, we can face any challenge that comes our way. Following Jesus' example, we too must speak God's Word aloud, sending Satan and temptation away with the power of truth. In the Spirit and by His name, Satan is vanquished. It worked for our Lord; it will work for us as well.

Stepping In: Read Deuteronomy 8:3; Proverbs 3:5–6; 1 Corinthians 10:13; and Galatians 5:22–23. This week, commit to memorizing one of these scripture passages. Take some time to talk with God about your struggles, and ask the Spirit to guide you toward helpful passages. God is faithful and will bring the appropriate passage to mind at the right time—if you ask Him to!

Stepping Out: This week, put your memory verses into practice each time a temptation comes your way. Then, look for the way out He is providing. Praise God for strengthening you in your times of testing.

November 26
Advantaged

> After this I looked, and there before me was a door standing open in heaven. And the voice I had first heard speaking to me like a trumpet said, "Come up here, and I will show you what must take place after this."
>
> —Revelation 4:1 (Rv 4:1–11)

Regardless of biblical evidence proving otherwise, for centuries the common depiction of heaven has been a peaceful, fluffy scene in white. Inside a large golden gate, there are cherubs dressed in white frocks, with white-feathered wings, playing harps and floating on cotton-ball-like clouds. This is not the heaven John witnessed and described in the book of Revelation. His scene was full of a rainbow's worth of colors, flashing lightning, and seven blazing lamps. It was also full of sounds—thunder clapping and voices singing. It wasn't the boring image that comes to most people's minds when they think of heaven.

That is the nature of the human mind—to paint the world (and heaven) the way we want to see it. Before much of the population was literate, the words and stories of God were passed down through an oral tradition. While the teller decided which details to highlight and which to downplay or leave out, the listeners were left to put together a cohesive meaning in their own imaginations. Naturally, artistic liberties were taken on both sides.

Today however, most people have access to the very words of God—no filling in the blanks is necessary. From cover to cover, the Bible makes clear that God wants us to know His plan for His people and His planet. Sadly, very few read the book of Revelation, the advantaged view of the culmination of world history. They prefer to make up their own ending. Christians should not be among them, but instead be the ones to take advantage of the truth spelled out in black, white and red. Then pass it on.

Stepping In: Read Psalm 119:159–160; John 17:15–17; 1 Corinthians 2:9–10; 2 Timothy 3:16–17; 2 Peter 1:20–21; and Revelation 1:9–20. How often do you take advantage of the privileged view God's Word offers you? Pray before opening your Bible that He reveals revelations for your life now and eternally.

Stepping Out: This week, invite five people to church, so they can take in the view.

November 27
Driven

"When you are persecuted in one place, flee to another. I tell you the truth, you will not finish going through the cities of Israel before the Son of Man comes."

—Matthew 10:23 (Mt 10:1–23)

Jesus' disciples may have thought these words were in stark contrast to the ones preceding them—not to mention puzzling. They had just been advised by their Lord and Master about what they should do when dangerous situations arose. Jesus told them to stand firm in the face of angry opposition. In today's verse, however, Jesus instructed them to flee persecution.

In referring to Himself as the Son of Man, Jesus gave His Jewish apprentices a clue as to His seemingly contradictory meaning. His reference to Daniel's prophecy about the coming Messiah was meant to inform the Twelve that their missionary duties would continue well beyond their inaugural journey, and their earthly lives. It would indeed be an enduring legacy. Driven by the imminence of Jesus' return, the faithful realized that to spread the gospel far and wide, they would have to remain alive for as long as possible so that they could pass on their saving faith to the next generation of believers. There was much ground to cover, and no way of knowing how long they would have before the Son of Man would come. Though the road they traveled was rocky and perilous, the apostles paved the way for all Christ-followers thereafter.

Jesus gave His chosen representatives specific instructions, blunt warnings, and sincere promises as He sent them out as sheep among wolves. His words were sincere and completely trustworthy. They still are. What He said would happen has, and what He says will happen surely will. Today, we carry out our ministries by following this same set of instructions as we wait for Jesus' second coming. The only difference is that the mission field is a lot bigger. Though it is important to be driven to spread the good news, it is wise to always seek the will of the One who is driving. And to avoid dangers when possible.

Stepping In: Read Daniel 7:13–14; Acts 1:1–11; and Revelation 1:7. Note: that the phrase "men of Galilee" refers to the apostles. Consider all the times Jesus' words have been trustworthy in your life. Has He ever not kept a promise? If there were times you felt He was not there with you, honestly acknowledge who left or went astray. Pray that your desire to know God more aligns with your drive to serve Him well.

Stepping Out: This week, practice wisdom and restraint in your evangelism, not letting zealous enthusiasm drive your approach. Pray that God nudges you toward people or away, depending on the volatility of the situation. When possible, live to share another day.

November 28
Far-Sighted

"Get behind me, Satan! You are a stumbling block to me; you do not
have in mind the things of God, but the things of men."
—Matthew 16:23 (Mt 16:13–23)

Of all the disciples, Peter was known to be the most zealous and impetuous. He nearly always voiced his unfiltered thoughts and acted seemingly without much forethought. However, he was also a fiercely devoted student of Jesus and one of His closest friends. After spending nearly three years with Jesus, Peter was the one who demonstrated belief in Jesus' power when he asked to walk to Him on water. He was also the only one to verbally acknowledge that Jesus was "the Christ, the Son of the living God" (Mt 16:16).

Jesus could see that Peter possessed a spiritual aptitude that would be of great service to the coming kingdom, and He told him so. Jesus also knew that Peter's nature would lead him into trouble and make him vulnerable to spiritual attacks from Satan.

This became evident when Jesus began to prepare His disciples for His upcoming arrest, torture, and death. Peter's instant reaction was to flatly refuse to accept this news. Satan blurred Peter's perspective, causing him to focus on the loss of an earthly king rather than the reality of gaining an eternal King. Recognizing the evil influence behind this response, Jesus rebuked Peter and Satan both. This harsh reprimand was issued partly to demonstrate the necessity of identifying and eradicating the Devil's input, and partly to refocus the disciples' minds on the eternal, not the temporal.

It is difficult not to have a visceral reaction to these words of Jesus. It may seem unduly harsh, even out of character, for our loving Savior to call one of His devoted disciples Satan. It certainly seems an incongruous response to Peter's desire to defend his Master. Yet, as shocking as it appears at face value, Jesus was only doing what was necessary. The lesson Jesus needed Peter and the other disciples to learn that day is one that all believers must also take to heart: Satan uses fear and doubt to weaken a believer's faith. He must be called out and cast out! And, though Satan may not cause our fearful situations, he most certainly capitalizes on our emotional frailty.

Jesus needs us to know that spiritual warfare is real. He wants us to know how to identify the Evil One's attacks and how to defend against them. The first step for all Christians is to utilize the Holy Spirit, seeking God's will in all circumstances. When we feel our faith waver in response to a perceived threat, we must call on the power of Jesus to guard us against the Devil's schemes. We must verbally tell Satan to take a hike. We must maintain a far-sighted, eternal perspective, even in the face of difficulties.

Stepping In: Read Luke 4:33-36, 10:17; Acts 16:16–18; and Ephesians 6:10–18. When have you seen Satan put stumbling blocks in the way of your spiritual growth or that of others? Pray for strength to focus beyond difficult circumstances, keeping your eyes on Jesus.

Stepping out: Each morning this week, ask Jesus to cloak you with the armor of God. Call on Jesus' name each time Satan causes you to stumble. Be an example to others of someone who lives by faith and not by sight (2 Cor 5:7). Trust in Jesus' eternal plans, not in Satan's empty promises.

November 29
Withstanding

"It is easier for heaven and earth to disappear than for the least stroke
of the pen to drop out of the Law."

—Luke 16:17 (Lk 16:16–18)

From the time John the Baptist began preaching the coming kingdom of God, the Jewish teachers of the Law and the Pharisees took issue with the attention this new movement was attracting. When Jesus began preaching the same gospel, the Pharisees rejected Him just as they had John. To the Jewish leaders, Jesus' gospel was a new teaching, altogether other than the laws and prophecies of God. Jesus explained to them in the simplest of terms that He indeed was the fulfillment of the Law and the Prophets. He reminded these closed-minded men that the kingdom of God was an unstoppable force that many were eagerly clamoring for. He denounced the false notion that one had to choose either the gospel or the Law, as they were in fact one and the same. In today's verse, Jesus restated His point by concluding that, of all they could see, only the Word of God would withstand the tests of time.

Messianic Jews understand the prophecy of today's verse probably better than anyone else. Like learned Christians, they have recognized Jesus as the prophesied Savior for generations. In the Old Testament, the Messiah was referred to in many ways: Shepherd, Redeemer, Root of Jesse, Branch of David, Immanuel. In addition to fulfilling each of these roles to the letter, Jesus became "the Lamb of God who takes away the sin of the world" (Jn 1:29), thus ending the sacrificial system with one final act of atoning mercy.

But the Pharisees did not recognize this. They chose not to accept the truth, even when He was standing right in front of them. We, however, have all the evidence we could possibly need to prove that what Jesus said about Himself is true. From Genesis to Revelation, the Bible tells a beautiful love story of God's plan to create, sustain, forgive, and reclaim His most prized possession: us. Heaven and earth will pass away, but those who claim this reality will not. When the world expires, we will withstand.

Stepping In: Read Isaiah 7:14, 11:1-3; Jeremiah 31:31-34, 33:15-16; Matthew 5:17-20, 24:35; John 1:26-30; and 1 Peter 1:23-25. What truth about Jesus, the prophecies, or the Word of God did you discover in these passages? Praise God for His infallible and immutable plan. Thank Him that you are also withstanding.

Stepping Out: This week, Google "Prophecies of Jesus" on the internet. Write down the ones you find most interesting and share them with your small groups, or a friend.

Receptive

"Blessed are the poor in spirit, for theirs is the kingdom of heaven."
—Matthew 5:3 (Mt 5:1–12)

Jesus began the Sermon on the Mount by declaring a series of blessings known as the Beatitudes. Today's verse is the first beatitude, which left some in His audience immediately puzzled. This was most likely intentional, as Jesus chose His words carefully. Jesus was speaking to mixed crowd, some spiritually poor and some spiritually proud. He cut right to the chase.

Inferring that the converse was also true, Jesus told His audience that only those who recognized their spiritual depravity and need for a Savior's mercy would be blessed to inherit God's kingdom. The blessing of the promised kingdom of heaven is out of reach to those who fail to admit their poorness of spirit. Jesus knew that His words, actions, and theology would greatly challenge His listeners. Therefore, He stated up front that unless one has an open mind—like that of a child, not already filled with man-made rules and regulations—it is pointless for one to try to understand His logic. This was the sort of statement that repeatedly struck at the Achilles heel of His ultra-religious contemporaries throughout His ministry.

The main issue addressed in today's verse is pride. Because humans are, for the most part, an opinionated and stubborn bunch, it is difficult for many of us to admit that we don't have all the answers. We deem our beliefs infallible and reject different or contrary ideas. Like the religious leaders of Jesus' day, we tend toward a rigidity of mind and therefore of spirit. To hear that it is a blessing to be poor in anything, let alone spirit, seems an oxymoron.

These carefully chosen words of Jesus tell us that indeed we must understand our spiritual insufficiency to receive the riches of a changed heart, one that is open to Christ's teachings. We must present our depleted and needy spirits before Jesus before we can begin to advance toward the ultimate blessing—the promise of eternal glory. The message applies to every audience throughout every age. It is the necessary first step in becoming kingdom-ready. It is not surprising that the first words of one of Jesus' most important teachings is about being receptive.

Stepping In: How rigid are you in your opinions and beliefs? Is there room for consideration of others' ideas? Take time to think this over this week. Make a list of your core beliefs—the ones you do not bend on—and seek biblical support for them. If you find that your beliefs are not biblically sound, pray for a willingness to be flexible and receptive to what Jesus is teaching you.

Stepping Out: This week, count your blessings! Share with someone how they encourage you.

December 1
Wise

> "Therefore, everyone who hears these words of mine and puts them into practice is like a wise man who built his house on the rock. The rain came down, the streams rose, and the winds blew and beat against the house; yet it did not fall, because it had its foundation on the rock."
>
> —Matthew 7:24–25 (Mt 7:24–29)

After several days of sitting on the hard and dusty ground, listening to Jesus' Sermon on the Mount, many in the audience might have thought that the comforts of a sturdy house were beginning to sound pretty good. However, Jesus was alluding to more than external security in today's passage. He was explaining that the metaphors, analogies, rebukes, suggestions, and warnings issued throughout His multi-day teaching were not merely for the listening pleasure of those in attendance; they were commands with which to comply.

The people were amazed. Never had they heard a young rabbi speak with such confidence and authority. Never had they heard such a new and controversial ideology. So enamored were they of His forthrightness and wisdom, they may have missed the subtle hint of where true security lies. Had anyone noticed that He said, "the rock," not "a rock"? Those who were becoming spiritually wise would have sensed that they were in the presence of a man of God. Yet it would be years before most understood that Jesus Himself was the Rock. All who heeded His commands would indeed be able to weather the storms of life. For all others, He would become a "Stumbling Stone" (Isaiah 8:14, 28:16; Romans 9:33).

It should never be taken for granted that we today have the true and complete Word of God at our disposal. What an advantage we have over the first-century church! Yes, they got to see Jesus in person, though many did not recognize Him. But we get to see His teaching in the context of scripture as a whole. We can see this final section of the Sermon on the Mount, which is called "The Wise and Foolish Builders," as more than just good engineering advice. We can see that it contains deep spiritual truth about seeking and applying God's wisdom in our lives, so that the winds of adversity and change do not blow us over. Jesus wants us to be prepared for *when* the storms of life come, not *if* they come.

Jesus assures His followers in all generations that, though hard times will test our faith, those who look beyond the difficult circumstances to the source of all stability, Jesus, will be left standing when those times pass. Jesus is the only firm foundation. All other ground is sinking sand.

Stepping In: Look up and read or sing the words to the old hymn, "On Christ the Solid Rock I Stand." Also read Genesis 49:24; Exodus 17:6; Numbers 20:8; Psalm 19:14; and Isaiah 26:4. Meditate on who Jesus, the Rock, is to you. Consider where you need to exchange foolish choices for wise ones. Praise Him for being your safe-haven in the storms of life.

Stepping Out: Review Matthew chapters 5–7. What commands is Jesus calling you to put in to practice this week? Choose one to work on diligently. Commit to (re)establishing a firm foundation in Christ through obedience to His Word. Identify and relinquish false, worldly securities as you look forward to the house He is now preparing for you in heaven.

Dependable

"You have persevered and have endured hardships for my name, and have not grown weary. Yet I hold this against you: You have forsaken your first love."

—Revelation 2:3–4 (Rv 2:1–7)

While imprisoned on the Greek island of Patmos for his promotion of Christianity throughout the province of Asia Minor, the apostle John received a vision from God. He was transported in the Spirit into the Lord's presence, where Jesus Himself instructed John to write a letter to the seven churches in Asia Minor, proclaiming God's revelation of the end times to come.

Beginning with the church in Ephesus, John transcribed Jesus' message for each church in turn, commending them for the kingdom work they had done, and rebuking them for their faults. As we see in today's verse, Jesus had one complaint against the Ephesian leadership. They had let their affection for the Lord grow cold. In so doing, the members of the church had forgotten the main premise of their faith: love for God and others. They were apparently so determined in their cause, they had neglected the importance of the people themselves. Jesus wanted them to remember that to love Him was to love others. Jesus wanted them to be dependable stewards of the bountiful fruits of the Spirit with which they had been entrusted.

Very few budding romances maintain their initial intensity over the course of time. Newly in love, we abound in affection and devotion. We are full of enthusiasm and energy, willing to do anything for our loved one. However, we simply cannot continue at that pace forever. The same seems to be true for Christian zeal. Most of us can remember being "on fire" for Jesus when we first came to faith. But, over time, our passion for Him and His causes waned. Like an old married couple, we tend toward contentment and complacency in our relationship with the Lord.

When the fire for God fades in our hearts, so too does the flame of fellowship flicker and go out. While we may go through the motions, fulfilling our churchly duties and keeping up Christian appearances, we are not fooling God with our bare-minimum efforts. He knows when our hearts are not in it anymore. Today's verses, meant to encourage and convict the Ephesians, are for Christians everywhere, throughout the generations. Jesus wants us to fall in love with Him again and pace ourselves so that we can be dependably devoted for the long haul.

Stepping In: Read Jeremiah 2:1–2; Hosea 2:14–20; Matthew 22:37–40 and 24:12; 1 Corinthians 13:1–10; and Hebrews 10:23–25. Take some time to consider your heart condition. Is the fire for Jesus still burning brightly, or are there only embers? Pray for the Spirit to reignite your passion for Him and for His people.

Stepping Out: This week, wear red to remind yourself of your love for Jesus. Plan a fellowship meal with your small group or some fellow believers.

Blessed

"But blessed are your eyes because they see, and your ears because they hear. For I tell you the truth, many prophets and righteous men longed to see what you see but did not see it, and to hear what you hear but did not hear it."

—Matthew 13:16–17 (Mt 13:1–17)

At the height of His ministry, Jesus' safety become an issue of great concern. Not only did He have to take precautions against the Pharisees' attempts to incriminate Him, but He also needed to contend with the pressing throngs of people wanting to get close to Him. One day in Galilee, Jesus not only avoided being crushed by a massive, clamoring crowd by teaching from the safety of a small boat, but He also successfully shielded the spiritual meaning of His message from the ears of His persecutors by using a parable to teach the discerning.

Afterward, Jesus' disciples asked Him why He hadn't spoken plainly to the people. Jesus quoted ancient prophecies that foretold of the Jews' rejection of God's wisdom and their inability to comprehend His truth. Not only was it pointless to make things clear for the spiritually blind, it was dangerous to provoke their anger and frustration. However, as Jesus pointed out in today's verses, those with the ability to see, hear, and understand Jesus' gospel truth, even when spoken in the form of parables, would be greatly blessed. Those who could not understand Him would go on wondering what Jesus' teaching was about.

It is easy for us today to look smugly at the first-century doubters and scoff at their ineptitude. How could they not have realized who Jesus was when He was standing right in front of them? The issue for unbelievers in every generation remains the same: spiritual blindness. People who do not have the indwelling Holy Spirit cannot see, hear, or understand the proof of a loving Creator God, even when it is clearly visible all around.

Those who reject God and refuse the Son's salvation must derive their happiness, security, and success from the things of this world. Today's verses remind us that beyond what our senses can physically perceive is a realm of beautiful insight only the blessed get to enjoy. Where the rest of the world sees in three dimensions, Christians have a fourth: eternity. In a world where "seeing is believing," Christians more than ever must cling to and be thankful for the vision Jesus has blessed us with.

Stepping In: Read John 8:56–58; Hebrews 11:8–16; and 1 Peter 1:10–12. How do these verses help you understand the legacy of spiritual blindness? Pray that your sight does not limit your belief nor influence how you respond to the Spirit's leading. Praise God for the gift of discernment you have been blessed with.

Stepping Out: This week, speak of the intangible truths of God. Look for and express the ways you experience God in the world. Share your eternal vision with someone today.

December 4
Realistic

"It is not the healthy who need a doctor, but the sick. But go and learn what this means: 'I desire mercy, not sacrifice.' For I have not come to call the righteous, but sinners."

—Matthew 9:12–13 (Mt 9:9–13)

Early in His earthly ministry, while teaching and healing in the region of Galilee, Jesus began to call His twelve disciples. Shortly after accepting the invitation to follow Christ, Matthew threw a dinner party in celebration. Jesus was the guest of honor, and many tax collectors and other sinners were in attendance. Word of this gathering reached the ears of the Pharisees and Jewish teachers of the Law, who were puzzled and incensed by the young rabbi's indiscretion. Some of them questioned Jesus' disciples about their Master's choice of dining companions.

Jesus, who was aware of this line of questioning, gave His disciples (and all within earshot, especially the Pharisees) the above reply. Quoting the prophet Hosea's speech to an unrepentant Israel, Jesus pointed out that mercy, not rigid adherence to rules, was what God desired. People, not piety, should come first. Jesus wanted His students to learn from Him, not from the closed-minded Jewish teachers, how best to meet the needs of needy and sick.

Ironically, not only were the Pharisees blind to Jesus' divinity, but also to their own need for His healing. The so-called sinners in attendance would have had a more realistic viewpoint of their depravity, and been humbly grateful for Jesus' merciful acceptance of them.

It is truly mind-boggling to consider the amount of time, money, and energy today's society puts into self-improvement. In a desperate attempt to defy the progression of age-related decline, we invest hugely in diets, exercise regimes, and various "procedures." To make ourselves feel better, we seek all manner of advice from doctors, gurus, and salesmen. In our hearts, we know we are grievously flawed, yet we do not often willingly admit it. We prefer to live on Fantasy Island rather than in Realityville.

Unfortunately, many of us approach our spiritual lives in the same way. We falsely believe that we need to fix our brokenness and cover up our imperfections before we can be acceptable to God. Or, worse yet, we deny our need for a merciful Savior like the Pharisees did. Today's verses teach us that Jesus wants us to have a realistic attitude about who we are and *whose* we are. Every person needs Christ's healing; those who approach the throne of mercy will receive it. As Jesus' ambassadors, we must lead the sick to the only One who can heal them fully.

Stepping In: Read Hosea 6:1-6 and Luke 5:27-32. What illness or flaw are you currently trying to ignore or cover up? Ask God to help you release it to Him. Pray for a humble and realistic view of your neediness. Gratefully accept Christ's healing and mercy. Thank Him.

Stepping Out: This week, extend the same mercy and gracious acceptance to others that Jesus does for all his hurting children—including you.

December 5
Unflinching

"Do you think I cannot call on my Father, and he will at once put at
my disposal more than twelve legions of angels?"
—Matthew 26:53 (Mt 26:36–56)

After Jesus and His disciples had shared one last Passover meal in a borrowed upper room in Jerusalem, and after Judas Iscariot had left to carry out His betrayal, Jesus led the remaining eleven into the garden of Gethsemane. Taking Peter, James, and John further into olive grove, Jesus instructed His closest companion to watch and pray while He went a distance away to be alone with the Father. Yet, try as they might, the three were too overcome with angst and exhaustion to be helpful to their Lord. Waking the trio for the third time, Jesus informed them that His betrayal was at hand. Impulsively, Peter drew his sword and severed an armed guard's ear, to which Jesus gave a stern rebuke. He also reminded Peter and all present that no human force could possibly match the defenses He could call upon, if indeed they were necessary. After healing the soldier's wound, Jesus unflinchingly allowed Himself to be bound and led to His fate. As He went, Jesus reminded everyone that what was taking place was necessary and according to God's divine plan.

Of all the fruits of the Spirit, many of us will attest that self-control is the hardest. Our society is sorely lacking in defenses against instant gratification and self-indulgence. When we consider the self-control Jesus employed during that night of trials, beatings, mocking, and crucifixion, we should be more than impressed. Indeed, we ought to be eternally grateful that He didn't give in to His human nature and call on His Father to put the whole agonizing affair to an end.

Thankfully, His holy nature was infinitely stronger. What a lesson for us today. When we think that our circumstances are unfair or unbearable, we need only remember what Jesus went through and why He did it. This should be a sufficient perspective changer. It also should be the inspiration necessary to finish the race with perseverance and determination, unflinchingly so.

Stepping In: Read Mark 14:43–52; Luke 22:47–50; and Hebrews 12:1–3. Use the Envision It method (see appendix) to reflect on one of the gospel accounts of Jesus' arrest. Who did you choose to identify with and why? What was your reaction to Jesus' betrayal and arrest? Thank Jesus for His unflinching self-control, love and obedience.

Stepping Out: This week, examine where you lack self-control. Choose an area to work on and give Jesus your best efforts to make a marked improvement.

December 6
Intercessory

"This kind can only come out by prayer."
—Mark 9:29 (Mk 9:14–32)

During His ministry, Jesus traveled widely with His twelve disciples throughout the region of Galilee, spreading the good news of the gospel and healing many. When He felt they were ready, Jesus took Peter, James, and John with Him up a mountain so that they could experience a supernatural event, Jesus' transfiguration, meant to eliminate any doubt these men may have had regarding Christ's deity.

When they had returned to where the other disciples were, they found them engaged in heated conversation with some local people. As it turned out, Jesus' disciples could not drive a demon out of a suffering child. The people were indignant and the boy's father remiss. The father let his wavering faith show by inquiring whether Jesus could do the job. Though Jesus was quite irritated by the collective unbelief, He compassionately restored the boy to full health.

Certainly, there were many lessons for all parties to learn that day, including Satan himself, who fled the scene after being commanded to leave and never return. Jesus informed His men that, though they had tried to exorcise the demon, they had not tried every tool available to them. The disciples discovered that sometimes an indirect approach was the correct one. His disciples, while trusting in the power of Jesus' name, had neglected to consult with the Father and seek His sovereign will and assistance.

We are a people of action. Especially in America, constant activity and busyness are synonymous with productivity. We have become "human doings" rather than "human beings"! But this is not the example Jesus set. Yes, He *did* many amazing things, to be sure. But He was often found prayerfully seeking His Father's will first.

The lesson Jesus taught His first disciples is one He is still teaching His followers today. Like the disciples, we tend to act first and think or pray later. Not only is this potentially ineffective, it also skips the most important link in the healing chain: tapping into God's sovereign Spirit. As Jesus trusts His Father to know what is best and to already be at work in every situation, we must do the same. When we are confident in God's caring nature, we can slow down and allow Him to intercede in our circumstances. And while we prayerfully intercede on behalf of others, Jesus is also interceding for us. In fact, if we are to follow Jesus' example, we must be on our knees before ever trying to solve a problem. Every good thing we can do for Jesus begins with intercessory prayer.

Stepping In: Read Mark 11:24; Romans 8:34; Philippians 4:6–7; Hebrews 7:25; James 4:2-3, 5:15; and 1 Peter 3:12. Take some time to consider your approach to prayer. Is it too casual or forced? Do you take it for granted, or fail to fully believe it will be answered? Humbly ask God for forgiveness and for Him to grant you a yielded heart in prayer.

Stepping Out: Prayerfully seek God's will this week. Practice praying for others (intercessory prayer). Bring all kinds of prayers and petitions before God. Be quick to act only when prompted by the Holy Spirit.

Cautious

"Watch out for false prophets. They come to you in sheep's clothing, but inwardly they are ferocious wolves. By their fruit you will recognize them."

—Matthew 7:15–16

To the audience hearing Jesus' Sermon on the Mount, the last part of this statement may have seemed incongruous. Certainly, the Jews in attendance understood the warning about false prophets, as this was something they had been told to guard against since the days of their forefathers. As members of an agrarian society, they understood the reference to predators and produce—just maybe not how these related to each other.

As was the hallmark of Jesus' teaching, His message held both spiritual truths and serious warnings, which He knew His audience would not fully understand. Far more was at stake than simply being fooled and taken advantage of. The false prophets claiming to be the Messiah were after the very souls of their victims. Jesus told this crowd to pay attention. He told them that a deceiver's true identity would be revealed to those who could recognize rotten fruit when they saw it. The wise who took to heart Jesus' advice would be cautious of those making only skin-deep claims of divinity.

Though we are familiar with the "wolf in sheep's clothing" analogy, the context and significance of today's passage may be somewhat lost on a modern audience. The claims of a delusional madman hardly warrant notice these days amid the constant bombardment of sensationalized media. Yet, one only need to scan the long list of crazies claiming to be Christ incarnate, some of them quite recent, to know that the battle for souls rages on. We still need to be on high alert for these predators. As convincing as their acts may be, we must test every grand promise and prophetic statement against the Word of God. No one should be fooled by a charismatic soothsayer when we can read for ourselves that the second coming will not be covert by any stretch of the imagination. But until Jesus returns, we must be cautious about being duped by phony promises of those claiming to be the way to God.

Stepping In: Read Ezekiel 13:1–23; Luke 21:10-28; and 2 Timothy 3:1-5. Talk to God about what the end times should mean to you. What should you look for? What should you guard against? Ask Him to replace fear with confidence in your position in His kingdom. Pray for strength to stand firm as you wait, accepting no false prophets.

Stepping Out: Read Galatians 5:22–26. This week, model these Christian characteristics. Thank God for a greater awareness of good versus bad fruit in yourself and others.

December 8
Hopeful

"Unless you people see miraculous signs and wonders," Jesus told him,
"you will never believe."

—John 4:48 (Jn 4:38–54)

After His encounter with the Samaritan woman at the well, Jesus went to Cana, where He had recently turned water to wine. The people there eagerly greeted Him. His disciples were aware that the people were only hoping to be entertained by more miracles. However, there were some whose belief was hopeful and true. One such person was a rich Roman official, a Gentile who would normally not mix with Jews. He had come all the way from Capernaum to appeal to Jesus for help for his dying son. Jesus responded to this plea with today's verse. Undeterred, the official pleaded with Jesus again. Seeing that this man had humility and faith, Jesus told him he could go; his son would live. Taking Jesus at his word, the man headed home. On his way, the official was met by a servant who told him the good news of the boy's recuperation. Realizing that his son's health had returned at the very hour Jesus had spoken, the man and his whole household put their faith in Him.

Many people today are familiar with the sayings "Show me, don't tell me" and "I'll believe it when I see it." Though we are not born skeptics, over time most of us become less trusting. Deceived and disappointed over the years, most adults withhold trust until all doubts have been assuaged. Knowing this, Jesus tells us that we must have faith like a child: trusting, humble, dependent, unquestioning, obedient, hopeful. He also tells us that we only need to have faith the size of a mustard seed to see spiritual results.

This is good news for us. Taking a lesson from the hopeful Roman official, we too can approach Jesus with our fears and petitions. He sees past our outward appearance and straight into our hearts, looking for faith and hope. When Jesus looked past the trappings of the high-ranking, powerful, political figure, He saw a man who believed that Jesus could do what no one else could. The Roman was right. Jesus looks past everything that we hide behind, right to the core of our belief.

Stepping In: Read Matthew 18:3; Luke 17:6, 19; John 1:50; Romans 5:1-8; 2 Corinthians 5:7; and 1 Peter 1:3–5. What do these verses teach you about true faith and hope? How hopeful do you remain even when things don't go the way they should? Pray for your heart to be filled with confidence and trust in Jesus, for whom nothing is impossible.

Stepping Out: This week, make a list of answered prayers, signs, or miracles Jesus has done for you. Share this list with fellow believers and unbelievers as well.

Unmovable

"Because of the increase of wickedness, the love of most will grow cold, but he who stands firm to the end will be saved."
—Matthew 24:12–13 (Mt 24:1–14)

Just days before He was put to death by the Jewish leaders, and with little time left to prepare His followers for the events that lie ahead, Jesus sat down on the Mount of Olives and began teaching about the end of the age. In today's verses, He encouraged His disciples to remain unmovable in their faith, knowing that salvation would be their reward. Some of the prophecies of which Jesus spoke would be fulfilled in the very near future. Others would not transpire for many thousands of years. The times and places of these occurrences were only for the Father to know. But Jesus made one thing perfectly clear: those who held on to their faith through the trials to come would be safely brought home. Those who helped to spread the gospel would play their part in seeing this prophecy through to the end, starting with the apostles themselves.

To this day, Bible experts and theorists have been proven unable to predict when the catastrophic and wonderful event of Jesus' return will take place. Certainly, there have been innumerable catastrophes that have caused many to believe the end was at hand. They were obviously incorrect. The truth is, no one knows when Jesus will return. We can only know for certain that His return will not go unnoticed and that the devastation will be complete.

Christians need not fear. We expect the times to get increasingly wicked and human compassion to fade into obscurity. Jesus Himself tells us these things so that we can be prepared, and so that we can resolve to remain unmovable in our faith. By so doing, we can continue our kingdom work with confidence and be a beacon of hope for many.

Stepping In: Read Isaiah 19:2–10; Daniel 9:25-27, 11:31, 12:1-13; 2 Thessalonians 2:1–4; and Hebrews 10:19–25. How concerned are you about the end times? How do these verses help you better understand God's plan and what you should do inside of it? Pray for comfort and guidance.

Stepping Out: This week, make sure to rebuke Satan's attempts at deception, while at the same time radiating Christ's love in all circumstances. Be unmovable in your faith!

December 10
Unbiased

"But love your enemies, do good to them, and lend to them without expecting to get anything back. Then your reward will be great, and you will be sons of the Most High, because he is kind to the ungrateful and wicked."

—Luke 6:35 (Lk 6:17–36)

After hand-selecting His twelve disciples, not for their superior intellect or spiritual prowess but for their willingness to learn and obey, Jesus began to reveal His true, divine identity to them. His words, devotion to God, and compassion for the people were the basis of the ministry they would soon be carrying forward. As the disciples came to know, Jesus always talked about the heart of a person. Some hearts were pure and honest—God-fearing. Others were jaded and self-serving—ungodly. Jesus called His apostles to a higher morality, insisting that they do the opposite of the world's expectations. Jesus instituted practices of forgiveness and generous giving that none had seen before, which today's verse summarizes nicely.

The world today is a very divided place. In America and Europe, cultural integration and mutual acceptance are promoted. Places like the Middle East are still very much opposed to the blending of people groups. The struggle for autonomy has led to many wars and disputes, especially for religious reasons. Examples of this include the Israelis and the Palestinians, the Protestants and the Catholics. Each group draws deep lines of separation based on differing interpretations of holy law. Too many people resort to extreme acts in the name of their God.

Jesus saw this in His day, and He knew that it would continue. He has never wavered in His stance for unbiased peace and reconciliation. He came so that *all* could come to a right relationship with Him. He knows that not everyone will make that choice. But as far as His disciples, including us, are concerned, we are to love. This is the only right way to God. It is our duty and privilege to obey.

Stepping In: Read Proverbs 16:1-7, 24:17, 25:21-22; Matthew 5:43-45; Romans 5:10–11; and Philippians 3:18–21. Meditate on these scripture passages. Is God bringing to mind any animosity that you harbor against a person or people group? Ask Him how to turn your disdain into unbiased love. Pray for a heart of compassion for the lost.

Stepping Out: This week, find a practical way to love an enemy. Start by praying for them, and then respond in obedience to the Spirit's prompting to positively engage.

December 11

Determined

"When you fast, do not look somber as the hypocrites do, for they disfigure their faces to show they are fasting. I tell you the truth, they have received their reward in full. But when you fast, put oil on your head and wash your face, so that it will not be obvious to others that you are fasting, but only to your Father, who is unseen; and your Father, who has seen what is done in secret, will reward you."

—Matthew 6:16–18

In ancient Jewish culture, the practice of fasting was commonplace, especially for religious leaders seeking God's guidance or provision. The purpose of fasting was to humbly rely entirely on God for strength and sustenance, while seeking His will alone. It was meant to be a time when one's entire focus was on God. During the designated time frame, the faster was not to let even the distraction of eating get in the way of God. Often fasting was practiced by the faithful during times of hardship or great need. At other times, it was used as an act of contrition while pleading for forgiveness and restoration. Though it was a demonstration of absolute submission to God's sovereign power, it was meant to be a private matter.

The religious leaders, however, enjoyed making a public show of fasting. They wanted others to recognize their sacrifice and dedication. They exaggerated their suffering. In today's verse, Jesus tells the phony fasters in the audience that their act might gain them sympathy and attention from those who saw their performance, but it did not fool or please God.

Today, fasting for dietary or health reasons is somewhat commonplace. The practice of fasting for spiritual reasons is certainly less so. Regardless of how or why we fast, it is, by design, a difficult task. Most of us are not in the habit of denying ourselves anything. In a culture of self-indulgence, pleasure, comfort, and ease, most of us cannot imagine making a practice of going hungry, even for religious or spiritual reasons. Because it is a tough sell, many churches pay little attention to this biblical practice.

But, like it or not, fasting serves an important purpose for those seeking God's will. As with any of the commands Jesus gave us, fasting is designed to benefit those who obey. When God sees our intentionality, devotion, determination, and utter dependence, He is pleased. Will-power may play a role in how successfully we perform, but the ultimate source of fortitude comes from God. Jesus reminds us of the stance we should take with fasting. He expects that we will participate in it from time to time—notice He says "when," not "if," you fast. He also expects us to do so quietly and humbly—and joyfully as well.

Stepping In: Pray and ask God what area of your life needs cleansing. Is there a habit or an attitude that comes between you and God? Do you need guidance or help in a big way? Pray for a willingness to deny yourself in order to rely on God alone.

Stepping Out: This week, determine to fast from something that God is telling you to let go of. Humbly and happily draw near to Him for refreshment, healing, restoration, and vision.

346

December 12
Directed

"He who speaks on his own does so to gain honor for himself, but he who works for the honor of the one who sent him is a man of truth; there is nothing false in him."

—John 7:18 (Jn 7:1–24)

During the Feast of Tabernacles, in the third year of His ministry, Jesus went to the temple to teach the Word of God, as was His custom. The Jews were amazed at His wisdom and asked Him how an unlearned man such as He could have come to His understanding of scripture. Aware of their spiritual blindness, Jesus reiterated His personal connection with God, and then issued today's pointed statement. In so doing, He directed the religious leaders' attention to the fact that He was well-aware of their self-aggrandizing behavior and false piety.

Jesus, especially in the book of John, spoke frequently about the One who sent Him: His Father, God. His close connection to and relationship with His Father was obviously of first importance to Jesus. Time and again, Jesus reiterated that He sought to please and do the will of the Father, and honor God through obedience to God's plan.

This lesson of submitting to God's authority and being willing to be directed by Him is one that Jesus wishes all His followers would learn and appreciate. Yet this subject has never been well received. The notion of having to acquiesce to authority is met with adamant resistance by an increasingly self-centered and fiercely independent world population. Consequently, our proud and rebellious nature is revealed. Today's verse points out our propensity to speak and act in promotion of our own best interest, caring more about what makes us look good than what is honorable and right. Christians must look to and follow the example of our leader, Jesus. He gave His very life to honor the will of the One who sent Him. We must work to glorify the One who sends us to do the same: Jesus.

Stepping In: Read 1 Chronicles 16:24–25; Psalm 29:2; Proverbs 3:9–10; Matthew 23:12, 28:19-20; John 12:26; and 1 Corinthians 10:31. How do these verses help you understand the importance of honoring God above all else? Are you allowing yourself to be directed by God more than by your own interests? Pray for awareness of any tendencies toward self-aggrandizement you may have, and also for help in reprioritizing your devotion.

Stepping Out: This week, speak only what honors God and brings glory to Jesus. Ask the Spirit to direct your thoughts, speech, and actions.

December 13
Deserving

"Anyone who receives a prophet because he is a prophet receives a prophet's reward, and anyone who receives a righteous man because he is a righteous man receives a righteous man's reward."
—Matthew 10:41 (Mt 10:1–41)

In today's verse, each apostle would have been cheered to hear their Lord refer to them as prophets and righteous men. Though they did not know it at the time, these titles would have significant meaning for them in the near and distant future. Certainly, they would have been grateful to learn of the reward they would receive for fulfilling their duty as God's chosen messengers. But they could not have fully understood the eternal reward that would be given to those who claimed righteousness in Christ.

Today, when we hear words like "prophet" and "righteous," our minds go directly to Old Testament teachings. Prophets were people like Isaiah and Jeremiah—they lived a long time ago and prophesied about things that have mostly already happened. A "righteous man" was someone in the ilk of Moses or Abraham, people with long beards and stunning track records of obedience.

Stories about guys like these are interesting and even inspiring, but most of us would not consider them relevant. This could not be further from the truth. In fact, the terms "prophet" and "righteous" apply to everyone who calls themselves Christian. Equipped with the truth and prophecies found in the New and Old Testaments, today's Christ followers become modern-day prophets to a world that needs to learn what is to come. We know that only those who are saved by grace through faith in Jesus are righteous in God's eyes. This makes our duty as messengers all the more imperative. Spurred on by the stark knowledge that only the deserving will receive the reward of eternal life, today's righteous prophets must pick up where our famous predecessors left off.

Stepping In: Read Psalm 62:11–12; Proverbs 9:12; Jeremiah 17:10; Romans 4:3; and Colossians 3:23-24. Consider the reward God has promised you. Recall how you came to faith. Thank Him for this wonderful and formerly undeserved gift.

Stepping Out: Thank the person or people who led you to Christ, if possible. Share with someone a prophecy you are thankful was fulfilled, or one whose fulfillment you are looking forward to.

December 14

Responder

> The dead man came out, his hands and feet wrapped in strips of linen,
> and a cloth around his face. Jesus said to them, "Take off the grave
> clothes and let him go."
>
> —John 11:44 (Jn 11:1–44)

Undeterred by the fact that Lazarus had already begun to decompose in the tomb, Jesus ordered the stone removed from the grave's entrance. Jesus then commanded His friend to "Come out" (Jn 11:43). When Lazarus did, the stunned crowd was speechless and motionless. Aware of their fear, Jesus gave them the command in today's verse. For a moment, no one moved. Slowly though, responders took action. Overcoming their amazement over the miracle, and pushing aside worry about being rendered ceremonially unclean, they bravely stepped forward. Without their help, the resurrected man would have remained bound in death's trappings.

Those of us who are born again know that the moment we are saved is only the beginning of the long journey of faith and obedience, known as sanctification. When we heard Jesus' call to come out of our dead-end lives and join the eternally living, we stepped into a bright and overwhelming new reality. The world around us remained the same, but we had changed. For many of us, this was an exciting yet scary time.

Jesus knows that, like Lazarus, all new Christians need help removing the things that keep them trapped in the ways of death: fear, doubt, pride, greed, confusion, old habits, destructive influences, and spiritual ignorance. Therefore, following Jesus' command, all mature Christians are to become responders. It is our privilege to obey Jesus in this beautiful task of ushering in new life by removing the barriers that impede it. It should be our joy to nurture and encourage burgeoning faith. It is our honor to help our brothers and sisters to exchange their filthy rags for robes of righteousness.

Like the crowd at Lazarus' tomb, we must overcome the barriers that keep us from stepping forward. Today's verse is a reminder that we have been entrusted with the important work of releasing the formerly bound and showing them how to walk from darkness into light.

Stepping In: Read Psalm 104:1–2; Isaiah 64:6; Zechariah 3:4; Matthew 10:8, 25:44-45; Romans 15:1–2; and Galatians 6:2. How quickly do you respond to the needs of new Christians in your life? How well do you model positive life change? In what ways are you teaching biblical truths to those who are uninformed? Ask God to show you who you should be assisting in removing their graveclothes.

Stepping Out: This week, volunteer to help facilitate a New Believers Bible study at your church.

December 15

Washed

"Blessed are those who wash their robes, that they may have the right
to the tree of life and may go through the gates into the city."
—Revelation 22:14 (Rv 22:1–21)

At the end of his apocalyptic journey, the apostle John was blessed to preview the world in its redeemed state—when all was made right, and God's children were restored to their pre-fallen state, washed clean of all sin. Then Jesus proclaimed His imminent return and issuing His seventh and final beatitude to the recipients of John's letter. Jesus called "fortunate" those who wore the garment of righteousness His own blood had purchased. Those blessed to don these robes would finally enjoy the good fruit they had always longed for, and have unlimited access to their eternal home.

A fitting image—and an analogy Jesus Himself used to describe the union of God and His people at the time of His return—is that of a wedding. Even today, wedding guests don their best attire and makes themselves most presentable. They certainly do not go to a wedding feast wearing hastily thrown on, shabby, dirty outfits! The bride, more than anyone else, dresses in her finest "robes," washed spotlessly clean and perfect. She would not want her groom to see her any other way.

As Jesus' beloved bride, we never again need live in the squalor of sin and depravity. Instead, we are given the right to a new life of blessings beyond measure, including full access to the kingdom of heaven. With that in mind, we are reminded in this verse that the covering we will put on is a gift from God—one that denotes purity and immeasurable privilege. This is what we look forward to.

In the meantime, we must never take for granted the cleansing power of Jesus' blood, and that He willingly shed it for us so that we might receive the reward of eternal life. Practically speaking, this means that Christians today should be ever mindful of the price our Savior paid for our new digs, duds, and grub. For an instant dose of appreciation, one need only read the verses that precedes today's verse.

Stepping In: Read Genesis 3:24; Job 29:14; Isaiah 59:17–18, 61 and 64:6; Zechariah 3:4–5; Ephesians 5:25–27; Hebrews 9:22; and Revelation 19:7-8. How do feel about Jesus' blood cleansing you? Praise God that you are His bride.

Stepping Out: This week, in your small group or with a friend, read aloud or listen to the old hymn, "Nothing but the Blood of Jesus." Discuss your thoughts on the truth of this proclamation.

Glad

"But many who are first will be last, and many who are last will be first."
—Matthew 19:30 (Mt 19:16–30)

At times, the disciples seemed to really understand Jesus' divinity and sovereign power. At other times, it was painfully apparent that their thinking was stuck in a human perspective. Peter, being the most vocal of the disciples, tended to voice what was probably on the hearts and minds of the rest of the men: a fierce devotion for their Rabbi and Master, but a devotion tainted by fears, doubts, and cultural influences. On one hand, these men understood God's power and authority; on the other hand, they continued to rely on their own knowledge and abilities. Pride threatened their unity and compromised their effectiveness.

With time running out, Jesus increased the spiritual depth of His teaching with His disciples, using every opportunity to replace their worldly thinking with eternal truths. The encounter with the rich young man served to illustrate just how detrimental was the human tendency to value self-interest and personal gain over reliance and trust in God. Seeing the disciples' smug response to being on the right side of that lesson, Jesus explained the contrast between their worldly view of themselves and the eternal perspective they would need to be effective missionaries. They had to grapple with the necessity of taking on the humility and dependence of a child, and the heart of a servant as well. Instead of vying for first place in the kingdom, they should be glad of the eternal rewards Jesus promised to those who took Him at His Word.

The truth found in today's verse has challenged Christians in every generation. More than ever, Jesus' backward notions of status, wealth, and merit stand in stark contrast to the ideologies of our world. The world views success as a quantifiable measure of material possessions and wealth. We are obsessed with rank and status. We are competitive, wanting to win at any cost. To be last is embarrassing and demoralizing. This is true in almost every arena of our lives: finances, education, career, social life, home, family, health, and appearance. We express it in what we drive, what we wear, where we vacation, even what we eat. It is a massive and complicated game of comparisons. We all wish to come out on top (or at least close to it). Our self-esteem and personal identities rely largely upon what others think of us and how we rank among our peers.

Christians are not exempt. In fact, we add "religiosity" to the list of comparisons. How opposed this is to what Jesus is trying to teach us! He reminds us time and again that the only One whose opinion we should value is the Holy Trinity. It is in that humble and submissive state that we can come to understand Jesus' teaching, and then know how to respond correctly in our attitudes and actions. It is there that our desires align with our Lord's. In our glad hearts, gratitude replaces envy.

Stepping In: Take some time to think about the types of comparisons you make every day. Would you consider yourself a competitive person? Why or why not? Pray and ask God to replace your desire for personal gain and status with a servant's humble heart.

Stepping Out: This week, allow others to be first. Be glad not to be burdened by the bondage of a heart tricked into valuing worldly wealth and status above your inheritance in heaven.

Bounteous

"This is to my Father's glory, that you bear much fruit, showing yourselves to be my disciples."

—John 15:8 (Jn 15:1–17)

To instill confidence in His men, Jesus made seven emphatic "I am" statements, reminding them that eternal life and death were under His command. In the last of these statements, Jesus implored His missionaries to "remain" in Him and He is them, so that they could be successful in their missions. Without Him, they could do nothing of eternal value. He promised that when they asked Him for help, He would supply it. Hearkening back to an earlier teaching that identified fruit as the key indicator of a true disciple, Jesus rephrased the imperative to produce good fruit in today's verse. The clear indicator of fruit in the apostles' lives and ministries would be bounteous love for one another. Loved first by Jesus, devoted to one another, and supplied by the Father, they would certainly produce lasting fruit.

Deeply ingrained in nearly every person is the desire to please our dads. Most of us go to our mothers for tender love, comfort, and unconditional acceptance. We look to our fathers for approval and recognition. Though a mother's accolades make us happy, a father's blessing is a source of deep pride. To make our father proud is a great and sometimes difficult accomplishment.

To bring glory to our heavenly Father is that much greater still, and infinitely more attainable than gaining the praise of a fickle human. Jesus explains just how simple it is: abide in the Father, stay close to His Word, live in His ways, and continually seek His will. Simple, yes; easy, no. Jesus knows it is hard work to keep the faith and stay on the straight and narrow path. Therefore, He implores us to call on Him by name and seek His help when we need it. Our efforts and desire to bring God glory tether us to Him with a divine cord of strength, peace, courage, and love. This enables us to persevere even in tough times. Called and equipped by the Trinity, we can offer bounteous support to others.

Stepping In: Read Luke 22:32; Romans 5:1-5, 8:28-30; Galatians 5:22–23; Colossians 3:12–14; Hebrews 13:15-16; and James 1:12. Meditate on these verses and praise God that He chose you to glorify Him by doing work in His name.

Stepping Out: This week, ask the Spirit to help you produce a bounteous crop for the kingdom. From the Galatians passage, which fruit will you focus on, and how will you use it to glorify your heavenly Father?

December 18
Mild

"And when you pray, do not be like the hypocrites, for they love to pray
standing in the synagogues and the street corners to be seen by men.
I tell you the truth, they have received their reward in full."
—Matthew 6:5 (Mt 6:5–15)

Jesus' words were directed squarely at the religious leaders in attendance during the Sermon on the Mount. These pious men came to see what all the fuss was over this new-on-the-scene young rabbi. They had no doubt heard Jesus speak with authority in the synagogues. Surely, they had heard about the miracles He was performing. They noticed and disapproved of His increasing popularity. When Jesus exposed the religious leaders' selfish reasons for praying in public, a collective gasp likely ensued.

"Hypocrite," a Greek word meaning actor, pretender, or deceiver, was synonymous with "Pharisee." There was no coincidence in Jesus' word choice here. This was the way the Lord Jesus saw these prominent religious and societal figureheads. Though their actions might have been above reproach from a human perspective, their hearts were deplorably far from God. Jesus knew the true motives of these hard-hearted men, and He was not about to let the charade continue.

When one reads today's verse, two very distinct current-day images probably come to mind. The first is of a vocally opinionated pray-er in Christian circles. These are the folks who use lots of churchy words, quote as much scripture as they can cram in, and pray indirectly for the sins (i.e., the behavior of which they disapprove) of those within earshot. The second is those who stand in the middle of a busy public space with an illustrated sign that reads, "Repent or DIE!"

In both cases, *what* they say may be true, but *how* and *why* they say it is where hypocrisy and questionable motives come in. They may believe that their intentions are good. They want to *inform* or *help* others see the error of their ways. Sadly, aside from the damage they do, the only reward these folks will receive is the attention they get for being bigmouths. Jesus commands Christians to take a more mild and thoughtful approach, one with only one motive in mind: pleasing God.

Stepping In: Are you self-conscious when you pray aloud in a group? Do you worry about using the right words or sounding biblically illiterate? Check in with your motives for praying out loud. If you find that it is just to be heard or because you think you must, it would be better to decline. You can opt to pray silently in a group if more appropriate. This week, seek a mild approach to sharing God's wisdom.

Stepping Out: Pray with a humble heart always—only to God and for His approval. When in doubt, simply pray the Lord's Prayer and say amen (Mt. 6:9–13). Do not be hypocritical in any area of your life.

December 19
Sacrificial

"If anyone would come after me, he must deny himself and take up his cross and follow me."

—Matthew 16:24 (Mt 16:21–28)

With only months until He would go to the cross, Jesus prepared His men for His departure. He explained that, for the kingdom of heaven to be established, He must die and be raised again. Speaking plainly in today's verse, Jesus pointed out that sacrifice was required of all who called themselves His followers. The disciples soon learned that more than the redemption of the Hebrew nation was at stake. The kingdom message of salvation was for the entire human race.

Before Jesus' triumph, the cross was only known for being the cruelest and most humiliating killing device in the ancient world. Today, it is the symbol of Christianity. Some regard the cross with reverence and gratitude. Familiarity has bred an apathic response in many others. For Christians and non-Christians alike, the cross has become little more than a casual accessory. Even so, the cross remains a constant reminder of Jesus' necessary sacrifice. Without it, we would have no fulfilled prophecy and no salvation.

Jesus bore our sin unto death on that tree, removing it from us forever. It was His choice. Now, we get to make the choice to also deny (ourselves) and take up (our) cross. Daily we can choose to trust in God's sovereignty as we intentionally love others and defend the truth—even if it means making significant sacrifices. Out of gratitude for our Savior, we give of ourselves joyfully.

Stepping In: Read Numbers 21:8; Isaiah 53:1–5; and John 3:14-15, 18:31-32. How do these verses help explain why the cross was necessary? Thank Jesus now for His willing sacrifice—that He chose to die so you could have life. Pray for the Spirit to reveal where you could be honoring God through sacrificial acts.

Stepping Out: Each day this week, deny yourself some small (or big) pleasure. Instead of mourning your loss, use the time to be thankful for all Jesus has blessed you with. Pray for those who have less. Then obey Jesus' command to follow Him wherever His Spirit leads you.

December 20
Ignited

"I have come to bring fire on the earth, and how I wish it were already kindled. But I have a baptism to undergo, and how distressed I am until it is completed."

—Luke 12:49–50 (Lk 12:1, 49–53)

With each successive teaching Jesus gave to His disciples, He revealed more about His ultimate purpose. Giving His men an opportunity to utilize their developing spiritual discernment, Jesus foretold the baptism He would soon undergo, by which He would be buried in sin and raised victorious. He hoped His frightening words and shocking illustration of bringing fire on the earth would spur His disciples to cling to their faith. Moreover, He hoped that His message would ignite a deeper conviction within them.

Those who heard Jesus' words who had not yet put faith in Him would have found this message confusing and upsetting, to say the least. Though the Jews in the crowd would likely have recalled prophecies about God's fiery judgment, many preferred to focus on the scripture passages that promised a redeemer king. The notion of a suffering savior was simply too bleak.

Jesus wanted His men to understand that He was the fulfillment of both justice and judgment prophecies. Jesus needed His successors to see beyond the present and trust Him to guide them through the difficulties ahead. Soon, the cost of their identity in the Christ would be made clear—purification from sin, as they would learn, was a costly affair.

Many people today have been turned off from Christianity because of "fire and brimstone" teachings such as this. To those who are perishing, verses like today's are proof positive that God is nothing more than a vengeful tyrant, bent on destruction.

Hard to believe as it may be, Jesus said these shocking words not to frighten, but to encourage. Those who know Jesus understand that the fire of which He speaks is either the fire of judgment for unbelievers, or the cleansing force that burns off our transgressions and brings purification. We who believe are left with no trace of the sin that used to impede our access to the throne of God. Once cleansed, our desire to assist others in the unraveling of the mysteries of judgment and grace should be ignited. Saved, we ought to lead others from the destructive flames of unbelief and toward the purifying fire burning in the heart of our Savior.

Stepping In: Read Joel 2:30–32; Malachi 3:2–4; 1 Corinthians 3:10–15; and 2 Thessalonians 1:5–10. Does the prospect of holy fire scare you? Why or why not? Take some time to rejoice in the refining and purifying work of the cross. Pray that God will ignite your desire to inform others about the two types of fire each person will face.

Stepping Out: This week, mimic Jesus' sense of urgency in doing the Father's will. If there is some kingdom work you have been putting off, this is the week to embrace it with a burning passion.

December 21
Respectful

> "Again, anyone who says to his brother, 'Raca,' is answerable to the Sanhedrin. But anyone who says, 'You fool!' will be in danger of the fires of hell."
>
> —Matthew 5:22 (Mt 5:21–26)

Speaking directly to the Jews listening to His Sermon on the Mount, Jesus concluded His thoughts on murder and anger with today's verse. Like many of His pronouncements, this one perhaps seemed unreasonably harsh. *Raca* is an Aramaic word meaning "empty" or "empty-headed." Jesus was saying that if you insult someone's intelligence, you will have to answer to the authorities and face a possible consequence. If you go so far as to insult a person's character, you risk offending God as well. So severe an offense was this that one should risk eternal damnation for it.

The Jews had limited knowledge of heaven and hell, and some did not believe in the afterlife. However, Jesus' point was clear enough. The message that carelessly spoken words of anger could have dire results would have given His audience something to think about, and perhaps have spurred some to be more respectful with their words.

Words have power—of this there is no question. As each of us knows, words have the ability to build others up or knock them down. The casual use of hurtful and derogatory words only seems to be getting more prevalent as time marches on. The damage is becoming more immediate and widespread due to the use of social media. Jesus' warning should be a serious wake-up call for our generation.

God created each person's nature, personality, and character. Thus, He takes defaming insults personally. Words are manifestations of our attitudes and beliefs; it is more about how we think than what we say. If we look down on others and view them as unworthy of respect, we may believe that what we say to them doesn't matter. Jesus says otherwise.

Stepping In: Read James 1:26 and skim James 3. How careful are you with words? How respectfully do you treat others with your words, both spoken and written? Check your attitude about the importance of words and the casualness of their use. Pray that your attitude increasingly aligns with God. Pray for strength to hold your tongue when needed. Pray that your respect for others as wonderful creations of God grows.

Stepping Out: This week, think before you speak! Is what you are about to say something that will build others up or bring them down? Are the words even necessary? Are they words you would like said to or about you? If not, keep respectfully silent.

December 22
Astute

"How foolish you are, and how slow of heart to believe all that the prophets have spoken! Did not the Christ have to suffer these things and then enter his glory?"

—Luke 24:25–26 (Lk 24:1–35)

Three days after Jesus' body had been laid in the tomb, two of His followers set out for Emmaus, seven miles northwest of Jerusalem. A disguised Jesus joined them as they walked and inquired as to what they were talking about. Thinking He was a visitor from out of town, they told Him about the death of the prophet Jesus, whom some had hoped would be Israel's redeeming king. They spoke of His power and authority, and of the amazing signs and wonders He had performed.

Because they were clearly downcast and confused, Jesus knew that these men had not understood His teaching or the prophecies about the Messiah. He issued them a mild rebuke in today's verses. He explained that the Christ was a direct fulfillment of the ancient prophecies, and that all of scripture pointed to Jesus.

When they arrived at their destination, the men urged their companion to stay with them for the evening, as it was getting late. He agreed. While they all were at the table, Jesus opened their eyes to His identity. But before they could embrace their living Lord, He vanished. So inspired were these men by this interaction that they ran back to Jerusalem and told the eleven disciples that what the women had said was true: the Lord Jesus lived!

Despite all the evidence that scholars, theologians, and archeologists have brought to light, proving the validity of Jesus' claims, many people remain skeptical today. Not only do the "stories" in the Bible seem outlandish, but without seeing Jesus with their own eyes, many refuse to believe that He exists in the present tense.

As today's verses confirm, even those who saw Jesus face-to-face failed to recognize Him. Christians today are at an extreme advantage over early believers in more than one way. Not only is Christianity now widely accepted through many parts of the world, but we have the complete Word of God to explain how we got to where we are, and where we are going. We can clearly see how Jesus is the central character in God's plan for the redemption of His prized yet dismally lost creation. Unlike the disciples on those devastating days following the crucifixion, we have written assurance of God's prophecies and promises. The astute can clearly see God's professed plan in black and white and *red*. More is yet to come—of this we can be sure.

Stepping In: Read Psalm 22; Isaiah 53; and other prophecy scripture passages. Pray for an astute mind and a softened heart, that you may fully know the love of the Lord. Praise Him for His flawless plan.

Stepping Out: This week, in your small group or with some friends, listen to and reflect on the song "Sweetly Broken" by Jeremy Riddle. Pray for opportunities to discuss fulfilled prophecies with others.

December 23
Thick-Skinned

"A student is not above his teacher, nor a servant above his master. It is enough for the student to be like his teacher, and the servant to be like his master. If the head of the house has been called Beelzebub, how much more the members of his household!"

—Matthew 10:24–25 (Mt 10:1–33)

The two points of Jesus' statement here may have seemed hopelessly incongruous to His disciples. Interwoven in a speech of promise and encouragement were stern warnings and blunt admonitions. Though anxious and fearful, the twelve newly appointed apostles were eager to please their Lord. Certainly, they did not consider themselves "above" or even equal to Jesus, their Master and Teacher. However, Jesus had just promised His men miraculous powers similar to His own, which could lead to a higher-than-necessary opinion of themselves if their attitudes were not kept in check. Jesus also wanted His men to realize that the work they were setting out to do would gain them the same negative attention that Jesus endured.

Everyone who stands up as a public figure is open to scrutiny; Jesus was no different in His day, nor His followers in this. Regardless of the cause they represent or the personality traits they display, anyone taking a stand for what they believe *will* be received unfavorably by some. Even people like Mother Teresa and Billy Graham had opponents who were happy to voice their displeasure. Jesus was called many things: prince of demons, blasphemer, lawbreaker, liar, lunatic. So too will his followers be disparaged. In today's mission fields, foreign and domestic, in our homes, communities, and churches, as Christ's humble servants we must don thick skins if we are to honor our Lord with our words and our actions amid persecution.

Stepping In: Read Isaiah 8:12-13; Mark 3:22; John 13:16-17. Pray that God strengthens your resolve to deal with negativity and persecution in a way that reflects Christ's character.

Stepping Out: This week, wear the thick-skinned armor of God as you stand firm amid opposition (Eph 6:10-17). Pray that those who angrily resist God will find Him.

Spiritual

Then I remembered what the Lord had said: "John baptized with
water, but you will be baptized with the Holy Spirit."
—Acts 11:16 (Acts 10:34–11:18)

During their forty-day encounter with the resurrected Jesus, the disciples' faith was not only renewed,
it developed into an unstoppable force, spurring them to spread the good news of salvation to all of
Israel. But Jesus had much bigger plans for them. The apostles' mission field was to stretch further
than any of their imaginations had ever gone, both mentally and spiritually. The disciples, including
their new members Matthias (who replaced Judas Iscariot) and Paul, set out to spread the gospel far
and wide.

Though Paul had been specifically commissioned to bring salvation to the Gentiles, Peter found
himself driven by a vision from Jesus to do the same. Peter had a fateful encounter with Cornelius,
the Gentile centurion, which resulted in the coming of the Holy Spirit on those in his household in
Caesarea. Peter returned to Jerusalem to describe his mission's surprises and successes to the other
apostles.

As He reflected on these events, words Jesus had spoken suddenly became clear to Peter. His
spiritual eyes were opened to the enhanced theology he and his fellow apostles were to promote. Thus,
He explained to the others how Jewish regulations and man-made rules about purity no longer applied
to those under the new covenant of Christ. As Jesus had practiced religious inclusion, so it should be
with His gospel messengers. The good news was for all—Jews and Gentiles alike.

Another proclamation of Jesus came to Peter, which he expressed in today's verse. While the
water baptism John had offered brought about a refreshing of the body and mind, the new baptism
the disciples would offer would transform the spirit as well.

As Christians, we should never take for granted the gifting of the Holy Spirit. It is easy to forget
that God's favor used to rest only on His chosen ones, the Jews. Only by Jesus' death on the cross were
all people given direct access to His throne of mercy. So, it is good for us to read passages like Acts
chapters 10 and 11. We need to be reminded of how the gospel message was brought out of Israel and
into the rest of the world—and to our own ears. Brave men and women throughout history risked
their reputations, their careers, their families, and their very lives so that the truth of who Jesus is
could be proclaimed in places where it had never been taught or accepted before.

In today's verse, Peter reflects on the symbolism of John's baptism and message, and how they
pointed to "the Lamb of God, who takes away the sin of the world" (Jn 1:29). This will forever be the
spiritual message of truth that all Christians must promote. Today, it is our joy to guide people toward
the only One who can wash, not just a body, but a soul, clean of sin forever: Jesus, our Lord and Savior.

Stepping In: Read Luke 24:45–49; John 1:19–34; and Romans 8:1–6. Has Jesus opened your spiritual
eyes so that through the discernment of the Spirit you can now understand His Word? Are you
currently more focused on your physical reality than your spiritual condition? Pray for the spiritual
wisdom.

Stepping Out: If you have not been baptized by water or the Spirit, make plans to be soon.

December 25
Chosen

"The kingdom of heaven is like a king who prepared a wedding banquet for his son."
—Matthew 22:2 (Mt 21:1–11, 23–46; 22:1–14)

In the days leading up to Jesus' betrayal, He still had several important messages to get across to the hard-hearted crowd before going to the cross. In the parable about a king giving a wedding feast for his son, Jesus related a rather tragic tale about those who refused the king's generosity, those who rebelled against the king's servants, and those who accepted the invitation only to mock the king's authority. Stinging from the obvious innuendos, but without recourse at that moment, the Jewish leaders vowed to put an end to Jesus' ministry and life at the earliest possible opportunity.

Christians today might call the first-century Jewish leaders' rejection of Jesus, an "epic fail." Not only did they miss the signs and fulfilled prophecies that pointed to Jesus, but they failed to recognize their Messiah when He was giving them more than ample proof of His majesty. Worse, these religious experts completely failed the people they were entrusted to lead. Thus, those who had long been God's chosen people were no longer able to claim sole ownership of that title.

God's chosen ones today—Christians—know that Jesus' life, death, resurrection, and ascension have ushered in a new and lasting covenant, replacing the old order of things. However, while Christians rest in this assurance, there are many who still refuse to accept the King's generous invitation. Sadly too, there are those who continue to mistreat and kill His messengers. Others claim to be invited guests, but are not clothed in Christ's righteousness.

When spoken, this parable was a foreshadow of the Passion week. Today, we can see that it represents the many stories of people who have and will ungratefully refuse the grace of God. The unfortunate truth, which Jesus accurately predicted, is that we will see this same scene repeated until He returns and takes His chosen banquet guests into the King's palace for a feast beyond compare.

Stepping In: Read Luke 14:12–24; John 15:18–19; and 1 Peter 2:9–10. After meditating on these references, reread Matthew 22:1–14 and reflect on it using the Envision It method (See appendix). Who did you relate to and why? What are your thoughts on God's judgment? Pray and thank Him that you are chosen. Pray also for the courage to invite others to the banquet.

Stepping Out: This week, ask yourself if anyone you know resembles one of the doomed in this parable. As the Spirit leads you, tell them about Jesus and the wonderful things He has for those who believe.

December 26
Legitimate

"These people honor me with their lips, but their hearts are far from me. They worship me in vain; their teachings are but rules taught by men."

—Matthew 15:8–9 (Mt 15:1–9)

When word of Jesus' unconventional teaching and practices reached the Pharisees and teachers of the Law in Jerusalem, some of them traveled to Galilee to confront Jesus. They did not want to cause Jesus' admiring fans to turn on them, so instead of attacking Jesus' character, they questioned the unlawful behavior of His disciples. Jesus matter-of-factly pointed out several examples of how His opponents regularly disregarded their own laws. Quoting the prophet Isaiah in today's verse, Jesus made both the Pharisees' guilt and His divinity clear.

Christians throughout the generations have been quick to condemn the Pharisees and religious leaders of Jesus' day. Based on what we read about these antagonists, and using the titles Jesus Himself gave them—hypocrites, blind guides, brood of vipers—we are happy to consider ourselves polar-opposites of these enemies of God.

Yet when we analyze our own attitudes and behaviors, we are often shocked to discover how similar we are to the Pharisees. Like them, we have firm convictions that we hold as infallible truth. Like theirs, our unbending view of God's doctrine is often incomplete and biased.

When we attach a list of rules for right living to our religion, we almost always lose the most important element of our Christian walk: a legitimate relationship with our Lord, Jesus. That is why it is so important to know what He said, why He said it, and what we should do about it. More than anything, Jesus does not want us to be like the Pharisees. He desires our hearts' devotion, not just our mouths'. He wants us to seek His will above the "rules taught by men," and to demonstrate a legitimate faith based on truth, love and respect.

Stepping In: Read Isaiah 29:13–14 and Colossians 2:20–23. Also review the Ten Commandments (Dt 5:1–21) and the Beatitudes (Mt 5:1–12). Which of these rules of God do you disagree with or ignore? What rules of men do you find yourself adhering to instead? Pray for God to speak His wisdom into your life, your attitude, and your behavior, changing a contrived faith into a legitimate love of Jesus.

Stepping Out: This week, choose to worship Jesus with your whole heart by obeying His commands and refraining from constructing your own. Also, be careful not to judge others who have not yet learned this lesson. Instead, pray for them.

Brave

"Take heart, daughter," he said, "your faith has healed you."
—Matthew 9:22 (Mt 9:18–26)

While Jesus was answering John the Baptist's disciples' question about fasting, a ruler from Capernaum named Jairus came to seek restoration for his dead daughter. Jesus agreed to revive the girl, and He and His disciples followed Jairus to his home.

On the way, a woman stricken with an unrelenting bleeding disorder pushed her way through the crowd, just to touch the edge of Jesus' cloak. Jesus, sensing His power go out from Him, stopped in His tracks and asked who had touched Him. The stricken woman bravely stepped forward. When Jesus saw her, he took pity on her. But more than that, He had loving compassion and sympathy for her. He knew that this woman had suffered both physically and emotionally for many years. Her condition rendered her unclean, and she had been cruelly shunned by society. Her bleeding made her unfit to be a wife and ineligible even to go to the house of worship. Yet, her faith made her brave. The healing that came from Jesus would have been enough to send her away smiling, but this woman received far more than that. When Jesus called her "daughter," she received acceptance into God's family—a complete restoration of her body and soul, and a royal inheritance as well.

In our day and age, there are a multitude of caring agencies tasked to assist the needy. Some of us have been on the receiving end of their services at one point or another. Those who haven't, though unlikely to express disdain for people who appear rough around the edges, may inwardly feel uncomfortable around them. The rejected and marginalized still live among us. The only difference for us now is that we have better ways of keeping them tucked away—out of sight and out of mind, someone else's problem.

When we consider just the religious ramifications of Jesus allowing contact with the diseased and the dead, we should take notice of how little we risk when we reach out to someone who is hurting. Ceremonial cleanliness is not an issue for most of us today. What is our excuse? Jesus does not shy away from the sick and the unclean. He seeks out His hurting children.

Breaking through social, political, and religious barriers, regardless of which side one is on, takes bravery. As Christians, we must lead our brothers and sisters in Christ to the loving arms of the Father, and encourage them to trust in the healing power of Jesus.

Stepping In: Read Mark 5:22–43; Luke 8:41–56; and 1 John 3:1. What is your relationship with your earthly father? Does it lack the unconditional love you desire? Pray and thank God for the way He loves you completely and calls you His child. Bravely reach to Jesus for the healing you need in your life.

Stepping Out: This week, step out of your comfort zone to close the gap between you and a less fortunate brother or sister. Pray that God will open your eyes to the needs of others, and for bravery to reach out to them in Jesus' name. Never underestimate the power of a touch!

December 28
Special

> "If I want him to remain alive until I return, what is it to you? You must follow me."
>
> —John 21:22 (Jn 21:1–25)

After Jesus' reappearance in His resurrected state, the disciples' hope for the future was restored. During one of their encounters with Him, Jesus took Peter aside and inquired as to his love for Him. Peter readily affirmed his adoration. Jesus asked again—and again. By the third round of questioning, Peter's feelings were hurt. But Jesus was not really questioning Peter's love for Him. Rather, Jesus was reminding Peter of his love and urging him to forgive himself. Jesus had chosen Peter to be the rock on which His church would be built. Jesus needed Peter to be confident and secure in his special calling. He needed Peter to leave behind pride, self-pity, and envy, and to follow Him only.

One of the flaws of the human character is this tendency to compare ourselves with others. Using a completely subjective and often changeable rating scale, we determine how we rank among our peers in terms of looks, smarts, financial successes, parenting abilities, and even spiritual aptitude. When we perceive others as less "gifted" than ourselves, we are content with our condition. However, when we perceive that we have somehow been given less of what we desire, we take issue. Our fairness meter is alerted to an impending travesty of justice, and we want someone to answer for it. Like Peter, instead of being happy for a friend's blessing, we tend to focus on our misfortune and the unfairness of the situation.

Today's passage is a reminder that Jesus has a unique and special calling for each of us. Negative emotions like jealousy, self-pity, and pride diminish our effectiveness in serving Him. When we keep our eyes on Jesus, we are no longer paying attention to anyone else. When we follow Jesus into the work He is doing, we no longer see others as competitors. They are our compadres in Christ. When we consider how privileged we are to be wanted and chosen by God to represent Him, we realize just how special we are. Suddenly, nothing else matters.

Stepping In: Read Psalm 139; Proverbs 14:30; Ecclesiastes 4:4; Isaiah 43:4; Jeremiah 1:5; John 13:36–38; 1 Corinthians 3:3, 13:4-7; Philippians 2:3–4; and James 3:13–14. Is there any bitterness, envy, or contempt you need to confess before the Lord? If so, do so now, and thank Him for loving you in His own unique and special way.

Stepping Out: This week, follow Jesus into the work He is already doing around you. Keep your focus on Him and the special gifts of the Spirit He is giving you to accomplish His will today.

Fearless

"Take courage! It is I. Don't be afraid."
—Matthew 14:27 (Mt 14:13–27)

Immediately after miraculously feeding more than five thousand people on the shores of the Sea of Galilee near Bethsaida, Jesus instructed His disciples to go ahead of Him across the lake to Capernaum. With the Twelve in the boat, rowing against the wind, Jesus dismissed the crowd and went up on a nearby mountain to pray. Because of the demands of His busy ministry and the recent loss of His cousin, John the Baptist, Jesus was in need of physical rest and spiritual refreshment. Throngs constantly vied for His attention, and His own disciples still needed intensive instruction. Jesus was careful to carve out moments such as these for quiet communion with His Father.

After He had revived Himself in His Father's presence, Jesus set out to meet up with His disciples. The wind and the waves were tossing the small boat about, and the Twelve did not initially see Jesus approaching. When they finally saw Him walking toward them on the water, they thought He was a ghost. The men started to panic. Jesus quickly responded with today's words of encouragement.

Many of us are familiar with the story of Jesus walking on water. From the comfort of our easy chairs, we wonder how the disciples could have been so daft as not to instantly recognize Jesus and be calmed. However, amid the storms of our own lives, we too tend to allow our fears to keep us from seeing Jesus in our situations. Fear, irrational and otherwise, can be a blinding force in our lives, especially if we forget to call on the rescuing power of our Savior to help us. Like the disciples, we measure our safety by what we can see.

In a chaotic world of perceived threats to our well-being, many of us spend a good deal of time working at controlling our circumstances. But many things are simply out of our control. Truth be told, *most* things are out of our control. This can induce fear, or it can cause us to focus on the One who is in control: Jesus. Throughout scripture, God encourages us to be fearless, even in the face of the unknown. Time and again, Jesus reminds us that He is with us and for us. He promises to never leave us nor forsake us. We need only fix our eyes on our Savior and not on the waves crashing over the bow, remembering all the while that He is good, and He is great.

Stepping In: Read Deuteronomy 31:6; Psalm 23, 46:1-3, 91:5-6; Isaiah 35:4, 41:10, 43:1; Jeremiah 17:7–8; and 1 John 4:18. Meditate on these encouraging scripture passages. Talk to God about your fears and ask Him to replace them with peaceful assurance in the safety of His love. Pray for others who live in fear.

Stepping Out: Is fear currently keeping you from stepping out of the boat and obeying Jesus' command to come? This week, step out of your comfort zone and walk boldly and confidently toward Jesus in trusting obedience.

December 30
Swift

> When I returned to Jerusalem and was praying at the temple, I fell into
> a trance and saw the Lord speaking. "Quick!" he said to me. "Leave
> Jerusalem immediately, because they will not accept your testimony
> about me."
>
> —Acts 22:17–18 (Acts 21:27–22:30)

Against the wishes of his travel companions and fellow-servants in Christ, Paul finished off his third missionary journey by returning to Jerusalem. He knew all too well the hatred and violence he could expect to face among the zealous Jews in the city, as he had been one of them not too long before. Yet, because of his great faith, he was willing to suffer anything to do the work of spreading the gospel.

Sure enough, within a week, Paul was seized at the temple and arrested. Bound in chains, he was taken to the Roman barracks to be beaten and questioned. Before being taken inside, Paul pleaded with the Roman commander to have a word with the riotous mob. Paul spoke to the pressing throng in Aramaic, a Hebrew dialect, and silenced the crowd, who had fully expected him to speak to them in Greek, the language of the Gentiles.

Once he had the multitude's attention, Paul explained how Jesus had opened his eyes to the truth of who He was, and had given him a new life purpose—proclaiming Jesus as Lord and Savior. Today's verses are his description of how he received a vision from the Lord, predicting the situation he was to face in Jerusalem. Jesus had also told him, "Go; I will send you far away to the Gentiles" (Acts 22:21). Paul informed the crowd that God had plans they knew nothing about.

At this, the people called for Paul's death. Paul had been told to be swift in making an exit from the city where the people wanted him dead. He used his Roman citizenship as a temporary appeal to the authorities. Unsure what to do, the Roman guards brought Paul to be tried by the Jewish rulers.

Whenever the Lord gives a command, He expects His children to respond swiftly. Always, He wants us to quickly engage our brains and seek His will. Sometimes He wants us to jump into action as well. In a world of perpetual motion, we often get the order of this command-response wrong; we are quick to act, slow to mentally process, and even slower to consult God's Spirit.

When Jesus told Paul to quickly leave Jerusalem, He didn't want Paul to run away in fear. Yes, Jesus was telling Paul not to tarry among his enemies. At the same time, Jesus knew that leaving at the right moment, after the right words had been spoken to the right people, was important to Paul's ministry. Because Paul was quick on his feet, so to speak, he kept his wits about him and did not escalate the conflict. By the Holy Spirit, he was able to recall key words Jesus had given him for that very moment. Through Paul, as He does through us when we are yielded to His will, Jesus teaches His people a valuable lesson about God's character, His plan, and His faithfulness. With swift discernment and carefully timed words, God's power can be revealed through us in amazing ways.

Stepping In: Read Deuteronomy 5:33, 13:4; Psalm 119:60, 133; John 14:15, 15:14; Galatians 5:25; and James 1:19–20. What is Jesus teaching you about swift obedience through these passages? Pray for a yielded heart.

Stepping Out: This week, do not hesitate to follow the Spirit's prompting to obey Jesus' commands.

December 31
Celebrated

"But we had to celebrate and be glad, because this brother of yours was dead and is alive again; he was lost and is found."

—Luke 15:32 (Lk 15:1–32)

Jesus began employing the use of parabolic teaching sometime in the middle of His ministry, with the combined purpose of stretching His disciples' ability to discern spiritual matters and baffling the spiritually unwise. Among this latter group were the Jewish religious leaders, particularly the Pharisees. Though well-versed in scripture, these learned men's hearts were far from God. Thus, they did not recognize Jesus as God's true Son. Try as they might to find evidence of blasphemy in Jesus' teachings, the Pharisees usually wound up being the object of His lesson.

One day, with the Pharisees observing at a distance, Jesus talked with a group of known sinners. For the benefit of all who were listening—especially the self-righteous religious leaders—Jesus told a series of three parable relating to the recovery of lost items of great value: a sheep, a coin, and a son. In the third parable, a father had two sons. One squandered his inheritance on wild living; the other obediently worked for his father. Upon the return of the rebellious younger son, the older son became furious with his father's lavish outpouring of mercy. More than that, the older son, who represented the Pharisees, was particularly indignant about the father's uncontainable joy at the safe return of his wayward sibling.

The Prodigal Son is quite possibly Jesus' most famous parable. This section of scripture has been pored over and discussed for many generations. Reactions to it vary widely. Some readers are quick to side with the older son because his loyal service was utterly forgotten in the excitement of the younger son's return. Parents may immediately relate to the relief and joy the father felt. Others identify with the reckless and self-centered choices of the younger son.

Regardless of your initial reaction to this parable, Jesus wants us to know that grace, love, and forgiveness for even the most unforgivable behaviors are available to those who seek them. The down-and-out defector came to his senses and was blown away by the royal reception he received. This is how God works; a party erupts in heaven each time a sinner repents and returns home to the Father. Christians today can be inspired knowing that each person we help find their way home is celebrated.

Stepping In: Read Proverbs 29:3; Zephaniah 3:17; Zechariah 3:1–7; Romans 6:11–14; and Ephesians 2:1–5. Reflect on the Prodigal Son parable using the Envision It method (See appendix). With whom did you relate, and why? Pray and ask God to reveal and remove any stubbornness, pride, jealousy, rebellion, or destructive tendencies in you. Thank Him for making you one of the celebrated.

Stepping Out: This week, based on what the Spirit revealed, choose an attitude or behavior you currently need to work on, then do so. Celebrate each victory, big or small, you win over sin.

Appendix 1
Scripture Reflection Methods

Emphasize It

Read the passage through as many times as there are words in it, each time emphasizing each individual word in turn. This method is best for shorter passages. Examples:

"*If* you love me, you will obey what I command."

"If *you* love me, you will obey what I command."

"If you *love* me, you will obey what I command" (Jn 14:15).

And so on. This verse has ten words in it, so you would read this passage ten times.

Consider how the emphasis of each word in turn changes the meaning of the passage. Read the passage one last time, emphasizing the word or words that brought the passage alive for you. Thank Jesus for speaking His truth to you in a new way. Ask the Holy Spirit to help you respond appropriately to what you have learned.

Envision It

As you read the day's verse or verses within the context of their larger passage, identify the characters in the story. Which one did you most identify with? Which character most shocked, annoyed, angered, or touched you? Read the passage again, and try to see the scene from one of the character's point of view. Try to envision what that character was experiencing. How did their role positively or negatively influence Jesus' teaching? What can you learn from them? Ask the Holy Spirit to expand your perspective to be able to understand others' viewpoints.

Say It

Read the verse or verses several times, more slowly each time. What word or words stood out to you? Say that word a few times, and consider its uses and definition. Ask the Holy Spirit to help you understand why that particular word was especially meaningful to you. Praise God for this insight.

Own It

In a passage where Jesus is addressing an individual, insert your name. Change the personal pronouns to "I," "me," and "mine," so that Jesus is speaking directly to you. Ask the Holy Spirit to help you own Jesus' teaching, instructions, or commands.

Rewrite It

After reading Jesus' words a couple of times, rewrite them in your own words. You may wish to paraphrase the larger passage to better capture the context or meaning. Write as if you were going to explain what the passage meant to someone who was not familiar with scripture. Use modern vernacular and a conversational tone.

Compare what you wrote to the original passage. Does your version seem clear and concise? Thank the Holy Spirit for helping you to assimilate Jesus' teaching in a way that makes sense to you. Pray for an opportunity to share what you have learned.

10/10/80 Financial Wisdom

Throughout scripture, God places immense importance on making wise choices with one's money and possessions. Beginning in the book of Genesis and in many Bible books beyond, God's plan for the rightful distribution of assets is made clear: God is to receive the first 10 percent of everything! This is where the practice of tithing comes from. Of all the good things God blesses a person with, including income, it is only right and fair to give back to Him the first and best portion of it. It all belongs to God anyway. Giving Him a fraction of our earnings is an appropriate gesture of our appreciation. And, though it is an act of obedience, one should always give freely and joyfully.

Jesus spoke about money almost more than any other topic. Because it is a highly influential and necessary evil, Jesus warns us often about not letting a lust for money and possessions drag our hearts away from our first love: God. Money is a test of our faithfulness. In fact, it is the only thing God has said we can test *Him* with (see Mal 3:10). The management of our money is something that God wants us get right. We are to control it so that it won't control us.

Most Americans live way beyond their means. The stress of financial trouble is the cause of too many health, relational, and spiritual dis-eases. God has a simple solution. It starts with trust.

First, regardless of your financial situation, tithe the full biblical amount. God wants this *for* you, not *from* you. He does not need your money, He needs only your faith and obedience. He knows what you need, and He will supply it. Test Him on this, and prepare yourself to be amazed!

Second, after tithing the first 10 percent of your income, save the second 10 percent. Again, regardless of your outgoing expenses, commit to building up a safe buffer for yourself and your family, so that when the winds of adversity blow through, you will not be wiped out—financially or otherwise.

Last, commit to living off the remaining 80 percent of your income. With frugal practices and disciplines, one should manage the cost of living and paying down debt with this amount. If this is a stretch, consider speaking with a Christian financial advisor for some practical tips.

How to use the Action Plan Tracker

The following chart is provided so that you can make a weekly log of your devotional activities as you progress through Lead the Way. Hopefully you will find the Action Plan Tracker useful in organizing and synthesizing your daily and weekly discipleship goals.

It is designed to be an at-a-glance reminder of what Jesus is teaching you through His words and examples; what He is informing you on a mental and intellectual level (brain), how His words make you feel (heart), and what His message inspires you to do (hand).

To use, you will want to either copy the chart or cut it out and laminate it. Either way is fine. Since I suggest that you make a copy of the filled in chart each week, it may be more efficient to go ahead and make 52 copies so that you have one for each week at the onset of your study. Then you will have a record of your week's progress on hand for later reflection. This is key. Since spiritual maturation is a process, and our relationship with Jesus an ongoing affair, being able to look back over your progress in these areas will help you know how to move forward in each.

Because each day of Lead the Way is loaded with information and suggests a high level of participation, it may seem overwhelming and difficult to keep track of and accomplish all that is asked of you. This Action Plan Tracker is meant to help with that. As mentioned in the introduction, this chart can help you to keep your devotional and discipleship life simple and fun. Naturally, there will be days (or weeks) where you find the suggestions given in Lead the Way difficult to meet. That is okay. By tracking your progress using the Action Plan Tracker, you can easily see where you have done well and where you have struggled. From there you can set goals and cast a vision for where your spiritual development may be taking you. By keeping track of your goals and progress, you can be encouraged and inspired to take your love for Jesus deeper and farther each week, month, year. It is a tool for you to use as you wish, not a requirement for this devotional.

My hope is that you will find this book, and this chart, helpful in your personal quest to follow your leader, Jesus, with all your heart, mind, soul and strength, and that by doing so, others will know that you are His disciple.

Sincerely,
Elaine

LTW - Weekly Action Plan Tracker

VERSE	S	M	T	W	T	F	S
🧠							
♡							
🖐